Muslims and Global Justice

PENNSYLVANIA STUDIES IN HUMAN RIGHTS

Bert B. Lockwood, Jr., Series Editor

A complete list of books in the series
is available from the publisher.

Muslims and Global Justice

Abdullahi Ahmed An-Naʿim

PENN

UNIVERSITY OF PENNSYLVANIA PRESS

PHILADELPHIA · OXFORD

Published by
University of Pennsylvania Press
hiladelphia, Pennsylvania 19104-4112
www.upenn.edu/pennpress

Printed in the United States of America on acid-free paper
10 9 8 7 6 5 4 3 2 1

Library of Congress Cataloging-in-Publication Data
Na'īm, 'Abd Allāh Ahmād, 1946–
    Muslims and global justice / Abdullahi Ahmed An-Na'im.
    p.   cm. — (Pennsylvania studies in human rights)
    ISBN: 978-0-8122-4286-7 (hardcover : alk. paper)
    Includes bibliographical references and index.
    1. Civil rights (Islamic law) Human rights—Religious
aspects—Islam. 2. Law and globalization. 3. Globalization—
Religious aspects—Islam.
KBP2460 .N353   2010
340.5'9—dc22   2010017225

Contents

Contents

Introduction

Reimagining Global Justice

The title and themes of this book, *Muslims and Global Justice*, may be briefly explained as follows, subject to further elaboration in this introduction and clarification in various chapters. By "global justice" I mean globally inclusive conceptions of justice to be realized by human beings for themselves, everywhere, through their own self-determination. Both conceptions of justice and the processes of their realization include the interaction of local and global actors and factors. This emphasis on the agency of the human subject in determining what justice means for her, and striving for realizing her own conception, leads me to focus on Muslims as believers seeking justice for themselves and other human beings, in solidarity and cooperation, rather than speaking of Islam as a religion. I prefer to focus on believers to emphasize our responsibility and ability to change ourselves and transform our understanding and practice of our religious beliefs, instead of invoking abstract doctrines of religion for which we may not feel personally responsible, or believe we can change. The question for me as a Muslim is how to affirm my commitment to global justice and responsibility for its realization, without implying that Islam is the sole or exclusive determining factor in the lives of Muslims. Indeed, my understanding and practice of Islam are influenced by my experiences as a global/local citizen and agent of social change at various levels.

To begin on a personal note that is integral to the coherence of this book, the basic purpose and meaning of my work have always been and continue to be the reconciliation of my being a Muslim with my commitment to peaceful international relations and the protection of universal human rights. To be candid and clear on this point, these two aspects of my personal orientation are not equal sides of an equation, whereby I fluctuate between the two to achieve reconciliation. The two sides are obviously so different in nature and role in a believer's life that it is impossible to hold them in comparative equivalence. From my perspective, being a Muslim is the core of my identity and life philosophy, and my commitment to peaceful relations and human rights is one of the consequences of that core. For me, as for other religious believers, I would expect, the relevance of international law and human rights is that each is a means to enable me to live in accordance with my religious beliefs, but neither can be a substitute for religion. If I am faced with a stark choice between Islam and international law and human rights, I will opt for Islam without any hesitation or doubt whatsoever. From this perspective, I find it imperative for international law and human rights to be seen by religious believers as consistent with their religious beliefs, which is Islam in my case. This fundamental consistency is the basis of my own commitments and work, as presented in this book.

My purpose in gathering this edited collection of essays published during the last twenty years, from 1988 to 2007, is not only to make them more accessible to readers but also to highlight and advance their underlying theme of what I am calling "global justice." While the pieces are organized in this volume in a combination of chronological order and thematic focus, I am also suggesting that these essays advance a theoretical approach to global justice from an Islamic perspective. I am not, of course, implying that I started with this theme back in the mid-1980s or that I began deliberately to develop it along the way. When writing and publishing these essays, I was simply taking advantage of opportunities as they arose, often in response to an invitation to present a paper at a conference or contribute to a journal or an edited volume. What I did have since my student days at the University of Khartoum, Sudan, in the late 1960s was the objective of seeking to reconcile my being a Muslim with my commitment to peaceful international relations and the protection of universal human rights. As I explain in most essays in this volume, however, my ability to reconcile my religious beliefs and these commitments is entirely due to the personal guidance and Islamic reform methodology of my Ustadh (revered teacher) Mahmoud Mohamed Taha. Under his religious guidance and through his profound insights, I began my own "dialogue of Islam and human rights." His exemplary life experience also inspired and enabled my personal commitment to this concept of "global justice."

The position I am now trying to advance is founded in the belief that the right and ability of individual persons to strive, in solidarity with others, for achieving and sustaining their own conception of justice is integral to that end. The global dimension is to emphasize the need not only to "think globally and act locally," the familiar mantra of social activism, but also to "think locally and act globally" to achieve justice for all human beings as also integral to achieving justice for ourselves. This combination is necessary because the interdependence of the local and global makes thinking and acting at either level alone insufficient under present conditions of accelerating and intensifying globalization. As I argue in some of the essays in this collection, this reciprocal conception of justice is a matter of pragmatic strategy as well as moral mandate. This conception calls for "reimagining global justice" in order to shift focus from the present statecentric view of international law and relations to a people-centered approach to human rights and constant self-determination of persons and communities.

In this introduction, I will discuss what I mean by global justice and its rationale as an organizing principle for this collection of essays and highlight the main ideas and concepts I have tried to advance in this body of work. I will also try to explain why a "reimagination" of global justice is needed, elaborate on some aspects of my conception, outline a proposed approach to its realization, and close with an overview of the chapters and how they relate to this subject. In the last part of this introduction, I will explain my preference in the title of this book for speaking of Muslims, as believers in their own respective historical context, rather than the religion of Islam as such.

To begin with, I think there are both a procedural aspect and a substantive dimension to my conception of global justice. At one level, I am concerned with promoting and securing the necessary conditions for the most inclusive and uncensored dialogue among religious and cultural traditions of the world. From this participatory perspective, I have proposed promoting an "overlapping consensus" among religious or cultural traditions and opposed imperial imposition of any tradition or philosophy on others. On the substantive side, I have also called for internal discourse within Islamic societies to promote consensus among Muslims on conceptions of justice they can share with other societies. Therefore, my approach to global justice is collaborative rather than perspective—it is the process of global consensus building and resisting the imposition of specific theologically or philosophically conditioned conceptions of justice by some societies on others.

In that process, I contribute my own views about social justice on any issue, which tend to emphasize interdependence rather than dichotomy between civil and political versus social, economic, and cultural human rights. This distinction between two types of human rights was a product of ideological rivalry during the Cold War and not justified from a human rights point of view. My approach also emphasizes interaction between human rights and other aspects of global public policy on issues of international peace and security, environmental sustainability, and capacity building of local, civil-society actors, as well as international institutions. But all I claim for myself is the right to participate in the collective process of defining and implementing globally inclusive conceptions of social justice. Instead of attempting to impose my views on others, I seek to participate in the debate in the hope of reaching consensus on the issue.

The position I am hoping to advance is premised on the following inter-related propositions.

1. Human perception and experience are always of the individual person, and any collective representation of that is a metaphorical approximation of that personal sensibility. The moral sensibilities and actions of individual persons are the building blocks of the transformative force we call collective action, even though collectivities are not entities that think, feel, and act as such. In other words, to say that collective notions are metaphorical is not to underestimate their influence on individual perception and experience, as individual persons are formed by and dependent on their social relationships. Rather, the point is that we need to address and motivate the individual person who is the entity that can perceive and experience justice and injustice and that can act accordingly. Yet, the meaning of what is perceived and experienced, as well as the ability to act and the likely outcome of action, all occur within the person's social network, in solidarity with and support of other members of the collectivity.

2. This interdependent view of justice is necessary for the motivation of individual persons to act in pursuit of justice within their context of living and interacting with causes of injustice and resources for action. Among the many factors influencing perceptions, experience, and action on justice issues, religion is likely to have a strong role for believers in a variety of ways and at different levels. This is not to say that religion is important for all people or is the sole relevant factor for religious believers, but simply to affirm that the influence of religion for believers can work in multiple ways. For instance, religion for believers serves as an interpretative frame of reference for their perceptions of what is just or unjust, influences their motivation to act accordingly, and provides institutional and material resources for their action.

3. All persons in their communities need to draw on legitimate normative

standards and effective institutional resources for promoting justice and resisting injustice. We tend to perceive justice in terms of what we accept as legitimate normative standards and organize our action through institutional structures and organizations that are capable of applying those standards. Distinguishing between normative and institutional resources is not to imply dichotomy. There is an organic and constantly interactive relationship between these resources and the processes of their application and operation. Efforts to set and clarify legitimate standards and develop effective resources are, therefore, integral to our struggle for justice at all levels, from the local to the global and back to the local. Norms and resources at each level are necessary but insufficient, as we need an interactive combination of local and global strategies. These local-global dynamics are becoming increasingly necessary because of the mounting interaction of local and national conditions of social and political integration at an accelerated speed and intensity.

To further clarify what I mean by global justice and why this concept needs to be reimagined, I will first discuss how I see human rights as the framework of global justice. Second, I will examine ways of mediating the tensions or paradoxes within this human rights framework itself. The third element in the process of defining and realizing global justice is the human subjects who are both the end and means of achieving justice for themselves.

Human Rights as a Framework for Global Justice

At a basic level, the imperative of global justice is premised on the realities of accelerating and intensifying globalization, as we are continuously crossing borders and sharing identities throughout the world. Even for those who are physically confined to specific places, the realities of globalization mean that their economic and security interests, as well as social relations and cultural identities, are not determined exclusively by that location. But notions of crossing borders and relating to different geographies and identities are only new ways of reframing the same basic questions of politics and justice, whoever one happens to be or wherever located. These questions include how to organize the distribution of political power and economic resources, to achieve transparency and accountability of officials, always in specific contexts of time and place. As human beings, we are always somewhere and constituted as persons in relation to other persons, individually and collectively in social and political relations to each other. When we cross boundaries, physical or metaphorical, we are forming new boundaries because we are redefining our location, without eliminating all boundaries by crossing them. As long as boundaries exist, we are likely to face the same kinds of questions of distribution, allocation, and accountability in our new locations. Intensified dynamics of local and global interaction do not mean complete detachment from time and place. The interplay of the local and global does mean, in my view, that these questions cannot be addressed in one place or time frame, in isolation of what is happening in other places other times. This is what I referred to earlier as thinking locally and acting globally as well as thinking globally and acting locally. What happens everywhere is relevant to what is happening anywhere. People are reexamining their history and what it means in their relationship with other people, whether former colonial powers or fellow colonial subjects.

The notion of global justice can, of course, be invoked in a wide variety of settings, in relation to an extensive range of issues and concerns. Consequently, an equally wide variety of actors, representing an extensive range of experiences and priorities, must continue to negotiate the meaning and implications of justice in each case. This can be in relation to problems of terrorism and retaliatory violence, as illustrated below by September 11, 2001, and its aftermath, or over issues of race, health, development, and the environment, among countless other possibilities. I would not therefore presume to define what justice should mean in such an expansive multitude of settings. Instead, I will simply indicate a sufficiently broad framework where the concept and its implications can be negotiated and mediated among competing claims and perspectives.

It is in this limited and specific sense that I propose human rights as a set of safeguards to ensure sufficient "space" for all perspectives to emerge and be considered, as well as being an institutional framework for realizing specific claims. For this to work, the human rights concept must be understood broadly as an interdependent set of moral and political entitlements that include economic, social, and cultural rights, as well as civil and political rights of individuals or collectivities. For example, civil and political rights like freedom of expression and association are obviously necessary for ensuring the space for the articulation of claims, but the right to education, commonly regarded as a social right, is equally necessary for that to happen. That is, people need education to be able effectively to exercise their freedoms of expression and association. Furthermore, while both "kinds" of rights belong to individual persons, they can only be realized in a meaningful and sustainable manner in group or collective settings, in relation to other persons and groups like families and communities. The conception of human rights I am working with also includes legal articulation and institutional implementation of these rights. I will now outline some features of this framework, subject to further elaboration later.

The ability of human rights to be an effective framework for global justice is contingent on a variety of factors, especially the possibility of the universality of these rights, the fundamental and essential prerequisite of the concept itself. The universality of human rights means that they are the rights of every human being, everywhere, without any other requirements of status or location other than being human. As such, human rights cannot be defined or implemented except through constant and dynamic inclusion of all perspectives, experiences, and priorities. In other words, the universality of human rights can only be defined and realized in practice through the most globally inclusive multilateral process. In view of the shared vulnerability of all human beings to harm and injustice, we need to invest in human rights as a normative system that can follow us everywhere and serve whoever we happen to be, whether citizens, immigrants, or refugees.

This view of human rights also requires these norms and their implementation mechanisms to be constantly reimagined because, as new constituencies emerge and new identities are formed or negotiated, more or different priorities and concerns will also need to be addressed. This is not to say that every claim of a new right has to be accepted; but for the concept to retain its universality and relevance, new claims must be given serious consideration and judged by the most inclusive criteria through the widest possible multilateral process. As briefly highlighted later in this Introduction, and at length in some of the essays of this volume, no cultural/religious or philosophical/ideological perspective should be either privileged or overlooked in determining what qualifies as a human right, and no context should be either preferred or rejected in deciding how any human right, old or new, can be implemented in practice. For example, the universality of human rights must transcend its liberal antecedent in Western political history and philosophy, in relation to those rights classified as economic, social, and cultural rights (ESCR), which are not given the same weight and consideration at present as civil and political. Moreover, the mechanisms for the implementation of human rights must be multilateral in an institutional manner, not just through ad hoc coalitions of convenience among powerful countries to be imposed on the rest of the world.

We also need to appreciate and engage the profoundly political nature of the process, without underestimating the practical value of striving to expand the legal obligation of states to respect and promote these rights under international treaties. However clear and categorical a legal obligation may be, it is unlikely to be respected in practice without a political constituency that is willing and able to push for that obligation to be fulfilled. The broader implementation of human rights in ways that preempt and avoid actual violations, instead of reacting to them after they happen, also requires the political will to allocate human and material resources, adopt and implement necessary policies, and so forth.

Moreover, there are several related tensions in the conception of how human rights can serve as a viable framework for global justice. One tension is how to implement the idea of "equal rights of all humans" without distinction or discrimination in a world of national sovereignty and citizenship. This tension can be mitigated by viewing respect for these rights as integral to the definition of sovereignty itself, coupled with a more effective implementation of these rights everywhere as "a common standard of achievement for all nations and peoples" as proclaimed in the Preamble of the Universal Declaration of Human Rights in 1948. When they are viewed as such and equally applied in all countries, no country would have reason to complain that its sovereignty is compromised more than another's. The common human resistance to being judged is mitigated by the knowledge that we are all being judged by the same standards equally and consistently and that we are judging others as well as being judged by them.

Another tension is the distinction between citizen and alien. It may be helpful first to note here that all rights are always violated or protected on the ground, within the territorial jurisdiction of one state or another. The antecedents of human rights are often traced to the English Magna Carta, the American Declaration of Independence, and the French Declaration of the Rights of Man and the Citizen; but all those documents were concerned exclusively with the rights of citizens—on a very limited understanding of citizenship at that—and not the rights of all human beings in general. In other words, the benefits of earlier constitutional documents were limited to citizenship, narrowly defined, and not extended to humanity at large. The idea of universal rights for all human beings only emerged after World War II and the establishment of the United Nations. Still, this revolutionary idea does not seek to equate human rights with all the rights of citizens but only to set a minimum standard of universal rights for all human beings everywhere. For example, freedom from torture and the right to due process of law are due to all human beings, but citizens have additional rights, like the right to vote and hold public office in their own country. The human rights doctrine requires the territorial state to respect the human rights of all persons who are subject to its jurisdiction, while recognizing that the citizens of the state in question have additional rights that are not due to aliens.

The present linkage of human rights obligations to national sovereignty is premised on European conceptions of the nation-state that have become the global model for national governance and international relations. Since these conceptions are the product of specific local and regional developments, they are open to change, as can be seen in the comprehensive regional integration of Europe and global economic integration through the World Trade Organization (WTO). This is not to say that the "withering away" of the nation-state, with its restrictive notions of citizenship, is likely to be complete or immediate. Instead, as I will briefly highlight later, the point is about the possibility of a gradual diminishing of the supremacy of sovereignty and relaxation of the exclusively of citizenship into regional, and eventually global, inclusion.

It may be helpful to conclude this overview of human rights as a framework for global justice by illustrating how it can apply to a specific recent situation. Since struggles for justice are being waged over all sorts of grievances and concerns everywhere, one can pick up the thread of debate and reflection almost anywhere at any point in time. The fact that this universal reality tends to have a disproportionate impact on poorer and disenfranchised persons and groups might lead one to begin from that perspective. The ability of the rich and powerful to attract more attention to their concerns at the expense of greater suffering by others is often part of the problem. While sensitive to this disproportionate manifestation of relative injustice, I prefer to consider the case of the terrorist attacks of September 11, 2001, in the United States and their aftermath to draw several lessons of general application to the theme of global justice.

To be clear on the point, by the aftermath of September 11, 2001, I am referring to the illegal U.S. invasion and occupation of Iraq in March 2003 in particular, as well as the gross human rights and humanitarian law violations perpetrated during and following the U.S. invasion of Afghanistan in October 2001. While it could be argued that the invasion of Afghanistan was justified by an expansive understanding of the right to self-defense, there is no doubt that the United States and its allies have committed massive violations of international humanitarian and human rights law for most of the duration of the administration of President George W. Bush, which ended in January 2009. It is ironic that the United States grossly abused its right to justice against the perpetrators of the vicious crime against humanity of September 11, 2001, by perpetrating for several years massive injustices against countless innocent victims in its bid to destroy its enemies. Moreover, the United States must be judged here by the standard appropriate for a sovereign state and world leader, a Permanent Member of the Security Council of the United Nations who is responsible for protecting international peace and security, instead of reducing its moral and political responsibility to the level of a few renegade terrorists. From this perspective, I am highlighting the following points.

First, the fact that a small group of determined men could launch such a devastating attack on the most powerful country in the world today emphasizes what I call our shared vulnerability—the recognition that all human beings everywhere are vulnerable to arbitrary violence. Moreover, our failure to see ourselves everywhere as potential victims can become a major source of suffering for others when we act recklessly to gratify our outrage at the expense of the needs of others for basic security and well-being. Conversely, the more we appreciate our shared universal vulnerability, in all its different and varied forms and manifestations, the more effectively we can respond to the challenge of terrorism and all other forms of political violence, as well as poverty, disease, and other dangers. In particular, it is clear that the appropriate response to our universal vulnerability should be that of the international community at large through its lawful institutions, like the United Nations, and not through fragmented and arbitrary vigilante justice and self-help by some states or non-state actors.

Second, another aspect of our shared vulnerability I have observed in the United States in the aftermath of September 11, 2001, is the tendency to grant governments extraordinary powers so that they can "protect us" against an amorphous and invisible danger at home and abroad. This understandable impulse can perhaps be resisted when there are sufficient resources for lawful and humane responses to injustice, but it is unrealistic to expect people simply to endure harm or injustice without resisting or retaliating against the perceived perpetrators or source. But this is true for people on both sides of any issue; the risk of violent resistance or retaliation is as likely against relatively powerful actors, like the United States, as it is against apparently less powerful protagonists. Again, the lesson here is about the importance of developing sufficient resources for effective remedy and redress to avoid the risk of counterproductive arbitrary retaliation, whoever is the victim or perpetrator.

Third, part of the futility of arbitrary retaliation at the presumed source of harm without addressing the underlying causes, of terrorism in this case, is that it leaves the victims vulnerable to further attacks in the future. Although it is true that a hardcore group of extremists like those who perpetrated the September 11, 2001, terrorist attacks—or national chauvinists like those who pursued the reckless American response—will probably harbor aggressive designs, whatever others may do or fail to do, it is also clear that such elements cannot act on those designs without the support of a much larger number of people who can be persuaded to refuse to cooperate with the extremist or chauvinist few, if the grievances of that wider constituency are addressed. Neither the terrorist attacks nor the American retaliation could have happened without the support of a wider constituency on each side. In my view, a much wider circle of responsibility expands to include many more people around the world, in different capacities and to varying degrees, for having incited, condoned, or acquiesced to injustice or aggression. This can happen by justifying or condoning the specific action in question, permitting the continuation of injustices that can motivate the perpetrators of arbitrary violence, or failing to ensure the establishment of a credible system of accountability and redress according to due process of the law, whatever the crime and whoever the perpetrator.

Fourth, we should draw instructive lessons from such tragedies as a matter of principle and beyond the details of the specific case. Part of the threat of terrorism to human rights is precisely because it provides a powerful temptation to sacrifice principled commitment to the due process of law in the name of defending national security and public safety. The ultimate object of terrorism, whether perpetrated by state officials or non-state actors, is to diminish the humanity of its victims and reduce them to its own level of barbarity. To respond to this challenge, each society needs to uphold its own enlightened and humane best interest in the face of such grotesque behavior. In particular, since direct retaliation will only feed into a spiral of mutual destruction, each society has to strive to understand and address possible causes of senseless carnage, however alien and incomprehensible such causes may be to the society's own values or sense of rationality. Failure to acknowledge and address the rationality of the terrorists is to deny their humanity and thereby undermine the universality of human rights for all. That is why it is necessary to try our utmost to understand and respond to the underlying injustice that may make any wider community sympathetic to the claims of terrorists, without conceding those claims as such or accepting that terrorism can ever be a legitimate or justified means of redressing any perceived grievances. The most compelling example of this is the occupation and humiliation, loss of land and humanity suffered by Palestinians. Addressing that underlying injustice does not mean conceding radical calls for the destruction of the State of Israel or conceding that Hamas actions are justified by the justice of the Palestinian cause.

Fifth, any appropriate response to violence or other injustice must, therefore, be firmly grounded in a clear appreciation of the multifaceted and universally shared vulnerability of all human beings, everywhere, instead of the illusion that any of us as persons or communities can escape it by fortifications, preemptive or retaliatory violence, accumulation of wealth, or exploitation of others. An appreciation of all sorts of shared vulnerability will indicate different modes of response for different people, each person in his or her own "location," however defined, but all responses must be focused on achieving justice for all human beings everywhere in order to secure it for ourselves. That is, the realities of our global interdependence require all of us to strive to realize global justice for the whole of humanity, not for some more than others.

The general conclusion to draw from this illustration is that the only viable and sustainable alternative to all forms of arbitrary violence and injustice, whatever the source or alleged justification, is for the whole of humanity to seek ways of addressing its underlying causes, including the genuine and legitimate concerns of all those who justify, condone, or facilitate acts of violence and other forms of injustice. The underlying causes of injustice and concerns for those who justify, condone, or facilitate terrorist attacks or imperial domination of others include broader issues of global social justice, as well as the immediate grievances suffered or perceived by the perpetrators. The just and legitimate rule of law must also be maintained against all perpetrators of injustice, whether committed by private persons or state-actors and regardless of their motivation or alleged justification.

By "just and legitimate rule of law" I mean one that authorizes proportionate self-defense when necessary and ensures justice and accountability in accordance with due process of international as well as domestic law. The fact that adequate and effective justice and accountability are unlikely under current international relations is part of the reason we need to reimagine global justice. We have to invest in the norms, institutions, and processes of lawful protection of security and effective accountability in accordance with the rule of law.

The Prophet of Islam is reported to have told his followers to support the aggressor as well as the victim. They responded: we understand how to support the victim, but how can we support the aggressor? The Prophet replied: by driving him back from aggression. In today's increasingly diverse and complex global relations, driving back the aggressor should be done by the collective action of the international community by reimagining justice through its lawful institutional mechanisms of justice and accountability, as noted earlier, and not by arbitrary self-help and vigilante justice.

Mediating Paradox and Negotiating Conflict

In this part, I will examine how we can mediate some of the paradoxes and negotiate some of the conflicts of human rights as a framework for global justice. That is, I need to address the question of how human rights can serve the role I envisage for them in defining and implementing global justice when the idea of universality itself is perceived to be inconsistent with the reality of cultural and religious difference. How can human rights serve this function when they are expected to be enforced by states against themselves, what I call the paradox of self-regulation by the state?

The idea of universal human rights is far from being fully realized, but there are good beginnings in the impressive set of international standards adopted since the Universal Declaration of 1948 and various implementation mechanisms at the international, regional, and national levels. Other relevant developments during the second half of the twentieth century include rapid decolonization resulting in tripling the membership of the United Nations, thereby bringing many new voices and concerns at that level. This expansion and diversity of the membership of the United Nations gradually transformed the composition of its relevant organs, like the Human Rights Commission (now Council), and specialized agencies like the United Nations Educational, Scientific and Cultural Organization (UNESCO) and the United Nations Population Fund (UNFPA). Technological advances in communications, travel, and a series of United Nations conferences on the environment, human rights, and women rights have also facilitated the development of global networks of nongovernmental organizations (NGOs) cooperating on these issues at the local and global levels. The development of regional human rights systems in Europe, the Americas, and Africa has also fostered a stronger sense of relevance and legitimacy for human rights norms, as the standards are set and implemented in the same cultural and geopolitical sphere. Thus, the provision and implementation of a human rights norm like equality for women under the African Charter of Human and Peoples Rights of 1981 cannot be dismissed within the continent itself as a neocolonial imposition of Western values. With this precedent and an increasing number of those in favor of human rights as a framework for global justice, why do human rights problems persist throughout the world?

It is, of course, difficult to generalize about the actual level of protection of human rights around the world not only because of the lack of systematic and comprehensive monitoring but also because of the general difficulty of assessing the success of this framework, as distinguished from other factors. On the first count, the large number of "monitoring and advocacy" organizations operating on the model set since the early 1960s by Amnesty International tend to focus on limited instances of violation of the civil and political rights of elites, rather than critical assessment of compliance with *all* human rights standards for the general population. The "human development index" of the United Nations Development Programme (UNDP) has pioneered efforts to present a systematic and comprehensive assessment of the status of various populations around the world according to a wide range of indicators. However, it is difficult to identify the causes of a particular situation in terms of human rights principles as such, as opposed to a wide range of historical and contextual factors that affect human development in general. Subject to these and related difficulties of monitoring improvements and identifying its causes, one can still appreciate at least a strong association of the level of respect for or violation of human rights norms with such factors as political instability, economic underdevelopment, and weakness or corruption of institutional structures and resources, like the civil service, judiciary, and police. This association indicates the need to combine an integrated approach to addressing structural and underlying causes of human rights violations with remedy and accountability for individual violations when possible and appropriate.

Moreover, the purpose of a realistic assessment of what has been achieved and what remains to be done should be directed at implementing appropriate strategies to break the cycle of violation and transform conditions that produce and perpetuate suffering among local populations. To say that poverty and underdevelopment should end through more investment and development assistance and/or better trade terms between rich and poor countries only begs the question of how that is going to happen. Decrying bad planning and mismanagement of the economy by corrupt local elite or the weakness of national structures and institutions does not address the issue of when any of this will change and how. In contrast, framing the question in terms of what we should do shifts the focus to what each of us can do in order to produce the desired outcome—it is a question about the role of the *human agency* of all of us everywhere, as the only way change can be realized in practice. To move away from violations as symptoms of underlying causes, we need to focus on human beings whose actions can create resources, reform weak or corrupt national and international institutions, or change the domestic and foreign policies of their countries. The question is how to motivate and empower people to confront the difficulties of rendering the universality of human rights a realistic framework of global justice.

While appreciating that calling for action by human subjects exposes them to serious risks of harsh response from perpetrators of human rights violations, there is simply no alternative to the human agency of the subjects to achieve global justice for themselves. At a more fundamental level, however, the agency of the human subject is integral to the idea of human rights itself—it is what I call "the "human" in "human rights." This linkage locates the humanity of the subject at the core of the norm and its application. From this perspective, the human in human rights should be a self-determining person, one who decides what her rights are and how she can protect them. This is not to say that human beings are already self-determining everywhere, but that situation is the objective and rationale of human rights as a framework for global justice. Both the pragmatic and principled aspects of my focus on the human agency of the subject are addressed in some chapters of this volume in relation to the role of religion and culture more broadly, as well as the role of civil society organizations in mobilizing and empowering people to act in defense of their own human rights. There is also the question of the relationship of citizenship to human rights to be highlighted later; but for now, I will outline some theoretical concerns.

The universality of any normative system, like human rights, is a paradoxical notion because it contradicts our inherent and protracted relativity as the inevitable product of our social and material location. We can only understand the world and relate to notions of right and wrong, just and unjust, and claim our rights and fulfill our obligations within our own network of human relations in terms of who we are and where we are located. As I argue in some chapters of this volume, the paradox of affirming universal human rights norms despite the difficulty of escaping our respective cultural/contextual relativity in a world of profound and permanent diversity can be mediated through an overlapping consensus on commonly agreed principles, even in the face of disagreement on our respective reasons for that shared commitment. That is, we can agree on the idea of universal rights and achieve some consensus on what those rights should be and how they can be implemented despite our disagreement as to the reasons for our own commitment. Some may come to that shared position out of a religious rationale, while others may have pragmatic reasons or prefer a secular philosophical approach; yet we agree on the principle and its application. Our consensus is "overlapping" because it covers the same shared understanding, but we do not need to have the same reasons for sharing that view. However, to establish genuine universality of human rights, this process must be fully inclusive and genuinely open-ended, and we must all be both appreciative of other perspectives and critical of our own. The more we are sensitive to our own relativity and tendency to project our values and perceptions on other people, challenge our assumptions and practices, the closer we get to consensus on the universality of human rights. The more multilateral and globally inclusive the source of the norm and the more consistent our application of the same norms to ourselves, the more will our judgment of others be acceptable to them and motivate them to change offending practices.

The second paradox that must be mediated is the dependence of human rights protections on self-regulation by the state. The performance of every state must be judged by the human rights standard, regardless of what its own constitution, legal system, and policies provide for or implement. The paradox is real because the violation or protection of human rights necessarily happens within the geographical and legal jurisdiction of one state or another, yet the principle of sovereignty and territorial integrity of the state under Article 2 (7) of the Charter of the United Nations precludes external intervention to protect human rights without the consent and cooperation of the state itself. One aspect of the paradox is that states are entrusted with the implementation of international standards against themselves within their own borders. Another aspect of the paradox is that the present international system also relies on the willingness of states to hold each other accountable for their human rights failures, often at some economic, political, security, or other costs to their own national interests. For instance, the United States is supposed to press Israel and Saudi Arabia for their human rights violations at the expense of its security and strategic interests. Even more absurd is the expectation that either of those states, or other states that are allied with or dependent on the United States, is likely to criticize the United States for its human rights violations. Moreover, even if states are willing to criticize each other, external pressure is difficult to sustain and is often counterproductive.

Both aspects of this paradox of self-regulation—of each state of itself or states of each other—require some external source of pressure. The internal aspect of the paradox within the same state is, of course, true of enforcement of fundamental constitutional rights against abuse and excess of power by national governments. That aspect has traditionally been addressed at that level by the emergence of strong local civil-society organizations that are willing and able to use domestic legal institutions and political processes to force governments to comply. It is ultimately up to citizens to hold officials of the state accountable for any violation that may occur and to ensure the adoption of appropriate policies and provision of necessary resources by the state for broader implementation of human rights norms. It is difficult to see this scenario effectively working in all states, especially in the most oppressive and authoritarian situations where human rights need the most protection. In view of this reality, it is necessary for all human agents to be able to act to protect the human rights of all human beings regardless of national citizenship as such. This is one rationale of the concept of "global citizenship" to be highlighted later.

Now to consider another tension in the scenario outlined above, even when it is supposed to be working. The ultimate measure of success is for human rights to be respected and protected routinely in the first place, as well as ensuring that effective accountability immediately follows whenever a violation occurs. In both aspects, in the final analysis, citizens acting through a variety of strategies and levels can ensure systematic and sustainable protection of human rights. Where local citizens are unable or unwilling to act to protect human rights, say, of women or religious minorities, then the international community is supposed to take up the cause by "naming and shaming" offending governments into compliance with human rights norms. The main idea here is that careful documentation and publication of credible reports of human rights violations will generate sufficient moral and political pressure to force offending governments to stop violating the human rights of their own citizens within their own borders. Another aspect of this strategy is that the naming and shaming of offending governments will persuade the governments of rich "donor" countries to make their development aid or political, diplomatic support for offending governments of poor underdeveloped countries conditional on the latter governments' ceasing their violations of human rights norms.

I call this scenario "human rights dependency" because it makes the protection of the right of local populations dependent on the good will and ability of external actors to pressure offending governments to respect human rights. Since naming and shaming are unlikely to influence the most seriously offending governments unless they realize that they risk significant economic or political costs of violations, the whole scenario is premised on the dependency of offending governments on the economic aid and political good will of donor countries. In this way, both the civil society and interstate aspects of the present international system are founded on the economic, political, and security dependency of African, Asian, and Latin American states on rich and former colonial European and North American states, without questioning or seeking to adjust the global injustice of this neocolonial power relationship. Moreover, the present approach can only work in a piecemeal and reactive manner, responding to human rights violations after they occur, rather than preempting them or preventing their occurrence in the first place. It also needs to focus on specific cases, or at best limited issues, to be effective, without attempting to address structural causes of human rights violations or creating institutional mechanisms for sustainable respect for and protection of rights. Other governments must be willing to risk their national interests in pressuring offending governments, in addition to having some point of leverage in bilateral relations, for the whole scenario to be relevant at all. But the complexity and contingency of foreign policy objectives and priorities of all governments make it difficult to predict how and when any of them will act in which ways, to which outcomes, and how far they would be willing to go, at what costs to their own perceptions of national self-interest.

Despite all these limitations, it would be irresponsible to suggest the immediate shift from international to local protection of human rights, as this would leave local populations at the complete mercy of their oppressors. While fully accepting that such pragmatic considerations must be taken seriously, the question remains: what else can be done in addition to whatever external measures are taken to protect the human rights of local populations? In particular, it is imperative to adopt appropriate strategies designed to diminish dependency over time in view of the obvious problems with the present approach, as outlined above. The degree and quality of empowering local actors to protect their own human rights should always be the underlying criteria for evaluating all activities and strategies because this approach is consistent with the rationale of human rights in the first place. The human dignity of every person should be upheld by his or her own agency, instead of being dependent on the goodwill of others, which is often doubtful or mixed with their own interests.

All these and related factors were, of course, known and appreciated by human rights advocates who had to negotiate around them to achieve the best possible results for their own objectives. Still, I am raising these issues here as part of my call for reimagining global justice through the human rights framework, a challenge to think in more creative pragmatic ways about how to recover the initiative and continue to achieve stronger and more sustainable protection of human rights everywhere. As already suggested, in particular, it is imperative to shift the focus of human rights advocacy to be more "people-centered" and less dependent on the ambiguities and contingencies of intergovernmental relations. This does not mean stopping all efforts accurately to monitor human rights violations in order to use the information in pressuring governments to comply with their international obligations. It is simply an invitation to human rights advocates to integrate in their current human rights work practical ways of promoting local capacity everywhere as the best means of mediating the paradox of self-regulation by the state. Since human rights violations are likely to continue into the future, the work of human rights advocates will never be fully and conclusively done, neither at home nor abroad. Investing in local actors to protect their own rights is, therefore, a long-term investment in our own future.

Global Citizenship and Global Civil Society

As noted earlier, the paradox of self-regulation by the state at the national constitutional level has been mediated by citizens acting through their civil society organizations. I also suggested that civil society organizations and public opinion at large must be willing and able to act in a similar manner for the protection of human rights throughout the world, not only within their own country. From this perspective, I argue that global citizenship is needed to play the role for universal human rights that is played by national citizenship for domestic constitutional rights. Since both the above-noted paradoxes of universality and self-regulation by the state should be mediated through the agency of human beings everywhere, global citizenship is a critically important status and institution that enables and safeguards that agency in practice. The mutual support and synergy of citizenship and human rights are possible in that the latter provide the normative content of citizenship, which is the practical framework for people to organize to enforce and protect these rights on the ground. This interconnectedness is facilitated by the dynamic and evolving nature of both human rights and citizenship, but I am concerned at this stage with the evolution of citizenship through theoretical reflection as well as political and legal developments.

The need for the evolution of the concept of citizenship from its traditional national level to a global scale is inherent in the idea of the universality of human rights as the rights of every human being and not only of the citizens of a particular state. The challenge of reimagining and evolving citizenship from a human rights perspective is integral to reimagining global justice because this challenge is global in the sense that it faces the adherents of all religions and belief systems, state and nonstate actors, national and transnational entities, scholars, and civil-society actors. However, the idea of global citizenship is about an overlapping conception of global and national citizenship, what can be called "layered citizenship," and does not purport to abolish all legal and political distinctions between citizens and noncitizens of a state. Such distinctions are indeed necessary and justified from a human rights point of view.

It is already established that the universality of human rights requires certain minimum standards in the treatment of noncitizens by the authorities of the state, regardless of their legal status. To speak of the possibility of global citizenship does not eliminate the need to consider the rationale and implications of distinctions among citizens and noncitizens, as well as among different categories of noncitizens, in relation to particular rights' claims. For example, human rights such as protection against torture or inhuman degrading treatment or punishment and the requirement of fair trial and due process of law must be secured on a universal basis. In contrast, the right to vote or be elected to public office is clearly due only to citizens, though limited voting rights may be accorded to long-term residents of a country or municipality in proportion to their contribution to the well-being of the community. It is also possible to justify a higher level of entitlement to education, health services, and employment opportunities for citizens than noncitizens, a lower level of some of these benefits for permanent residents, and none for transient visitors to a country who do not pay taxes or fulfill other obligations of citizenship or legal residence. While fully conceding the legitimacy of such distinctions, I hope that the linkage of universality of human rights and global citizenship should facilitate the granting of citizenship at the national level while gradually diminishing any distinction between citizens and non-citizens that cannot be justified in human rights terms.

As I have explained in the last chapter in this volume, the idea of a global or world citizenship is, in fact, ancient and has been supported by philosophers and jurists for the last 2,500 years. For example, Diogenes the Cynic (412–323 B.C.E.) called himself a "citizen of the world," and Hugo Grotius (1583–1645) argued for limiting the sovereignty of the state according to the law of nature because all persons are members of a world society. In 1623, Emeric Cruce proposed a global association, including non-Western nations like Persia, China, and Ethiopia, where decisions would be made by a majority vote on policies and rules. But such visions of a global political system capable of sustaining the idea of global citizenship have been overcome by perception of interstate relations in Europe since the nineteenth century, whereby law and the concept of citizenship remained focused on state sovereignty and territorial jurisdiction. That European model became universalized through colonization of South America, Africa, and much of Asia, but that should not preclude possibilities of future development and adaptation of citizenship to better serve the evolving needs of human beings and communities.

The contemporary discourse on global citizenship is approached by scholars and politicians from widely divergent perspectives, ranging from a call to cultivate global citizenship through a global market to the role of the nation-state as a mechanism for the realization of a legal conception of global citizenship. Some scholars argue for shared sovereignty, whereby a legal conception of global citizenship can coexist with the nation-state if nation-states would "pool their sovereignty in common institution and norms." From this perspective, an alternative to totally integrated shared sovereignty that has proven elusive so far, it may be possible to get closer to a legal and political global citizenship through a layered structure of multiple or overlapping systems of citizenship. One possibility is "regional" citizenship that would foster social development, civil rights, and security, by linking states. The European Union seems to be heading in this direction of regional citizenship coexisting with traditional national citizenship. This sense of layered citizenship is linked to the widespread entry of transnational migrant communities into the public sphere, long-distance nationalism, the rise of dual national identities, and the emergence of cross-border civic and political communities, as well as multilateral institutions and regional integration in different parts of the world. This can be seen in varying degrees of regional integration in the Community of Sahel-Saharan States (CEN-SAD) in Africa, Association of Southeast Asian Nations (ASEAN) and North American Free Trade Agreement (NAFTA), in addition to highly integrated regions like the European Union.

The apparent paradox that needs to be mediated is that citizenship is both the means for protecting human rights and a limit on the universality of these rights. If only citizens are entitled to rights like freedom of expression, opinion and belief, health care and education, how can these rights also be due to all human beings? This paradox can be mediated by thinking of two sets of overlapping entitlements: civil rights based on national citizenship and human rights based on global citizenship. But if that is the case, how can human rights be the standard for judging the protection of rights in every state or country if only civil rights of citizens can be protected within each state? The only way I can see out of this paradox is to develop layered or overlapping conceptions of citizenship to match the entitlements to civil rights to that of entitlements to human rights. Among the range of arguments I make for this proposition in the last chapter are the ways in which the issue of national and regional citizenship is being negotiated in the context of the European Union. As can be seen in that experience, however, the process is difficult and protracted even within a limited and highly homogenous region like Western Europe.

My proposal for negotiating such difficulties is to avoid presenting the issue in terms of a drastic and immediate choice between traditional national citizenship, on the one hand, and various levels of equal, legal global citizenship, on the other. The idea of global citizenship may be more acceptable in the short term if presented as a moral and political conception of rights and obligations that are subordinate to legal national citizenship. There can also be more emphasis on the reciprocal relationship of rights and obligations of citizenship and what that might mean for global citizenship. A critical part of both the promise and consequences of citizenship for my purposes here is its role in facilitating and regulating the role of civil society in the protection of human rights as a framework for global justice. I will now briefly highlight this aspect of reimagining global justice.

My point of departure here is that our understanding of civil society must be rooted in the local cultural context and practical experiences of local communities, instead of insisting that it must be everywhere in the exact images of Western civil society organizations and processes. This does not mean that the concept and operation of civil society as developed and applied in one part of the world have no relevance to other societies. Rather, I am emphasizing that civil society in every setting should be taken for what it actually is, instead of assuming that it must fit certain preconceived notions of what civil society should be. However, taking civil society as it really exists on the ground would include elements that are antagonistic to such notions as human rights-based global justice, as well as elements that are supportive of these values.

It is also important to understand civil society in any setting in relation to the nature and role of the state since the two spheres are defined and shaped by their relationship to each other. Civil society is transformed by the changing social, economic, and political conditions as represented by the state, while the state is influenced by the activities of civil society in pursuit of competing objectives of various segments of the population. This complementary and dialectical relationship between civil society and the state is realized through existing social structures and institutions.

For the purposes of this collection of essays in particular, it is important to emphasize that the relationship between civil society and the state throughout Africa and Asia, where the vast majority of Muslims live, is the postcolonial nature of state, where colonial policies and practices continue by default for several decades after independence. In particular, the exclusion of much of the population from the political process during the colonial period has sometimes been maintained by the new ruling elite after independence, contrary to the principle of self-determination that brought them to power. Formal independence usually signified the transfer of control over authoritarian power structures and processes of government from colonial masters to local elites, who had little commitment to popular participation in governance and sharing of power among different segments of the population. Unable to govern effectively and humanely, the postcolonial governments of countries where Muslims constitute the majority of the population have tended to compensate by using oppressive and authoritarian methods, employing the same type of colonial legal and institutional mechanisms.

Another caution to note is that taking civil society as it is on the ground necessarily reflects the demographic and sociological features of the country as a whole. That is, the social movements that emerge from and operate within various segments of society will reflect the characteristics of their own communities and constituencies. They are the means that some segments of the population use to assert their demands for political, economic, and social change, which will probably conflict with demands of other segments of the population. In other words, social movements can contribute to intensifying rather than mediating conflict or work for injustice rather than justice. This caution does not mean that the nature and likely contribution of civil society anywhere are necessarily negative for global justice as such. Rather, the challenge is to be clear on the possibilities and limitations of each situation and to be pragmatic in our approach and strategies. As emphasized in several chapters, internal transformation within societies and communities is possible, sometimes imperative, and issues can often be reframed in ways that people find to be less threatening or more attractive from their religious or cultural perspective. The outcome of engaging civil society on its own terms is what I call "contingent" in the sense of being influenced and shaped by a variety of interactive factors, not a foregone conclusion or static status. I am convinced that most outcomes can be modified or changed significantly by the action of the right actors working through the appropriate approaches that is broad and flexible enough to adapt to the changing dynamics of the process.

In light of these remarks about civil society in general, I will now turn to highlighting another related element of my approach to reimagining global justice, namely, the role of global civil society (GCS). The first question to consider is how the variety and contextual nature of civil society in general influence our understanding of GCS and its potential role in realizing global justice. On the one hand, our conception of GCS must be inclusive to be truly global, but on the other hand, that cannot be simply the aggregation of all forms and types of civil society everywhere. For example, it is clear to me that social movements working along Gandhian conceptions and processes of nonviolent resistance are fundamentally different from those inspired by the ideology of Osama bin Laden's al-Qaida, though both types of movements claim to be advancing their own views of global justice. The challenge here is to distinguish between these types of movements without undermining the essentially inclusive approach to GCS in general. Regarding the role of religion in particular, the challenge is to distinguish that role in the Civil Rights Movement in the United States and Liberation Theology in Latin America, for instance, from the role of religion in the violence in Northern Ireland or the Kashmir conflict between India and Pakistan. To exclude al-Qaida or other types of violent organizations from the scope of GCS constructive for the proposed human rights as framework for global justice should not mean abandoning the inclusive approach itself, as each case must be judged on its own terms.

I suggest that the relationship between religion and GCS can be clarified in terms of the relationships between the composition and function of GCS and the impact of space and place on its nature and operation. Clarification of the relationship between its composition and function, what it is and what it is supposed to do, should, in turn, lead to questioning the present composition of GCS to verify whether it is conducive to realizing its objectives. Moreover, one should also take into account the relationship between space and place in order to appreciate how GCS may operate in pursuit of its objectives. GCS should be the space where people and transnational entities debate and negotiate the terms of their relationships and pursue accountability for those terms in furtherance of their respective concerns. However, the physical location of actors conditions their perceptions of and participation in that process. Since people do not interact with transnational entities at an abstract conceptual plane, the question is where and how they actually do participate in GCS activities in the physical world. The nature and dynamics of these two relationships, in turn, affect the way GCS operates in practice at any given point in time.

For example, the fact that some NGOs are now engaged in the provision of services that were traditionally supposed to be provided by the state is a particular outcome of that process in specific place(s). This can happen on a global scale by organizations like CARE and Oxfam. To characterize this phenomenon as pertaining to GCS reflects a certain understanding of the composition and function of GCS and how it might operate in practice. In contrast, other forms of GCS, like the antiglobalization or environmental movements, are questioning the diminishing role and accountability of the state for its failure to provide essential services or protect the environment, instead of simply stepping in to substitute for the state. The first type of function assumes the dominant "free-market ideology" and capitalist economic power relations, while the second seeks to confront and challenge those assumptions.

In other words, conceptions and operation of GCS should take into account a minimum normative content beyond a descriptive notion of simply being nongovernmental and global. Since every analysis of GCS must necessarily emanate from some implicit or presumed normative content, it is better to state that content openly for debate, instead of leaving it to the ideological or cultural bias of the participants. From my perspective, the critical question here is by whom and how that normative content is to be determined. The true "globalness" of GCS requires a more inclusive sense of participants and process for this purpose. The methodology I proposed for "constructing" the universality of human rights can also be used to promote agreement among different constituencies about the normative content of GCS as follows.

As with human rights, the purpose of such discourse and dialogue among different entities of GCS is to broaden and deepen their overlapping consensus over the normative framework of their global association despite their cultural, ideological, and other differences. For this process to work, however, the various entities of GCS in question need to agree on a core set of values, which must be universal human rights values if that is supposed to be the field of their cooperation. In other words, there would be no need for an overlapping consensus if there are no differences among various constituencies of GCS, but that process is unworkable without agreement on at least the conditions necessary for the process of negotiation to continue. Conditions that I hold to be essential for consensus over global justice issues include mutual respect and appreciation of cultural and contextual difference and the possibility of peaceful coexistence. Most importantly, in my view, all constituencies of GCS must appreciate the need to construct an overlapping consensus over the normative content of their solidarity and cooperation, rather than seek to impose their own view of it on others.

Applying this approach to the challenge of the role of religion noted earlier, the question is how to mediate the tension between the presumed exclusivity of religious communities and their tendency strictly to enforce narrowly defined moral codes, on the one hand, and the requirements of inclusion, civility, and freedom of choice of civil society, on the other. According to the proposed model for constructing an overlapping consensus over the normative content of GCS, the mediation of this tension can happen through an internal discourse within religious communities and dialogue with other constituencies. The challenge for those engaged in internal discourse within their own religious communities is how to promote understanding and practice of their religion that are more inclusive, civil, and voluntary in order to support these essential qualities of civil society. The corresponding challenge facing other constituencies of GCS is how to cooperate with religious communities on that joint venture with due regard to the legitimate concerns of all communities, not only religious communities.

An obvious question for this approach, for instance, is what constitutes a "legitimate concern" of one community or another. In my view, this issue should itself be the subject of internal dialogue within religious communities and dialogue with other constituencies. A practical guide for addressing this question is that the concerns of religious communities should be conceived in terms that are consistent with prerequisite conditions for the process of negotiation to continue, as noted earlier. Accordingly, whatever concerns a community deems to be legitimate must be pursued through peaceful means, because violence is counterproductive for the possibility of negotiation with others in the first place.

Recalling my earlier emphasis on human agency, I would emphasize here that the contingent possibilities of reconciliation between religious and other constituencies of GCS must be actively sought by all sides, instead of passively waiting for religious or other persons and communities to succeed or fail the test of inclusion. In conclusion of this brief review, I would emphasize that religion and religious identity can and should be included in our conceptions of GCS precisely because current conditions of globalization clearly show that religion everywhere is socially constructed, dynamic, and implicated in socioeconomic and political power relations to varying degrees in different contexts. From this perspective, I will now offer some reflections on how the preceding analysis applies to Muslims, in my view as a Muslim advocate of human rights as a framework of global justice.

Muslims and Global Justice

It is true that the United Nations Universal Declaration of Human Rights avoided identifying religious justifications for these rights in an effort to find common ground among believers and nonbelievers. But this does not mean that human rights can be founded only on secular justifications because that does not address the need of believers to relate their moral and political actions to their religious beliefs. As already emphasized, the underlying rationale of the human rights idea itself would entitle believers to found their commitment to these norms on their own religious beliefs, in the same way that others may seek to affirm their commitment on secular philosophy. We are all entitled to expect equal commitment to the human rights doctrine from others in our communities and societies, at the national and international level. But this does not mean that any of us can prescribe the grounds on which others may wish to found their commitment. In any case, I find that the dichotomy between the religious and the secular is often exaggerated when it is taken to mean an inherent incompatibility of the two, though they are, in fact, interdependent with human rights.

My personal commitment to human rights is founded on my faith and practice as a Muslim, but as discussed in various essays in this volume, I am also concerned with the case of Islam within the general role of religion as a foundation of the universality and legitimacy of human rights among believers. If human rights are supposed to be universal, as I believe they should, that universality cannot be claimed without taking into account people's religious perspectives and experiences. The idea of universal human rights would be incoherent if it does not take Islam into consideration when Muslims constitute 20 percent of the total world population, living in every continent and region, predominantly in Africa and Asia. They are the majority of the population in more than forty countries, a quarter of the membership of the United Nations. My call for taking religion seriously applies to all religious traditions, not only Islam. In all cases, however, the issue can be meaningful when it is about believers and not the religion in the abstract. That is, it is about Muslims, not Islam; Jews, not Judaism; and so forth, thereby raising the *same* question for all religious traditions. Once framed in this way, the issue becomes about people in their social, economic, and political context and about how those factors affect their understanding or practice of their religion. For all believers, the question is how human beings negotiate the relationships between their religious beliefs and practice, on the one hand, and their daily concerns with security and material well-being, on the other. This perspective also emphasizes that this question should be asked about specific Muslims or Hindus, for instance, and not about all Muslims or Hindus as if they are a monolithic, undifferentiated global community.

As noted at the beginning of this introduction, my focus on particular believers in their own context is intended to engage their personal responsibility and ability to transform their understanding and practice of their own religious tradition. If the issue is framed in terms Islam as an abstract immutable entity, Muslims will probably either feel obliged to "defend their religion" against attack, or assume that there is nothing they can do to respond to the challenge. But if the issue is addressed to human believers, not to Islam as such, Muslims may not be as defensive, and consequently be more willing to reconsider their own understanding and practice of Islam. In other words, focusing on Muslims rather than Islam is more appropriate as a matter of principle because every claim about Islam is in fact about the understanding and practice of Muslims, and not about Islam in its divine essence. This focus is also pragmatically useful for inspiring and enabling the agency of Muslims to seek to transform their human perceptions.

In this light, I would frame my own engagement of human rights as a framework for global justice in terms of the following propositions:

1. The reference to Islam as an important component of the worldview and framework for the social and cultural values and institutions of Islamic communities does not mean it is the sole determining factor or suggests that Islam is understood and practiced in the same way in all situations where it is relevant. Problems of compliance with human rights norms are more likely to be associated with conditions of political instability and economic and social underdevelopment in postcolonial Islamic societies than determined by Islam as such. Moreover, to the extent that Islam is a factor, its role cannot be understood in isolation from other factors that influence how Muslims interpret and attempt to comply with their religious tradition. In other words, one cannot predict or explain the degree or quality of human rights compliance by Islamic societies as the logical consequence of the relationship between Islam and human rights in an abstract theoretical sense.

2. Nevertheless, this relationship is important enough for most Muslims that their motivation to uphold human rights norms will probably diminish if they perceive those norms to be inconsistent with Islamic principles. This is not to suggest that the Islamic tradition at large is inherently or permanently inconsistent with all human rights norms because that is simply not true. But certain specifics of the historical interpretation of Shari'a—namely, regarding the human rights of women and religious minorities and freedom of religion—are clearly problematic from a human rights point of view.

3. It is unrealistic and inconsistent with human dignity as the underlying rationale of the universality of human rights in my view to confront Muslims with a choice between Islam and human rights over such issues. If Muslims or other believers are forced to make a choice between their religion and human rights, they will probably uphold their religion over human rights because the latter cannot be a substitute for religion or rival its transformative power in the lives of believers.

4. A more constructive and practically viable approach, I believe, is to encourage Muslims to reconsider their human interpretation of Shari'a in the present context of their own societies, rather than attempt to superimpose the universality of human rights over what Muslims believe to be required by Shari'a. This approach, I suggest, is necessary as a matter of principle because it is more respectful of the freedom of religion and self-determination for Muslims, as well as being more desirable in pragmatic tactical terms.

5. As I have argued in my own work, including some essays in this volume, I believe that the Islamic reform methodology of Ustadh Mahmoud Mohamed Taha offers a viable and coherent approach to reconciling Muslims' understanding of Shariʿa with universal human rights, but I would also welcome any other Islamic reform proposals that would achieve the necessary degree of reform.

6. My position on the whole question of Shariʿa and human rights has been criticized as approaching Islamic scriptural sources from a particular perspective of commitment to upholding human rights. But this is true of any believer who can approach these sources only from his or her own experience and perspective since there is no possibility of an abstract or neutral interpretation of sacred texts of Islam or any other religion. The question is which values I or any other Muslim seeks to promote through our Islamic beliefs, not the illusion that any of us can be neutral in discovering a pure or abstract interpretation outside the historical experience of human beings. In other words, it is not true that so-called traditionalists or Islamists hold the correct interpretation of Islam, and I am trying to argue against that view. In fact, we all hold our own interpretation of Islamic sources and the historical experience of Islamic societies and should compete equally and fairly in trying to persuade Muslims of the validity of our views. Whether I or any other Muslim is advancing a legitimate or coherent understanding of Islamic sources is for the generality of Muslims to decide, and not for any person, group, or religious institution to prescribe.

7. Whatever position one takes on these issues, the practical outcome is likely to be influenced by a variety of geopolitical, cultural, and other factors, in addition to the theoretical coherence and legitimacy of Islamic methodology. For instance, the sort of internal reinterpretation of Shariʿa I am calling for is unlikely to materialize when Islamic societies feel threatened by external hegemonic forces that seek to undermine their independence and well-being. The challenge for me is to take such apprehensions and concerns seriously in pursing the necessary reform. My plea for a human rights framework for global social justice as explained above is integral to my own strategy for promoting Islamic reform in favor of human rights.

In light of these framing remarks, I will now conclude with an outline of the essays of this volume and explain how they reflect an underlying concern with human rights as a framework for global justice. To begin with, as I said at the very beginning of this chapter, I believe international law and human rights are useful means to enable me to live in accordance with my religious beliefs, as a Muslim in my case, but never as a substitute for my religion. It is from this perspective that I am exploring the relevance and utility of these normative systems as a framework for global justice. As noted earlier, this theme has not been in my deliberate design as I have been publishing the essays of this collection since the mid-1980s. But since the idea of global justice seems to have emerged in my work over time, I now see it as an appropriate organizing principle in selecting these essays and ordering the sequence of their presentation in this volume.

Among the many ways in which such a collection of essays could be organized and sequenced, I have opted for a combination of chronological and thematic methods to present the progression of my thinking on the issues, as well as to demonstrate how each theme and related questions evolved in my work. The collection is organized in three sections that combine this chronological and conceptual development system within each section and among all sections taken together. In general, some basic themes first emerged in the late 1980s and early 1990s and continued to evolve through the 1990s. Thus, the first essay on Islamic ambivalence to political violence, published in 1988, reflects my basic commitment to peaceful international relations, indeed to the very possibility of international law, which is a basic theme that resonates throughout my work. This early essay also applied the approach to Islamic reform methodology of Ustadh Mahmoud Mohamed Taha to issues of jihad and political violence more broadly. Another constant theme that emerged through several essays is the need for cultural legitimacy of the universality of human rights and an approach to promoting that, which are the subjects of Chapters 2 and 3. The development of these two basic themes in relation to international law and human rights can also be observed in Chapters 5, 6 and 7.

My focus on human agency and a people-centered approach to human rights is emphasized in Chapter 4 and continues to evolve in later essays, including Chapter 11 which was published in 2007. The idea of mediation of competing claims and of paradox can be observed emerging in Chapter 6 and evolving in Chapters 8 and 10. The paradoxical role of the state is discussed also in Chapters 4 and 11.

It may be relevant to note here the slightly different emphasis of my most recent work toward issues of the relationship between religion and the state.

I began working on issues of Islam and the secular state in the late 1990s and examined what I call the interdependence of religion, secularism and human rights in some essays published in the early 2000s. Those efforts culminated in my book *Islam and the Secular State* (2008), in which I presented constitutionalism, human rights, and citizenship as the framework for mediating the paradox of the separation of Islam and the state and the connectedness of Islam and politics. I also expect to continue working on this theme as part of the same approach to human rights-based global justice presented in this book. I considered including some essays that show this different emphasis in this collection but decided against that to make this volume more manageable.

In conclusion, I should note that the essays presented in this volume have been substantially edited for language and general clarity, without changing their respective concept, analysis, and argument. I considered doing more substantive revisions in order to incorporate the theme of global justice for this collection but decided against that because that would have distorted the actual progression of my thinking over the last twenty years. However, the original date of publication of each essay is noted in the first note to each chapter so that readers can take the time frame and context in which I was writing into account in considering my argument in each essay. For example, as noted above, the first chapter in this collection is an article I published in 1988 criticizing what I called Islamic ambivalence toward political violence (including international terrorism) and proposing an Islamic methodology to affirm peaceful politics and international relations. It is important for the rationale of the present collection to keep that essay in its original form in order to shows how the Muslim scholars I discussed then were confronting these issues as an internal agenda of Islamic societies, rather than in response to the horrific crimes of 9/11, some thirteen years later.

PART I

The Challenge of Universality
and Cultural/Religious Legitimacy

Chapter 1

Islamic Ambivalence to Political Violence: Islamic Law and International Terrorism

From a formal point of view, it can be said that Islamic law prohibits all violence except in cases of official punishment for crime, strict private self-defense, or formally declared legitimate war as regulated by law. Islamic religious ethics emphasize orderly and peaceful social relations and condemn clandestine violence against defenseless victims. However, there are certain ambiguities in the notions of self-defense and legitimate war, especially as seen in light of certain "precedents" in Islamic history. Moreover, some Islamic sources appear to sanction direct action and self-help. These ambiguities and sources contribute to creating a degree of ambivalence in Muslim attitudes and practice regarding political violence and terrorism, as defined, and to some extent distinguished, in this essay.

It is obvious that none of the above is peculiar to Islam and the Muslims since almost all major historical, religious, and cultural traditions reflect similar ambivalence. Nevertheless, the strong association between religion and political action in Islam makes it particularly important to address these questions in the present Muslim context. This association has been dramatically emphasized by recent demands for a greater role for Islam and Islamic law in public life throughout the Muslim world. In other words, historical Islamic religious values and legal norms seem to have a greater impact on the current attitudes and practices of Muslims than appears to be the case with other historical religious and cultural traditions. To the extent that this is true, it is useful to work with Islamic sources and arguments in order to repudiate the basis of political legitimacy and psychological motivation for political violence and terrorism in the Muslim context.

The focus of this essay on political violence and terrorism in the Muslim context should not be seen as assuming or implying that these phenomena have a peculiar association with Islamic values and norms. In view of the brief historical and comparative background offered in the first section of this essay, it would be incorrect to assume that Islamic cultural and political norms have a unique propensity for political violence and terrorism. Moreover, when we allow for the large number of Muslims and the extensive geographical size of the Muslim world, most of which suffers from conditions of severe political instability and economic underdevelopment, the political violence and terrorism associated with Islamic groups and individuals do not appear to be disproportionate to that of non-Muslim groups and individuals.

This essay is predicated on the premise that Muslim peoples are entitled to exercise their right to self-determination in terms of an Islamic identity and the modern application of Islamic law, *provided* that they do so in ways that are consistent with certain minimum domestic and international standards. In particular, this essay upholds the right and obligation of modern Muslims to resolve their cultural ambivalence toward political violence and terrorism both within an Islamic framework and in favor of the rule of law in both domestic and international contexts. Islamic self-determination in terms of archaic concepts and antiquated norms is, in my view, both undesirable and impracticable.

In order to address questions of the international dimension of political violence and terrorism from an Islamic perspective, this essay begins by defining these phenomena for our present purposes and placing them in a historical context. The second section of the essay will briefly explain the nature and sources of Islamic law as a necessary prelude to discussing political violence and terrorism in the Muslim context. Further explanation of the Islamic equivalent to international law in historical context will be offered in the third section, followed by a brief statement of the specific principles of Islamic law relevant to international political violence and terrorism. The final section of this essay will address the general question of Islamic law reform and propose a specific approach toward an Islamic contribution to the rule of law in international relations.

Emphasizing a formal legalistic approach, however, should not in any way suggest that this is the only or even necessarily the most useful method of discussing political violence and terrorism. It is obvious that these phenomena can and should be treated from political, sociological, psychological, and other perspectives. However, I would suggest that an understanding of the legal point of view is useful, and perhaps necessary, for a meaningful discussion of these phenomena from any other point of view. Conversely, a legal approach would have to be sensitive to the political, sociological, psychological, and other dimensions of the phenomena in question. It is common experience that people do not always comply with legal norms. Moreover, and to the extent that people do comply with legal norms, the impact of other factors has to be taken into consideration in assessing the practical consequences of such compliance. By the same token, an understanding of extralegal factors is important for promoting greater compliance with legal norms and indicating possible directions for future policy and action.

Political Violence and International Terrorism

Although terrorism is a specific form or manifestation of political violence, it is advisable to use both terms for a number of reasons. As will be explained below, there are certain difficulties in defining the term "terrorism," especially as distinguished from other forms of political violence. In any case, it may be necessary to address other forms of political violence because what may be described as terrorism is often related, and is sometimes seen by the participants as direct retaliation, to other forms of political violence. Moreover, "terrorism" in common contemporary usage is generally conceived as applying a strongly negative label to the person(s) identified as "terrorists" and to their cause. Most people would agree, perhaps implicitly, with Brian Jenkins of the RAND Corporation that "Terrorism is what the bad guys do."[1] These considerations would suggest that it may be useful for analytical purposes to use the broader term "political violence."

However, since the term "political violence" covers such a wide a field, ranging from full-scale international war to individual acts of politically motivated violence, it may also be helpful to use the term "terrorism" to indicate a specific form of political violence. It is certainly desirable that all forms of political violence should be effectively prohibited and combated in the same way that nonpolitical violence is prohibited and combated. Unfortunately, although significant steps have been taken to outlaw war, especially under the Charter of the United Nations, much more needs to be done effectively to prohibit and combat that form of political violence.[2] Until a unified regime is developed to cover all forms of political violence, including war, it is necessary to distinguish between various forms of political violence. However, while recognizing the difficulties of providing a precise and comprehensive definition of terrorism as a specific form of political violence, we would be completely paralyzed if we were to wait for clear and conclusive distinctions between various forms of political violence.

In light of all the above considerations, I have decided to use both terms. For the purposes of the present essay, the term "political violence" refers to the broader phenomenon of using violence to settle or decide a political dispute or conflict, while the term "terrorism" refers to political violence by individual actors, whether they claim to be acting privately or under color of official office.

Terrorism in Historical and Comparative Perspectives

Although international terrorism has received extensive popular and scholarly attention in recent years,[3] the phenomenon itself is ancient, probably as old as human society and political conflict.[4] Moreover, many ancient and modern cultural and religious traditions have made their terrorist "contributions." For example, David C. Rapoport has explained and documented the international nature of three terrorist groups in major religious traditions: the early Jewish Zealots-Sicarii, the Isma'ili Shi'a Assassins of the eleventh to thirteenth centuries, and the Hindu Thugs who persisted for at least six centuries, possibly since the seventh century.[5]

Furthermore, although religion has sometimes played a central role in the motivation or orientation of terrorists, secular and nationalist causes have also produced terrorists and continue to do so to the present day. The modern usage of the term "terrorism" itself is traceable to the tactics of the supporters of the revolutionary tribunal during the 1793/1794 Reign of Terror in France and the methods of opponents of the czarist rulers of Russia.[6] Moreover, many of the contemporary terrorist groups have explicitly secular or nationalist orientations. Even groups associated with certain religions or religious sects, such as the Catholic Irish Republican Army, are clearly more nationalist than religious.

Defining Terrorism in the Modern Context

As a generic term, terrorism was defined several decades ago as "a mode of governing, or of opposing government, by intimidation." Terrell Arnold, a former deputy director of the Office of Counterterrorism and Emergency Planning in the United States, suggested the following definition:

> Terrorism is the use or threatened use of violence for a political purpose to create a state of fear that will aid in extorting, coercing,

intimidating, or causing individuals and groups to alter their behavior. Its methods are hostage taking, piracy or sabotage, assassination, threats, hoaxes, and indiscriminate bombings or shootings.[7]

Arnold then proceeded to state that terrorism is a subject that lends itself readily to definition by example. After a large number of recent examples of "what people as a rule think terrorists do," ranging from acts of the Italian Red Brigade, nationalist groups such as the Armenians and Palestinians, Islamic groups such as the Lebanese Hezballah (the Party of God), as well as state-sponsored agents, he concluded that it is possible to build a cluster of examples around an unequivocal central concept of terrorism.[8]

Numerous other definitions of terrorism can be cited, but there is little consensus on what the "best" definition is.[9] However, based on a content analysis of 109 definitions of the term, Alex Schmid describes the frequency with which certain elements appear.[10] The element of violence/force appears in 83.5 percent of the sample, followed by political intent at 65 percent, emphasis on fear/terror at 51 percent, and so on. Some of the elements listed in this content analysis tend to overlap with others or be another way of expressing the same idea. For example, ideas of threat and psychological effects and anticipated reactions, mentioned in 47 percent and 41.5 percent respectively, appear to me to overlap with the preceding element of emphasis on fear/terror and the element of emphasis on intimidation, mentioned in 17 percent of the sample. Nevertheless, and although such content analysis does not provide a definition per se, it "does point to the central element connected to terrorism upon which considerable agreement exists."[11] This agreement seems to focus on systematically planned, politically motivated violence that does not distinguish between the intended target and innocent bystanders or that is lacking in humanitarian constraints in its use of terror to coerce/extort compliance with the demands of the actor(s).

Another possibly helpful practice is to distinguish terrorism from related concepts, especially ones that may be used to legitimize conduct that may otherwise be described as terrorist. Thus, Arnold seeks to distinguish between terrorism and insurgency as legitimate warfare in terms of targets of action, organization, objectives, location of operations, and compliance or lack of compliance with the international rules of armed conflict, and so on.[12] His purpose in doing so is to repudiate the common notion that if one cannot find some nonviolent redress to accumulated grievances, the path of violence is always open.[13] He also wishes to repudiate the confusion between ends and means, often expressed in the phrase "One man's terrorist is another man's freedom fighter."

The Moral Dimension

As Grant Wardlaw correctly points out, a "major stumbling block to the serious study of terrorism is that, at base, terrorism is a moral problem."[14] Efforts at providing a universal definition of terrorism are unlikely to succeed because people wish to avoid having to apply this negative term to proponents of causes with which they sympathize. Thus, a distinction is often emphasized between ends and means, presumably in an attempt to maintain that if the ends were "just" or "deserving" the means may not be as objectionable as they would be if they are used to further an "unjust" or "undeserving" end.[15] "From this perspective," states Provizer, "the debate over definition is less significant than the debate over the propriety of the action, that is its morality."[16]

To my mind, a clear moral judgment that "just" or "deserving" ends must always be pursued by equally "just" and "deserving" means is the only way out of the definitional difficulty. In other words, the same criteria for judging the justice of the end should apply to the justice of the means. Such judgment is in the best interest of all parties to any conflict because it enhances clarity of policy and efficacy of action. Its simple but irrefutable logic is reported to have been corroborated by a French peasant speaking in the sixteenth century of the religious wars in France: "Who will believe that your cause is just when your behaviors are so unjust?"[17]

A Legal Definition of Terrorism

The confusion over the definition of terrorism may be due in part to the fact that the parties are not always clear on the purpose of the definition. It does not clarify thought on the subject to confuse political and sociological considerations regarding the nature of the precipitating conflict or the psychological processes of motivation for the perpetrators of the act. While all these perspectives are necessary for understanding terrorism and dealing with it at various levels, a clear definition is imperative from the legal point of view.

For the purposes of the present essay, the question should simply be one of applying the penal law of the state under whose jurisdiction the act is perpetrated. If the conduct constitutes a criminal offense under the penal law of the particular state, it should be prosecuted and punished as such, regardless of the political or other motives of the culprit(s). If there are international or transnational aspects to the conduct, they should only be relevant to the question of jurisdiction, that is to say, determining which state has jurisdiction over the culprit. [18] Once that question is settled through the application of the relevant rules of international and domestic law, the state awarded jurisdiction should proceed in enforcing its own penal law.

In other words, no distinction should be made between politically motivated criminal activity and other forms of criminal conduct. Murder, bodily harm, robbery, kidnapping, or abduction are crimes under all legal systems and should be treated as such regardless of the culprit's motives. In this respect, it is important to distinguish between *motive* in the general sense and *intent* in the legal sense. Intent in the legal sense relates to the actor's purpose or objective to produce the unlawful consequence, such as the desire to kill or otherwise harm the victim or to take property through the use or threat of force; motive is the private reason or motivation that prompts the culprit to form that intent. If this distinction is not maintained, the administration of criminal justice will be thrown into total confusion, with executive and judicial organs of the state being preoccupied with searching for and evaluating a wide variety of complex private motives.

It is true, of course, that some legal systems allow for consideration of motive in the classification of certain crimes or in the determination of appropriate punishment. For example, the "mercy killing" of a terminally ill person may not be classified or punished as murder under some legal systems. However, such cases are radically different from politically motivated crimes in that the "well-being" or "best interest" of the victim is of no concern to the culprit.

The obvious problem with such a clear-cut legalistic approach is whether the given state would have the political will to enforce its own penal law without regard to political or any other considerations. Besides the possibility of sympathy with the political objectives, or "cause," of the culprit(s), leading to the above-noted confusion between ends and means, a state may be tempted to abdicate or compromise its duty to enforce its penal law in the interest of safety of its nationals or of other interests perceived to be threatened by associates of the accused person(s). While such a temptation presents governments with a difficult decision, I believe that the best policy is that of strict enforcement of the penal law of the state.

It is not within the scope of the present chapter to elaborate on these aspects of the decision; however, I maintain that every effort must be made to assist governments in upholding the rule of law under difficult circumstances. One of the most fruitful avenues of such effort, I would suggest, is to repudiate

authenticity of reported Sunna texts.[24] Nevertheless, in view of the fact that Sunna remained in the form of oral tradition for nearly two centuries of tremendous political turmoil and theological controversies, there have always been major doubts as to the authenticity and exact wording and circumstances of numerous texts of Sunna.[25] Moreover, when we scrutinize the techniques of authentication employed by the early Muslim jurists and judge them by modern standards of evidence, more doubts can be raised as to the authenticity of some of the accepted texts of Sunna and to their significance as source Islamic norms.[26] By the same token, it may be safely assumed that some genuine Sunna texts were excluded as "inauthentic" or of doubtful authenticity.

Besides the scarcity of Shariʿa principles in the Qurʾan noted above, the total body of Sunna that was accepted as authentic by Muslim jurists and scholars can hardly provide a comprehensive and detailed source of social and legal norms. Consequently, the founding Muslim jurists developed a number of "supplementary" sources and techniques of Shariʿa. These secondary sources of Shariʿa include *ijma*, the consensus of the Muslim community, and *qiyas*, reasoning by analogy to an earlier established principle or precedent.[27] These and other secondary sources can also be seen as part of the broader concept of *ijtihad*, independent juristic reasoning to provide answers where the Qurʾan and Sunna were silent. Sunna is cited as authority for the legitimacy of exercising ijtihad in such cases.[28]

Although ijtihad was actively employed during the formative stages of Shariʿa, scope for its exercise was perceived as gradually diminishing as the founding jurists developed general principles and specific rules based on the Qurʾan, Sunna, and other sources and techniques between the eighth and ninth centuries. Moreover, due to their religious concern with the authority of Shariʿa as the divinely sanctioned way of life for the believers, Muslim jurists insisted on extremely high qualifications for the person who may be authorized to exercise ijtihad. For these and possibly other reasons, a consensus evolved around the tenth century, the third century of Islam, that the gates of ijtihad had been closed; that is to say, ijtihad was no longer allowed.[29] Since this consensus can be seen as a result of sociological and political circumstances rather than being based on the direct authority of the Qurʾan or Sunna, modern Muslim writers have argued for the reopening of the gates of ijtihad.[30] Indeed, some have argued that the gates of ijtihad may have never been closed.[31]

Such recent indications of creative, intellectual, and religious revival are clearly most welcome in the modern Muslim context; however, we have to emphasize that ijtihad and all juristic sources of Shari'a are subject to the two fundamental sources, namely, the Qur'an and Sunna. While ijtihad may be used in interpreting the Qur'an and Sunna, Muslims in general believe neither ijtihad nor any source of Shari'a can be allowed to contradict any clear and definite text of Qur'an and/or Sunna. The implications of this principle will be discussed in the final section of this chapter in relation to the prospects of significant modern reform of Shari'a.

As indicated earlier, the founding jurists of Islamic jurisprudence interpreted the Qur'an and Sunna and employed ijtihad, ijma, qiyas, and other techniques to develop Shari'a as a comprehensive code for Muslims. Although elements of Shari'a had obviously existed from the beginning in the sense that clear and definite texts of the Qur'an and Sunna, as well as specific instances of ijtihad and interpretation of texts of the Qur'an and Sunna, were applied in the daily life of Muslims, the systematic development of Shari'a came about during the second and third centuries of Islam, the eighth and ninth centuries.[32] In particular, the four major surviving schools of Islamic jurisprudence, *madhabib*, followed throughout the Sunni Muslim world, were established during the period.[33] As will be explained below, Shi'a jurisprudence developed around the same time.

The Shi'a Perspective(s)

The success of Shi'a clerics to seize power in Iran in early 1979 has brought Shi'a Islam to the attention of public opinion throughout the world. Moreover, in view of the subject of this chapter, it is important to consider briefly the ways in which Shi'a perspectives are similar to or different from those of the Sunni majority.

Strictly speaking, it may be misleading to speak of the Sunni and Shi'a perspectives in contrasting terms because both groups of Muslims share much of same beliefs and religious dogma. In actual fact, there are some differences among Sunni as well as among Shi'a Muslims.[34] Indeed, some Shi'a Muslims, such as the Zaydis of southern Arabia, are closer to the Sunni majority than they are to some other Shi'a groups.[35] What unites all Shi'a, however, is the special status they ascribe to Ali, the Prophet's cousin and son-in-law, and the belief that the iman, the legitimate ruler of the Islamic state, must be a descendent of Ali and Fatima, the Prophet's daughter.[36]

It may be helpful for our purposes here to note the following general points of agreement and disagreement between the main Shi'a sect, known as the Ithna Ashari or Twelvers, now in power in Iran, and Sunni Muslims.

Like the Sunni majority, the Twelvers Shi'a accept the Qur'an as the literal and final word of God, although they disagree on the interpretation of the Qur'an.[37] They also accept the Prophet Muhammad as the final Prophet and consequently accept Sunna as the second source of Shari'a, but do not accept a report of Sunna as authentic unless recognized by their own jurists.[38] Twelvers Shi'a do not accept the ijtihad, ijma, and qiyas of Sunni Muslims and prefer that of their own jurists.[39] Most important, the theological and legal thinking of Shi'a in general, and the Twelvers in particular, is dominated by the expectation of the return of the absent iman—reappearance of the hidden iman in Isma'ili Shi'a belief—who has the ultimate authority to declare what Shari'a is and to implement it in practice.[40] In the meantime, Shi'a Muslims try to live by the dictates of Shari'a as elaborated by their own jurists and to coexist with other Muslims, as well as with non-Muslims in the manner indicated by Shari'a.[41]

The Nature and Modern Application of Shari'a

The Nature of Shari'a. As a result of their primary concern with regulating the relationship of the individual Muslim with his or her God, "the jurists had formulated standards of conduct which represented a system of private, and not of public law, and which they conceived it to be the duty of the established political power to ratify and enforce."[42] The conception of the role of the jurists and the duty of the political authorities, in these terms of private law, was also reflected in the nature and degree of detail in the various fields of Shari'a. Not only did this preference lead to greater development of the religious and worship rituals and private and family law than the public law aspects of Shari'a, but it also led to the formulation of Shari'a principles in terms of moral duties sanctioned by religious consequences rather than by legal rights and duties with specific temporal remedies.[43] All fields of human activity were categorized in terms of *halal* or *mubah*, permissible or allowed, and *haram*, impermissible or prohibited, with intermediate categories of *mandub*, recommended, and *makruh*, reprehensible.[44]

In this way, Shari'a addresses the conscience of the individual Muslim, whether in a private or a public and official capacity, rather than the institutions and corporate entities of the community and the state. The other major categorization of Shari'a in terms of *ibadat*, worship rituals and practices, and *mu'amalat*, social dealings, also conforms to the fundamental nature of Shari'a as religious obligations to be reflected in private and public action from an individual perspective.

The same individual perspective underlies the vast diversity of opinions over the Shari'a ruling on any given matter. Although Shari'a professes to be a single logical whole, there is immense diversity of opinion not only between the schools but also among different jurists of the same school.[45] Because all the divergent, and sometimes conflicting, views are regarded as equally valid and legitimate, any Muslim has the choice of taking whatever view is acceptable to his or her individual conscience.[46]

In terms of content or subject matter, and excluding the spiritual and ritual aspects, we find that Shari'a's hold is strongest in family law and inheritance and weakest in penal law, taxation, constitutional law, and the law of war, with the law of contracts and obligations in the middle.[47] This order of variation in detailed regulation is partly due to the greater degree of detail regarding the particular field in the Qur'an and Sunna, leading to a stronger identification of the relevant rules of Shari'a with religious belief and practice. The other reason for this differential in specific regulation under Shari'a is the ancient dichotomy between the theory and practice of Shari'a.

Historical Application of Shari'a. It is certainly true, as Noel Coulson observes, that "Shari'a law had come into being as a doctrinal system independent of and essentially opposed to current [eighth-century] legal practice."[48] Nevertheless, it is as dangerously easy to exaggerate the cleavage between the *umara* (amirs, military commanders, and civil governors) and the *fuqaha*, jurists, as it is to ignore it.[49] While the jurists were obliged by the Qur'an itself to acknowledge the unity of the Islamic state, and consequently the necessity for an effective head of that state, however distasteful the individual occupant of that office may have been to them, the rulers always had to make some outward deference to Shari'a because they owed their position to the religion of Islam. As Joseph Schacht notes, because of this state of affairs, there has been "an uneasy truce between *ulama* [*fuqaha*] . . . and the political authorities [*umara*]. . . . As long as the sacred law [Shari'a] received formal recognition as a religious ideal, it did not insist on being fully applied in practice."[50]

The dichotomy between theory and practice, naturally enough, varied from time to time and from one field of Shari'a to another. The earliest stage of the Medina state (622–661) is believed by the majority of Muslims to have represented the strongest unity between the theory and practice of Shari'a;[51] but that perceived unity was over an extremely limited territory and for a very short period of time. Although the strict observance of Shari'a is not believed to have been a high priority with the Umayyad dynasty (661–750),[52] their executive officials were clearly guided by it, to the extent that it had been developed by their time.[53] In particular, increasing importance and prestige were attached to the office of the *qadi*, a judge who specialized in Shari'a. This special office was carried further under the early Abbasid dynasty (as of 750), which based the legitimacy of its challenge to the Umayyads on a claim of greater commitment to the implementation of Shari'a.[54] That commitment, however, as Coulson notes,

> did not mean that the future course of the Islamic ship of state was to be steered by the Shari'a courts. The Abbasid rulers maintained a firm grip on the helm, and the Shari'a courts never attained that position of supreme judicial authority independent of political control, which would have provided the only sure foundation and real guarantee for the ideal of the *Civitas Dei*.[55]

Subsequent stages of Muslim history reflected continuous fluctuation between greater and lesser observance of Shari'a.

Contemporary Application of Shari'a. As a result of increasing internal weakness and external Western influence, the implementation of Shari'a in the public affairs of Muslims has reached a very low level since the late nineteenth century.[56] The main seats of Muslim power, in the Ottoman Empire, Persia, and India, collapsed and were co-opted into accepting the European models of the nation-state and international order and abandoning all pretence of conforming to Shari'a in public affairs.[57] European legal systems became the norm in domestic law enforcement and international relations, leaving only family law and inheritance to be governed by Shari'a.

This displacement of Shari'a by modern Western law seems to have been the outcome of a compromise. The ancient concepts and principles of Shari'a became increasingly difficult to maintain in domestic public affairs and in international relations with modern, superior non-Muslim states. As correctly explained by James Anderson,

> to a Muslim, it has always been a far more heinous sin to deny or question the divine revelation than to fail to obey it. So it seemed [to Muslims] preferable to continue to pay lip-service to an inviolable Shari'a, as the only law of fundamental authority, and to excuse departure from much of it in practice by appealing to the doctrine of

necessity (*darura*), rather than to make any attempt to adapt that law to the circumstances and needs of contemporary life.[58]

Nevertheless, many Muslim countries are currently experiencing rising demands for a stronger Islamic identity and greater application of Shari'a.[59] Indeed, it is natural for Muslim peoples to seek a sense of national identity following the achievement of political independence from colonial rule. Moreover, many individual Muslims may feel a strong sense of religious commitment to Shari'a and be motivated by its dictates at the private psychological level, regardless of the official policies of their governments. I would accept both the collective and individual aspects as legitimate exercise of the right to self-determination *provided* that such exercise does not violate the rights of others, whether at the domestic or international levels.

Islamic International Law in Historical Context

Although the founding Muslim jurists did not know and discuss international law in the modern sense of the term, some of them did elaborate on the relevant rules under the rubric of *siyar*, or conduct of state. The leading early Muslim jurist generally credited with founding siyar as a branch of Shari'a is Muhammad ibn al-Hasan al-Shaybani, the student of Abu Hanifa and one of the founders of the Hanafi Madhhab school of Islamic jurisprudence.[60] Other jurists have treated some of the relevant issues in their general or specialized treatises on Shari'a.[61] However, the international law aspects of Shari'a should be understood in the historical context of the eighth and ninth centuries, during which the founding Muslim jurists operated. When viewed in this light, it will be apparent that Shari'a's conception of international relations and its version of Islamic international law were a natural outcome of the interpretation of the fundamental sources of Islam in a certain historical context, rather than the only valid interpretation of those sources. Once this contextual framework of interpretation is appreciated, the door will be open for an alternative interpretation of the fundamental sources of Islam in the present historical context in order to develop a modern version of Islamic international law.

Impact of the Historical Context on the Principles of Shari'a

Islam was born in an extremely harsh and violent environment and received a very hostile and aggressively violent reaction from the tribes of seventh-century Arabia.[62] The first Muslims had to fight for their survival until Islam prevailed throughout Arabia by the time of the death of the Prophet. The preexisting norms of intertribal relations were heavily, if not completely, dependent on the use or threat of violent force by the claimant of any "right," even the right to exist at all.[63]

The use or threat of force was also the norm among the various entities or polities of the region, including the two powerful empires to the northeast and northwest of Arabia, the Sasanian and Byzantine Empires.[64] Thus, when the first Muslim state was established in seventh-century Arabia, force was the basic method of conducting what is known today as international relations.[65] It was therefore inevitable in that historical context that Islam should endorse the use of force in Muslim relations with non-Muslims. In doing so, however, Shari'a introduced new norms to proscribe the reasons for going to war as well as its actual practice.[66] Some of these regulations of the use of force under Shari'a will be explained in the next section of this essay.

Thus, it is important to emphasize the exclusive and limited nature of what may be described as ancient and premodern systems of international law. Customary rules and practices regulating relationships between various political entities prior to the rise of modern international law were not, as Majid Khadduri observes, "truly 'international,' in the modern sense, for each was exclusive and failed to recognize the principles of legal equality and reciprocity which are essential to any system if it is to become world-wide."[67] Siyar, Shari'a's equivalent to international law, was therefore consistent with the conception of the international law of the time.[68]

Islamic International Law in the Present Context

Nonetheless, to argue that Shari'a was fully justified in endorsing the use of force in international relations and that it did in fact restrict and regulate its use is not to say that such use of force is still justified. Rather, since the use of force was justified by the historical context of violent intercommunal and international relations, it must cease to be so justified in the present context where peaceable coexistence has become a vital necessity for the very survival of humanity. Besides the independently growing enlightened trend toward peace and cooperation in human relations, modern means of atomic warfare have made hostile international relations unthinkable. Moreover, until the use or threat of violent force has been totally eliminated in international relations, it is obviously true that the use of violence must be restricted and regulated to the maximum possible degree.

It must be emphasized, however, that, for Muslims, the historical context as such can be neither the source of Shariʿa in the past nor its source in the future. According to Muslim belief, Islamic law in the past, present, and future must be based on the Qurʾan and Sunna. I fully accept this position and only wish to suggest that the historical context is merely the framework for the interpretation and application of these basic sources of Islam. In other words, it is not suggested here that Islamic law should simply follow developments in human history, regardless of the provisions of the Qurʾan and Sunna. What is suggested is that the Qurʾan and Sunna have been the source of Shariʿa as the Islamic response to the concrete realities of the past and must be the source of modern Shariʿa as the Islamic response to the concrete realities of today.

In order to highlight the conflict and tension between Shariʿa and modern international law and to illustrate their implications for the subject of this essay, it is necessary to state clearly and authoritatively the relevant principles and rules of Shariʿa. Once the basis of current Muslim ambivalence toward internal political violence and terrorism is clearly identified, the need for international Islamic reform to promote the rule of law in international relations will be appreciated. That aspect will be discussed in the final section of this essay.

Shariʿa and Political Violence

It is true that the focus of this essay is international or transnational political violence and terrorism by individual persons. However, I submit that the ideological justification and psychological motivation for such individual violence in the Muslim context are closely linked to collective attitudes derived from the principles of Shariʿa. As an essentially religious law, Shariʿa addresses the individual Muslim as well as the state as the official organ of the community of Muslims. In this light, it would be useful to begin with a review of the relevant aspects of Shariʿa and then discuss their implications for the conduct of individual persons and groups.

Antagonism and Use of Force Against Non-Muslims

In addition to the explicit sources of Shariʿa on the use of force against non-Muslims and renegade Muslims to be reviewed below, many verses of the Qurʾan, which were revealed after the Prophet's migration to Medina in 622, emphasized the internal cohesion of the Muslim community and sought to distinguish it from other communities in antagonistic terms. During the

Medina stage, the Qur'an repeatedly instructed Muslims to support each other and dissociate themselves from non-Muslims warning against taking non-Muslims as friends or allies. Thus, verses 3:28, 4:144, 8:72–73, 9:23 and 71, and 60:1 prohibit Muslims from taking unbelievers as *awliya*, friends, helpers, and supporters and instructs them to look for friendly relations and support among themselves. Similarly, verse 5:51 instructs Muslims not to take Jews and Christians as *awliya*, as they are *awliya* for each other, and any Muslim who turns to Christians and Jews for friendship and support becomes one of them.

These verses and related Sunna provided the general context within which the sources dealing specifically with the use of force against non-Muslims were understood and applied by early Muslims. As will be emphasized below, all the above-cited verses were revealed during the Medina period and not the earlier Mecca period. As such, these sources should now be seen as having provided the necessary psychological support for the cohesion of a vulnerable community of Muslims trying to survive in a hostile and violent environment.

The commonly used Islamic term for the use of force in international relations is *jihad*. The literal meaning of the word jihad is effort and exertion, which includes, but is not necessarily restricted to, exerting effort in war.[69] Thus, on the one hand, both the Qur'an and Sunna have used the term jihad in a wider sense of making the utmost effort, sometimes in ways that have nothing to do with the use of force.[70] In numerous verses of the Qur'an, such as 2:18, 5:54, and 8:72, the term jihad and its derivatives are used to refer to self-exertion, whether in combat or peaceful efforts. As against the unbelievers, for example, verse 25:52 instructs the Prophet and Muslims to use the Qur'an in jihad against the unbelievers. This passage obviously refers to using the force of arguments of the Qur'an, and not the force of arms, in jihad. Moreover, some verses, such as 29:8, 31:15, and 47:31, use the term *jihad* and its derivatives in a sense that has nothing to do with the use of force. In one statement of Sunna, the Prophet described the use of force in battle as the minor jihad and self-exertion in peaceful and personal compliance with the dictates of Islam as the major or superior jihad. In another Sunna, the Prophet is reported to have said that the best form of jihad is to speak the truth in the face of a tyrannical and oppressive ruler.[71] On the other hand, both the Qur'an and Sunna have used the term *qital*, fighting, and its derivatives to refer to the use of force in international relations. For example, this is clearly the sense of verses 2:190, 193, and 244; 4:76; and 9:12, 29, and 123 of the Qur'an.

In view of this linguistic ambiguity and the fact that the term *jihad* has frequently been misused by Muslims and non-Muslims alike, it may be better to use the phrase "use of force" to refer to this aspect of Shari'a. This latter term is further recommended by the fact that it has become a term of choice in international law, especially since its use by the Charter of the United Nations. As such, this term can be applied in cross-cultural analysis of the issues.

Much can be learned about Shari'a's view of the legitimate use of force in international relations through a review of the relevant sources of Shari'a in chronological order. In relation to the Qur'an, this review may be possible because of the relatively greater general agreement over the site, and hence at least the approximate date, of the revelation of each verse. It is much harder, if not impossible, to attempt a chronological survey of Sunna because there is very little agreement on its chronological sequence. However, Sunna can be helpful in understanding the meaning of a given verse of the Qur'an and will be used for this purpose in the following survey.

The first verses of the Qur'an that clearly sanction the use of force by Muslims against non-Muslims were revealed in Medina, after the Prophet and his companions migrated from Mecca in 622. According to Ibn Kathir's leading interpretation and commentary on the Qur'an,[72] the first verses instructing Muslims to use force in jihad/qital against unbelievers were 2:190–93 and 22:39, which may be translated, respectively, as follows:

> Fight in the cause of God those who fight you, but do not transgress the limits (initiate attack or aggression), for God does not love the transgressors (aggressors). And slay them wherever you catch them, and turn them out from where they have turned you out, for tumult and oppression are worse than slaughter; but fight them not at the Sacred Mosque (of Mecca) unless they (first) fight you there; but if they fight you (there), slay them, (because) that is the reward of the unbelievers. But if they cease, God is most forgiving, most merciful. And fight them until (so that) there is no more tumult or oppression, and there prevails faith in God; but if they cease, let there be no hostility except to those who practice oppression. Permission (to fight back) is (hereby) given to those against whom war is made; and God is most powerful and able to support them. (They are) those who have been wrongfully expelled from their homes (for no cause or reason) except that they say "God is our Lord"; if God did not check one set of

people by means of another, there would surely have been destruction of temples (of worship) and property.

Verses 4:90, 8:39, and 8:61 of the Qur'an are identified by Ibn Kathir as having been revealed in Medina, without stating an exact date for their revelation. The first mentioned verse comes in the context of instructing Muslims to dissociate themselves from hypocrites and to confront and slay them wherever they find them. "But if they (the hypocrites) withdraw from you without fighting you," says verse 4:90, "and send you (guarantees) of peace, then God gives you no license or permission (to fight them)." Verse 8:39 may be translated as saying "And fight (the unbelievers) until (so that) there is no tumult or oppression, and faith in God completely prevails everywhere; but if they cease (their oppression) God is most capable (knowledgeable) of what they do." Following verse 8:60, which instructs Muslims to prepare for war in order to deter the unbelievers, verse 8:61 states, "But if they (the unbelievers) incline towards peace, you shall also incline towards it (peace) and place your trust (confidence) in God. He is the one who hears and knows (everything)."

Then there is the whole of chapter nine of the Qur'an that is identified by Ibn Kathir as having been revealed in the ninth year of Hijra, that is to say around 631, and is generally accepted to have been among the last of Qur'anic revelation. The verses of this chapter, such as 5, 12, 13, 29, 36, 73, and 123, contain the clearest sanction for the use of force against non-Muslims and are generally taken to have repealed or superseded all previous verses that prohibit or restrict the use of force. In particular, verse 5 of this chapter is said to have repealed, or abrogated for the purposes of Shari'a, over one hundred preceding verses of the Qur'an that instruct Muslims to use peaceful means and arguments to convince unbelievers to embrace Islam.[73] This verse appears in the context of instructing the Prophet to declare that he repudiates his previous pledges of nonaggression to unbelievers, subject to a four-month period of grace or until the end of the time set by a specific treaty of peace that the other side has not violated. Then comes verse 9:5, which may be translated as follows:

> But once the forbidden months (the period of grace) are over then fight and slay the unbelievers (polytheists) wherever you find them, and seize them, beleaguer them, and lie in wait for them in every stratagem (of war); but if they repent, and establish regular prayers

and pay *zaka* (Islamic alms and religious tax) then open the way for them; for God is most forgiving, most merciful.

The other verse of this chapter that should be quoted in full is verse 29 because it applies to the use of force against *ahl al-kitab*, non-Muslim believers who have received heavenly revealed scriptures, mainly Jews and Christians. This verse may be translated as follows:

> Fight those People of the Book who do not believe in God or the Last Day, nor hold as forbidden what has been forbidden by God and His Apostle (the Prophet of Islam), nor acknowledge the Religion of Truth (Islam) until they pay *jizya* (poll tax) with willing submission, and feel themselves subdued.

Several conclusions can be drawn from this survey of the Qur'an on the use of force by Muslims against non-Muslims. The first clear conclusion is that this advocacy of force is an exclusively Medinese phenomenon, that is to say, it relates to the Medina period after migration from Mecca. During the earlier period of Mecca, prior to migration to Medina in 622 CE, there was no authorization in the Qur'an for the use of force against non-Muslims.[74]

The second clear conclusion from the above survey of the relevant verses of the Qur'an is that there was a progression in Qur'anic sanction for the use of force by Muslims against non-Muslims, from the use of force in self-defense to the use of force in propagating Islam. However, and as has already been indicated, since chapter nine of the Qur'an was among the last revelations, it was taken by many Muslim jurists to have repealed, or abrogated for the purposes of Shari'a, all previously revealed inconsistent verses of the Qur'an. As will be explained in the final section of this essay, it should be possible for modern Muslim jurists to reverse this process of abrogation in order to reinstate the principles of peaceful coexistence with non-Muslims.

The third conclusion to be drawn from the above survey of relevant verses of the Qur'an is that the use of force was not permitted except for two reasons: self-defense and propagation of Islam. In view of the claims of some modern Muslim writers that Shari'a permitted the use of force only in self-defense,[75] it is important to emphasize that both the Qur'an and Sunna did in fact, by the end of the Prophet's life, sanction the use of force in propagating Islam. It is simply not plausible to argue that the early Muslims conquered the whole of Syria, Iraq, northern Africa, southern Spain to the west, and Persia and northern India to the east in self-defense.[76] The truth of the matter is that Shari'a sanctioned and regulated the use of force by Muslims against non-Muslims not only in self-defense but also as a means of propagating Islam. In accordance with this position, early Muslim jurists developed the theory of Shari'a that promotes the notion that Islam and unbelief cannot exist together in this world.[77] This principle is clearly illustrated by the last practice of the Prophet and that of his caliphs, as well as by the whole history of the early expansion of Islam.

In accordance with this principle, we find numerous reports of the Prophet, and his caliphs after him, instructing Muslim armies to offer the non-Muslim side the chance to embrace Islam and, if they accepted the offer, to use no force against them. If the non-Muslim side rejected the Muslim invitation to embrace Islam and happened to be People of the Book, they were offered the second option of concluding a compact with the Muslims, commonly known *dhimma*, or pledge of honor; according to this compact, they would agree to pay *jizya* and submit to Muslim sovereignty in exchange for being secure in their persons and property and allowed to practice their religion and apply their personal laws. The Muslim armies were instructed by the Prophet, and his caliphs, that if the offer to embrace Islam was refused and the alternative option to pay *jizya* was rejected by those qualified to receive such an offer, that is to say People of the Book, then the Muslim armies must fight them. For example, the following Sunna is reported in *Sahih Muslim*, one of the most authoritative compilations or records of Sunna:[78]

> Whenever the Prophet appointed a commander over an army or detachment, he enjoined upon him to fear God regarding himself and regarding the treatment of the Muslims who accompanied him. Then he used to say: "Fight with the name of God and in the path of God. Combat those who disbelieve in God. Fight yet do not cheat, do not break trust, do not mutilate, do not kill minors.
>
> "If you encounter an enemy from among the non-Muslims, then offer them three alternatives. Whichever of these they may accept, agree to it and withhold yourself from them:
>
> "So call them to embrace Islam. If they accept, then agree to it and withhold yourself from them . . .
>
> "If, however, they refuse, then call them to pay the *jizya*. If they accept, then agree to it and withhold yourself from them. If they refuse, then seek help from God and combat them."

It is remarkable that, although he quotes this and other similar Sunna, Muhammad Hamidullah, a leading contemporary Muslim writer on Islamic international law and relations, still attempts to avoid recognizing the true nature of Shariʿa in this respect and calls the use of force in propagating Islam the "idealistic" cause of war under Shariʿa.[79] Another modern Muslim author attempts to avoid admitting that Shariʿa required Muslims to use force against People of the Book, such as Christians and Jews, if they refused to pay *jizya*.[80] In contrast, it is my position that it would be better to recognize this endorsement of force and other aspects of Shariʿa in their true nature and explain them in terms of historical context.

Regulation of Use of Force and Peace Treaties

Besides restricting the legitimate use of force by Muslims against non-Muslims to the two reasons of self-defense and propagation of Islam, Shariʿa regulated the actual conduct of war in a number of ways.[81] First, the requirement of offering the other side the option of embracing Islam, and accepting *dhimma* when appropriate, constituted what is known in modern terminology as a formal declaration of war and fair warning as a necessary prerequisite to commencement of hostilities.[82] Furthermore, Shariʿa regulated in detail the conduct of Muslim armies in combat. We have already seen that the Prophet instructed Muslim armies not to cheat, break trust, mutilate, or kill minors. In other reports, he specifies that the prohibition of killing noncombatants includes women, children, and monks.[83] Abu Bakr and Umar, the first and second caliphs of the Prophet, who can safely be assumed to represent the accurate position of Shariʿa, are often quoted as instructing Muslim armies not to embezzle, cheat, break trust, mutilate, kill a minor or an old man or a woman, hew down a date palm or burn it, cut down a fruit tree, slaughter a goat or cow or camel except for food. They are also quoted instructing Muslim armies not to interfere with people who have secluded themselves in convents.[84]

However, if Muslim armies were victorious, they were entitled to take enemy property as *ghana'im*, spoils of war, in accordance with prevailing practice.[85] This practice is clearly recognized by Qur'an verses 48:19–20; 8:41, 69; and others, which regulate the distribution of such booty.

In light of all these sources, it is not surprising to find, as documented by Khadduri and other writers in the field, that the founding jurists of Shariʿa who addressed intercommunal/international relations spoke of a permanent state of war between *dar al-Islam*, the abode of Islam or territory under

Muslim rule, and *dar al-harb*, the abode of war or territory falling outside Muslim control.[86] According to those founding jurists of Shariʿa, Muslims may have to conclude peace treaties, *sulh* or *ahd*, suspending hostilities with non-Muslim polities, if Muslim interests required it. Such treaties, however, must be of a temporary nature and only in order to permit Muslims to resolve their internal differences or prepare for the next round of fighting with the non-Muslims.[87]

As indicated by the rules on making peace treaties and as shown by many sources of Shariʿa and historical experience, the theoretically permanent state of war between Muslims and non-Muslims did not necessarily mean violence or fighting.[88] Nevertheless, it is important to remember that the theory of Shariʿa is that Islam and unbelief cannot exist together in this world.[89] Thus, Shariʿa requires that, whether through active fighting or other means, dar al-harb, the abode of war that is all territory outside the jurisdiction of Islam, must be brought within dar al-Islam, the abode of Islam where Shariʿa prevails.[90]

Moreover, since upholding Islam is considered by Shariʿa to be a legitimate cause for the use of force, such force can be used even against Muslims whose conduct is deemed to be subversive of the Muslim community or detrimental to the interests of Islam.[91] Thus, we find the standard treatises of Shariʿa discussing both uses of force in the same context and language.[92] This approach is understandable in view of the religious nature of the state itself. Since apostates and rebels were regarded as the enemies of the Muslim community, they were to be treated on the same footing as external enemies.[93] Such reasoning is, of course, no longer valid or tenable under modern principles, which would not sanction the use of force against such groups unless they used force themselves.[94] Furthermore, since Muslims are now organized in different nation-states, the use of force among Muslim states, as in the case of the Iran-Iraq war, is now an international conflict that should be governed by the relevant rules of international law.

Implications for Conduct of Individual Persons and Groups

As indicated earlier, Shariʿa addresses the individual Muslim person directly. It is the duty of the individual person to implement the dictates of Shariʿa in his or her personal conduct as well as in collaboration with others or through official organs and institutions. Moreover, the individual Muslim is also influenced by the vast wealth of early Islamic history and precedents derived from the conduct of highly revered early personalities.

For example, the events of *al-fitna al-kubra*, or the Great Upheaval, which refers to the protracted and violent conflict over power following the murder of Uthman, the third caliph, in 656, are very much alive in the imagination of the majority of Muslims and continue to influence the course of events to the present day.[95] During that period, Ali, the Prophet's cousin and son-in-law and designated fourth caliph, was challenged by several groups of Muslims. As a result of those challenges, almost all of Ali's short reign was occupied by civil war against his primary adversaries, the Umayyads, and against renegades from his own ranks, the Kharijites. In 661, a group of Kharijites conspired to assassinate the three leading figures of the civil war, Ali and the two leaders of the Umayyads, Mu'awya ibn Abu Sujiyan and Amr ibn al-Ass. However, since only the assassin assigned to murder Ali succeeded in his mission, Mu'awya was able to consolidate his position and established the Umayyad dynasty. Al-Shi'a, the partisans of Ali, became a persecuted minority following the assassination of Ali and subsequent death of his two sons from Fatima, the daughter of the Prophet.

Those events and subsequent developments of the second half of the seventh century continue to exercise extremely powerful psychological and political influence on many Muslims to the present day. For example, Shi'a throughout the world commemorate annually the martyrdom of Hussayn, the son of Ali, on the anniversary of his death, called *ashura*, at the hands of the forces of Yazid, the second Umayyad caliph.[96] On this date, thousands of Shi'a reenact the tragedy and declare their commitment to uphold the right of the descendants of Ali and Fatima to rule as imams of the whole of Islamic lands. Many non-Shi'a Muslims are also powerfully moved by the memory of that tragic event.

One of the central themes of the Qur'an and Sunna is the notion that Muslims have the obligation to uphold good and justice and combat evil and injustice.[97] Moreover, while the Qur'an does not explicitly specify the ways in which this obligation is to be discharged, some Sunna seem to suggest direct action. For example, in one very well-known Sunna, the Prophet is reported to have said:

Whoever among you perceives a *munkar*, an injustice/evil, he or she shall rectify it (the situation) by his or her own hands. If unable to do so, then he or she shall rectify the situation by speech. If unable to do so, then he or she shall disapprove of the injustice/evil in his or her own heart, and this (last mentioned option) is the lowest degree of belief (the last acceptable resort).

Neither the Qur'an, nor the above-quoted Sunna, nor any other Sunna explicitly sanctions the use of private violent force in rectifying injustice and evil. It is true that these fundamental Islamic sources sanction direct action in rectifying injustice and evil, but such action need not, of course, be violent action. However, it can also be said that the commonly known Islamic sources are *not* explicit in condemning and prohibiting direct violent action. This permissiveness is not surprising since the absence of the rule of law, in the modern sense of the term, during the times of the early Muslims may have necessitated the use of private violence.

Thus, on the one hand, Muslims are enjoined to rectify, by direct private action if possible, whatever they *perceive* to be injustice or evil; on the other hand, historically there has been an ambivalence in Islamic sources as to what sort of direct private action is permissible in rectifying injustice and evil. So long as an individual modern Muslim person is confronted with the duty to act in furtherance of his or her perception of what is good and just, and with a wealth of detailed historical events that seem to favor violent private direct action, it is likely that some Muslim individuals and groups will see private violent direct action as one of the options open to them. This line of thinking is the basis of the creed of militant proponents of the literal application of historical Shari'a, commonly known as Islamic fundamentalists,[98] and the religious justification for their terrorist actions.[99] For any person motivated by this logic, international boundaries are of no significance whatsoever. If he or she believes that violent private direct action is necessary, whether in another country or against the nationals of another Muslim or non-Muslim state, he or she will act accordingly.

The only way to counteract the force of this religious motivation and rationalization of domestic and international/transnational political violence and terrorism is to develop an alternative religious motivation and rationalization for nonviolent action. This is the task addressed in the next section of this essay.

Toward an Islamic Contribution to the
Rule of Law in International Relations

Although the historical diversity of opinion among Muslim jurists reflected the possibilities of differences in interpretation of the texts of the Qur'an and Sunna, those possibilities have been exercised within a definite historical context. Now that the domestic and international circumstances within which

Muslims operate have changed drastically from what prevailed at the time of the elaboration of the principles of Shariʿa highlighted in the preceding section, I submit that these legitimate possibilities of interpretation should be exercised with the conscious knowledge of this drastic change in circumstances. The following considerations should be emphasized in this process of reinterpretation.

First of all, there is the obvious fact that concepts and ideas can only be derived from any text, whether believed to be of divine or human origin, through a process of interpretation. This principle should be easily appreciated by Muslims because even the Qurʾan, which they believe to be the literal and final word of God, clearly describes itself in verses 12:2 and 43:3 as something conveyed through the vehicle of the Arabic language in order to be reflected upon and understood through the faculty of reason. In verse 29:49, the Qurʾan describes itself as something that is understood and appreciated by the hearts and minds of those granted knowledge.

Consequently, Muslims should realize that they are always dealing with a *human interpretation* of their sacred sources rather than the sources per se. Moreover, in accordance with the Islamic principle of individual responsibility,[100] each and every Muslim should know that he or she is personally responsible for the choice he or she makes in accepting or rejecting any given interpretation of the sacred sources. As frequently reiterated by the Qurʾan,[101] one cannot excuse him- or herself by accepting what has been handed down from previous generations of Muslims or stated by contemporary Muslims. Each and every Muslim is responsible for what he or she may accept as the valid interpretation of the sacred sources. The crucial question would, therefore, be what the criteria or guidelines are for accepting or rejecting a given interpretation.

It is not possible to state and explain here the various approaches and issues related to this question of assessment; however, it is safe to assume that most Muslims would agree that the given interpretation must be consistent with the realities of the concrete situation within which a proposed principle is supposed to be applied. When Imam al-Shafiʿi, the founder of the Shafiʿi school, was asked why he varied some aspects of his teachings when he moved from Iraq to Egypt, he is reported to have said that the changes were necessitated by differences between the two environments and societies. None of the above considerations is new or conclusive because other considerations and counterarguments can easily be envisaged. When all is said and done, the ultimate question would be a moral one, namely, what *ought* to be the principle in the particular case or situation. With particular reference to the issue of political violence and terrorism, the question becomes this: should this sort of behavior be acceptable or condoned by the norms of Islam?

To answer the moral question, one should consider the full implications and consequences of political violence and terrorism in light of the fundamental moral principle that one should treat others in the same way he or she would like to be treated by them. Thus, since one would not accept acts of political violence or terrorism being inflicted on his or her person or that of a person for whose safety and well-being one is concerned, then one should not inflict such acts on other persons. This proposition can be stated in terms of considering the consequences of the wholesale practice of political violence and terrorism. In other words, since the very basis of civilized human existence would be totally repudiated if every person, or even a large number of persons, should resort to direct private violence in rectifying injustice and since one would not accept those consequences, one should not engage in that conduct.

Thus, in the final analysis, this position is a plea for the rule of law in domestic and international relations. Whatever may be the problems that we have with the practice of lawlessness by other persons and official organs, the answer can never lie in repudiation of the principle of the rule of law itself. Whatever injustice may be inflicted on one person or group of persons, it would have to be rectified in an orderly and peaceful manner. This point was brilliantly made in the simple statement of the French peasant quoted earlier: "Who will believe that your cause is just when your behaviors are so unjust?"[102]

I do not in any way suggest that Muslims should abandon their religious obligation to uphold good and justice and combat evil and injustice. On the contrary, Muslims must do their utmost in this regard, but only through peaceful and orderly means. As suggested earlier, ends and means are intricately connected; a good end can never be achieved through bad means. Muslim individuals and groups must, therefore, employ peaceful and orderly means in their struggles for peace and justice. Internal political action, to the extent of nonviolent civil disobedience, and external political action, through all diplomatic and other peaceful means of influencing public opinion and government action, are available and perfectly legitimate means of upholding good and justice and combating evil and injustice in accordance with the dictates of Islam.

With this perspective, I suggest that Muslim scholars and popular leaders should approach Islamic sources. While it is true that there has been ambivalence in the interpretation of the sources and that there are precedents for political violence and terrorism in Islamic history, the clear choice of Muslims today should be to uphold the rule of law in domestic and international relations. All Islamic sources that may be seen as supporting political violence and terrorism should be set aside, having lost legitimacy and authority in the radically transformed present context; moreover, sources and precedents that support the rule of law should be emphasized and implemented.

The Islamic theological arguments for this position have been explained in the work of the late Sudanese Muslim reformer, *Ustadh* Mahmoud Mohamed Taha.[103] Citing the impact of historical context on the formulation of Shari'a and the need for reformulation under contemporary circumstances, *Ustadh* Mahmoud argued for enacting those verses of the Qur'an and texts of Sunna that support peaceful relations and the rule of law. According to *Ustadh* Mahmoud, the practical application of the fundamental and permanent message of Islam of peace and cooperation had to be postponed in view of the concrete realities of the seventh-century Middle East. Instead, the Prophet had to implement a transitional message of Islam that restricted and regulated, but did not eliminate, the use of force in intercommunal/international relations. However, in doing so, the Prophet also conveyed the fundamental message of peace and cooperation through the Qur'an and Sunna but did not elaborate on that message because to have done so would have confused the early Muslims who were supposed to implement the transitional message.

In terms of the subject matter of the present chapter, *Ustadh* Mahmoud held that the verses of the Qur'an and Sunna that sanctioned the use of force in international/intercommunal relations, quoted and cited above, were merely transitional in application. In other words, he maintained that those sources will cease to be legally binding as part of Shari'a once the practical conditions and circumstances that justified their application in the seventh century have changed. He also emphasized the vital need for peace and the rule of law in domestic and international relations under contemporary circumstances, thereby concluding that the applicable Islamic message is one of peace and cooperation, *not* one of violence and confrontation.

Although it may not be possible to explain the technical aspects of *Ustadh* Mahmoud's theory for Islamic reform in the present short chapter, it should be emphasized that the whole approach I have adopted in the preceding discussion is based on that theory. Moreover, it should be noted that, although I find the ideas of Ustadh Mahmoud particularly appropriate for achieving the desired results of resolving the Islamic ambivalence to political violence and terrorism, any equally appropriate approach would be acceptable. The fundamental point here is that there is an urgent need for resolving this ambivalence in favor of the rule of law and that the proposed reform methodology must enjoy Islamic legitimacy if it is to have the desired result of changing Muslim attitudes and policies.

Chapter 2

Problems of Universal Cultural Legitimacy
for Human Rights

It is commonplace now to decry the unacceptable discrepancy between the theory and the practice of human rights. Despite several decades existence of elaborate and enlightened international standards of human rights and despite the rhetoric of strong commitment to these standards by governments, which are often supported in or pressured into such a commitment by an increasing number of nongovernmental organizations and groups, we continue to witness gross violations of human rights in all parts of the world. If we are to reduce this unacceptable discrepancy and promote greater respect for the full range of human rights throughout the world, then we must understand and combat not only the immediate causes of the discrepancy but also the underlying factors that contribute to it.

For example, it is often stated that the discrepancy between the theory and practice of human rights results inevitably from ineffective implementation and enforcement procedures under the international human rights instruments. This explanation invites the question of why the implementation and enforcement process has lagged behind the standard-setting achievements. Other explanations for the discrepancy point to the tendency of official authorities to resist accountability in general and to resent in particular accountability to external entities as inconsistent with national sovereignty and self-determination. Those in power clearly would prefer to have a free hand to implement their own view of the common good, if not to manipulate power to their own advantage. To avoid accepting this state of affairs as a fait accompli, those in power must be induced to accept internal and external accountability in the interest of implementing and enforcing human rights standards. Other observers base the discrepancy between human rights theory and practice on the political, social, and economic processes within a given country. Once again, however, the question remains: how can we adjust or transform the relevant political, social, and economic processes and relationships within a given community so as to promote greater compliance with human rights standards?

Whatever the reason one accepts as the cause of the discrepancy between the theory and practice of human rights, a more positive element needs to be injected into the reform process if this discrepancy is to be reduced. The *cultural legitimacy* of the full range of human rights standards must be developed—that is, the concern for human rights as they figure in the standards of many different cultures should be enhanced. In particular, I believe it would be useful to challenge representations of some human rights that lack genuine cultural legitimacy within a given sociological system.

Enhancing the cultural legitimacy for a given human right should mobilize political forces within a community, inducing those in power to accept accountability for the implementation or enforcement of that right. With internal cultural legitimacy, compliance with standards set for a particular human right can no longer be branded by those in power as a compromise of national sovereignty. Compliance with human rights standards would be seen as a legitimate exercise of national sovereignty and not as an external limitation. The continuing processes of change and adjustment of political, social, and economic relationships within a community mean that internal changes can be made to accommodate a given human right, if that right is shown to be legitimate within the culture of the particular community.

The term *culture* is used here in its broadest sense as a "totality of values, institutions and forms of behavior transmitted within a society as well as the material goods produced by man [and woman]. . . . [T]his wide concept of culture covers *Weltanschauung*, ideologies and cognitive behavior."[1] If, within a given cultural tradition, a certain human value or need is believed to be fundamental and is accorded or guaranteed to every human being, then that value has cultural legitimacy. Many factors and forces influence the formulation and content of a purported human right. However, it seems that a necessary prerequisite for a human right is that individuals accept its underlying validity. After all, individual convictions and motivations shape and precipitate action that either favors or opposes the recognition and implementation of the claim as a human right. Institutional actors or economic and social forces may appear to be the immediate causes of efforts to recognize and implement a claim as a human right, but in the final analysis, institutions emerge from the interaction of individuals; moreover, economic and social forces are also the expression of the interests of individuals.

This chapter argues that the difficulties in effectively implementing established human rights and in recognizing other claims and interests as human rights and implementing them as well derive from the insufficiency of cultural support for the particular right or claim. Culture mediates power and acts as the framework within which self-interest is defined and realized in any community. Cultural legitimacy, moreover, cannot be deduced or assumed from the mere fact of official recognition of the claim as a human right in existing formal documents. As explained later, the process through which the current international human rights standards were formulated and adopted did not address issues of cultural legitimacy in relation to most of the cultural traditions of the world.

To address this fundamental need for universal cultural legitimacy as the basis for international efforts to protect and promote human rights, this chapter begins with a brief explanation of the notion of cultural legitimacy and its impact on public policy and action in relation to human rights. The second section of the chapter reviews the beginning and subsequent stages of modern international efforts to protect and promote human rights in order to assess the nature and quality of concern with cultural legitimacy displayed during those formative and subsequent stages. The third section focuses on the Islamic tradition of illustrating a working model for assessing and enhancing the cultural legitimacy of human rights within indigenous cultural traditions. The possibilities and problems of using the processes of cultural dynamics in support of universal standards of human rights are discussed in the final section.

On the Nature and Role of Cultural Legitimacy

Many definitions of *culture* in the wider sense adopted here are found in anthropological or sociological literature, some emphasizing social heritage, others stressing shared ideas or shared (standardized) behavior, and so on.[2] According to one source, culture can generally be seen to comprise the "inherited artifacts, goods, technical processes, ideas, habits, and values" of society, which endow human beings "with an additional extension of [their] anatomical apparatus, with a protective armor of defenses and safeguards, and with mobility and speed." Culture is the cumulative creation of human beings, which "transforms individuals into organized groups and gives these [groups] an almost indefinite continuity."[3]

A more recent approach to the study of culture presents it in terms of symbols and meanings.[4] Clifford Geertz, for example, defines culture as "an historically transmitted pattern of meanings embodied in symbols, a system of inherited conceptions expressed in symbolic forms by means of which men [and women] communicate, perpetuate, and develop their knowledge about and attitudes toward life."[5] The proponents of this approach, within a number of disciplines, would challenge the assumption of the behaviorists who maintain that most things about people—personality, culture, and language—can be understood as a complex of stimulus and response connections or patterns of behavior.[6] Instead, they view culture as shared information or knowledge encoded in systems of symbols.

In the context of international relations, Roy Preiswerk has identified four conceptual levels of culture:

> Conceptually, we can differentiate between at least four levels of culture: (1) *micro-culture* can be used to describe the particularity of smaller units such as tribes, minorities, village communities, social classes and sub-cultures; (2) one speaks of *national culture*, a very frequently used expression (e.g., "French culture"), mostly in the narrow sense of artistic and intellectual creation. But, insofar as the nationals of a country, despite differentiated micro-cultures, have certain common values, institutions and forms of behavior, one can here also speak of culture in the broad sense; (3) the cultural particularity of a nation is limited to specific cultural characteristics; in other respects it is part of a wider cultural area in so far as it shares other characteristics with neighboring nations within a *regional culture*; (4) beyond this level one can speak, in the broadest sense, of *macro-culture* to describe characteristics which are common to a number of cultures despite local, national and regional differences.[7]

Cultural legitimacy for human rights might be sought at all these levels and certainly should be discussed in relation to all societies. No society, regardless of material development, has yet been able to demonstrate that it is capable of sustaining the full range of human rights envisaged by the United Nations International Bill of Human Rights. This failing is particularly true with regard to the so-called third-generation rights, such as a right to development, a right to peace, and a right to the protection of the environment.[8] In other words, the scope and significance of culture should be understood in the broadest sense, with a view to applying the proposed analysis to Western liberal and Marxist societies as well as to societies of the developing world.

It may be argued that this definition of culture is too broad. This would be a valid objection if it is suggested that culture is everything. What is suggested is that there is a cultural dimension to every aspect of human consciousness and activity. I understand the phrase quoted earlier, "this wide concept of culture covers *Weltanschauung*, ideologies and cognitive behavior," to mean that these aspects of human consciousness and activity are anchored in cultural norms and institutions.

Like the term *culture*, the term *legitimacy* can be defined in different ways for different purposes. In relation to the present discussion, legitimacy is the quality or state of being in conformity with recognized principles or accepted rules and standards. Cultural legitimacy may be defined as the quality or state of being in conformity with recognized principles or accepted rules and standards of a given culture.

The prime feature underlying cultural legitimacy is the authority and reverence derived from internal validity. A culturally legitimate norm or value is respected and observed by the members of the particular culture, presumably because it is assumed to bring satisfaction to those members. Because there may be conflicts and tensions between various competing conceptions of individual and collective satisfaction, there is in any culture constant change and adjustment of the norms or values that are accorded respect and observance. Such change and adjustment appears related to prevailing perceptions of whether a specific normative behavior does or does not bring sufficient satisfaction to warrant its continuation.

Cultural Legitimacy and Public Policy and Action

The interdependence and essential compatibility of the individual and society underlie the relationship between cultural legitimacy and public action and policy. As Ruth Benedict correctly observes,

> Society . . . is never an entity separable from the individuals who compose it. No individual can arrive even at the threshold of his potentialities without a culture in which he participates. Conversely, no civilization has in it any element which in the last analysis is not the contribution of an individual. Where else could any trait come from except from the behaviour of a man or a woman or a child?[9]

This suggests two interconnected propositions. First, every society is dependent on individual members for the development of its institutions, norms, values, and action. Second, each individual is also dependent on society for his or her very existence and for the prospects of realizing a meaningful and gratifying life.

This fundamental interdependence and compatibility does not suggest, however, that there is no tension between individuals and their society. Although there is an overlap between individual perceptions of norms, values, and institutions, these perceptions are by no means identical. The degree of incompatibility and tension varies from person to person and often between one stage and another in the life of the same person. Although most people find it possible to conform, or are pressured into conforming, with prevailing attitudes and behavioral patterns, others fail or refuse to do so. Depending on many factors, including the personal endowments of the individual and the susceptibility of the culture to change under the particular circumstances, "deviant" individuals may either succeed in bringing about change that favors their perspectives or be branded as abnormal, even psychopathic.[10] Society's great reformers as well as its psychopaths are manifestations of this creative tension.

In addition, society may retrospectively perceive change as positive and beneficial, but such changes can be perceived initially as negative and detrimental by the carriers or guardians of the previous order. In a contemporary debate over social change, appreciating this point enables each side to understand and deal with the other's point of view. Both proponents and opponents of social change are not necessarily malicious, deviant, or reactionary people. Whereas the proponents of change may serve the legitimate needs of their evolving society, opponents may serve the needs of the same society by resisting change until the case for it has been made. These and other elements of cultural dynamics are discussed later regarding how a given norm or value attains cultural legitimacy and influences public policy and action. Cultural norms are not the only determinants of behavior.[11] Cultural habits are conceptualized as ideal norms or patterns of behavior. Since a person behaves in response to his or her perception of the total situation, including physical stimuli and psychological factors such as the degree of the person's identification with the cultural model, actual behavior may not necessarily coincide with the ideal norms or patterns of behavior.

Given the individual's dependence on society and society's formidable capacity to instill or enforce conformity in its members, public policy and action are more likely to accord with ideal cultural norms and patterns of behavior than private action. Whereas the individual may succumb to deviant impulses and drives in private and may even contemplate rebellion against the established ideal, open deviance and rebellion are rare. The powerful force of conforming to the established ideal is illustrated by the fact that most people seek to keep their deviant behavior and views secret and, if discovered, try to explain them as temporary lapses in judgment rather than as a deliberate rejection of the ideal norm or pattern of behavior. Even the few who choose to come out in open revolt, whether or not they claim a commitment to an alternative model, would normally attempt to explain or rationalize their position as reflecting a more genuine commitment to the ideals of society or as resulting from a reinterpretation of those ideals.

Open and systematic nonconformity gravely threatens those in authority over the society—the ruling class or group that over time comes to have a vested interest in the status quo. Using the powers explicitly or implicitly vested in them by society, these people will naturally seek to suppress nonconforming behavior, often in the name of preserving the stability and vital interests of society at large. In other words, the self-interest of those in power in political, economic, religious, or other spheres, who claim a monopoly over the determination of what is in the public good, tends to shape public policy and action in terms of the cultural ideal.

This analysis emphasizes the desirability of seeking the support of the cultural ideal for any proposition of public policy and action, especially for the protection and promotion of human rights. Whether the rights are individual or collective, civil and political, or economic, social, and cultural, their protection requires mobilizing and harnessing the relevant resources of society. That is more likely to be achieved, and more likely to achieve the desired objectives, if the purpose is seen to be consistent with cultural ideals. Because individual action is the ultimate resource at the disposal of any society, it is vital to motivate people to act in favor of a given human right. Such motivation involves a mental attitude that accepts the particular human right as worth working for. This process may require discarding or modifying previously held attitudes or perceptions in order to create or discover new ones.

Basic to this hypothesis is the proposition that all cultural positions have some problems with some human rights, yet where this is so, it is probable that an *internal* value or norm can be used to develop or supplement the cultural legitimacy of any given human right. The goal is to adopt an approach that realistically identifies the lack of cultural support for some human rights and then seeks ways to support and legitimize the particular human right in terms of the values, norms, and processes of change belonging to the relevant cultural tradition.

Cultural Relativism and the Universality of Human Rights

The controversy among anthropologists over cultural relativism can be used to clarify the implications of the need to achieve cultural legitimacy for human rights. Many scholars have recognized that our perception of the world is conditioned by our preexisting conceptual categories. Although this generally accepted proposition applies to many facets of life, such as perceptions of beauty, I am concerned here with its ethical implications. Although it may therefore be more appropriate to use the term *ethical relativism*,[12] I use the term *cultural relativism* because it is commonly used in the field with specific reference to ethical issues.

Emphasis on cultural relativism in modern anthropological literature evolved as a reaction against cultural evolutionism—that is to say, the view that human societies tend to progress from "primitive," or "savage," to "modern." With their Eurocentric disposition, nineteenth-century anthropologists ranked Western societies highest and made Western values the standards of their universal model for the "evolution" of societies. Cultural relativism was introduced to combat these Eurocentric and racist notions of progress.[13]

Although there are various formulations of cultural relativism, some perceived to be problematical,[14] the basic thrust of the theory is clear and very useful. As John Cook notes, "it is aimed at getting people to admit that although it may *seem* to them that their moral principles are self-evidently true, and hence *seem* to be grounds for passing judgment on other peoples, in fact the self-evidence of these principles is a kind of illusion."[15] According to its strongest proponents, cultural relativism acknowledges the equal validity of diverse patterns of life and lays "stress on the dignity inherent in every body of custom, and on the need for tolerance of conventions though they may differ from one's own."[16]

The critics of cultural relativism perceive it as undermining the ability to condemn repressive practices in other countries that are sanctioned by the particular culture.[17] For example, some scholars have charged that relativism provides a notion that can be used to justify slavery and genocide.[18] There is certainly substance to this criticism if one believes cultural relativism implies the complete tolerance of all norms and practices sanctioned by the respective cultures. But some scholars have argued that cultural relativism does not

logically entail tolerance and could entail intolerance.[19] In other words, tolerance of diverse moral practices may be part of a particular culture rather than
a necessary consequence of cultural relativism. "It is not the theory of relativism that makes tolerance supreme," Alison Renteln suggests, "but rather
the uncritical acceptance of this value by Americans."[20] Although aware that
cross-cultural criticism is weakened by being more or less ethnocentric, a relativist may still criticize what violates his or her deeply held beliefs.[21] Despite
its ethnocentricity, criticism can be effective in bringing various economic
and political pressures to bear on the "offending" culture. In this respect, I
agree with Renteln when she writes:

> Although it is appropriate to draw a distinction between criticisms
> corresponding to internal standards, on the one hand, and external
> ones, on the other, the theory of relativism blocks neither. It says
> nothing about the desirability of social criticism. It holds that every
> society will utilize its own standards. Sometimes there will be a fun-
> damental conflict among the various standards, and sometimes there
> will be convergence or consensus on standards. What one makes of
> the conflicting or consensual standards depends not on relativism but
> on the role one wishes to play in the international community. There
> is nothing in the theory of relativism that requires one posture as op-
> posed to another.[22]

Moreover, insofar as criticism is based on values accepted by a wide range
of cultures, the charge of ethnocentricity is weakened, especially if it can be
shown that such criticism is based, even indirectly, on values or norms accepted by the culture being criticized. This fact would seem to recommend
the sort of cross-cultural search for universal human values in support of
universal human rights advocated here.

One may ask why a proponent of one cultural view should accept a judgment of the majority of other cultures. Insofar as a person believes in the validity of a norm, that person is unlikely to accept an opposing norm: the more
strongly we believe in our values, the less likely we are to tolerate the values
of others. In response to this point, there appears to be a universal rational
principle to the effect that strong evidence of a contrary view should induce
a person to reexamine her or his position. In my own culture of northern
Sudan, this notion is expressed in this maxim: if two people tell you that your
head is missing, you better check to see if it is still there. In other words, the

more widely our positions are challenged by others, the more likely we are to reconsider those positions.

As for the dangers of excessive cultural relativism, it is extremely unlikely that any culture will condone an inhumane practice. This belief may be an article of faith, but it is one worth having. Moreover, probably any inhumane practice that may persist within a given culture can be challenged by an alternative interpretation of the underlying cultural norms. Unless we take this article of faith seriously by looking for its empirical verification, we would prematurely condemn the human experience on this planet to catastrophic failure.

As Jack Donnelly correctly states, "the problem of cultural relativism and universal human rights cannot be reduced to an either-or choice. Claims of cultural relativism show a great diversity in meaning, substance, and importance."[23] Accordingly, he suggests that a "weak" cultural relativist position may be justified, primarily at the level of form and interpretation, without violating the essential universality of human rights. For example, a weak cultural relativist position would accept a certain degree of practices as legitimate *interpretations* of "the right to political participation," while it would reject other practices as illegitimate and as amounting to a complete denial of the right.[24]

Arguing in terms of the general values human rights seek to protect today and the relative universality of "human nature," Donnelly asserts that basic human rights must at least initially be assumed to be similarly universal. His review of the provisions of the Universal Declaration of Human Rights and the two covenants seems to support this proposition. However, some of the rights recognized by the declaration and covenants may be viewed as "interpretations" or "forms" with which some cultures may differ without necessarily denying universal human rights.[25] Donnelly proposed the following test for assessing claims of cultural relativism:

> Rights are formulated with certain basic violations, or threats to human dignity, in mind. Therefore, the easiest way to overcome the presumption of universality for a widely recognized human right is to demonstrate either that the anticipated violation is not standard in that society that the value is (justifiably) not considered basic in that society, or that it is protected by an alternative mechanism. In other words, one would have to show that the underlying cultural vision of human nature or society is both morally defensible and incompatible

with the implementation of the "universal" human right in question. I would argue that such a test can be met only rarely today, and that permissible exceptions usually are relatively minor and generally consistent with the basic thrust of the Universal Declaration.[26]

In my view, two main conclusions are warranted by the preceding analysis. First, as a manifestation of the right to self-determination and as a safeguard against the dangers of ethnocentrism, the theory of cultural relativism provides a good approach to cross-cultural evaluations without necessarily undermining our ability to criticize and condemn repressive or morally abhorrent practices. Cultural relativism does not necessarily require allowing cultures total autonomy in accepting a given human right as culturally legitimate or rejecting it as culturally illegitimate. As I argue elsewhere, the basic premise of international efforts to protect and promote human rights is the belief that there are limits on cultural relativism.[27] What I find to be at issue, however, is the *manner* in which outsiders can challenge practices that they deem to be in violation of human rights. Second, cross-cultural evaluations, which are unavoidable for any international effort to protect and promote human rights, are most effective when based on universal human values. The more it can be shown that a particular human right is based on a value or norm accepted by the widest range of cultural traditions, the less our efforts to protect and promote that right will be open to charges of ethnocentricity or cultural imperialism.

Adda Bozeman argues that "ideas . . . are not transferable in their authenticity . . . [and] in the final analysis cultures are different because they are associated with different modes of thought."[28] According to Bozeman, given the difficulty and complexity of perceiving the other in his authenticity, "cross-cultural communications lead to misunderstandings by virtue of their very nature."[29] Although intended to challenge the tenability of international law, Bozeman's thesis has obvious implications for international efforts to protect and promote human rights. In fact, she states expressly in her conclusion that

Present efforts aiming at an extension of international law to the sphere of individual life by drafting, for example, universally valid covenants of human rights, appear in this perspective to be exercises in futility—all the more so as most non-Western governments are not constrained by locally dominant moral orders to assure respect for individual liberties within their respective local jurisdictions.[30]

It is interesting to note that Bozeman's conception of human rights as exclusively "individual liberties" betrays the reality of her Western ethnocentricity despite the pretense of an effort toward universalism. In her introduction, she states that "European peoples escaped the restrictions which came to bind societies in China, India, the Near East, and Africa because they have been continuously responsive to the unsettling forces emanating from biography . . . among them most particularly the commitment to cultivate rational yet daring thought."[31] While I concede the element of truth in what she says, I do so from a constructive perspective. I would take the difficulty and complexity of perceiving the other in his or her authenticity and the consequent dangers of misunderstanding as guidelines in searching for cross-cultural support for human rights, and international law in general, rather than as reasons for abandoning the effort. The moral imperative and the practical need for upholding the rule of law in international relations—and protecting and promoting human rights in particular—are too strong to abandon merely because of the complexity and difficulty of the effort. Moreover, each person should work from within her or his own culture precisely in order to avoid the dangers of misunderstanding.

It should be emphasized, however, that in advocating the search for cross-cultural support for human rights, I am not suggesting that universal human rights are only those expressly articulated or overtly supported by existing cultural traditions. I do not believe that universal human rights can only be justified in terms of the least common denominator among the cultural traditions of the world. In my view, human rights should be based on the inherent dignity and integrity of every human being. Cross-cultural studies can be helpful from both substantive and tactical points of view. From a substantive point of view, cross-cultural studies can help to discover the actual content and necessary implications of the inherent dignity and integrity of the human being. It is vital to do this without violating the paramount human right of self-determination by imposing external standards. From a tactical point of view, cross-cultural support for human rights helps to foster legitimacy and efficacy for national as well as international efforts to protect and promote human rights.

It may be necessary, failing internal reinterpretation, to appeal to external standards in order to uphold fundamental human rights against inhumane or seriously objectionable practices sanctioned by any culture. Although this endeavor should not be undertaken lightly, its possibility is the ultimate safeguard against the excesses of cultural relativism. The obvious question here is the criteria by which a given practice may be judged inhumane or seriously objectionable for the purposes of justifying appeal to external standards. In my view, the proper criterion is what may be called the principle of *reciprocity*—namely, that one should not tolerate for another person any treatment that one would not accept for oneself.

By placing oneself in the position of the other person, one is able to see if he or she would find any treatment to which the other person is subjected inhumane or seriously objectionable. In placing oneself, however, in the position of the other, one should not impose one's own perceptions on the other's position. For example, it should not be open to a Muslim to say that, since he accepts Islamic law, or Shari'a, for himself, he would conform with the principle of reciprocity in imposing Shari'a on non-Muslims. In this context, the principle of reciprocity means that, since a Muslim would demand the right to decide what law should apply to him or her and would not accept being subjected to the religious law of non-Muslims, he or she should grant the same right to non-Muslims.

As usual, there are clear and strong cases and marginal and weak ones. Whereas appeal to external standards to prevent a culture from sanctioning torture or slavery would be universally accepted as justified and proper, that may not yet be true of some aspects of equality for women. However, to recall that even torture and slavery were not accepted as justification for outside intervention a few decades ago is to appreciate that the scope of protection is expanding. Applying the principle of reciprocity, one can see that as more and more men are faced with the normative imperative of not tolerating for others what they would not accept for themselves, consensus on complete equality for women will grow. In other words, men can be made to concede that women are entitled to the same status and rights that men would demand for themselves if they were women. The same normative imperative applies to the status and rights of ethnic, religious, and linguistic minorities and other victims of human rights violations.

Cultural Legitimacy in the Formulation of Current Standards

The degree and quality of concern with cultural legitimacy in the formulation and adoption of current international human rights instruments have been determined by several factors. One is the nature and content of traditional international law, which influences the formal framework for international action generally, including the field of human rights. Another is the reality of national and international relations and differential levels of development, which affect the capacity of participants to articulate an effective cultural perspective in the process of drafting and adopting human rights standards.

This second factor manifests itself in many ways. For example, in an early study on the history and evolution of human rights prepared by the UN Secretariat in 1947, the accessibility of Western perspectives and the presumed inaccessibility of non-Western perspectives were determining elements in excluding the latter.[32] The authors of that study decided to exclude material prior to the Middle Ages because they felt it would be too difficult to go back to antiquity. In doing so, however, they effectively excluded much of the civilizations of African and Asian peoples. Even for its limited time frame, the twelfth to the eighteenth centuries, the study focused on Europe, especially England, because this focus was thought to be particularly interesting and to provide "solid" information. Thus, the lack of articulation of non-Western perspectives in manners and languages accessible to officials of the United Nations led to the exclusion of those perspectives at the earliest stages of consultation and conceptualization of human rights.

Related to this factor are the nature and quality of the representation of non-Western countries at the international forums where decisions on international human rights standards and the machinery for their implementation were made. As I suggest later, it seems that the "representatives" of non-Western countries may have been more representative of Western cultural perspectives than of their own. Moreover, different levels of material development may have retarded the efforts of peoples in the developing countries to articulate indigenous cultural perspectives on human rights at home and communicate those perspectives at the international level. Peoples of the developing world lacked both clear articulations of their perspectives and the material resources to contribute significantly to the formulation of the International Bill of Human Rights.

International Law and the Realities of International Relations

Since international efforts for the promotion and protection of human rights were undertaken through either international treaties, or state action at the international level, or within established international organizations, it is necessary to consider relevant aspects of international law and relations to assess their effect on the concern with cultural legitimacy during the formulation and adoption of international human rights instruments.[33] In this regard, the primary consideration is that traditional international law recognizes states and organizations of states as its only subjects. Therefore, only states and organizations of states have the capacity to acquire rights and obligations under traditional international law. Although recent developments support the view that individuals may also acquire some rights and obligations under international law, such rights and obligations have thus far been exclusively enforced through the medium of states.[34]

In accordance with the primary role of states under international law, all *legal* international action, including action in the field of human rights, tends to take the form of communications, agreements, and other actions by a state in relation to other states. Even in political, diplomatic, economic, and other spheres, the state format continues to influence the options and efficacy of action. Private or nonofficial forces within society often have their effect on international action, but mostly through the medium of the national state or through appeals and pressure on other states.[35] The principles and rules of international law for the formulation, interpretation, and enforcement of international treaties are of fundamental importance for human rights, not only because of the central role of treaties in setting the relevant substantive standards and procedures but also because international organizations, such as the United Nations, which play an increasingly important role in the human rights field, are created and operated in accordance with treaties. Thus, the essential format of treaties, as instruments negotiated and ratified by states that have the sole competence to pursue their implementation under international law, determines the scope and form of contributions to the content of such treaties. Therefore, if there is to be any concern with cultural legitimacy in a human rights treaty, it must come from or through the action of states party to the negotiation and ratification of the treaty.

This emphasis on states should not obscure the fact that they are not completely autonomous entities that act independently from the social and political forces within their populations or from the constraints of their resources or other factors.[36] In fact, the nature and structure of the state and its options in international action are very much the product of internal sociological, economic, and political processes. Moreover, in today's increasingly interdependent world, even the most powerful states are influenced by the actions of other states. Thus, any contribution made by a state to international action for the protection and promotion of human rights would be partly determined by the effect of internal and external sociological, economic, and political factors on its domestic and foreign policy. I say "partly determined" because the influence of ideas operating through the personalities of individual state officials should not be discounted.

To evaluate the degree and quality of concern with cultural legitimacy in the development of the current human rights instruments, it is necessary to look at the states involved in the process, at the background of their representatives, and for indications of the positions they took during the drafting and adoption processes. As regards the states that participated in those processes in the initial stages after the establishment of the UN in 1945, the vast majority of the peoples of Africa and Asia were still suffering external domination by colonial Western powers. Thus, of the fifty-one original members of the UN, there were only three from Africa and eight from Asia, with seven more Asian states joining over the next ten years.[37] Of the sixteen states that joined the organization in 1955, only one was from Africa and five from Asia. However, with the rapid decolonization of the late 1950s and early 1960s, thirty-four African states joined the UN between 1956 and 1967. In terms of our inquiry, it is clear that few African and Asian states participated in the drafting of the Universal Declaration of Human Rights and the formative early stages of the two covenants.

Additionally, two related considerations need to be noted in regard to the quality of representation accorded to the few states that did participate. The more obvious consideration has to do with the nature of the government that was accorded UN recognition. For example, China was represented at the UN by the national government established in Taiwan, which in effect disenfranchised and excluded from all UN procedures the People's Republic of China, where the vast majority of Chinese people lived. Less obvious, but equally significant, some governments of the time purported to represent their native populations yet barely allowed them participation in making decisions over their national and international policies. The imperial government of Ethiopia, one of only three African states at the UN before 1955 (the others being Egypt and Liberia), is an example of a government that was in effective control of the country but did not allow most of its population to participate in making policy decisions.

State Representation of Non-Western Countries at International Forums

The orientation and cultural identification of the elites who ruled African and Asian states and represented them at international forums determined their participation in the drafting and adoption of the International Bill of Human

Rights. Some insights into the cultural perspectives and philosophical orientation of those African and Asian "representatives" who were most influential in the early stages can be gained through an examination of their educational background and careers. The significance of this factor was underscored at a human rights conference in 1981:

> The previous speaker said that different nations accepted the human rights conventions. This is a surrealistic statement that could only be made by a lawyer. These laws were not adopted by nations but by a small clique of lawyers, bureaucrats and intellectuals who are highly westernized and most of whom have absolutely nothing to do with the cultures in which most of their fellow nationals live. . . . The most interesting problem to me is how notions of human rights, which are clearly of Western provenance and which are now institutionalized are related to the values by which human beings live in most of the world.[38]

Although it is a slight exaggeration to describe the small clique who represented African and Asian countries as having "absolutely nothing to do" with their native cultures, there is obvious validity to the point. The drafting committee of the Universal Declaration of Human Rights consisted of representatives of the governments of Australia, Chile, China, France, Lebanon, the United Kingdom, the United States, and the Soviet Union. The only representatives of non-Western countries in that committee were Chang Peng-Chung of China and Charles Habib Malik of Lebanon.[39] Both had been educated in American universities, and both reflected their "Westernization" in the positions they took during the debates. For example, Chang and Malik emphasized individual rights over collective or peoples' rights and the need for the protection of the individual from the state.[40] Regardless of one's agreement or disagreement with their position, it clearly reflects more the Western than the Chinese and Middle Eastern perspectives.

It is true that the Universal Declaration went through many stages of debate and drafting at the levels of the Human Rights Commission, the Third Committee of the General Assembly, and the General Assembly itself. But African and Asian countries were probably represented at all those levels by people of similar orientation to Chang and Malik.[41] For example, General Carlos Romulo was ambassador extraordinary and plenipotentiary of the Philippines to the UN. Besides his master's degree from Columbia University, he had several honorary degrees from American universities. During the war, Romulo was a high-ranking officer in the U.S. Army and served as aide-de-camp to General Douglas MacArthur on Bataan and Corregidor.

Moreover, as noted by delegates from the developing countries, certain Western delegates were particularly influential in drafting the Universal Declaration. For example, at the beginning of the Third Committee debate on the draft declaration, Chang of China "paid a particular tribute to the contribution to the work of preparing the draft declaration made by Professor Cassin, the representative of France, who had so ably exposed French doctrines of the eighteenth century."[42] Chang also found France to be a particularly appropriate place for discussion of rights because it was "the birth-place of modern ideas of freedom." At the General Assembly level, many delegates made favorable comparisons between the Universal Declaration they were about to adopt (in 1948) and the eighteenth-century declarations, especially the French Declaration of the Rights of Man and of the Citizen of 1789.[43]

In its formulation of civil and political rights, however, the final version of the Universal Declaration departed in important ways from eighteenth-century Western conceptions of natural rights. For example, it included economic, social, and cultural rights unknown to eighteenth-century European conceptions.[44] These aspects of the declaration were included because of the support of Latin American and socialist countries. As for the peoples of Africa and Asia, the format and process for adopting the declaration did not permit the effective participation of their indigenous cultures.

Although initially undertaken at the same time as the declaration, the Covenant on Economic, Social and Cultural Rights and the Covenant on Civil and Political Rights had much longer and more complex histories. By the time they were finally adopted by the UN General Assembly in 1966, most African and Asian countries had gained independence and joined in the last stages of the drafting and adoption. From a formal point of view, African and Asian cultural perspectives had a better chance of being represented in the drafting and adoption of the covenants. At a more substantive level, I submit that the elites who represented African and Asian countries at that stage did not have a clear conception of their respective cultural positions on most of the principles covered by the covenants. This deficiency may be somewhat obscured by the fact that representatives of African and Asian countries took strong positions on certain draft provisions of the covenants and managed to change some of them. Given the lack of popular input and debate on these issues at the national domestic level in most African countries at the time, it is difficult to see how those elites could have genuinely represented their respective cultural traditions.

However, neither the integrity and caliber of the representatives of African and Asian countries nor agreement or disagreement with their orientation is at issue here. Rather, the issue is the degree to which those representatives could reasonably have identified with, and genuinely represented, their indigenous cultural traditions at the time of the drafting and adoption of the Universal Declaration and covenants. Western higher education does not necessarily preclude a person from a developing country from being committed to her or his own cultural tradition. In fact, such an education may enable one to act as a bridge between the two cultural traditions. But this does not seem to have been true for those representatives who participated in the drafting and adoption of the Universal Declaration.

Furthermore, to criticize the degree and quality of concern with cultural legitimacy during the formulation of the declaration and covenants does not mean that these instruments are untenable within non-Western cultural traditions. As I hope to show in the next section, there may be significant cultural support for the philosophical foundations and moral values underlying the current human rights standards. Moreover, insofar as there is inconsistency between the two, I believe that further reconciliation and resolution of conflicts and tensions are possible. The point here is simply that there was little initial concern with cultural legitimacy and that this may have diminished the validity of international human rights standards as seen from non-Western cultural perspectives.

Finally, despite their differences, the essence of cultural traditions reflects the continuity and interdependence of the total human experience. Eighteenth-century Western formulations of rights are as much a reflection of pre-eighteenth-century non-Western experiences as they are a result of the experiences of Western peoples. Seen in this light and presented as the outcome of shared insights rather than as the model developed by a "superior" people, the diffusion of this conception of rights is more likely to be accepted as legitimate by non-Western cultures and less likely to be rejected as manifestations of cultural imperialism.

Subsequent Concern with Cultural Legitimacy

The initial deficiency in establishing universal cultural support for the declaration and covenants (the International Bill of Human Rights) has been partly addressed in subsequent educational and scholarly efforts. For example, the United Nations Educational, Scientific, and Cultural Organization (UNESCO) has sponsored many international conferences, seminars, and publications on human rights in different cultural and religious traditions.[45] Other institutions, such as the International Commission of Jurists, and individual scholars have also published volumes on human rights and cultural perspectives.[46] In my view, most of these efforts suffer from two main weaknesses: inadequacy of their treatment of cultural legitimacy within specific traditions and the lack of an integrated cross-cultural approach.

I find that most of the published works tend to treat cultural traditions from a static and a historical point of view, with little regard for the constant evolution and change of cultural norms and institutions. If the point of the exercise is to support human rights standards within a given cultural tradition in order to encourage greater respect for and protection of these rights in *current* practice, cultural norms and institutions must be analyzed and discussed in terms of their manifestations and significance in the present life of the community. Even as historical accounts, some of the relevant works tend to be selective and misleading because they emphasize points of agreement between historical cultural norms and current human rights standards without identifying and addressing points of conflict and tension.

This criticism can be illustrated with reference to the available literature on human rights in the Islamic tradition.[47] Not only is this literature ahistorical, in that it tends to deal with formal scriptural tenets of Islam in isolation from their current social reality, but it is also selective and misleading even in terms of those formal tenets. By quoting and citing selected general scriptural statements that are presented as supportive of human rights in Islam, while omitting others that cannot be so presented, and by failing to show the ways in which the allegedly supportive statements have been qualified in juridical interpretations, this literature presents a completely misleading view of its subject.

Fortunately, some authors have recently sought to expose the misleading effect of selective citation of scriptural sources out of juridical context, and others have tried to discuss those tenets in relation to current social reality. However, much more needs to be done to clarify the internal situation within Islamic and other cultural traditions and to relate it to current social reality. This work is a necessary prerequisite for addressing the second main criticism noted earlier—namely, the lack of a cross-cultural approach. Such an approach is necessary for developing universal cultural legitimacy for human rights beyond the least common denominator of cultural legitimacy within various traditions. The least common denominator will not suffice to protect the human rights of women, for example.

Efforts to identify existing cultural support for human rights and to resolve tensions between human rights standards and cultural norms and values assume some agreement on what are universal human rights. Initially, and for the sake of expediency, the current international standards must be accepted as identifying universal human rights. But since a genuinely universal approach was not used in the initial formulation of the current standards, which came primarily from liberal and to some extent Marxist perspectives, a truly universal substantive set of human rights standards is still needed.

Take, for example, the question of cruel, inhuman, or degrading treatment or punishment. Starting from the existing instruments, one finds that protection against such treatment or punishment is recognized as a human right. When looking into specific cultural traditions, one may well find that a culture supports this concept as a human right, in the sense of a right to which each person is entitled by virtue of being human. Nevertheless, this "consensus" on the right as a matter of principle does not extend to the precise content of the right or provide criteria for determining whether a particular form of treatment or punishment violates the right. Only through the development of a universal consensus on the content of this right, established, for example, by the systematic analysis of the underlying rationale of punishment in cross-cultural perspectives, can human rights discourse avoid being trapped in a situation of competing claims over what constitutes cruel, inhuman, or degrading treatment or punishment.

Toward a Model for Enhancing the
Cultural Legitimacy of Human Rights

Despite the inadequate concern with cultural legitimacy in formulating the current international standards of human rights, it is advisable to work with these standards rather than to seek to repudiate and replace them. To discard the achievements of the last forty years by dismantling the International Bill of Human Rights (the declaration and two covenants) is to risk never being able to replace it with better instruments. I would therefore make the existing bill the foundation of future efforts to establish cultural legitimacy for human rights by interpreting the current provisions and developing an appropriate literature, sensitive to the need for cultural legitimacy. For example, it would be useful to contrast the values and institutions of various cultural traditions with the values underlying the International Bill of Human Rights and the specific implications of those values. Processes of internal cultural dynamics and change may then be used to reconcile and resolve any conflicts and tensions that exist between the values and institutions of a given cultural tradition and those envisaged by the current standards of human rights.

Fundamental Values of the International Bill of Human Rights

I am not concerned here with the historical origin of these values, whether as perceived by the delegates who formulated the International Bill of Human Rights or discovered through some other analysis.[48] Instead, I propose to state the underlying values of the bill as discovered through an interpretative reading of the final text of the instruments. This method seems possible regardless whether the delegates who drafted and adopted the instruments shared a common view of the philosophy of the bill and whether they succeeded in implementing their philosophy in the final texts of the instruments. In other words, for the following discussion, I take the texts of the International Bill of Human Rights as the source of the underlying values of the bill.

An interpretative reading of the provisions of the bill reveals several fundamental values that are accepted as valid and worthy of implementation based on the specific principles of these documents. As expected, however, these values have their own internal tensions, which can be resolved only through detailed consideration of their specific implications in given situations. Although it is not possible to bring such attention to bear in the following brief survey of these values, the point should be borne in mind. In other words, the survey does not assume that these values were adopted by the International Bill of Human Rights in an unqualified form. It assumes that the flexibility of the interpretation of these values and the possibilities of their mutual limitation offer good prospects for reconciling them with values and institutions of a variety of cultural traditions.

The fundamental value underlying the Universal Declaration and covenants is the notion of the inherent dignity and integrity of every human being. All the civil and political rights as well as the economic, social, and cultural rights recognized by the Universal Declaration and elaborated on in the covenants are the necessary practical implications of the inherent dignity and integrity of the human person. For example, human dignity and integrity require not only that individuals have their needs for food, shelter, and health care satisfied but also that they be guaranteed freedom of belief, expression, and association and afforded opportunities for education and communication with others to develop fully their personalities and achieve their human potential.

Equality is another implication of the inherent dignity and integrity of the human being, which, in turn, requires nondiscrimination on grounds such as race, sex, religion, and national or social origin. Both notions are explicitly affirmed in the Universal Declaration and the two covenants. The essence of human rights is that they are the entitlement of every human being by virtue of being human. For example, this essence will be defeated if a woman is denied her human rights because of her sex, race, or beliefs.

It is sufficient here to focus on these values and their implications because they can be taken as the foundation of all human rights and because they are likely to encounter problems or difficulties of legitimacy in the context of traditional African cultures. Although I propose to focus on issues of cultural legitimacy in relation to Islamic African societies, this does not imply that other cultural traditions are fully consistent with all the underlying values and implications of the International Bill of Human Rights. On the contrary, the assumption is that every cultural tradition raises some problems in this regard. However, it is the thesis of this chapter that alternative sources and interpretations within any given tradition may prove useful in overcoming the problems raised by a particular tradition.

An often cited example of the inconsistency between some human rights and the liberal tradition is the latter's presumed rejection of the notion of imposing positive duties on the state to provide housing, health care, and so forth for those citizens who are unable to secure these essential needs for themselves. The limited success of social democracy in some Western European countries, for example, clearly shows that the liberal tradition can sustain social services based on a positive obligation of the state to provide for the physical needs of its population. Nevertheless, the dominant theme in both the theory and practice of Western liberalism remains that of restricting human rights to the negative duty of the state not to interfere with the liberty of the individual rather than linking human rights to a positive obligation to provide for basic needs. From the point of view of the proposed approach, however, the question is how to enhance the view of human rights as requiring both positive and negative duties from the state within the liberal tradition through internally legitimate arguments.

Cultural Legitimacy of Human Rights in Islamic Societies

Traditional African cultural perspectives on human rights are too diverse and volatile to permit neat generalizations about their positions on the underlying values of the International Bill. Even when focusing on a specific cultural tradition, one must allow for significant variations in norms and attitudes over time, while also taking into account the inevitable discrepancy between the theory and practice of those norms and attitudes. Provided one keeps these limitations in mind, one can gain some understanding of the relationship between the values underlying the current standards of human rights and the corresponding values of specific African cultural traditions. In this section, I discuss my own Islamic tradition in order to demonstrate both the difficulties it has with some aspects or implications of human rights values and the prospects of resolving those difficulties.

Religion, in general, is central to the cultures of many African societies, though it is not the sole formative force behind the prevailing values and attitudes. Other local factors and external influences also contribute to the continuing processes of social and political change. In Islamic African societies, however, the religion of Islam seems to be a particularly important source of cultural legitimacy because of the comprehensive and forceful nature of its precepts. In contrast to most traditional African religions, Islam has a highly specific ethical code and well-developed and articulated views on almost every aspect of private and public life.

Islam is an extremely complex and multifaceted phenomenon that has been the subject of numerous, often violent, disagreements among its adherents for the last fifteen centuries. Many sociological factors and philosophical considerations influence and inform the understanding and practice of Islam at any given time and place.[49] Nevertheless, any meaningful discussion of an issue from an Islamic point of view must be based on the fundamental sources of Islam, namely, the Qur'an, which Muslims firmly believe to be the literal and final word of God, and Sunna, the traditions of the Prophet.

Although the text of the Qur'an was recorded within a few decades after the Prophet's death in 632 and is accepted as accurate by the vast majority of Muslims, the texts of Sunna were, and continue to be, much more controversial because they remained an oral tradition until they were recorded about two centuries after the Prophet's death.[50] Besides the controversies about the accuracy of many reported Sunna texts, both the Qur'an and Sunna have been the subject of extensive scholarly and popular interpretation and counterinterpretation for many centuries. This process has led to the evolution of Shariʿa the comprehensive and complex codes ranging in subject from religious dogma and ritual practices to ethical norms, principles and detailed rules of private and public law, and matters of etiquette and personal hygiene.

Internal controversy and differences within the corpus of Shariʿa were encouraged for two reasons. First, some verses of the Qurʾan and texts of Sunna appear to contradict each other. Whenever Islamic scholars and jurists encountered this contradiction, they deemed one set of texts to have abrogated or repealed, for the purposes of Shariʿa, any other inconsistent text. This process of reconciliation through abrogation is known in Islamic jurisprudence as *naskh*.[51] Second, since both sources used the Arabic language to communicate their teachings, the understanding of those teachings has been influenced by the many shades of meaning of Arabic expressions as comprehended by different Islamic jurists and scholars.

As a result, today the official and formal Shariʿa position on many issues is based on decisions made by Muslim scholars and jurists either to adopt one set of texts rather than another or to adopt one possible interpretation of the applicable texts rather than another. In other words, though the Qurʾan and Sunna as sources of Shariʿa are believed by Muslims to be divine, the interpretation and implementation of those sources have been the product of human comprehension and action in a particular historical context. Once this basic fact about the evolution of Shariʿa is appreciated, the door should be open for developing alternative concepts and principles from within the Islamic tradition itself. So long as such efforts are consistent with the fundamental precepts of Islam and sensitive to concerns for Islamic authenticity, there is no reason to prevent the adopting or adapting of norms and ideas from other cultural traditions. Early Muslim scholars and jurists did just that in developing their understanding of Shariʿa.

Looking at the totality of the Qurʾan and Sunna in relation to the values underlying current international standards of human rights produces a mixed picture. On the one hand, many general texts seem to emphasize both the inherent dignity of the human person and the equality of all human beings in the sight of God.[52] On the other hand, many other specific texts establish strict limitations on who is a human being entitled to full dignity and equality within the context of the Islamic society and state. In particular, certain texts of the Qurʾan and Sunna support a hierarchy of status according to sex and belief, with Muslim men being the only group entitled to the full implications of human dignity, integrity, and equality, followed by Muslim women, certain non-Muslim believers (mainly Christians and Jews), and finally other believers and unbelievers. Given the historical context within which Shari'a was developed, it was probably unavoidable that the early Muslim scholars and jurists should adopt that view of the source texts. In other words, the historical context of the eighth- and ninth-century Middle East determined the choices and interpretations Muslim scholars and community leaders made among the range of texts. By the same token, the present historical context, which upholds universal human rights regardless of sex and belief, should determine the choices and interpretations modern Muslim scholars and community leaders have to make among the range of texts and interpretations.

I have elsewhere documented human rights problems with Shari'a and elaborated on the modernist approach to Islamic reform advocated by the late Muslim reformer, Ustadh Mahmoud Mohamed Taha.[53] This approach not only is feasible in the Islamic context but may provide a useful model for working within other cultural traditions to identify conflicts with values underlying the current human rights standards. The approach may also help to develop ways of resolving authentic and legitimate conflicts within the particular cultural perspective. The essential premise of this model is the recognition that cultural norms evolve in response to specific historical circumstances. Therefore, norms may vary or be modified with the change of circumstances. The sources of norms and values, and the techniques by which they evolve and change, may be specific to the particular culture. Nevertheless, there are certain principles that regulate the processes of cultural dynamics and change in general and that may therefore be used in conscious efforts to enhance the legitimacy of human rights within any given cultural tradition.

Cultural Dynamics and Change

As mentioned earlier, this chapter takes a very broad view of culture as the totality of the experience of a given society. It also assumes that every cultural tradition contains some norms and institutions that are supportive of some human rights as well as norms and institutions that are inhospitable to other human rights. The constructive approach suggested here would seek to enhance the supportive elements and to redress the inhospitable elements in ways that are consistent with the integrity of the cultural tradition in question. It is self-defeating and counterproductive to try to enhance the legitimacy of human rights within any culture in ways that are unlikely to be accepted as legitimate by that culture.

Against this background, this section investigates present knowledge of the processes of cultural dynamics and change and how it may help to promote the cultural legitimacy of human rights. Is it possible to develop some guidelines for human rights advocates who may wish to undertake this task? A cross-cultural approach provides the appropriate balance between the relativism and universalism of human rights, but what does this approach entail and how can it be used to enhance the cultural legitimacy of human rights?

It is helpful to begin by emphasizing the major assumptions underlying cross-cultural studies, such as the pioneering cross-cultural survey of the Institute of Human Relations of Yale University in 1937.[54] According to the organizers and editors of the Yale survey, cross-cultural studies are founded on the conviction that, despite their diversity, all human cultures have fundamentally a great deal in common and that these common aspects are susceptible to scientific analysis. Furthermore, such studies are said to be based on seven assumptions shared by most social scientists in the field. These assumptions may be summarized as follows:[55]

- Culture is not instinctive or innate, or transmitted biologically, but is composed of habits, such as learned tendencies to react, acquired by each individual through life experience.
- Culture is repeatedly inculcated by transmission from parent to child over successive generations. Such inculcation involves not only the imparting of techniques and knowledge but also the disciplining of the child's animal impulses to adjust the child to social life.
- As such, the habits of the cultural order are social, in that they are shared by human beings living in organized aggregates, or societies, and kept relatively uniform by social pressure. Since many cultures provide for the societal survival of their respective societies, they tend to reflect certain universals, such as sentiments of group cohesion, mechanisms of social control, organization for defense against hostile neighbors, and provision for the perpetuation of the population.
- To a considerable extent, the group habits of which culture consists are conceptualized (or verbalized) as ideal norms or patterns of behavior. Actual behavior, however, may not always conform to the cultural ideal because that ideal is only one of the determinants of behavior. Since individuals behave in response to the state of their organism and drives

at the moment and in response to their perception of the total situation in which they find themselves, such behavior may deviate from the ideal norms.

- Since habits persist only as long as they bring satisfaction, elements of culture can continue to exist only when they yield to the people in a society a margin of satisfaction, a favorable balance of pleasure over pain.
- Culture changes through an adaptive process that is comparable to but different from that of evolution in the organic realm. In this way, cultures adjust and adapt to the surrounding physical and geographic as well as social environments. To subscribe to this assumption of cultural adaptability is not to maintain a rigidly deterministic view of the process—that any culture would necessarily have to adjust in any given way—since different cultural forms may represent adjustments to similar problems and similar cultural forms may represent adjustments to different problems. Some similarities in different cultures may represent independent adjustments to comparable conditions. Thus, while cultures always adjust to physical events and historical contacts with peoples of differing cultures, both kinds of stimuli exert only a conditioning rather than a determining influence on the course of a given culture. In other words, there is always an element of selection and choice of reaction to the particular event or historical context.
- In this adaptive process, cultures *tend* to form a consistent and integrated whole, but total integration is never achieved because historical events are constantly exerting a disturbing influence. Integration takes time, and long before one process is completed, many others will have been initiated.

These assumptions are useful provided that they are seen in the context of a broad definition of culture and are perceived as being applicable to *all* the cultural traditions of the world, including those of materially developed societies. When seen in this light, these assumptions offer prospects for influencing the direction of cultural change toward enhancing the legitimacy of human rights. Given the radical transformation of the technology for communicating information and ideas in an increasingly globalized world, it is possible to manipulate the assumptions in favor of specific goals. Such manipulation is already taking place, somewhat haphazardly, to serve the narrow ends of commercial interests. Powerful symbols and images are constantly used to promote consumerism in fashion, entertainment, and so forth. Can appropriate techniques be used to promote universal legitimacy for human rights? And what is the content of the human rights message to be conveyed through those techniques?

Although limited by its subjects—normally small individual societies—and by its retrospective approach to understanding past processes of societal change, the available anthropological literature on cultural dynamics and change may nevertheless provide some guidance for effecting change in a particular direction. This literature can inform us about the factors facilitating change and about those opposing or resisting it within any given society. For example, Edward Shils's discussion of endogenous and exogenous factors effecting the inevitable process of change within a wide variety of traditions—as well as of patterns of change and stability in traditions[56]—may be useful in advancing the *prospective* process of change in favor of enhancing the cultural legitimacy of human rights. Additionally, the work of other scholars may provide useful insights into the psychological and sociological processes of interaction and change within a given culture.[57] Studies of the receptivity and resistance of specific societies to change may also provide some guidance.[58]

Examples of planned social engineering undertaken by totalitarian states may be particularly instructive on the negative side of this approach; for instance, the attempt by the Soviet Union to transform human relations in traditional Islamic societies of Central Asia in the 1920s.[59] While heeding the warning raised by such efforts, I view them as examples of what should not be done, not as reasons for abandoning my approach. The success of human rights-oriented cultural engineering depends as much on the sensitivity of its methods as on the validity of its goals. As to sensitivity of methods, I reemphasize the need to work from within the culture and to preserve its integrity. Since the Soviet experiment ignored both imperatives, it is not a strong argument against what I am proposing. But how do the goals of my proposal and the content of the human rights message I hope to realize address the imperatives of cultural sensitivity?

As Alison Renteln observes, the work of anthropologists who have argued on behalf of universals may be criticized for basing those universals on concepts such as human needs, rationality, and human nature that may well be culturally determined. Nevertheless, Renteln seems to favor undertaking comparative analysis of cultural ideals ("oughts") to discover cross-cultural universals for which she adopts the definition of "those least common denominators to be extracted from the range of variation that all phenomena of the natural or cultural world manifest."[60] She then admits the possibility of the following problem of cross-cultural universals, in the sense of least common denominators:

> The objection might be raised that some cross-cultural universals might be discovered that Westerners would call "inhumane." ... I view this as an unlikely possibility. Since the values in question are cultural *ideals*, it would seem most improbable that any "inhumane" ideal would be universal. Even if a universal ideal is found which some would regard as "inhumane," this is a part of morality. It is better to be honest and to admit that it exists than to pretend that it does not. The possibility for change means that concerted effort might lead the international community to reject it.[61]

Although Renteln's use of the designation "Western" is understandable given her primarily Western readership, this usage unfortunately gives the impression that it is the Western value judgment that counts. The use of a neutral or broader designation would be preferable to express the same optimistic view that it is improbable that universal cultural ideals are inhumane. Realistically speaking, however, one has to face the possibility of a broadly held ideal's being inhumane. Moreover, as mentioned before, a strictly relativist position may insist on maintaining a cultural ideal that is regarded by outsiders as inhumane.

Regarding this problem of universality, a dual approach would allow a human rights advocate to work within the cultural tradition while drawing on an enlightened universal conception of human rights. Cross-cultural studies can develop a universal conception of the inherent dignity and integrity of the human being. Insofar as any cultural tradition fails to uphold and implement the full implications of the inherent dignity and integrity of human beings within the particular community, human rights advocates within that community should use the resources of their cultural tradition to redress that fault internally in ways that are perceived to be legitimate by the members of that culture. In so doing, human rights advocates can be supported by colleagues from other cultural traditions and by the international community at large. Here the technology of communication can be used to good effect. The golden rule for outside help and support, however, is the same as that for internal action; that is, one must demonstrate respect for the integrity of the cultural tradition and sensitivity to its criteria for legitimacy.

In this endeavor, the universal principle of reciprocity is particularly useful: one would not be entitled to claim against another person what one demands for oneself. According to this principle, *human rights are those that a person would claim for herself or himself and must therefore be conceded to all other human beings.* This principle can be used to inform and guide the cross-cultural search for the content and necessary implications of the inherent dignity and integrity of human beings. Whatever the members of a culture would demand for themselves in accordance with their inherent human dignity and integrity they would have to concede to members of other cultures. This is, in my view, the basis of universal cultural legitimacy for human rights.

Conclusion

The basic premise of this chapter views culture, broadly defined, as the context within which human rights have to be specified and realized. Despite the initial lack or inadequacy of concern with universal cultural legitimacy during the formulation and adoption of international standards of human rights and despite the inadequacy of subsequent efforts to supplement that initial deficiency, those standards remain to be improved upon rather than abandoned.

It is not too late to correct the situation by undertaking cross-cultural work to provide the necessary internal legitimacy for human rights standards. The golden rule for both levels of action is the need for relativist sensitivity in developing universal standards. Each culture has its share of problems with human rights as well as the potential to resolve those problems. In working within the culture, and receiving guidance and support from without, external standards should not be imposed to enhance cultural legitimacy. The inherent dignity and integrity of the human person, taken as the fundamental underlying value of all human rights, can be extended beyond barriers of sex, race, religion, and so on, through the principle of reciprocity—namely, that one should concede to others what one claims for oneself. Thus, the full range of human rights can gain cultural legitimacy everywhere in the world.

One important set of questions that I deliberately avoided here concerns the nature and scope of human rights in the abstract philosophical sense. It is premature to embark on such an inquiry before establishing its proper cultural frame of reference. Despite the abundance of literature on the subject from within a specific cultural tradition, usually the Western liberal tradition, and of literature comparing competing perspectives on the issues, I have not been able to discover an integrated cross-cultural examination of this question. I would therefore rather wait until a satisfactory methodology for cross-cultural analysis is devised before embarking on an inquiry into the abstract philosophical nature and scope of "human rights." The definition proposed here is a useful working model for the development of universal cultural legitimacy for human rights.

Chapter 3

Toward a Cross-Cultural Approach to Defining International Standards of Human Rights: The Meaning of Cruel, Inhuman, or Degrading Treatment or Punishment

An intelligent strategy to protect and promote human rights must address the underlying causes of their violation. These violations are caused by a complex variety of factors and forces, including economic conditions, structural social factors, and political expediency. For the most part, however, human rights violations are due to human action or inaction—they occur because individual persons act or fail to act in certain ways. They can be the overlapping and interacting, intended or unintended, consequences of action. People may be driven by selfish motives of greed for wealth and power or by a misguided perception of the public good. Even when motivated by selfish ends, human rights violators normally seek to rationalize their behavior as consistent with, or conducive to, some morally sanctioned purpose. Although their bid to gain or maintain public support may be purely cynical, such an attempt is supported by the belief that their claim of moral sanction is plausible to their constituency.

It is not possible in this limited space to discuss the multitude of factors and forces that contribute to the underlying causes of human rights violations in general. I maintain that the lack or insufficiency of cultural legitimacy of human rights standards is one of the main underlying causes of violations of those standards. In this essay, I argue that internal and cross-cultural legitimacy for human rights standards needs to be developed; moreover, I advance some tentative ideas for implementing this approach. The focus of my supporting examples will be the right not to be subjected to cruel, inhuman, or degrading treatment or punishment. For example, insiders of a culture may perceive certain types of punishment as dictated or at least sanctioned by the norms of a particular cultural tradition, whereas to outsiders, such measures constitute cruel, inhuman, or degrading treatment. Which position should be taken as setting the standards for this human right? How can the cooperation of the proponents of the counter-position be secured in implementing the chosen standards?

My thesis does not assume that all individuals or groups within a society hold identical views on the meaning and implications of cultural values and norms or that they would therefore share the same evaluation of the legitimacy of human rights standards. On the contrary, I assume and rely on the fact that there are either actual or potential differences in perceptions and interpretations of cultural values and norms. Dominant groups or classes within a society normally maintain perceptions and interpretations of cultural values and norms that are supportive of their own interests, proclaiming them to be the only valid view of that culture. Dominated groups or classes may hold, or at least be open to, different perceptions and interpretations that are helpful to their struggle to achieve justice for themselves. This dynamic, however, is an *internal* struggle for control over the cultural sources and symbols of power within that society. Even though outsiders may sympathize with and wish to support the dominated and oppressed groups or classes, their claiming to know what is the valid view of the culture of that society will not accomplish this effectively. Such a claim would not help the groups the outsiders wish to support because it portrays them as agents of an alien culture, thereby frustrating their efforts to attain legitimacy for their view of the values and norms of their society.

Cross-Cultural Perspectives on Human Rights

The general thesis of my approach is this: since people are more likely to observe normative propositions if they believe them to be sanctioned by their own cultural traditions, observance of human rights standards can be improved through the enhancement of the cultural legitimacy of those standards.[1] The claim that existing human rights standards already enjoy universal cultural legitimacy is weak from a historical point of view, in the sense that many cultural traditions in the world have had little say in the formulation of those standards. Nevertheless, I believe not only that universal cultural legitimacy is necessary, but also that it is possible to develop it retrospectively in relation to fundamental human rights through enlightened interpretations of cultural norms. Given the extreme cultural diversity of the world community, it can be argued that human rights should be founded on the existing least common denominator among these cultural traditions. On the other hand, restricting international human rights to those accepted by prevailing perceptions of the values and norms of the major cultural traditions of the world would not only limit these rights and reduce their scope, but also exclude extremely vital rights. Therefore, expanding the quality and area of agreement among the cultural traditions of the world may be necessary to provide the foundation for the widest possible range of human rights. I believe that this can be accomplished through the proposed approach to universal cultural legitimacy of human rights.

While accepting the existing international standards, the cultural legitimacy thesis seeks to enhance their cultural legitimacy within the major traditions of the world through internal dialogue in order to establish enlightened perceptions and interpretations of cultural values and norms. Having achieved through this internal stage an adequate level of legitimacy *within* each tradition, human rights scholars and advocates should then work for *cross-cultural* legitimacy, so that peoples of diverse cultural traditions can agree on the meaning, scope, and methods of implementing these rights. Instead of being content with the existing least common denominator, I propose to broaden and deepen universal consensus on the formulation and implementation of human rights through internal reinterpretation of, and cross-cultural dialogue about, the meaning and implications of basic human values and norms.

This approach is based on the belief that, despite their apparent peculiarities and diversity, human beings and societies share certain fundamental interests, concerns, qualities, traits, and values that can be identified and articulated as the framework for a common "culture" of universal human rights. It would be premature in this exploratory essay to attempt to identify and articulate these interests, concerns, and so on, with certainty. Major theoretical and methodological issues must first be discussed and resolved so that the common culture of universal human rights may be founded on solid conceptual and empirical grounds. At this stage, I am concerned with making the case for internal and cross-cultural discourse on the subject, raising some of the questions and difficulties that must be faced and generally describing the process that should be undertaken. Neither concrete results nor guarantees of success can be offered here, only a promising approach to resolving a real and serious issue.

Concern with the implications of cultural diversity has been present since the earliest stages of the modern international human rights movement. In 1947, the United Nations Educational, Scientific, and Cultural Organization (UNESCO) carried out an inquiry into the theoretical problems raised by the Universal Declaration of Human Rights. This project was accomplished by inviting the views of various thinkers and writers from member states[2] and organizing subsequent conferences and seminars. Other organizations have also taken the initiative in drawing attention to the dangers of ethnocentricity and the need for sensitivity to cultural diversity in the drafting of international human rights instruments.[3] Individual authors, too, have addressed these concerns.

My approach draws upon these earlier efforts and supplements them with insights from non-Western perspectives. Some Western writers have revealed conflicts between international human rights standards and certain non-Western cultural traditions, without suggesting ways of reconciling them.[4] Despite their claims or wishes to present a cross-cultural approach, other Western writers have tended to confine their analysis to Western perspectives. For example, one author emphasizes the challenge of cultural diversity, saying that it would "be useful to try to rethink the normative foundations of human rights and consider which rights have the strongest normative support."[5] Yet, the philosophical perspectives he actually covers in his discussion are exclusively Western. Another author calls for taking cultural diversity seriously yet presents arguments based exclusively on Western philosophy and political theory.[6]

Alison Renteln is one of the few human rights scholars sensitive to issues of cultural legitimacy. She suggests a cross-cultural understanding that will shed light on a common core of acceptable rights.[7] Nevertheless, her approach seems to be content with the existing least common denominator—a standard I find inadequate to ensure sufficient human rights throughout the world. In my view, a constructive element is needed to broaden and deepen cross-cultural consensus on a "common core of human rights." I believe that this can be accomplished through the internal discourse and cross-cultural dialogue advocated here.

Cultural Relativity and Human Rights

Culture is defined in a variety of ways in different contexts.[8] A wide array of definitions is available in the social sciences.[9] In this essay, culture is taken in its widest meaning—that of the "totality of values, institutions and forms of behavior transmitted within a society, as well as the material goods produced by man [and woman] . . . this wide concept of culture covers *Weltanschauung* [world view], ideologies and cognitive behavior."[10] It can also be defined as "an historically transmitted pattern of meanings in symbols, a system of inherited conceptions expressed in symbolic form by means of which men [and women] communicate, perpetuate and develop their knowledge and attitudes towards life."[11]

Culture is, therefore, the source of the individual and communal worldview: it provides both the individual and the community with the values and interests to be pursued in life, as well as the legitimate means for pursuing them. It stipulates the norms and values that contribute to a people's perception of their self-interest and the goals and methods of individual and collective struggles for power within a society and between societies. As such, culture is a primary force in the socialization of individuals and a major determinant of the consciousness and experience of the community. The impact of culture on human behavior is often underestimated precisely because it is so powerful and deeply embedded in our self-identity and consciousness.

Our culture is so much a part of our personality that we normally take for granted that our behavior patterns and relationships to other persons and to society become the ideal norm. The subtlety of the impact of culture on personality and character may be explained by the analogy of the eye: we tend to take the world to be what our eyes convey to us without "seeing" the eye and appreciating its role.[12] In this case, the information conveyed by the eye is filtered and interpreted by the mind without the individual's conscious awareness of this fact. Culture influences, first, the way we see the world and, further, how we interpret and react to the information we receive.

This analogy may also explain our ethnocentricity, the tendency to regard one's own race or social group as the model of human experience. Ethnocentricity does not mean there is no conflict or tension between a person and his or her own culture, or between various classes and groups within a society. It rather incorporates such conflict and tension in the ideal model, leading us to perceive the conflict and tension we have within our own culture as part of the norm. For example, some feminists in one cultural tradition may assume that women in other cultures have (or ought to have) the same conflicts and tensions with their societies and are seeking (or ought to seek) the same answers.

A degree of ethnocentricity is unavoidable, indeed indispensable. It prompts our acceptance of the norms and institutions of our culture, an acceptance that ultimately is a matter of material and psychological survival.[13] Even the most radical "dissidents" rely on their culture for survival. In fact, their dissent itself is meaningful to them only as the antithesis of existing cultural norms and institutions. Rigid ethnocentricity, however, breeds intolerance and hostility to societies and persons that do not conform to the given models and expectations. Whether operating as initial justification or as subsequent rationalization, the tendency to dehumanize "different" societies and persons underlies much of the exploitation and oppression of one society by another, or of other classes within a society by one class of persons in the same society.

The appreciation of our own ethnocentricity should lead us to respect the ethnocentricity of others. Enlightened ethnocentricity would therefore concede the right of others to be "different," whether as members of another society or as individuals within the same society. This perspective would uphold the equal human value and dignity of members of other societies and of dissidents within society. In sociological terms, this orientation is commonly known as cultural relativism, that is to say, the acknowledgment of equal validity of diverse patterns of life.[14] It stresses "the dignity inherent in every body of custom, and . . . the need for tolerance of conventions though they may differ from one's own."[15]

Cultural relativism has been charged with neutralizing moral judgment and thereby impairing action against injustice.[16] According to one author, "[It] has these objectionable consequences: namely, that by limiting critical assessment of human works it disarms us, dehumanizes us, leaves us unable to enter into communicative interaction; that is to say, unable to criticize cross-culturally, cross-sub-culturally; intimately, relativism leaves no room for criticism at all . . . behind relativism nihilism looms."[17] Some writers on human rights are suspicious of a cultural relativism that denies to individuals the moral right to make comparisons and to insist on universal standards of right and wrong.[18]

As John Ladd notes, however, relativism is identified with nihilism because it is defined by its opponents in absolute terms.[19] I tend to agree with Clifford Geertz that the relativism/antirelativism discourse in anthropology should be seen as an exchange of warnings rather than as an analytical debate. Whereas the relativists maintain that "the world being so full of a number of things, rushing to judgment is more than a mistake, it's a crime," the antirelativists are concerned "that if something isn't anchored everywhere nothing can be anchored anywhere."[20] I also agree with Geertz's conclusion:

The objection to anti-relativism is not that it rejects an it's-all-how-you-look-at-it approach to knowledge or a when-in-Rome approach to morality, but that it imagines that they [these approaches] can only be defeated by placing morality beyond culture and knowledge beyond both. This . . . is no longer possible. If we wanted home truths, we should have stayed at home.[21]

In my view, the merits of a reasonable degree of cultural relativism are obvious, especially when compared to claims of universalism that are in fact based on the claimant's rigid and exclusive ethnocentricity. The charge that it may breed tolerance of injustice is a serious one, however. Melville J. Herskovits, one of the main proponents of cultural relativism, has sought to answer this charge by distinguishing between absolutes and universals:

To say that there is no absolute [not admitted to have variations] criterion of value or morals . . . does not mean that such criteria, in differing *forms*, do not comprise universals [least common denominators to be extracted from the range of variations] in human culture. Morality is a universal, and so is enjoyment of beauty, and some standard of truth. The many forms these concepts take are but products of the particular historical experience of the societies that manifest them. In each, criteria are subject to continuous questioning, continuous change. But the basic conceptions remain, to channel thought and direct conduct, to give purpose to living.[22]

Although this statement is true, it does not fully answer the charge. Morality may be universal in the sense that all cultures have it, but that does not in any way indicate the *content* of that morality, or provide criteria for judgment or for action by members of that culture or other cultures. The least common denominator of the universality of morality must include some of its basic precepts and not be confined to the mere existence of some form of morality. Moreover, in accordance with the logic of cultural relativism, the shared moral values must be authentic and not imposed from the outside. As indicated earlier, the existing least common denominator may not be enough to accommodate certain vital human rights. This fact would suggest the need to broaden and deepen common values to support these human rights. This process, however, must be culturally legitimate with reference to the norms and mechanisms of change within a particular culture.

Another author has sought to respond to the charge that cultural relativism impairs moral judgment and action by saying that, although it is appropriate to distinguish between criticism corresponding to standards internal to the culture and criticism corresponding to external ones, the theory of cultural relativism does not block either.[23] This observation holds true of a reasonable degree of cultural relativism but not of its most extreme forms.[24] Moreover, we should not only distinguish between criticism corresponding to standards internal to a culture and that corresponding to external ones, but also stress that the former is likely to be more effective than the latter.

I would emphasize that, in this age of self-determination, sensitivity to cultural relativity is vital for the international protection and promotion of human rights. This point does not preclude cross-cultural moral judgment and action, but it prescribes the best ways of formulating and expressing judgment and of undertaking action. As Geertz states, morality and knowledge cannot be placed beyond culture. In intercultural relations, morality and knowledge cannot be the exclusive product of some cultures but not of others. The validity of cross-cultural moral judgment increases with the degree of universality of the values upon which it is based; further, the efficacy of action increases with the degree of the actor's sensitivity to the internal logic and frame of reference of other cultures.

Cultural Universality and Human Rights

Although human rights require action within each country for their implementation, the present international human rights regime has been conceived and is intended to operate within the framework of international relations. The implications of culture for international relations have long been recognized. For example, as Edmund Burke has said,

> In the intercourse between two nations, we are apt to rely too much on the instrumental part. We lay too much weight on the formality of treaties and compacts. . . . Men [and women] are not tied to one another by paper and seals. They are led to associate by resemblances, by conformities, by sympathies. It is with nations as with individuals. Nothing is so strong a tie of amity between nation and nation as correspondence in laws, customs, manners and habits of life. They are obligations written in the heart. They approximate men [and women] to one another without their knowledge and sometimes against their

intentions. The secret, unseen, but irrefragable bond of habitual intercourse holds them together even when their perverse and litigious nature sets them to equivocate, scuffle, and fight about the terms of their written obligations.[25]

This bonding through similarities does not mean, in my view, that international peace and cooperation are not possible without total global cultural unity. It does mean that they are more easily achieved if there is a certain minimum cultural consensus on goals and methods. As applied to cooperation in the protection and promotion of human rights, this view means that developing cross-cultural consensus in support of treaties and compacts is desirable. Cultural diversity, however, is unavoidable as the product of significant past and present economic, social, and environmental differences. It is also desirable as the expression of the right to self-determination and as the manifestation of distinctive self-identity. Nevertheless, I believe that a sufficient degree of cultural consensus regarding the goals and methods of cooperation in the protection and promotion of human rights can be achieved through internal cultural discourse and cross-cultural dialogue. Internal discourse relates to the struggle to establish enlightened perceptions and interpretations of cultural values and norms. Cross-cultural dialogue should be aimed at broadening and deepening international (or rather intercultural) consensus. This effort may include support for the proponents of enlightened perceptions and interpretations within a culture, but it must be sensitive to the internal nature of the struggle, endeavoring to emphasize internal values and norms rather than external ones.

One of the apparent paradoxes of culture is the way it combines stability with dynamic continuous change.[26] Change is effected by internal adjustments as well as by external influences. Both types of change, however, must be justified through culturally approved mechanisms and adapted to preexisting norms and institutions; otherwise, the culture would lose its necessary coherence and stability.

Another feature of culture's dynamism is that it normally offers its members a range of options or is willing to accommodate varying individual responses to its norms. As Herskovits observes, "culture is flexible and holds many possibilities of choice within its framework . . . to recognize the values held by a given people in no wise implies that these values are a constant factor in the lives of succeeding generations of the same group."[27] Nevertheless, both the degree of flexibility permitted by a culture and the possibilities of choice it offers its members are controlled by the culture's internal criteria of legitimacy.

A third and more significant feature of cultural dynamism is the ambivalence of cultural norms and their susceptibility to different interpretations. In the normal course of events, powerful individuals and groups tend to monopolize the interpretation of cultural norms and manipulate them to their own advantage. Given the extreme importance of cultural legitimacy, it is vital for disadvantaged individuals and groups to challenge this monopoly and manipulation. They should use internal cultural discourse to offer alternative interpretations in support of their own interests. This internal discourse can utilize intellectual, artistic, and scholarly work as well as various available forms of political action.

Internal cultural discourse should also support cross-cultural dialogue and set its terms of reference. It should encourage good will, mutual respect, and equality with other cultural traditions. This positive relationship can be fostered, for example, by enlisting the support of what I would call the principle of reciprocity, that is to say, the rule that one should treat others in the same way that he or she would like to be treated. Although this is a universal rule, most traditions tend to restrict its applications to "others" from the same or selected traditions rather than all human beings and societies. Internal discourse should propagate a broader and more enlightened interpretation of the principle of reciprocity to include all human beings.

It is vital for cross-cultural dialogue that internal cultural discourse along these lines be undertaken simultaneously in all cultural traditions. As a matter of principle, it should be admitted that every cultural tradition has problems with some human rights and needs to enhance the internal cultural legitimacy of those rights. From a tactical point of view, undertaking internal cultural discourse in relation to the problems one tradition has with certain human rights is necessary for encouraging other traditions to undertake similar discourse in relation to the problematic aspects of their own culture.

The object of internal discourse and cross-cultural dialogue is to agree on a body of beliefs to guide action in support of human rights, in spite of disagreement on the justification of those beliefs. Jacques Maritain, the French philosopher, explained this idea at the time of the adoption of the Universal Declaration of Human Rights:

> To understand this, it is only necessary to make the appropriate distinction between the rational justifications involved in the spiritual

dynamism of philosophic doctrine or religious faith [that is to say, in culture], and the practical conclusions which, although justified in different ways by different persons, are principles of action with a common ground of similarity for everyone. I am quite certain that my way of justifying belief in the rights of man and the ideal of liberty, equality and fraternity is the only way with a firm foundation in truth. This does not prevent me from being in agreement on these practical convictions with people who are certain that their way of justifying them, entirely different from mine or opposed to mine, in its theoretical dynamism, is equally the only way founded upon truth.[28]

Total agreement on the interpretation and application of those practical conclusions may not be possible, however, because disagreement about their justification will probably be reflected in the way they are interpreted and applied. We should therefore be realistic in our expectations and pursue the maximum possible degree of agreement at whatever level it can be achieved. This approach can be illustrated by the following case study of the meaning of the human right "not to be subjected to cruel, inhuman or degrading treatment or punishment."

Cruel, Inhuman, or Degrading Treatment or Punishment

Some international human rights instruments stipulate that "no one shall be subjected to torture or to cruel, inhuman or degrading treatment or punishment."[29] There is obvious overlap between the two main parts of this right, that is to say, between protection against torture, on the one hand, and, on the other hand, protection against inhuman or degrading treatment or punishment. For example, torture has been described as constituting "an aggravated and deliberate form of cruel, inhuman or degrading treatment or punishment."[30] Nevertheless, there are differences between the two parts of the right. According to the definition of torture adopted in United Nations instruments, it "does not include pain or suffering arising only from, inherent in or incidental to lawful sanctions."[31] As explained below, this qualification is not supposed to apply to the second part of the right. In other words, lawful sanctions can constitute "cruel, inhuman or degrading treatment or punishment."

The following discussion will focus on the meaning of the second part of the right, that is to say, the meaning of the right not to be subjected to cruel, inhuman, or degrading treatment or punishment. In particular, I will address the question of how to identify the criteria by which lawful sanctions can be held to violate the prohibition of cruel, inhuman, or degrading treatment or punishment. The case of Islamic punishments will be used to illustrate the application of the cross-cultural perspective to this question.

The Meaning of the Clause in United Nations Sources

Cruel or inhuman treatment or punishment is prohibited by regional instruments, such as the European Convention for the Protection of Human Rights and Fundamental Freedoms, as well as under the international system of the United Nations. While regional jurisprudence is applicable in the regional context, and may be persuasive in some other parts of the world, it may not be useful in all parts of the world. For example, the jurisprudence developed by the European Commission and Court of Human Rights under Article 3 of the European Convention would be directly applicable in defining this clause from a European point of view, and may be persuasive in North America. It may not be useful, however, when discussing non-Western perspectives on cruel, inhuman, or degrading treatment or punishment. The following survey will therefore focus on UN sources because they are at least intended to reflect international perspectives.

The early history of what is now Article 7 of the Covenant on Civil and Political Rights indicates that drafters and delegates were particularly concerned with preventing the recurrence of atrocities such as those committed in concentration camps during World War II.[32] Thus, the Commission on Human Rights proposed in 1952 that the Article should read: "No one shall be subjected to torture or to cruel, inhuman or degrading treatment or punishment. In particular, no one shall be subjected without his free consent to medical or scientific experimentation involving risk, where such is not required by his state of physical or mental health."[33] At the thirteenth session of the Third Committee in 1958, however, most discussion centered on the second sentence. Some delegates felt that the sentence was unnecessary and also weakened the Article in that it directed attention to only one of the many forms of cruel, inhuman, or degrading treatment, thereby lessening the importance of the general prohibition laid down in the first sentence. Others insisted on retaining the second sentence as complementing the first sentence rather than being superfluous.[34] Although several suggestions were made to meet the objection that the second part of the Article was emphasized at the expense of the first, the second sentence was retained and eventually adopted, as amended, by the General Assembly.[35]

Whether because of preoccupation with this issue or due to the belief that the first sentence of the Article was self-explanatory, there is little guidance from the history of the Article on the meaning of "cruel, inhuman or degrading treatment or punishment." It was generally agreed early in the drafting process that the word "treatment" was broader in scope than the word "punishment." It was also observed that the word "treatment" should not apply to degrading situations that might be due to general economic and social factors.[36] In 1952, the Philippines suggested before the Third Committee that the word "unusual" should be inserted between the words "inhuman" and "or degrading." Some delegates supported the addition of "unusual" because it might apply to certain actual practices that, although not intentionally cruel, inhuman, or degrading, nevertheless affected the physical or moral integrity of the human person. Others opposed the term "unusual" as being vague: what was "unusual" in one country, it was said, might not be so in other countries. The proposal was withdrawn.[37] It is remarkable that the criticism of vagueness should apply only to the word "unusual" and not to the words "cruel, inhuman or degrading." Surely, what may be seen as "cruel, inhuman or degrading" in one culture may not be seen in the same light in another culture.

Do other UN sources provide guidance on the meaning of this clause and criteria for resolving possible conflicts between one culture and another regarding what is "cruel, inhuman or degrading treatment or punishment"? A commentary on Article 5 of the UN Code of Conduct for Law Enforcement Officials of 1979 states: "The term 'cruel, inhuman or degrading treatment or punishment' has not been defined by the General Assembly, but it should be interpreted so as to extend the widest possible protection against abuses, whether physical or mental."[38] Decisions of the Human Rights Committee under the Optional Protocol provide examples of treatment or punishment held to be in violation of Article 7 of the covenant by an official organ of the UN.[39] Although these examples may be useful in indicating the sort of treatment or punishment that is likely to be held in violation of this human right, they do not provide an authoritative criterion of general application.[40]

When the Human Rights Committee attempted to provide some general criteria, the result was both controversial and not particularly helpful. For example, the committee, in an attempt to define the scope of the protection against cruel, inhuman, or degrading treatment or punishment, only complicated the issue:

[It] goes far beyond torture as normally understood. It may not be necessary to make sharp distinctions between various forms of treatment and punishment. These distinctions depend on the kind, purpose and severity of the particular treatment. . . . the prohibition must extend to corporal punishment, including excessive chastisement as an educational and disciplinary measure.[41]

This statement is not particularly helpful in determining whether a certain treatment or punishment is cruel, inhuman, or degrading; and the example it cites is controversial. In the majority of human societies today, corporal punishment is not regarded as necessarily cruel, inhuman, or degrading. It may be even more debatable whether this characterization applies to what might be considered by some as excessive chastisement but routinely used for educational and disciplinary purposes in many parts of the world. This example clearly shows the dangers and difficulty of providing generally accepted criteria for defining the concept. Nevertheless, such criteria are necessary to implement this human right.

Again, this discussion focuses on the question of how lawful sanctions can be held to violate the prohibition of cruel, inhuman, or degrading treatment or punishment. This question must be addressed because such sanctions have been excluded from the definition of torture under Article 1 of the 1984 Convention against Torture and Other Cruel, Inhuman or Degrading Treatment or Punishment. Does this give the state a free hand to enforce whatever treatment or punishment it deems fit, so long as it is enacted as the lawful sanction for any conduct the state chooses to penalize? Does the international community have the right to object to any lawful sanction as amounting to cruel, inhuman, or degrading treatment or punishment?

Article 16 of the 1984 Convention provides for the obligation to prevent "other acts of cruel, inhuman or degrading treatment or punishment which do not amount to torture." Unlike Article 1, however, which defines torture in detail, Article 16 neither defines the clause "cruel, inhuman or degrading treatment or punishment" nor excludes pain or suffering arising only from, inherent in, or incidental to lawful sanctions. This phrasing means that States Parties to the Convention may not enforce lawful sanctions that constitute cruel, inhuman, or degrading treatment or punishment. But this obligation cannot be implemented or enforced in accordance with provisions of the Convention unless there is agreement on the definition of the clause.

Cross-Cultural Perspectives on the Concept

Some predominantly Muslim countries, such as Afghanistan and Egypt, have already ratified the 1984 Convention; others may wish to do so in the future. The meaning of cruel, inhuman, or degrading treatment or punishment in Islamic cultures, however, may be significantly, if not radically, different from the meaning of this clause in other parts of the world.

Islamic law, commonly know as Shariʿa, is based on the Qurʾan, which Muslims believe to be the literal and final word of God, and on Sunna, or traditions of the Prophet Muhammad. Using these sources, as well as pre-Islamic customary practices of the Middle East that were not explicitly repudiated by the Qurʾan and Sunna, Muslim jurists developed Shariʿa as a comprehensive ethical and legal system between the seventh and ninth centuries. To Muslim communities, however, the Qurʾan and Sunna were always believed to be absolutely binding as a matter of faith and were applied in individual and communal practice from the very beginning. Shariʿa codes were never formally enacted, but the jurists systematized and rationalized what was already accepted as the will of God and developed techniques for interpreting divine sources and for supplementing their provisions.[42]

Due to the religious nature of Shariʿa, Muslim jurists did not distinguish among devotional, ethical, social, and legal aspects of the law, let alone among various types of legal norms. The equivalent of penal or criminal law would therefore have to be extracted from a wide range of primary sources. For the purposes of this discussion, Islamic criminal law may be briefly explained as follows.[43] Criminal offenses are classified into three main categories: *hudud*, *jinayat*, and *taʿzir*. *Hudud* are a very limited group of offenses that are strictly defined and punished by the express terms of the Qurʾan and/or Sunna. These include *sariqa*, or theft, which is punishable by the amputation of the right hand, and *zina*, or fornication, which is punishable by whipping of one hundred lashes for an unmarried offender and stoning to death for a married offender. *Jinayat* are homicide and causing bodily harm, which are punishable by *qisas*, or exact retribution (an eye for an eye) or payment of monetary compensation. The term *taʿzir* means to reform and rectify. *Taʿzir* offenses are those determined and punished by the ruler in exercising his power to protect private and public interests.

It is important to emphasize that the following discussion addresses this question in a purely theoretical sense and should not be taken to condone the application of these punishments by any government in the Muslim world today. The question being raised is this. Are Muslims likely to accept the repudiation of these punishments *as a matter of Islamic law* on the ground that they are cruel, inhuman, or degrading? This question should not be confused with the very important but distinct issue of whether these punishments have been or are being applied legitimately and in accordance with all the general and specific requirements of Islamic law.

Islamic law requires the state to fulfill its obligation to secure social and economic justice and to ensure decent standards of living for all its citizens *before* it can enforce these punishments. The law also provides for very narrow definitions of these offenses, makes an extensive range of defenses against the charge available to the accused person, and requires strict standards of proof. Moreover, Islamic law demands total fairness and equality in law enforcement. In my view, the prerequisite conditions for the enforcement of these punishments are extremely difficult to satisfy in practice and are certainly unlikely to materialize in any Muslim country in the foreseeable future. Nevertheless, the question remains, whether these punishments can be abolished as a matter of Islamic law.

Shari'a criminal law has been displaced by secular criminal law in most Muslim countries. Countries like Saudi Arabia, however, have always maintained Shari'a as their official criminal law. Other countries, such as Iran, Pakistan, and the Sudan, have recently reintroduced Shari'a criminal law. There is much controversy over many aspects of the criminal law of Shari'a that raise human rights concerns, including issues of religious discrimination in the application of Shari'a criminal law to non-Muslims.[44] To the vast majority of Muslims, however, Shari'a criminal law is binding and should be enforced today. Muslim political leaders and scholars may debate whether general social, economic, and political conditions are appropriate for the immediate application of Shari'a, or whether there should be a preparatory stage before the reintroduction of Shari'a where it has been displaced by secular law. None of them would dispute, at least openly and publicly, that the application of Shari'a criminal law should be a high priority, if not an immediate reality.

Although these are important matters, they should not be confused with what is being discussed here. For the sake of argument, the issue should be isolated from other possible sources of controversy. In particular, I wish to emphasize that I believe that the Qur'anic punishments should *not* apply to non-Muslims because they are essentially religious in nature. In the following discussion, I will use the example of amputation of the right hand for theft when committed by a Muslim who does not need to steal in order to survive and who has been properly tried and convicted by a competent court of law. This punishment is prescribed by the clear and definite text of verse 38 in chapter 5 of the Qur'an. Can this punishment, when imposed under these circumstances, be condemned as cruel, inhuman, or degrading?

The basic question here is one of interpretation and application of a universally accepted human right. In terms of the principle Maritain suggests— agreement on "practical conclusions" in spite of disagreement on their justification—Muslims would accept the human right not to be subjected to cruel, inhuman, or degrading treatment or punishment. Their Islamic culture, however, may indicate to them a different interpretation of this human right.

From a secular or humanist point of view, inflicting such a severe permanent punishment for any offense, especially for theft, is obviously cruel and inhuman and probably also degrading. This may well be the private intuitive reaction of many educated modernized Muslims. However, to the vast majority of Muslims, the matter is settled by the categorical will of God as expressed in the Qur'an and, as such, is not open to question by human beings. Even the educated modernized Muslim, who may be privately repelled by this punishment, cannot risk the consequences of openly questioning the will of God. In addition to the danger of losing his or her faith and the probability of severe social chastisement, a Muslim who disputes the binding authority of the Qur'an is liable to the death penalty for apostasy (heresy) under Shari'a.

Thus, in all Muslim societies, the possibility of human judgment regarding the appropriateness or cruelty of a punishment decreed by God is simply out of the question. Furthermore, this belief is supported by what Muslims accept as rational arguments.[45] From the religious point of view, human life does not end at death but extends beyond that to the next life. In fact, religious sources strongly emphasize that the next life is the true and ultimate reality, to which this life is merely a prelude. In the next *eternal* life, every human being will stand judgment and suffer the consequences of his or her actions in this life. A religiously sanctioned punishment, however, will absolve an offender from punishment in the next life because God does not punish twice for the same offense. Accordingly, a thief who suffers the religiously sanctioned punishment of amputation of the right hand in this life will not be liable to the much harsher punishment in the next life. To people who hold this belief, however severe the Qur'anic punishment may appear, it is in fact extremely lenient and merciful in comparison to what the offender will suffer in the next life should the religious punishment not be enforced in this life.

Other arguments are advanced about the benefits of this punishment to both the individual offender and society. It is said that this seemingly harsh punishment is in fact necessary to reform and rehabilitate the thief, as well as to safeguard the interests of other persons, and of society at large, by deterring other potential offenders.[46] The ultimately *religious* rationale of these arguments must always be emphasized, however. The punishment is believed to achieve these individual and social benefits because God said so. To the vast majority of Muslims, scientific research is welcome to confirm the empirical validity of these arguments, but it cannot be accepted as a basis for repudiating them, thereby challenging the appropriateness of the punishment. Reform of the offender is not confined to his or her experience in this life, but includes the next life, too.

Neither internal Islamic reinterpretation nor cross-cultural dialogue is likely to lead to the total abolition of this punishment as a matter of Islamic law. Much can be done, however, to restrict its implementation in practice. For example, there is room for developing stronger general social and economic prerequisites and stricter procedural requirements for the enforcement of the punishment. Islamic religious texts emphasize extreme caution in inflicting any criminal punishment. The Prophet said that if there is any doubt (*shubha*), the Qur'anic punishments should not be imposed. He also said that it is better to err on the side of refraining from imposing the punishment than to err on the side of imposing it in a doubtful case. Although these directives have already been incorporated into definitions of the offenses and the applicable rules of evidence and procedure, it is still possible to develop a broader concept of *shubha* to include, for example, psychological disorders as a defense against criminal responsibility. For instance, kleptomania may be taken as *shubha*, barring punishment for theft. Economic need may also be a defense against a charge of theft.

Cross-cultural dialogue may also be helpful in this regard. In the Jewish tradition, for instance, jurists have sought to restrict the practical application of equally harsh punishment by stipulating strict procedural and other requirements.[47] This theoretical Jewish jurisprudence may be useful to Muslim jurists and leaders seeking to restrict the practical application of Qur'anic punishments. It is difficult to assess its practical viability and impact, however, because it has not been applied for nearly two thousand years. Moreover, the current atmosphere of mutual Jewish-Muslim antagonism and mistrust does not make cross-cultural dialogue likely between these two traditions. Still, this has not always been the case in the past and need not be so in the future. In fact, the jurisprudence of each tradition has borrowed heavily from the other in the past and may do so in the future, once the present conflict is resolved.

I believe that, in the final analysis, the interpretation and practical application of the protection against cruel, inhuman, or degrading treatment or punishment in the context of a particular society should be determined by the moral standards of that society. I also believe that there are many legitimate ways of influencing and informing the moral standards of a society. To dictate a set of moral standards to a society is both unacceptable as a matter of principle and unlikely to succeed in practice. Cross-cultural dialogue and mutual influence, however, are acceptable in principle and continuously occurring in practice. To harness the power of cultural legitimacy in support of human rights, we need to develop techniques for internal cultural discourse and cross-cultural dialogue and to work toward establishing general conditions conducive to constructive discourse and dialogue.

It should be recalled that this approach assumes and relies on the existence of internal struggle for cultural power within society. Certain dominant classes or groups would normally hold the cultural advantage and proclaim their view of the culture as valid, while others would challenge this view, or at least wish to be able to do so. In relation to Islamic punishments, questions about the legitimate application of these punishments—whether the state has fulfilled its obligations first and is acting in accordance with the general and specific conditions referred to earlier—are matters for internal struggle. This internal struggle cannot and should not be settled by outsiders; but they may support one side or the other, provided they do so with sufficient sensitivity and due consideration for the legitimacy of the objectives and methods of the struggle within the framework of the particular culture.

Conclusion: Toward a Cross-Cultural Approach

I have deliberately chosen the question of whether lawful sanctions can be condemned as cruel, inhuman, or degrading punishment or treatment in order to illustrate both the need for a cross-cultural approach to defining human rights standards and the difficulty of implementing this approach. The question presents human rights advocates with a serious dilemma. On the one hand, it is necessary to safeguard the personal integrity and human dignity of the individual against excessive or harsh punishments. The fundamental objective of the modern human rights movement is to protect citizens from the brutality and excesses of their own governments. On the other hand, it is extremely important to be sensitive to the dangers of cultural imperialism, whether it is a product of colonialism, a tool of international economic exploitation and political subjugation, or simply a product of extreme ethnocentricity. Since we would not accept others imposing their moral standards on us, we should not impose our own moral standards on others. In any case, external imposition is normally counterproductive and unlikely to succeed in changing the practice in question. External imposition is not the only option available to human rights advocates, however. Greater consensus on international standards for the protection of the individual against cruel, inhuman, or degrading treatment or punishment can be achieved through internal cultural discourse and cross-cultural dialogue.

It is unrealistic to expect this approach to achieve total agreement on the interpretation and application of standards, whether of treatment or punishment or any other human right. This expectation presupposes the existence of the interpretation to be agreed upon. If one reflects on the interpretation she or he employs to determine the norm, it will probably be the one set by one's culture. Further reflection on how one would feel about the interpretation set by another culture should illustrate the untenability of this position. For example, a North American may think that a short term of imprisonment is the appropriate punishment for theft and wish that to be the universal punishment for this offense. A Muslim, on the other hand, may feel that the amputation of the hand is appropriate under certain conditions and after satisfying strict safeguards. It would be instructive for the North American to consider how she or he would feel if the Muslim punishment were made the norm. Most Western human rights advocates are likely to have a lingering feeling that there is simply no comparison between these two punishments because the Islamic punishment is "obviously" cruel and inhuman and should never compete with imprisonment as a possible punishment for this offense. A Muslim might respond by saying that this feeling is a product of Western ethnocentricity. I am not suggesting that we should make the Islamic or any other particular punishment the universal norm. I merely wish to point out that agreeing on a universal standard may not be as simple as we may think or wish it to be.

In accordance with the proposed approach, the standard itself should be the product of internal discourse and cross-cultural dialogue. Moreover, genuine total agreement requires equal commitment to internal discourse and equally effective participation in cross-cultural dialogue by the adherents or members of different cultural traditions of the world. In view of significant social and political differences and disparities in levels of economic development, some cultural traditions are unlikely to engage in internal discourse as much as other cultural traditions and are less able to participate in cross-cultural dialogue as effectively as others. These processes require a certain degree of political liberty, stability, and social maturity, as well as technological capabilities that are lacking in some parts of the world.

The cross-cultural approach, however, is not an all-or-nothing proposition. While total agreement on the standard and mechanisms for its implementation is unrealistic in some cases, significant agreement can be achieved and ought to be pursued as much as possible. For example, in relation to cruel, inhuman, or degrading treatment or punishment, there is room for agreement on a wide range of substantive and procedural matters even in relation to an apparently inflexible position, such as the Islamic position on Qur'anic punishments. Provided such agreement is sought with sufficient sensitivity, the general status of human rights will be improved, and wider agreement can be achieved in relation to other human rights. We must be clear, however, on what can be achieved and how to achieve it in any given case. An appreciation of the impossibility of the total abolition of the Qur'anic punishment for theft is necessary for restricting its practice in Muslim societies as well as for establishing common standards, for instance, in relation to punishments that are, from the Islamic point of view, the product of human legislation.

PART II

Prospects of Mediation for the Paradox
of Universality and State Self-Regulation

Chapter 4

State Responsibility Under International Human Rights Law to Change Religious and Customary Laws

States are responsible for bringing their domestic law and practice into conformity with their obligations under international law to protect and promote human rights. This responsibility applies not only to laws enacted by formal legislative organs of the state but also to those attributed to religious and customary sources or sanction, regardless of the manner of their "enactment" or articulation and/or implementation.[1] In other words, every state has the responsibility to remove any inconsistency between international human rights law binding on it and religious and customary laws operating within the territory of that state. This responsibility is fully consistent with the principle of state sovereignty in international law, since it does not purport to force any state to assume legal obligations against its will. It simply seeks to ensure that states effectively fulfill legal obligations they have already assumed under international law.

These obligations could be based, in general terms, on customary international law and on the Charter of the United Nations in relation to all its member states. But since neither international custom nor the UN Charter is adequately specific,[2] an international obligation to respect and protect particular human rights, and the consequent obligation to change domestic laws, can be problematic in the absence of specific treaty provisions. Moreover, there are questions about the circumstances and context of the implementation of that obligation. In view of space limitations, I will focus in this chapter on issues raised by the realistic circumstances of implementation in countries where practices attributed to religious and customary laws are most likely to violate the international human rights of women. This choice of emphasis is supported by the fact that, to my knowledge, this set of issues has not received sufficient attention in available literature. I will begin by briefly highlighting some questions relating to the sources and nature of the obligation.

The principle that states are responsible for bringing domestic laws into conformity with international human rights law could simply be based on the notion that the state is bound to do so by international custom or treaties; however, it may not be sufficient to rely on a formalistic understanding of this notion, especially in relation to the international human rights of women. The argument that this obligation can be founded on customary international law may be somewhat controversial and strained in relation to the human rights of women. Customary international law, in general, is notoriously vague and difficult to prove.[3] Moreover, it would probably be difficult to establish a principle of customary international law prohibiting all forms of discrimination on grounds of gender. The restrictive formulations suggested by the few authors who support the existence of such a principle in customary international law clearly show that its scope and implications would be problematic and controversial.[4]

The rationale of binding agreements would, of course, apply when the state is party to a relevant treaty. For example, Articles 2(f) and 5(a) of the International Convention for the Elimination of all Forms of Discrimination against Women (the Women's Convention) require states parties to implement "appropriate measures" to eliminate discrimination against women in customary practices.[5] However, this rationale would not be applicable where the state has not ratified relevant treaties or has entered reservations that exclude the obligation to change religious or customary laws. For example, Egypt ratified the Women's Convention but entered a reservation on, inter alia, Article 16, concerning equality between men and women in all matters relating to marriage and family relations, which are governed in Egypt by Shari'a law.[6]

Even where a state is party to an appropriate treaty and has not entered a reservation with regard to a particular human right, it should not be assumed that the application of the notion of binding treaties to the obligation to change religious and customary laws will be a simple or straightforward matter. First, an effort to identify or define the exact extent and nature of the obligations of states-parties to a treaty will probably face problems of interpretation and operation.[7] Second, there are serious questions about who is going to raise the issue of the state's failure to comply with its treaty obligations—where, and how. For example, it is probably true that Egypt's reservations on the Women's Convention are inadmissible under the law of treaties.[8] But who is going to raise the issue, where, and how? Unlike commercial and other treaties where the states-parties would usually have the motivation and resources to pursue the issue of failure to comply in appropriate fora, state self-interest is normally lacking in relation to human rights treaties. Although there are some enforcement mechanisms for human rights treaties,[9] this aspect of international law remains extremely underdeveloped and largely dependent on the activities of underfunded and overworked nongovernmental and voluntary organizations.

In light of these considerations, the nature of international law in general,[10] and its dependence on largely voluntary compliance and cooperation of sovereign states in the field of human rights in particular,[11] I suggest that it is better to seek deeper consensus and sustainable commitment to the human right in question in order to support its implementation in practice, including efforts to change religious and customary laws accordingly. This work can and should be done, in addition to invoking the notion of binding international custom or agreement whenever, and to the extent, possible, and in support of that notion itself.

Moreover, it is important to understand not only the behavior of governments as political entities, who act within the context of specific political, economic, and social conditions, but also the power relations prevailing in the particular country. No government can afford to disregard the politically articulated wishes or positions of powerful groups or segments of its population who might want to maintain religious and customary laws. This phenomenon will be true, I suggest, of even the most authoritarian or undemocratic governments, in the unlikely event of their being "interested" in effecting such change.

Although it is obvious that the responsibility to change domestic laws must apply to religious and customary law, the implementation of this principle can be problematic in many parts of the world. In practice, a state's willingness or ability to influence practices based on religious and customary laws depends on many factors, any of which could cause difficulty in situations where domestic religious and customary laws are likely to be in conflict with internationally recognized standards of human rights.

Take the example of customary land tenure practices favoring males or the practice of female genital mutilation in some African countries.[12] There is first the question whether these practices do in fact violate the international human rights obligations of the particular state. In other words, is the state required or obliged to eradicate these practices not only as a matter of good or just domestic policy but also as a matter of conformity with international human rights law? The latter proposition presupposes that the practices in question violate specific human rights that are binding on the state as a matter of international law.

Assuming the existence of an international human rights obligation to eradicate these practices, there may still be some problems of implementation. A government may not be sufficiently motivated to engage in land tenure reform unless, for example, there are clear fiscal or other incentives to do so. Similarly, not all governments are particularly concerned with the serious health and psychological consequences of female genital mutilation. Even if there is the political will to act, it may not be easy for a government to influence the sociocultural roots of these practices. As explained below, this task is complicated by the nature of these practices and the inaccessibility of their manifestation or incidence. Moreover, in practice, governments do not necessarily speak with one voice or act with a unified will. Policies adopted at higher political or administrative levels can be frustrated by hostile or uncooperative bureaucrats, officials, or local actors.

In recognizing these and other difficulties of bringing religious and customary laws into conformity with international human rights law, I am not arguing for relieving the state of its obligation to effect such change. I would personally support the establishment of this obligation as a matter of international human rights law when that is not already the case, and support its effective implementation where it exists. It is precisely because of this commitment that I would argue for developing a realistic understanding of the problems involved in the application of this principle with a view to overcoming them. In the rest of this chapter, I will try to explore some facets of the required change process and suggest guidelines for its achievement.

To place the objectives of this chapter in context, however, I wish to address the question of the universal cultural legitimacy of internationally recognized standards of human rights. That is to say, to what extent are these standards accepted as legitimate and binding in all the major cultural traditions of the world? This question must be taken seriously precisely because it is sometimes raised with the intention of undermining international human rights law or of justifying its violation. Those who raise the issue of universality in the context of a given culture do so because they anticipate that the argument has strong appeal or apparent validity to the constituencies they address. Therefore, the best course of action for proponents of international human rights standards is to address these questions, rather than ignore them.

The Universal Cultural Legitimacy of Human Rights

The following brief discussion of the cultural legitimacy of human rights is premised on a view of culture as both a primary source of normative systems and as the context within which such norms are interpreted and implemented. In this light, it is reasonable to assume that the prospects for implementation of a given regime of human rights as a normative system are related to the degree of its legitimacy in the context of the culture(s) where it is supposed to be interpreted and implemented in practice. Otherwise, how can a people be expected to accept and effectively implement a system that they believe to be inconsistent with their own cultural values and institutions? Since the present system of internationally recognized standards of human rights is supposed to apply throughout the world, it must also be legitimated in all the major cultural traditions of the world.[13]

In my view, this premise is beyond dispute because I am unable to conceive of coercing people into implementing a human rights system they do not accept as legitimate. What might be at issue, I suggest, are two questions that follow from this premise. First, are the present internationally recognized standards of human rights, or aspects thereof, in fact culturally legitimate on a universal level? Second, if, or to the extent that, this is not the case, what is to be done about the lack of cultural legitimacy in any given situation?

The argument against the universal cultural legitimacy of the present internationally recognized standards of human rights in general is often made on the grounds that the basic conception and major principles expressed in these standards emerged from Western philosophical and political developments. This may well be true as a matter of historical fact.[14] Moreover, it may also be true that the predominance of Western conceptions of human rights was reinforced by such factors as the nature and context of the drafting process, the limitations of studies purporting to cover a variety of cultural perspectives on the subject, and the quality of representation of non-Western points of view.[15]

It must also be emphasized here that the history and development of the present internationally recognized standards of human rights can also give rise to other concerns. For example, given the male bias of all cultures, Western and non-Western, to varying degrees, there is good reason for concern about the lack of representation of feminist perspectives in the present formulations of internationally recognized human rights standards. Although I am not competent to address the substance and implications of this concern, I believe that it is at least as important as, and often overlaps with, the question of cultural legitimacy as such.

But raising these concerns in general terms, from either a cultural or feminist perspective, cannot justify a blanket condemnation and rejection of all international human rights standards, or even of a particular one, without very careful inquiry and substantiation of the alleged objections. It is true, at least in the interest of further refinement and elaboration, that the opportunity to challenge any present international human right should remain open. Otherwise, the international human rights movement will be condemned to its present state or course of development, without allowing for future needs and opportunities for change or modification. From this perspective, a culturally based (or feminist-based) challenge should be investigated in good faith. However, the case against any specific international human right must be extremely strong in order to justify discarding or reformulating the right in question.

The reasons for requiring a very high standard of proof from those who mount a challenge to an internationally recognized human right include the following. First, there is already significant consensus on internationally recognized human rights through the very deliberate process by which they were articulated and adopted over the course of several decades, as well as the wide ratification of most international treaties on the subject. Second, however one may feel that these rights, or aspects thereof, are inadequate, they nevertheless provide a level of protection. Even those who object to these rights in their present formulation need the protection afforded by them in making their case. Third, if the right is set aside, or its present formulation changed, too lightly or prematurely, there is the risk of failing to achieve even the level or type of human right one is objecting to.

Furthermore, in relation to culturally based challenges in particular, I wish to recall and explain some aspects of the politics of culture referred to earlier. In addressing these questions, it should first be emphasized that the cultural legitimacy or illegitimacy of any thing or matter is necessarily problematic in that it can only be considered within the framework of a number of vague and contestable variables. To claim that something is culturally legitimate or illegitimate presupposes a settled and well-defined set of standards and a fair and consistent process by which those standards are applied. Both aspects, I would add, should themselves be culturally legitimate. Many difficult and inherently political questions are raised by this scenario. Which standards of cultural legitimacy should apply? Who selects them and how? What about alternative or competing standards of cultural legitimacy? What is the nature of power relations among the holders of various views or positions, and how are their interests affected by the issues in question? Who adjudicates the process of selecting applicable standards and ensures the fairness and consistency of their application in practice?

Although it is not possible to resolve any of these questions and concerns here, I suggest that responses to the question of the cultural legitimacy of the international human rights of women, and what can be done about such claims, should be cast against the background of the problematic nature of what might be called the politics of culture. The politics of culture, in turn should be seen in light of what I call the ambivalence and contestability of cultural norms and institutions, which permits a variety of interpretations and practices. Since culture needs to respond to different and competing individual and collective needs and aspirations, it tends to combine stability and continuous change, offer its adherents a range of options, and seek to accommodate varying responses to its norms.[16] These features reflect the fact that culture is constantly contested in a political struggle between those who wish to legitimize their power and privilege and those who need to challenge the status quo in order to redress grievances, realize their human dignity, and protect their well-being. Cultural symbols and processes are constantly used in this struggle at local, national, or international levels. Therefore, human rights advocates need both to understand the process of cultural legitimacy and change and to utilize that process effectively in their efforts to enhance the implementation and enforcement of human rights standards throughout the world.

In light of the preceding remarks and reservations, I now turn to the question of the universal cultural legitimacy of human rights. It is neither possible, nor desirable in my view, for an international system of human rights standards to be culturally neutral. However, the claim of such an international system to universal cultural legitimacy can only be based on a moral and political "overlapping consensus" among the major cultural traditions of the world.[17] In order to engage all cultural traditions in the process of promoting and sustaining such global consensus, the relationship between local culture and international human rights standards should be perceived as a genuinely reciprocal global collaborative effort.

Rather than an "all-or-nothing" approach to the relationship between local culture and international human rights standards, I would recommend the intermediatory approach suggested by Richard Falk. Falk argues that, without mediating international human rights through the web of cultural circumstances, it will be impossible for human rights, norms, and practice to take deep hold in non-Western societies, except to the partial, and often distorting, degree to which these societies—or, more likely, their governing elites—have been to some extent Westernized. At the same time, without cultural practices and traditions being tested against the norms of international human rights, there will be a regressive disposition toward the retention of cruel, brutal, and exploitative aspects of religious and cultural tradition.[18]

Thus, the process of promoting and sustaining global cross-cultural legitimacy for an international system of human rights can work in the following manner.[19] Since we already have an international system of human rights law and institutions, the process should seek to legitimize and anchor the norms of this established system within, and between, the various cultural traditions of the world. In other words, the norms of the international system should be validated in terms of the values and institutions of each culture and also in terms of shared or similar values and institutions of all cultures. This can be achieved, I suggest, through what I call "internal discourse" within the framework of each culture, and "cross-cultural dialogue" among the various cultural traditions of the world.

It is of vital importance that internal discourse should be undertaken within each and every cultural tradition for at least two main reasons. First, internal validation is necessary in all cultural traditions for one aspect or another of the present international human rights system. It might be necessary for civil and political rights in one culture, economic and social rights in another, the rights of women or minorities in a third, and so forth. Second, for such discourse within one culture to be viable and effective, its participants should be able to point to similar discourses going on in the context of other cultures.

A parallel process of cross-cultural dialogue is also important for two main reasons. First, from a methodological point of view, all participants in their respective internal discourses can draw on each other's experiences and achievements. Second, cross-cultural dialogue will enhance understanding of, and commitment to, the values and norms of human dignity shared by all human cultures, thereby providing a common moral and political foundation for international human rights standards. In this way, the combination of the processes of internal discourse and cross-cultural dialogue will, one hopes, deepen and broaden universal cultural consensus on the concept and normative content of international human rights.

It should be emphasized, however, that the proposed approach is methodological and not substantive: it prescribes a methodology of internal discourse and cross-cultural dialogue on reciprocal, dynamic, and sensitive terms, but it does not anticipate or restrict the arguments to be used or the manner in which discourse(s) and dialogue(s) are to be conducted in each situation. It would be possible, therefore, to consider and analyze experiences in various cultural or country-specific contexts as a means of informing and promoting more constructive discourse and dialogue.[20]

In the next section, I highlight some issues relevant to the application of this approach to the responsibility of states to change religious and customary laws that violate internationally recognized standards of human rights. As I indicate at the end of that section, the proposed approach might also help resolve conflicts between national fundamental or human rights standards, on the one hand, and communal (religious, customary, or traditional) standards within a nation-state, on the other. The last section is devoted to a brief illustration of a possible application of this approach to changing Islamic religious laws in relation to the international human rights of women.

Changing Religious and Customary Laws

From a legal point of view, international law can only address states with due regard for their sovereignty, and it does not have the authority, concepts, or mechanisms for achieving compliance with its norms except through the agency of the state in question. This legal limitation does not mean, however, that nothing can be done to encourage and support states in their efforts to comply with international human rights law. In this light, it would be useful to explore possible strategies for changing religious and customary laws in order to bring them into conformity with international human rights law. Integral to this inquiry is the question of how such strategies may be employed by internal actors and how external support and assistance can be rendered without undermining the integrity and efficacy of the process as a whole. It is necessary for both aspects of the process to be grounded in a clear understanding of the nature and operation of religious and customary laws in relation to what the state can realistically be expected to do. Although it is not possible to present here a comprehensive treatment of this matter, some tentative remarks might be helpful.

On the Nature and Operation of Religious and Customary Law

The authority of religious and customary laws is commonly perceived to derive from either the people's religious beliefs or their communal practice from time immemorial. That is to say, the common perception is that the validity of religious laws is ensured by divine sanction, while the utility of customary laws is assumed to have been proven through long experience. Since the two sources of authority overlap, they can be invoked interchangeably or in combination. In the case of Islamic societies, for example, local custom is assumed to be sanctioned by divine authority, provided that such custom does not contradict the explicit dictates of religious law, commonly known as Shari'a. The validity of religious law, on the other hand, is believed to be vindicated by practical experience, as well as being supported by divine sanction. To the extent that traditional religions still prevail in some parts of Africa, it may be difficult to distinguish between divine sanction and communal authority.[21]

This common perception of the authority of religious and customary laws is founded on a complex web of economic, social, and political factors and tends to reflect existing power relations within the community. The perception is also maintained and promoted through processes of individual socialization and communal identification. While it is useful to understand its basis and dynamics, it may not be necessary or desirable to challenge or repudiate the perception itself in order to change the religious and customary laws it legitimizes. It is important to remember that the objective is to bring religious and customary laws into conformity with international human rights law, not to extinguish religious and customary laws themselves or transform their jurisprudential character. In any case, whether, to what extent, and how indigenous perceptions about religious and customary laws should and can be challenged, changed, or modified should be left to the process of internal discourse indicated earlier. An external effort to impose change would probably be perceived as an exercise in cultural imperialism and rejected as such.

It should also be emphasized that religious and customary laws can, and usually are, implemented independently of the structures and mechanisms of the state. The state might try to regulate the operation of these laws, for example, by providing for procedural safeguards to be enforced by administrative organs or tribunals. But it can neither immediately eradicate the practice of these laws altogether nor transform their nature and content, at least not without engaging in massive oppression and intimidation of the particular population over a long period of time. Even if the state were able and willing to maintain such a program as a high priority in its domestic policies, such policy or practice would be totally unacceptable from a human rights point of view.

An effort to change religious and customary laws in accordance with international human rights law should seek to persuade people of the validity and utility of the change. Such persuasion must, of course, be grounded in a complete and realistic understanding of the rationale or authority of these laws and the way they operate in practice. For example, customary land tenure practices that assign ownership or possession of land to men rather than women might be apparently justified or rationalized on the ground that only men can cultivate or otherwise use the land to support their families. Beyond that apparent rationale, however, such practices will probably also rely on assumptions about the competence and "proper" roles of men and women in society. This type of underlying rationale can be strong enough to override or negate efforts by the state to change or regulate customary land tenure practices.

For instance, the state may introduce a different land distribution scheme to give women their share, and seek to enforce this through an official land registration system. Nevertheless, previous customary land tenure practices may persist "off the record," with the apparent acquiescence of the women who are supposed to benefit from enforcement of the new system. An effort to change this aspect of customary law must take into account not only apparent economic and sociological factors or justifications but also the circumstances and underlying rationales that might cause the practice to continue despite attempts at legal regulation or change by the state.

Similarly, one or more justifications may be given for the practice of female genital mutilation. A more sophisticated inquiry, however, may reveal other rationales or underlying assumptions about, for example, male/female sexuality and roles, power relations, or economic and political interests. Moreover, this practice can be attributed to customary sanction but not to customary law in a jurisprudential sense. The customary sanction in this case is not enforced in any judicial or public setting. Rather, the sanction operates through the socialization or conditioning of women in order to induce them to "consent" to such mutilation being inflicted on their young daughters. Again, customary sanction for this practice may be strong enough to override state efforts to eradicate it, even through the imposition of criminal punishment, as in the Sudan, where the practice has been a criminal offense punishable by up to two years of imprisonment since 1946.[22] An effort to eradicate genital mutilation must take into account and address not only each and all types of justifications but also the cultural circumstances and underlying rationales that might cause the practice to continue in a particular community.

Toward Coherent Strategies for Change

In view of these factors, it is clear that the only viable and acceptable way of changing religious and customary laws is by transforming popular beliefs and attitudes, thereby changing common practice. This transformation can be accomplished through a comprehensive and intensive program of formal and informal education, supported by social services and other administrative measures, in order to change people's attitudes about the necessity or desirability of continuing a particular religious or customary practice. To achieve its objective, the program must not only discredit the religious or customary law or practice in question but also provide a viable and legitimate alternative view of the matter. Such an alternative view of an existing practice can be either the simple discontinuation of the practice in question or the substitution of another.

Since the original practice derives its authority from religious or customary sanction, an effort to discredit it (and to substitute another where appropriate) must draw its authority from the same source on which the original practice was founded. Moreover, this effort must be presented through a reasoning or rationale intelligible to the affected population. For example, efforts to change customary land tenure practices must seek to challenge and discredit whatever economical, sociological, or other rationale is perceived by the population at large to support or justify those practices. Such efforts must also seek to challenge and discredit the original practice in ways that are relevant to, and understood and accepted by, the population in question.

It is difficult to envision the application of the proposed approach in abstract terms, without reference to the nature and operation of a specific religious or customary law system in the context of a particular society. Generally speaking, however, it is possible to identify some internal requirements for a successful process of changing religious and customary laws to ensure their compliance with international human rights law. In an ideal scenario, there are two levels of requirements that need to be satisfied. First, the state in question must be legally bound by the relevant principle of international human rights law. It should also have committed itself effectively to discharging its responsibility to bring domestic religious and customary laws into conformity with the requirements of international human rights law. Second, there is a need for broadly based political support for the official commitment of the state. Moreover, a strongly motivated and well-informed local constituency, willing and able to engage in organized action, is needed to mobilize political support and press for the implementation of policies and strategies for change.

However, these ideal requirements are neither likely to be realized immediately and fully all at once nor to be lacking completely when the issue of changing religious or customary law arises in a given situation. In all probability, there would be some level of official obligation and commitment to change, some degree of broad political support, and some sort of constituency willing to work for it. Otherwise, the issue would not have arisen in the first place. If there is no political support for, or official commitment to, changing religious or customary laws in order to ensure their conformity with international human rights law, then the question will not arise at all in the particular country.

Moreover, a dynamic relationship exists between and within each level of requirement. A highly motivated and capable constituency, for instance, can cultivate popular political support for change and pressure the state into ratifying the relevant treaty or into increasing or effectuating its commitment to implement change in accordance with international human rights law. Conversely, the existence of an official commitment can encourage the growth of an active local constituency or facilitate the development of broadly based political support for change. This dynamic is part of the process of internal discourse whereby the proponents of an internationally recognized human right seek to justify and legitimize that right in terms of their own culture, as explained above.

In addition to these internal aspects, there is also the external dimension of the process of changing religious or customary laws. External actors can support and influence the process of internal discourse through cross-cultural dialogue, as explained above. However, it is crucial that external support and influence be provided in ways that enhance, rather than undermine, the integrity and efficacy of the internal discourse. The process of cultural legitimation will be undermined, if not totally repudiated, by even the appearance of imposition of extracultural values and norms. External actors should support and encourage indigenous actors who are engaging in internal discourse to legitimize and effectuate a particular human right. However, external actors must not, in any way, attempt or appear to dictate the terms of internal discourse or preempt its conclusions. Possible ways and means of external support include international action to protect the freedoms of speech and assembly of internal actors, the exchange of insights and experiences about the concept of the particular human right and the sociopolitical context of its implementation, and assistance in developing and implementing campaign strategies.

The need for cultural sensitivity and discretion in providing external support is underscored by the fact that those acting as internal agents of change are liable to be regarded by local religious or political forces as subversive elements acting on behalf of the imperial interests of alien powers and cultures. This tendency may appear obvious and elementary in such a political struggle, where the internal "guardians" of tradition and the status quo would want to seize on every opportunity and pretext in their efforts to undermine the credibility of the proponents of changing religious or customary laws. However, the subtle dangers of ethnocentricity and bias should not be underestimated in this connection. Cross-cultural dialogue should enhance the ability of internal actors to understand and address the nature and operation of cultural and political factors in their own context, not to press them into understanding and addressing these factors in terms of the experience of other societies.

As indicated above, the proposed approach might contribute to resolving conflicts between national fundamental or human rights standards, on the one hand, and communal (religious, customary, or traditional) standards within a nation-state, on the other. The *Lovelace* case in Canada[23] and the *Shah Bano Begum* case in India[24] reflect such situations of conflict within a single nation-state. Similar issues may arise in many other settings. Although each situation should be discussed in its own context, I believe that such situations raise the same basic set of dilemmas.

For instance, the dilemma confronting national policy-makers would be how to respect and protect the integrity (and independence, where relevant) of the community in question without tolerating violation of fundamental or human rights norms that are binding on the state as a matter of constitutional or international law. Such a dilemma would be particularly acute where the integrity and independence of the community in question is also dictated by constitutional or political imperatives.[25]

At a personal level such situations face women, for example, with a difficult choice between enduring inequality and discrimination in order to enjoy many vital benefits of membership in their own communities or abandoning all that by opting out of the community in order to enjoy equality and freedom from discrimination within the wider state society. On the one hand, they are likely to be castigated or harassed within the community because of their attitudes and lifestyle, thereby diminishing the benefits of belonging to the community. They would also be aware, on the other hand, of the limitations or inadequacy of equality and nondiscrimination promised by the wider society, especially to women of their status and background.

Such dilemmas would be resolved, I suggest, by transforming the internal communal (religious, customary, or traditional) standards relating to the status and rights of women in order to bring them into conformity with the norms of equality and nondiscrimination prevailing in the wider state society; this transformation may be accomplished through the processes of internal discourse and cross-cultural dialogue described above. In the absence of a better alternative, I would suggest that this approach be tried by both official agencies and private actors as a way of resolving conflicts between national and communal standards. Although space does not permit further elaboration, it bears repeating that the proposed approach is methodological and not substantive. Full consideration can therefore be given to insights gained from other experiences of discourse and dialogue in adjusting and adapting the proposed approach to the circumstances and context of each case.

Islamic Religious Laws and the Rights of Women

In light of the above remarks about developing general strategies for changing religious and customary laws, I wish now to illustrate how the process might operate in relation to changing Islamic Shari'a laws in particular. It is not possible here either to explain the nature and development of Shari'a or to discuss the many human rights problems raised by its application in the modern context.[26] In this brief section, I will present a theoretical discussion of the process of changing Shari'a family law, which, in my view, violates the human rights of Muslim women in even the most "secularized" Islamic societies.[27] This branch of Shari'a is enforced as the official law of the great majority of predominantly Muslim countries today and even in some non-Muslim countries, like India as noted earlier,[28] where Muslims are a minority. Moreover, the underlying assumptions and norms of this branch of Shari'a have a negative impact on the human rights of women in broader sociopolitical terms.

The basic problem can be outlined as follows. Shariʿa family law is fundamentally premised on the notion of male guardianship over women (*qawama*) and is consequently characterized by many features of inequality between men and women in marriage, divorce, and related matters. Thus, for example, as a general rule, a man may take up to four wives and divorce any of them at will, all without having to show cause or account to any judicial or other authority for his decision. In contrast, a woman can only be married to one man at a time and is not entitled to obtain a divorce except through a judicial ruling on a few specific grounds.[29] Although there are differences between and within the major schools of Islamic jurisprudence, as applied by the judicial systems of various countries, the above-mentioned premise and characterization are true of all situations where Shariʿa family law is enforced today.

The notion of male guardianship has serious implications for the marriage relationship as a whole and for the economic and social rights of married women. According to most jurists, a husband is entitled to the obedience of his wife and can prevent her from taking employment, if he wishes. A wife who is disobedient to her husband (*nashiz*) is not entitled to maintenance. Consequently, a woman can be forced to submit to her husband's will even when she cannot obtain his consent in order to be able to work and thereby support herself, receive maintenance from him, or obtain a divorce. In some jurisdictions, a wife who leaves the matrimonial home can be physically forced to return through the execution of a judicial "obedience decree." Moreover, as noted earlier, this and other features of Shariʿa family law have serious political and social consequences for women, in that their freedom to engage in activities outside the home is inhibited by the legal control men are entitled to exercise over their female "wards." These aspects of Shariʿa also reinforce and sanction the socialization of women, who are conditioned, from early childhood, into submission, learned helplessness, and dependency.

It is obvious that these principles of Shariʿa family law violate the fundamental human right of nondiscrimination on grounds of gender. In some situations, these principles are used to justify cruel, inhuman, or degrading treatment. Most Islamic states are parties to international treaties that provide for a wide range of human rights that are violated by Shariʿa personal law applied by the official courts of the same countries. A few Islamic states are even parties to the 1979 International Convention on the Elimination of All Forms of Discrimination against Women, which is clearly violated by all these aspects of Shariʿa family law. In other words, it is not difficult to establish the responsibility of many Islamic states to change these aspects of religious law in accordance with their obligations under international human rights law. The question is how to effect such change in practice. I will first address this question from an Islamic jurisprudential point of view and then consider the role of internal and external actors in the process of change.

Two fundamental points to note about the jurisprudential question are (1) that Shariʿa was constructed by early (male) Muslim jurists and (2) that they acted in accordance with their historical context.[30] Whether through the selection and interpretation of the relevant texts of the Qurʾan and Sunna (traditions of the Prophet) or through the application of such techniques as consensus (ijmaʿ) and analogy (qiyas), the founding jurists of Shariʿa constructed what they believed to be an appropriate legal and ethical system for their communities in very local terms. Clearly, the jurists were not engaged in the construction of a "divine and eternal" Shariʿa, as claimed by many Muslims today. In fact, the most authoritative jurists expressed their views as individual theoretical derivations and cautioned against codifying or implementing them as the only valid version of Shariʿa. Given this state of affairs, it is perfectly legitimate, indeed imperative in my view, for modern Muslim jurists and scholars to construct an Islamic legal and ethical system that is appropriate for the present historical context of Islamic societies.

In constructing Shariʿa, the early Muslim jurists emphasized certain texts of the Qurʾan and Sunna as relevant and applicable to the issue at hand and deemphasized or excluded others. This process was taken by the majority of succeeding generations of jurists to mean that the deemphasized texts were repealed or abrogated (nusikhat) for legal purposes, though they remain part of the tradition in other respects. Moreover, the technical rules employed by the early jurists in constructing their visions of Shariʿa, known as "the science of foundations of jurisprudence" (ʿilm usul al-fiqh), were entrenched by subsequent generations of Muslims as the only valid way of deriving principles and rules of Shariʿa. Given the fact that both aspects of this process were the work of the early Muslim jurists, it is obvious that they are open to question and reformulation by contemporary Muslims.

In light of these considerations, Ustadh (revered teacher) Mahmoud Mohamed Taha, the late Sudanese Muslim reformer, developed a coherent methodology for what he called "the evolution of Islamic legislation," that is, the reconstruction and reformulation of the constitutional and legal aspects of Shariʿa.[31] Through the application of this methodology, it is possible, indeed imperative, he argued, to abolish the principle of male guardianship over females and to remove every feature of inequality of women or discrimination against them, as a matter of Islamic law. This theological and jurisprudential framework will, in my view, achieve complete consistency between Shari'a religious laws and international human rights law. Taha's methodology of Islamic law reform is readily available now and is, I believe, fully substantiated in Islamic terms. The remaining issue is how to implement this methodology in order to transform the principles and rules of Shari'a in concrete practical terms.

As indicated earlier, this is the role of internal discourse, as supported by cross-cultural dialogue. It is up to Muslim women and men to engage in a political struggle to propagate and implement reform of Islamic law (whether on the basis of Taha's methodology or another adequate Islamic alternative to it) in their own communities and countries. These internal actors may indeed receive external support and assistance, but only in accordance with the guidelines emphasized above. This consideration is particularly important in view of the recent and current experience of Muslim peoples with Western colonialism and domination. Islamic human rights advocates in general are already suspected of subverting their own cultures and traditions in favor of Western values and institutions. It is, therefore, imperative that both the internal actors and their external supporters should avoid acting in a way that might be used as a pretext for undermining the credibility and legitimacy of the process of changing Shari'a laws.

I am not underestimating the difficulty and complexity of the task. Speaking from personal experience, I can say that prevailing conditions of political repression and social authoritarianism are hardly conducive to human rights organization and activism. Moreover, human rights advocates in Islamic countries are few and disorganized, their resources and experience are limited, and the demands on their time and energy are many and complex. Nevertheless, there is no substitute for internal discourse for transforming attitudes and perceptions about the nature and implications of Shari'a and for achieving the necessary legal reform and change. It is primarily the task of internal actors, supported and encouraged by external allies, to promote and sustain the necessary degree of official commitment and popular political support for a program for changing Shari'a laws.

Finally, I should indicate that while Taha's methodology has its limitations,[32] I believe that it can at least be useful as an initial framework for an internal discourse, which can then continue to seek other Islamic reform methodologies to supplement or replace it. I also believe it is important to note that international human rights law itself is not immune to critical examination and reformulation.[33] Unless human rights advocates in all parts of the world are open to this possibility, it would be unrealistic to expect Muslims to be open to critical examination of their religious law.

Conclusion

It is not possible to evaluate accurately the potential of the approach to change religious and customary laws presented here until it is applied to specific situations of conflict and to tension between such laws and international human rights law. However, judging by my knowledge of the possibilities for Islamic law reform, I envision a far-reaching potential for the proposed approach in relation to other systems of religious and customary law. I find this approach useful not only for maximizing the possibilities of resolution within the existing framework of a religious or customary law system but also for expanding or transforming that framework itself. This process is what I regard as a legitimate internal (within the culture or tradition) challenge and change of a people's perceptions about the nature and implications of their religious beliefs or long-standing communal practice. However, one must expect strong and sustained opposition or resistance from those whose vested interests are threatened by any change in the status quo.

As indicated at the end of the last section, a given reform methodology might not succeed in achieving the required reform of one or more aspects of a system of religious or customary law. In such a case, I suggest, that failure would be a failure of the particular methodology, not necessarily of the internal discourse/cross-cultural dialogue approach as a whole. Other methodologies can and must be developed by the people themselves, through internal discourse, supported by cross-cultural dialogue.

Chapter 5

Islamic Foundations
of Religious Human Rights

Following an introduction of the terms of reference and thesis of this chapter on the Islamic foundations of religious human rights, my discussion will fall into three parts. First, I will offer an outline of the origins, nature, and development of Islamic law and theology and of their modern influence. The second section will focus on the nature and circumstances of discourse about rights and responsibilities in the Islamic world today. In that light, I will suggest in the third section a theory of Islamic foundations of religious human rights, as can be perceived in the modern context.

Introduction: The Imperative of Resolving a Paradox

It is the intent of this chapter to discuss both Islamic legal and theological foundations of religious human rights and the influence of an Islamic discourse about rights in more recent Islamic legal life. As a matter of terminology, however, no distinction was made in the work of early Islamic scholars, or in the minds of their followers, between law and theology. Subject matters ranging from legal, in the modern sense of the term, to that pertaining to belief and doctrine, ethics and morality, religious ritual practices, style of dress, hygiene, courtesy, and good manners were all seen as falling within the domain of Shariʿa, the divinely ordained way of life.[1]

The phrase "religious human rights," as used in this chapter, refers to those rights that pertain to freedom of belief and conscience, including religious dissent, conformity or lack thereof, and tolerance, as *human rights*.[2] That is to say, I am concerned with religious rights as conceived, articulated, and applied within a "human rights" paradigm, rather than within a particular religious or other frame of reference or legal system. The conception and implementation of religious rights as human rights are both necessary and paradoxical in that the two can neither be easily joined nor separated.[3]

The connection is difficult to make, on the one hand, because of the inherent tension between the underlying premise of universality of human rights and the particularity of religious foundations for those rights.[4] Since the universality of human rights means the validity and application of these rights to all human beings throughout the world, they must apply regardless of whether they are perceived to be founded in the religious beliefs of a given community. Universality of human rights is particularly challenged by religious activists, such as Islamist groups in several Islamic countries today, who claim that their religious belief requires the establishment of a "theocratic" state to enforce their vision of the sacred law. Yet, it is imperative to maintain the universality of human rights against such claims precisely because of the exclusive and abusive nature of a theocratic state, against believers and nonbelievers alike.

On the other hand, it is difficult to separate religion and human rights because they both not only operate on the same moral plane of justification but also overlap and interact in content. Both normative systems are premised on the same moral precepts of human relations; and while believers are moved to uphold human rights norms out of religious conviction, the protection of the right to hold and act on those convictions is integral to the fundamental concept of human rights. Since believers will always make the connection between religion and human rights, whether positively or negatively, it is better for human rights advocates to acknowledge and respond to it rather than pretend that it does not exist.

Failure to resolve the apparent paradox between religion and human rights, I maintain, is detrimental from both perspectives. Unless common ground can be found whereby people would uphold human rights as a matter of, or at least without violation to, their religious conviction, they would be expected to make a choice between the two "creeds."[5] In that case, the cost to the community or person making such a choice is not only in the loss of some or all of the benefits of the abandoned creed but also in relation to the value of the adopted or preferred one. If a community opts for upholding what it believes to be the precepts of its religion over a commitment to human rights norms, then the community and its members will lose from a religious as well as a human rights point of view. Opting for human rights over religious precepts, on the other hand, would entail loss from a human rights as well as a religious perspective.

Loss of the benefits of the abandoned creed may be obvious, but how does a choice between the two creeds diminish the value of the adopted one as well? In my view, a commitment to human rights enhances the quality of religious belief and the relevance and utility of its precepts to the lives of its adherents. By its very nature, and in order to influence effectively the moral convictions and daily behavior of those who subscribe to it, religious belief must be voluntarily adopted and maintained. Coerced belief is a contradiction in terms and can only breed hypocrisy, social corruption, and political oppression.

Moreover, as can be seen from the history of every major religion, internal disagreement is essential for the rejuvenation of belief and rectification of practice among its adherents. The survival and renewal of every major religion were ensured by the convictions and insights of its dissidents as much as by the conformity of its orthodoxy. In the Islamic context, for example, every form of Sunni, Sufi (mystic), or Shiʿa belief held by its adherents today as "orthodox" was, at some point in history, a dissident view that survived against the opposition of the "orthodoxy" of that time. By protecting the right to dissent within a religious community, human rights norms and mechanisms safeguard the prospects of spiritual growth of any religion and the practical utility of its precepts to the lives of its adherents.

Yet, as can also be seen in the history of every major religion, dissident religious views have almost always been persecuted and repressed in the name of protecting the integrity of the faith, the community, and/or the moral well-being of others. While such concerns should be taken seriously because of their legitimate importance to believers, they should never be allowed to contradict or undermine the facts of religious and political plurality or to diminish the commitment of the community to recognize and respect them in the shared public domain. The present reality and future prospects of religious and political plurality must be fully acknowledged and accommodated as integral to, and essential for the legitimacy and integrity of, the faith and/or the community.[6] Otherwise, claims of acting in the interest of protecting the integrity of the faith and community will be nothing more than pretexts for political and religious domination by certain elites or groups of believers.

From a human rights perspective, while a religious motivation to uphold human rights enhances the prospects of voluntary compliance and the emergence of the political will to enforce them, resistance to these rights from a religious point of view is extremely difficult to overcome. Muslim believers, in my experience, are unlikely to accept and abide by a system of rights that excludes religion or fails to take it seriously. In my view as a Muslim, religious experience is not only an indispensable resource for enlisting the support for human rights among believers, especially in forging the rational linkage of rights to responsibilities as people experience them in their everyday life, but also a rich and valuable source of the content of those rights. Moreover, as noted earlier, these connections are being made by believers and must be acknowledged and responded to as such.

Thus, despite their difficult and paradoxical relationship, religion and human rights must not merely be reconciled; rather, they must support each other. This mutual support can and should be achieved, I believe, through efforts on both sides of the issue. Secular human rights advocates, on the one hand, must transcend an attitude of indifferent tolerance of religion to a moral recognition of religious faith and serious engagement of religious perspectives. Those who take religion seriously, on the other hand, must see human rights as integral to their belief or concern, rather than as a purely secular system to be accommodated.

In seeking to explore the prospects and problems of finding Islamic foundations for human rights, this chapter does not claim to offer a comprehensive discussion of the issues in relation to every aspect of Islamic history or all parts of the Islamic world. It is simply not possible to capture the full richness and complexity of many centuries of the history of major and highly diverse parts of the world in a single work. Instead, my purpose here is to distill the most pertinent features of that history and to draw on some of the experiences of Islamic communities, in order to develop a coherent theory of Islamic foundations of religious human rights.

As elaborated later, this theory is premised on two main principles. First, respecting "internal" freedom of belief and dissent among Muslims—since identity and its normative system can only be meaningful and useful in historical context—Islamic identity and Shari'a must remain open to renegotiation and reconstruction by each community in its own particular circumstances. Given the fact that human agency is unavoidable in the interpretation and implementation of religious texts, every formulation of Islamic identity and articulation of Shari'a is necessarily a product of human reason and action. As such, no formulation or articulation should be allowed to monopolize religious authenticity and authority to the exclusion of others. Alternative formulations and articulations should be allowed to compete for acceptance by the community as the practical arbiter of Islamic authenticity. Freedom of belief and dissent must therefore be safeguarded among those who identify as Muslims in order to ensure the vitality and integrity of this process of re-negotiation and reconstruction of religious identity and law.

Second, with respect to religious human rights of non-Muslims, modern circumstances of permanent religious communities, and other pluralities of national and international political communities, require equal respect for the religious human rights of all members of the community; this equal respect is, in turn, the basis of the demand of Muslims themselves to those rights. Moreover, the recognition of plurality and its consequences is not only supported by scriptural Islamic sources, as noted earlier, but also sanctioned by the historical experience of Islamic communities.

Shariʿa, Past and Present

I would not restrict a discussion of Islamic foundations of religious human rights to the basis of those rights, or lack thereof, under Shariʿa. Other aspects of Islamic consciousness, such as perceptions and experiences of piety and spirituality, as well as socioeconomic and political factors, are always integral to an understanding of Muslim beliefs and behavior. Indeed, I maintain that the origins, nature, and context of the development of Shariʿa were themselves conditioned by the historical context of early Islamic societies of the Middle East.[7] In due course, local context also strongly influenced the adoption and adaptation of Shariʿa in other parts of the Islamic world.

By the same token, historical contexts are affecting, and will continue to affect, the understanding and implementation of Shariʿa as part of the foundations of religious human rights in Islamic societies. Local context and socioeconomic and political factors influenced the displacement of Shariʿa during the colonial and early independence era in most Islamic countries, as well as its recent resurgence as a framework of discourse about rights and human rights.

In this light, I will now offer a brief outline of the origins, nature, and development of Shariʿa as a theoretical model for an Islamic way of life. Although this ideal model was rarely fully implemented in the actual lives of Islamic communities and individuals, it remains a powerful symbol and source of motivation and framework for action to the present day. This section will therefore conclude with an evaluation of the role of Shariʿa in modern Islamic discourse about rights and responsibilities.

The primary sources of the conceptual frame of reference and detailed content of Shariʿa are the Qurʾan and Sunna of the Prophet Muhammad.[8]

Traditions of the earliest generations of Muslims were also taken as authoritative sources of Islamic guidance in popular practice. Throughout the first century of Islam, Islamic communities and individuals referred to these sources for guidance in their daily lives, in light of their own recollections of the living example of earlier generations and their understanding of the message of Islam. The process of consulting scholars who were believed to be knowledgeable of the text and interpretation of the Qur'an and Sunna, and of the history and relevance of the traditions of early Islamic communities, gradually evolved into a practice of following a set of general principles and specific rulings attributed to a particular master or teacher and his leading disciples.

By the end of the second century of Islam and the beginning of the third (eighth and ninth centuries), the practice of adherence to a preferred scholar developed into a systematic and consistent following of what came to be known as his school of jurisprudence, *madhhab*. For the next millennium, and largely to the present day, the development of Shari'a has been structured and governed by the methodology, principles, and rules set by the founding teachers, their immediate disciples, and subsequent scholars of the major surviving schools of Islamic jurisprudence, *madhahib al-fiqh al-Islami*.[9] Much of the legal and theological life of Islamic communities occurred within the framework of the school prevailing in a given community, often within a subdivision or particular line of thinking and authority.[10] The extinction of some schools, however, and shifts of territorial influence among the surviving schools, testifies to a dynamic of discourse and choice by Islamic communities according to the sense of each community as to which school (or sub-school) is more responsive to its needs and interests at a given time.

Several features of the formative stage of Shari'a, in contrast to subsequent developments and more recent trends, should be noted here. First, the founding scholars were engaged in a process of derivation of general principles and specific rules for the guidance of their communities, responding to queries and requests or elaborating on hypothetical questions to clarify theoretical and methodological principles as they deemed necessary or useful for the community. Thus, the founding scholars and their immediate disciples were not, and did not see or present themselves as, establishing separate or distinctive, let alone immutable, schools of thought. Yet, one school or another came to be rigidly followed as the only valid articulation of Shari'a. A more integrated approach appears to be emerging today as a result of the intellectual and political context of the modern Islamic movement, but automatic observance of an accepted school or scholar(s) continues to be the norm.

Second, the elaboration of Shari'a by the founding scholars through the interpretation of the Qur'an and Sunna, in light of the living traditions of the early Islamic communities, was initially a spontaneous and unstructured process. To early Muslims, all divine guidance was contained in the Qur'an and Sunna, which were rendered in their own Arabic language and exemplified in the then oral history of their recent forefathers. Rigorous methodology for the derivation of Shari'a principles and rules evolved gradually in response to certain developments.[11] The evolution of rigorous and systematic methodology was also probably prompted by the growing maturity and complexity of Shari'a itself.

In response to these and other factors, scholars began to develop technical rules and criteria for the interpretation of the Qur'an, the authentication and recording of Sunna and its reconciliation with the Qur'an, the relevance and use of early traditions of Islamic communities in relation to the Qur'an and Sunna, and so forth. This development occurred within each of the schools, but al-Safi'i is generally credited with the most systematic and influential methodological development of what came to be known as *'ilm usul al-fiqh al-Islami*, the science of the foundations of Islamic jurisprudence.[12] But over time that legitimate and necessary methodological regulation became too inhibiting for, indeed detrimental to, the further development of Shari'a, especially in the modern era.[13]

This underdevelopment is particularly clear, in my view, in relation to the nature and role of *ijtihad*, literally self-exertion or effort but referring in this sense to the exercise of deliberate juridical reasoning to derive principles and rules of Shari'a. Although technically understood by Islamic jurists as applying only to matters on which there is no clear and categorical text in the Qur'an and Sunna, ijtihad was clearly applied to those fundamental texts themselves. Community leaders and scholars were always exercising ijtihad in relation to the Qur'an and Sunna because they had to rely on their own judgment in deciding which provisions of the Qur'an and Sunna applied to a given situation or question and in interpreting and applying the text(s) they deemed relevant. With the development of usul al-fiqh, however, ijtihad was regulated and restricted to the point of extinction and remains extremely problematic to the present day.[14] But since ijtihad was defined and regulated through human reason in the past, rather than being the direct product of divine revelation as such, it can be redefined and reregulated through human reason today and in the future.

A third significant feature to note about the formative stages of Shari'a is that, while the scholars were elaborating and perfecting an ideal and comprehensive normative system, the affairs of the state were conducted more in accordance with pragmatic political expediency than with the dictates of that system. For much of Islamic history since the Amawy dynasty (661–750), there existed "an uneasy truce between *ulama* [scholars of Shari'a] . . . and the political authorities. . . . As long as the sacred law [Shari'a] received formal recognition as a religious ideal, it did not insist on being fully applied in practice."[15] But the dichotomy between theory and practice should neither be exaggerated nor simplified in terms of secular and religious characterizations—an important point in relation to current Islamic discourse as indicated later.

For one thing, this dichotomy varied from time to time and from one field of Shari'a to another in ways that maintained the credibility of the appearance of allegiance to the ideal model from both the scholarly and political points of view. Second, the "light and distant" nature of government and administration in the imperial states of the past, coupled with the diffusion of Shari'a in inaccessible treatises and commentaries, was not conducive to rigorous systematic implementation. Communities were left to conduct their daily affairs in accordance with their own local customary or traditional practices that included Shari'a norms, but not in a coherent and formal sense of codes of law in the modern sense of the term.

More significantly from the point of view of current debates about human rights in the Islamic world, the ideal of Shari'a has remained very much alive in the hearts and minds of Muslims, even when they lived under colonial administrations that sought to displace Shari'a by modern notions of law and government in formal and systematic ways.[16] As explained by Anderson, "To a Muslim, it has always been a far more heinous sin to deny or question the divine revelation than to fail to obey it. So it seemed preferable to continue to pay lip-service to an inviolable Shari'a, as the only law of fundamental authority, and to excuse departure from much of it in practice by appealing to the doctrine of necessity (*darura*), rather than to make any attempt to adapt law to the circumstances and needs of contemporary life."[17]

But this traditional attitude is presently being challenged by Islamic activists who are saying that, after several decades of political independence as nation-states, Muslims are now free to implement the totality of Shari'a. It is far from clear, and extremely doubtful to my mind, whether the modern Islamists' project will lead to the implementation of Shari'a as articulated by the founding scholars and known to Islamic communities through the ages.

In addition to the incompatibility of fundamental aspects of Shari'a with the modern circumstances of living in pluralistic nation-states in a globalized and interdependent world,[18] the very effort of codification and enforcement by centralized coercive authority contradicts the nature of Shari'a and the mainstream of Islamic history. Nevertheless, I would insist that the Islamists' project must be taken very seriously because of its drastic consequences to human rights, and to religious human rights in particular.

Nature and Circumstances of the Present Discourse

It is difficult to generalize about the modern discourse of rights and responsibilities in all Islamic countries. Even in relation to certain regions or countries, one can identify several stages and forms of discourse. Generally speaking, however, this discourse tends to fall within two main stages, at least in relation to the countries of the Middle East and North Africa. During the struggle for independence, and immediately after it was achieved, the debate was focused on nationalist projects, whether liberal (such as that of Bourgiba in Tunisia), Arab/socialist (such as that of Nasir in Egypt), or socialist (such as that of the FLN, Front de Libération Nationale in Algeria). Those projects were explicitly or implicitly secular in orientation, with little reference, if any, to the role of Shari'a or an "Islamic ideology." However, upon the failure of the proponents of those projects to deliver the promised benefits, a variety of Islamist groups appear to have succeeded in seizing the initiative and redefining the terms of discourse. I will focus on this second stage because of its significance to the subject of this chapter, without claiming that the "Islamization" of discourse is either total or irreversible throughout the Islamic world or parts thereof.

In my view, discourse between Islamists and their opponents,[19] especially in the Middle East and North Africa, is complicated by contextual and operational factors and characterized by conceptual confusion. The reasons for this include the political and historical conditions under which discourse is taking place, the orientation and power relations of the participants, and the subject matter and terms of reference of the discourse itself. What is of particular concern for the subject of this chapter, however, is the conceptual confusion of this discourse.

On the Islamist side, the present discourse is apparently "modern" in its form and techniques, using to great effect sophisticated methods of organization, mass media, and communications technology. These modern forms and techniques are being deployed in pursuit of the declared objective of re-capturing and resurrecting an idealized vision of a past "Golden Age" of a powerful civilization. But that objective is usually presented as an ideological slogan, without a clear statement of how a Shari'a model might be reconciled with the realities of a modern multireligious nation-state or of international relations.

Despite these obvious problems with the Islamist side of the discourse, their opponents appear to be in disarray and generally on the defensive. Pos-sible reasons for this include such political factors as being associated in the public eye with the previous discredited nationalist, post-independence proj-ect, both liberal and socialist. Leftist Muslims appear to be demoralized and suffering a loss of ideological inspiration, especially after the collapse of the Soviet bloc and the general retreat of socialism in Europe. Liberal Muslims seem to suffer from perceptions of American patronage, which is seen as a li-ability in itself, in addition to its negative association with perceptions of total American bias in favor of Israel in the Arab-Israeli conflict.

The discourse is also distorted by prevailing conditions of political op-pression in many countries of the region, which, in turn, inhibit communica-tion and public debate, especially with respect to any subject matter deemed by security forces to be "sensitive" or controversial. Denied access to the mostly state-owned media, the Islamists seek political support for their cause by preaching at mosques and other "religious" locations and occasions, as well as using their own media (tapes and publications). Islamists are also very effective in generating support through the provision of social and health ser-vices to the target communities. Their opponents lack the organization and orientation to use these means but may have better access to newspapers, as and when permitted by the government, which are not read by the illiter-ate majority of the population. Thus, the two sides rarely interact directly between themselves or with each other's constituencies among the public at large.

A sense of mutual hostility and suspicion is intensified, it seems, by a lack of conceptual common ground: while Islamists speak of Shari'a and the revival of the glorious Islamic tradition, the frame of reference of their opponents is modern notions of constitutionalism, democracy, and human rights. Consequently, there are not only growing polarization and miscom-munication between the two sides, and between each of them and the public constituency of the other, but their respective positions are also likely to be seen as contradictory or irreconcilable. The Islamic public at large is therefore presented with a stark choice: either Islam and Shariʿa or democracy and human rights, without discussion or explanation of why there must be a choice or why the choice must be framed in these terms in particular.

Moreover, perceptions of a wider context of a historical confrontation with the West seem to reinforce this stark choice. Islamists tend to point to Western support for democracy and human rights as a ploy of exploitation and domination. Liberal Muslims, on the other hand, are discouraged by Western double standards, as reflected, for example, in its domineering behavior in the Gulf War of 1991 in contrast to its failure to act in Bosnia.

The most significant consequence of this wider context for our purposes here is that issues of identity and authenticity are seen as of paramount importance in a fundamental geopolitical confrontation. Thus, the Islamists' discourse often seems to be more about the *right* to define the identity of the community and the duty to protect it against hostile non-Muslims aliens and, perhaps more important, against subversion by corrupt Westernized elites or heretics and renegade Muslims than about the actual meaning of that identity and its relevance in the modern national and international context. Having succeeded in emphasizing the "Islamic" dimension of that identity over all other ethnic, cultural, economic, and political elements, the Islamists now claim a monopoly over Islamic authenticity and the authority to define and defend the identity of the community in those terms.

In their present defensive mode, on the other hand, opponents of the Islamists appear to be more concerned with defending themselves against charges of treason and subversion than with contesting the Islamists' right to define and defend the identity of the community in question. The very act of contesting the Islamist definition of the identity of the community and monopoly of Islamic authenticity is seen as corroboration of the charge, rather than as an attempt to incorporate other elements that may have been integral to that identity or to oppose its political manipulation. In this way, the boundaries become more important than the content, and those threatened with exclusion become more concerned with asserting their conformity with the criteria of inclusion than with contesting those criteria and the way they are applied.

This confrontational and unproductive state of discourse, I suggest, is compounded further by two conceptual confusions. The first confusion is over the relationship between religion and the state in the Islamic context. The second confusion pertains to the relationship between rights and responsibilities in connection with conceptions of the individual and the community.

The first is more explicit and visible; the second is more implicit and less appreciated as a separate issue.

It is not possible to trace here the precise sources and chronology of the confusion about the relationship between religion and the state. It is clear, I would suggest, that this confusion evolved through a dialectical process since the middle of the last century when Muslim reformers began debating whether it is desirable to separate religion and state, or Islam and politics, in order to achieve rapid modernization. While the advocates of separation, which came to be known as secularism (*al ilmaniya*), cited lessons from European history and quoted Western political theory in support of their position, its opponents claimed that Islam allowed no distinction between religion and state.

The coercive and intrusive manner in which secularization was imposed by authoritarian regimes in Turkey and Iran after the end of the First World War, and attempts to do so in other parts of the Islamic World after the Second World War, aggravated the confusion and intensified the controversy over the issue. At present, Islamists present secularism as an antireligious concept designed to alienate Muslims from their religion and thereby secure and perpetuate their domination and exploitation by the West. Those who advocate separation of Islam and politics, they allege, are anti-Islamic subversive agents of alien cultures serving the interests of foreign powers. In this way, the Islamists seek to discredit their opponents while installing themselves as the acknowledged guardians of Islamic identity and authenticity.

Liberal and socialist Muslims, on the other hand, have traditionally failed to take an Islamic discourse seriously or to educate themselves in its concepts and techniques. Whether this was due to a belief that it was unnecessary to engage in such discourse or because of a fear that to do so would mean conceding the legitimacy and authority of the Islamist frame of reference, the fact of the matter is that an Islamic discourse has become, or is becoming, unavoidable in many Islamic countries. It is therefore important to clarify the relationship between religion and the state from an Islamic point of view.

The other serious conceptual confusion pertains to the relationship between rights and responsibilities in connection to conceptions of the individual and community. Following their premise of seeking modernization through the application of European models and political theory, Muslim reformers emphasized earlier in the twentieth century the need to protect individual liberties against encroachment by the state and community at large.

To counter that claim, Islamists now tend to emphasize the interests of the community over the rights of the individual.

This confusion is closely related to issues of identity, as well as to the relationship between religion and politics with direct consequences to freedom of belief. According to the Islamists, since Islam is the sole foundation of the identity of the community, the state must "regulate" freedom of belief as the essential criterion of membership in the community. By disputing this in favor of protecting individual freedom of belief, they charge, their secular (read, anti-Islamic) opponents are weakening the Islamic identity of the community and undermining the Islamic nature of the state.

In this way, such a confrontational discourse presents modern Islamic communities with a stark choice between "secular" individualism and "Islamic" communitarianism. As I will argue in the next section, the sharp dichotomy implicit in this choice is neither necessary from an Islamic religious point of view nor realistic or useful to make in practice.

Foundations of Religious Human Rights

In light of the previous discussion, it is clear that freedom of belief ought to be supported from an *Islamic religious* point of view because it is essential for the authenticity of religious belief and experience as such and for the vitality and relevance of an Islamic normative system to the lives of Muslims today. An equally valid and fundamental reason for such support is that freedom of belief is essential for the peace and stability of necessarily and permanently pluralistic national and international political communities.

The task set for this chapter is to examine both the positive and negative aspects of an Islamic frame of reference for religious rights *as human rights*. This evaluation should be done, first, with a view to evaluating the existence or absence, adequacy or inadequacy, of Islamic foundations for these rights. The second purpose of such an evaluation, I believe, is to seek ways of developing Islamic foundations for freedom of belief, to the extent that they are absent, and of promoting them to greater adequacy and stronger influence on Islamic law and behavior.

There is an obvious "advocacy" element in my perception of the second purpose of this task (also implicit throughout my analysis) in that I am not concerned with an "objective" or "impartial" evaluation of the situation, but rather with changing or supporting it in favor of better protection of human rights, including religious human rights. From my perspective as a Muslim who not only takes both Islam and human rights seriously but also believes them to be mutually supportive normative systems, the promotion of such a change is the point of the whole exercise.

The background, context, and some of the premises of my approach to this task have already been explained in the preceding sections. This final section offers a two-fold discussion. First, I shall briefly review the status of religious rights under Shari'a as commonly conceived in Islamic discourse today and assess that conception from a human rights point of view. Second, I will elaborate on a theory of stronger Islamic foundations for religious human rights with a view to promoting and enhancing the protection of these rights in Islamic countries today.

On the first count, the Shari'a scheme of religious rights provides that a person is essentially "free" to adopt or reject Islam, but certain consequences will follow from his/her choice:[20]

1. If a person chooses to become a Muslim, or is born and raised as a Muslim, then he or she will have full rights of citizenship in an Islamic state, subject to limitations against the rights of women (as conceived in modern constitutional and human rights law). However, once a Muslim or being officially classified as such, a person will be subject to the death penalty if he or she becomes an apostate, that is, one who persists in repudiating his or her faith in Islam. An apostate is also subjected to forfeiture of property, nullification of marriage, and other legal consequences.

2. If a person chooses to be or remain a Christian, Jew, or believer in another scriptural religion, as defined by Shari'a—one of *ahl al-kitab*, the People of the Book or believers in divine scripture who are called *dhimmis*—he or she will suffer certain limitations of rights as a subject of an Islamic state. There are differences as to the scope and extent of these limitations among various schools of thought and individual scholars of Shari'a, and the practice has also varied over time. The essential point is that *dhimmis* are not supposed to enjoy complete legal equality with Muslims.

3. If a person is neither a Muslim nor one of *ahl al-kitab*, as defined by Shari'a, then that person is deemed to be an unbeliever (*khafir* or *mushrik*). An unbeliever is not permitted to reside permanently, or even temporarily according to stricter interpretations, in peace as a free person within the territory of an Islamic state except under special

permission for safe conduct (*aman*). In theory, unbelievers should be offered the choice of adopting Islam, and if they reject it, they may either be killed in battle, enslaved, or ransomed if captured.

Compared to the legal and theological systems of other "state religions" of the past, it is clear that the Shariʿa scheme of religious rights was superior from a modern perspective of freedom of belief. Moreover, except for minor exceptions or relatively brief periods, such as the early Fatimi dynasty in Egypt in the tenth century past and present Islamic states have generally tended to adopt the least restrictive interpretation of these principles or to disregard them in favor of relatively greater freedom of belief.

But when judged by modern standards of human rights, the Shariʿa scheme is objectionable not only because of its limitations on freedom of belief for Muslim and non-Muslims alike but also in view of its very conception of civil and political rights on the basis of a religious classification of people. To illustrate briefly the first point, the capital crime of apostasy not only violates the right of a Muslim to adopt another faith or belief but can and has been used to punish Muslims who express unorthodox views that are deemed to be a repudiation of belief in Islam.[21] While limitations on the rights of non-Muslim believers clearly constitute serious discrimination on grounds of religion, the possibility of death or enslavement for an unbeliever is a total nullification of any notion of human rights in principle and content.

Moreover, the very notion of basing civil and political rights on a religious classification is inherently inconsistent with the premise of the universality of human rights, however "insignificant" the legal consequences of that universality may appear to be. I would, therefore, conclude that, although there are foundations for some religious rights in Shariʿa and in the practice of Islamic states past and present, that level of protection of freedom of belief does not offer a sufficient foundation for religious *human* rights.

Nevertheless, I suggest that it is possible to construct a coherent and conceptually valid theory of Islamic foundations of religious human rights based on the following elements. First, since Shariʿa is a historically conditioned *human* interpretation of the fundamental sources of Islam, alternative modern interpretations are possible. Second, a reconstruction of Shariʿa in support of Islamic foundations for religious human rights is imperative in view of the need for contesting and renegotiating Islamic identity and its normative system in the present circumstances of plurality of national and international political communities. Third, such a theory will be fully Islamic because it would be based on the text of the Qur'an as interpreted and accepted by Muslims in the present context, instead of applying Shari'a principles, which were the product of interpretation by earlier Muslims in their own historical context. To clarify these elements further, it is necessary to outline the hermeneutical premise of this theory.

Hermeneutics may be defined as the art or science of interpretation, especially of scriptural texts. In view of the inevitability of using human reason and action in understanding and implementing any text, as noted earlier, a hermeneutical process is necessary for understanding the purpose and normative content of a text like the Qur'an or the Bible.[22]

Each religion, or specific tradition within a religion, is supposed to have its own distinctive set of interpretative techniques and their underlying assumptions that are accepted as valid or authoritative by the adherents of the religion or tradition in question. In reality, however, there will be more than one competing hermeneutical framework, each of which is open to mutual challenge and reformulation among cobelievers. Thus, for example, the diversity of Sunni, Shi'a, and Sufi Muslim schools of thought signify differences in the hermeneutical framework, not only among Muslims in general but also among those who belong to each of the Islamic traditions.

Although the proponents of one Islamic interpretative framework would normally tend to characterize those of others as invalid or illegitimate, even un-Islamic, the only reasonable and practical way to settle such differences is for each side to present its case to the relevant community of believers as the ultimate arbiter and mediator between competing frameworks. This mediation would usually happen in the process of seeking the support and allegiance of the community, and the issue would be settled over time through the community's adoption or rejection of one point of view or another. But how does a particular type of Islamic interpretative framework emerge and prevail over others at a certain time?

The emergence of a new interpretative framework, I suggest, is normally a function of individual and collective orientation, that is to say, the conditioning of the existential or material circumstances of the person and the community in relation to the text. A Muslim, for example, would understand the text of the Qur'an and derive its normative implications in terms of his or her knowledge and experience of the world, including perceptions of self-interest in political, economic, and social context, and of the realities of intercommunal or international relations. A similar process operates at the communal level in that the prevalence or demise of an interpretative framework is normally a function of the collective orientation of the community as defined above, that is to say, the conditioning of the existential or material circumstances of the community at a given time.

This circumstantial quality does not mean that the process is either completely deterministic, in that interpretations are automatically determined by settled and immutable orientations, or wholly relativistic, in that religious texts are open to all and every type of interpretation. The process is not deterministic because individual and collective orientations are sometimes influenced by visions of change and transformation beyond the immediate conditioning of circumstances as perceived by the general population. Otherwise, there would be no opportunity for the emergence of radical ideas and social movements capable of transcending the conditioning of individual and communal circumstances, and indeed eventually transforming those circumstances themselves. Individuals and communities do exercise a choice in articulating, adopting, or rejecting one interpretative framework or another.

The process is not arbitrary and relativistic because the validity of a proposed interpretation is judged by a living community through serious discussion and deliberation. The proponents of each interpretation will, of course, seek to win the support of the community through the use of what they claim are Islamic concepts and arguments, but it is the community that will ultimately make that determination. In practice, the community may follow the advice of its political or opinion leaders, and those whose proposals were thereby rejected should accept that decision until they can either win those leaders over or persuade the community not to follow their advice. The alternative is to seek to impose their interpretation on the community, which will only be counterproductive in the end.

In the process of emergence and adoption or rejection of interpretative frameworks, there is the factor of "historical contingency," which refers to the notion that an idea will not emerge or prevail prematurely. But since historical contingency can only be judged in retrospect, who is to predict with any certainty whether or not an idea is in fact premature? The emergence of an idea and the ability of its proponents to propagate it are indications of the ripening of historical contingency, but only time can tell whether the circumstances of the period were conducive to the conditioning and/or individual and collective choice that would allow it to prevail. In fact, as illustrated by the history of major religions, including Islam, social and political resistance is to be expected and should not be taken as conclusive evidence of the final rejection of an idea, however radical or innovative it may appear to be.

To illustrate briefly the application of this analysis to the subject of Islamic foundations of religious human rights, I would cite verse 137 of Chapter 4, which can be translated as follows:

> Those who believed, then disbelieved, believed again and disbelieve once more, and become even more disbelieving, God shall not forgive them or guide them on the right path.

Although the majority of early Islamic scholars interpreted this verse as consistent with the imposition of the death penalty for apostasy,[23] I would see it as conclusively excluding any possibility of punishment for disbelief in this life, since there is no mention of such punishment in this verse or anywhere else in the Qur'an. The difference between my understanding of this verse and that of early scholars, which is still advocated by some Islamists today, reflects divergence in interpretative frameworks, but neither is more or less Islamic because of that reason alone. Disagreement between these frameworks and their normative implications should be settled by the community of Muslims at large in light of the Islamic argumentation presented on behalf of each position.

The example of apostasy is particularly appropriate for the purposes of my analysis because it also involves the conceptual confusions mentioned earlier, namely, the question of the relationship between Islam and the state and that between rights and responsibilities. In the absence of Qur'anic authority, as noted earlier, the punishment of apostasy under Shari'a is based on reports of Sunna. But the support of Sunna for this punishment is valid only on the assumption of a certain type of unity between Islam and the state and a particular view of rights and responsibilities that conditions the former on performance of the latter. Sunna can be understood to support imposing the death penalty for apostasy only if disbelief is equated with high treason on the assumption that citizenship is based on belief in Islam. That assumption, in turn, is valid only under a view of entitlement to the rights of citizenship on the condition of satisfactory performance of the responsibilities of belief as a prerequisite for membership in the community whose members enjoy those rights.[24] Moreover, this reasoning is premised on a conception of freedom of belief as a conditional right of citizens and not as a human right to which all human beings are entitled.

While this reasoning and its underlying premise were valid, in my view, in the historical context of the formative stages of Shari'a, they are no longer valid today. The individual and collective orientations of Muslims today, I believe, are probably different from those of earlier generations because of the radical transformation of existential and material circumstances of today compared to those of the past. In contrast to the localized traditional existence of past Islamic societies, Muslims today live in multireligious nation-states that are fully incorporated into a globalized world of political, economic, and security interdependence and are constantly experiencing the effects of mutual social/cultural influence with non-Islamic societies. While some individual Muslims may still choose to advocate traditional notions of community and conditionality of rights, the reality of the pluralistic national and international political communities of today supports entitlement to freedom of belief as a human right rather than a conditional right of membership of a religious community.

In support of the view that freedom of belief is a human right to which all human beings are entitled by virtue of their humanity, rather than a right conditioned upon the performance of certain responsibilities of membership in a community, I would note that the right is needed and useful only in the former sense of universal human rights rather than in the latter sense of conditional rights. If the benefits of freedom of belief are available only to believers who are accepted as such, what is the rationale for having a right to freedom of belief at all? The right to freedom of belief is needed, and can be claimed, only by nonbelievers and believers who are not accepted as such by the community in question. I would also recall here the argument made earlier about the importance of freedom of belief, including the right of dissent, for the vitality and relevance of the religion itself and its normative system.

Finally, I wish to add the following suggested clarification of the above-mentioned conceptual confusion of the relationship between religion and the state and that of the individual and community in the Islamic context. In my view, notions of complete unity of religion and state, on the one hand, and their strict separation in a community of believers, on the other, are both conceptual fallacies, which also lack support in Islamic history, including in the articulation and implementation of Shariʿa itself.

The organic relationship between religion and politics is too obvious to deny and is not problematic except when it results in restrictions on the legal and human rights of citizens on the ground of their faith or belief. Even with regard to the state, religion can legitimately play a ceremonial or symbolic role in public life. What is objectionable is for religious beliefs to be constituted as the basis of political authority and legal system of a nation-state in ways that, for example, condition or base legal and human rights on faith or belief or gender. To do so would immediately repudiate the survival of the political community, as well as undermine the integrity and authenticity of religious belief and practice.

It is important to inject this clarification into the current discourse about rights and human rights in Islamic countries today, because, as indicated earlier, the protagonists tend to misconceive the issues and unduly restrict the options open to Islamic societies. Instead of facing Islamic societies with a false choice between total unity or complete separation of Islam and politics/state, participants in the discourse should seek to clarify and articulate a formulation of the relationship in ways that satisfy an Islamic sense of identity and self-determination without violating internationally recognized human rights norms.

It is also important to emphasize that secularism, as practiced in many parts of the world (and not only the West), is not anti-religion. On the contrary, secularism was conceived and applied in parts of Western Europe and the United States in order to protect freedom of belief and promote religious piety.[25] Moreover, there is nothing in the concept and practice of secularism to justify associating it as such with the exploitation and domination of others. Western powers did not colonize and seek to dominate Islamic countries *because* the former were/are secular, or *through* secularizing the latter countries. Nevertheless, the existence of these misconceptions must be acknowledged and addressed by those who are concerned that the relationship between Islam and politics or the state is not only compatible but also fully supportive of universal human rights, including religious human rights.

Conclusion: Realities and Prospects

Islamic Shari'a and history present a mixed picture regarding foundations of religious human rights, whereby the theory of the freedom of belief was comparatively superior to those of other state religions in the past and the practice was generally better than the theory; both are no longer acceptable from a modern human rights point of view. Strong Islamic foundations for religious human rights are conceptually possible, but their practical prospects depend on the outcome of the current discourse in Islamic countries.

Although I strongly believe in the Islamic validity of the theory presented in this chapter, I would neither suggest that it is the only possible Islamic foundation of religious human rights nor claim that it is necessarily widely accepted as such in practice. In my view, the more Islamic foundations for religious human rights one can find the better, for these multiple foundations will support and reinforce each other in promoting these rights as universal human rights. My theory may not be consciously accepted as such, but all its factual elements and essential logical premises are familiar to educated Muslims and scholars of Islam.

By addressing it to Muslims, I hope that my theory will contribute to promoting an Islamic commitment to religious human rights and thereby influence current and future practice in favor of greater respect and protection of these rights in Islamic countries today. A better understanding by non-Muslims of the prospects and problems of Islamic foundations for religious human rights, together with efforts from other religious perspectives, should contribute to enabling believers and nonbelievers alike to collaborate in a global project to protect and promote universal religious human rights.[26]

Chapter 6

Cultural Transformation and Normative Consensus on the Best Interest of the Child

The premise of this analysis is that normative universality in human rights, including the rights of the child, should neither be taken for granted nor achieved through the "universalization" of the norms and institutions of dominant cultures, whether at the local, regional, or international levels. In relation to the definition and implementation of the best interests of the child principle, this chapter emphasizes the need to maximize opportunities for contesting the nature and rationale of action regarding children from as many different perspectives as possible. This should include rigorous analysis to see who is taking the action in question, on what basis, and for whose benefit; how it affects children at large or groups thereof; and so forth. Particular attention should be given to understanding the nature, context, and dynamics of power relations between and among the various actors and subjects of the action in question and possibilities of altering or adjusting those power relations.

Thus, the essential feature in developing specific strategies for substantive normative consensus is the need to enable alternative perceptions and interpretations of cultural norms and institutions to emerge and compete with dominant ones. Such procedural universality, this chapter concludes, is both readily achievable and conducive to the realization of genuine normative consensus on the definition and implementation of principles such as the best interests of the child.

Introduction

The Convention on the Rights of the Child (the Child Convention) reflects sensitivity to the impact of contextual factors and cultural considerations on the norms it purports to set. The Convention is a far more multidimensional instrument than is implied by characterizations that would, whether in support or criticism, portray its text as mandating a particular outcome to global problems of child abuse or neglect. It could be argued, on the other hand, that flexibility and recognition of diversity may either hide an unbridgeable normative schism or lead to a slippery slope of persistent indecision and confusion. In the end, it might be said, there may be much apparent consensus on very little substance.

For example, all would readily agree that the child must be protected from "all forms of physical or mental violence" (Art. 19.1), that school discipline should be "administered in a manner consistent with the child's human dignity" (Art. 28.2), and that the child should not be subjected to "torture or other cruel, inhuman or degrading treatment or punishment" (Art. 37.a). How should these "universal norms" be interpreted and implemented in relation to certain types of corporal punishment that are routinely used by parents and school teachers in many parts of the world, with the complete approval of their local cultures? Are these provisions of the Child Convention intended to prohibit the use of all forms of corporal punishment, and if so, how can such prohibition be enforced in practice?

This sort of tension between the requirements of contextual diversity and cultural specificity, on the one hand, and the dangers of normative ambiguity or confusion, on the other, is inherent to any project that purports to set truly universal norms, especially in relation to a subject like the rights of the child. Without due regard to the consequences or implications of such diversity and specificity, there is little prospect of global normative consensus; but if the dangers of ambiguity or confusion are not addressed, the consensus thereby achieved might be superficial and perfunctory. While maintaining that this inherent tension cannot be eliminated altogether, I would argue that it can and should be mediated and somewhat contained through certain procedures and processes. The basic thesis of this analysis may be summarized in the following propositions:

1. Generally speaking, it is important to seek to formulate, interpret, and implement all internationally recognized human rights in their proper cultural context. While precluding arbitrary imposition of a specific definition of principles such as "the best interest of the child," respect for cultural and contextual diversity should not lead to normative indecision and confusion. This tension can and should be mediated

through the development of certain safeguards for the process by which this clause is defined and implemented in any given setting.

2. Although clearly identifiable and distinguishable from each other, human cultures are also characterized by their own internal diversity, propensity to change, and mutual influence. These characteristics can be used to promote normative consensus within and among cultures through processes of cultural transformation.

3. Given the inherent diversity and contestability of cultural attitudes toward matters such as the best interest of the child, the meaning and implications claimed for this principle in a certain society at a given point in time should not be taken as final or conclusive. Rather, the meaning and implications of the best interest principle in any society should be open to challenge, reformulation, and refinement through the processes of internal discourse and cross-cultural dialogue.

4. In due course, these processes of discourse and dialogue will promote genuine international consensus on the meaning and implications of the principle of the best interests of the child. Thus, the rigorous implementation of agreed-upon procedures and processes for defining this clause in various contexts will lead to a substantive common standard or level of achievement in relation to the best interests of the child, without violating the integrity of local cultures or encroaching on the sovereignty of the various peoples of the world.

5. Although participants in the processes of definition and specification of this clause will probably have their own normative agenda, they can all share a commitment to agreed procedures and processes that are conducive to developing international consensus in this regard.

According to these propositions, my commitment to the principles set by the Child Convention, as I understand them, should be distinguished from my advocacy of the proposed methodology. While the former would be the subject of my personal contribution as a participant in the process, I see the latter as necessary for the integrity and efficacy of consensus building among all participants. My wish that the process would lead to the adoption of my views on this issue should not detract from my commitment to the procedure and its safeguards. If accepted, however, this or any other proposed methodology should be institutionalized and protected against violation by those who may not like its outcome at any given point in time.

To explain the application of this thesis to the principle of the best interests of the child, I will discuss what might be called the "paradox of normative universality" and possible ways of resolving it in a given setting or context. In light of that discussion, I will review some relevant studies on the Arab world, propose a tentative model for defining the best-interest principle in cultural context, and illustrate its application in relation to child labor, corporal punishment, and female circumcision.

The Paradox of Normative Universality

Modern international human rights, such as the rights of the child, are premised on the assumption of universal normative consensus on who is a human being and what is due to a human person by virtue of his or her humanity, without distinction on grounds of race, gender, religion, and so forth. This notion is certainly very attractive and comforting. Upon reflection, however, one can see that genuine normative universality is a somewhat paradoxical concept that is yet to be realized in real and concrete terms.

To appreciate the paradoxical and problematic nature of such normative universality, it is important to distinguish it from purely formal agreement between governmental delegates who negotiate international human rights treaties. Delegates are usually more concerned with negotiating the official positions of their governments into what I would call "expedient ambiguity" than with achieving conceptual clarity on the basis of the realistic beliefs, attitudes, and practices of their national constituencies. Moreover, it is important to note that the circumstances under which even this level of official universality is pursued are normally far from consistent with its purported premise of equal sovereignty and proportionality of the negotiating positions of the parties.

The delegates of governments from the global South who flocked to New York and Geneva since independence to take part in the drafting, adoption, and implementation of "universal" human rights norms were not only late participants in a predetermined process but also operated with a fraction of the human and material resources available to their counterparts from the global North.[1] Delegates from the North, moreover, operated with concepts and mechanisms that evolved from their own political, cultural, and ideological history and enjoyed the wide support of their national governments and populations in this regard. In contrast, delegates from the South not only lacked that sense of familiarity, authenticity, and support at home but may also have had no alternative positions to present since their national constituencies did not have the chance to articulate different proposals out of their indigenous experiences and in response to the realities of their own contexts.

Although the situation may have been relatively better for some countries or recently improved for others, serious inequality in negotiating positions and other concerns still persist for the majority of countries from the South. As a matter of international law, of course, all states are bound by duly ratified treaties, but one must look beyond formalistic obligation in order to appreciate the realistic prospects of implementation of those treaties.

The elusiveness of universal normative consensus can readily be appreciated in view of the diversity of cultural and contextual realities that condition people's beliefs and behavior in daily life. With respect to the rights of the child, there are bound to be significant differences between the perceptions of childhood and circumstances affecting behavior toward children in the South and the North, as well as within these regions. The issue here is not a value judgment on which is the more humane perception of childhood or the better way of treating children. Rather, it is simply to emphasize that different perceptions and circumstances are bound to influence people's beliefs and behavior in this regard. This point is especially relevant, for example, to the responsibilities, rights, and duties of parents and others to provide direction and guidance for the child, recognized by Articles 5, 14.2, and 18.1 of the Child Convention.

Parents in the South would probably try to have as many children as they can because of the risk of loss through infant and child mortality. In contrast, parents in the North would probably plan to have the number of children they wish (for personal, financial, or lifestyle reasons), in the expectation that their children will survive and receive good education, health care, and so forth. For parents in the South, children are to be prepared for taking care of members of the extended family—that is, for providing private "social security" for many in sickness and old age. Children of the Northern "nuclear family" are expected to "move out and make their own lives" when they grow up, leaving their parents to enjoy the privacy and independence of retirement on their pension and/or life savings. These stereotypes are obviously not universal models of the situation in the South or North, but they certainly reflect dominant sociological norms and assumptions that appear to underlie public policy in these regions.

There are also bound to be significant differences among perceptions of how to raise children to uphold and live by certain values, depending on the

worldview and religious beliefs of parents or the cultural norms of their societies. What would be important for Muslim parents to instill in their children
is likely to differ in some significant ways from that of Buddhist, Hindu, or
agnostic parents. Within each religious or cultural group, economic, educational, and other differentials will probably influence parents' objectives and
expectations for their children, thereby affecting child-rearing practices.

Given the wide range of contextual specificity and cultural relativity between and within various regions of the world, how can normative universality be achieved regarding the rights of the child in general or the best interests
principle in particular? In view of the above-noted need for attention to the actual beliefs and behavior of parents and other people concerned with children
throughout the world, this issue of universality raises numerous questions.
Where does one look for and how does one verify claims of such universality? By whose criteria or according to which philosophical framework can the
universality of the norms in question be declared or verified? To the extent
that they can be shown to exist at any point in time, how can such norms be
elaborated and specified for daily implementation in different contexts?

Part of the basic problem here is that any conceptualization of the issues
will probably be limited by the cultural conditioning and/or intellectual and
professional orientation of its author. It is unrealistic, for example, to expect
a Western lawyer to know and account for the implications of Islamic jurisprudence to his or her analysis or for an Islamic jurist to appreciate and apply an analysis rooted in liberal thought and European or Anglo-American
legal theory. This tendency does not mean that the project of normative universality on the best interest principle should be abandoned because of the
difficulty of cross-cultural communication and understanding. Rather, my
objective here is to emphasize the need to take that difficulty into account in
seeking normative universality.

Universality and Cultural Transformation

As suggested elsewhere,[2] the paradox of normative universality can be mediated through processes of internal discourse and cross-cultural dialogue
to broaden and deepen genuine and substantive consensus over the formulation, interpretation, and implementation of international human rights
norms. The basic premise and concept of this approach may be briefly summarized as follows:

Global cultural diversity reflects the dominance of certain interpretations of the major norms and institutions of each culture at a given point in time. Although the proponents of dominant interpretations normally present them as the *only* "authentic" or "legitimate" position of the culture on the issue in question, different positions can usually be presented within a certain range of possibilities. This quality is due to the fact that cultural norms and institutions are characterized by varying degrees of ambivalence and flexibility, in order to accommodate the different needs and circumstances of the population. Cultures also change over time in response to external influence and internal demands.

There will always, therefore, be other perspectives that can be articulated to challenge dominant interpretations and thereby present alternative views of the culture's position on a particular issue at any given time. The prevalence of one perspective or another is, therefore, open to challenge through change or adjustment in the dynamics of power relations within the culture. It should be noted here that the struggle over cultural resources can take place through action or behavior as well as through verbal articulation. The absence of particular manifestations of such struggle, or the lack of certain forms of challenge and contestation of prevailing interpretations, does not mean that cultural transformation is not happening.

To effectively change the beliefs, attitudes, and behavior of a given population, the proposed alternative perspective must be perceived by that population to be consistent with the *internal* criteria of legitimacy of the culture and appreciated as relevant to their needs and expectations. It would, therefore, seem to follow that the proponents of change must not only have a credible claim to being *insiders* to the culture in question but also use internally valid arguments or means of presentation. In other words, the presentation and adoption of alternative perspectives can best be achieved through a coherent *internal discourse*.

This tendency does not mean that outsiders to the culture have no influence on the processes of internal discourse. Outsiders can influence an internal situation in many ways. For example, they can engage in their own internal discourse, thereby enabling participants in one culture to point to similar processes taking place in other cultures; they can support the right of the internal participants to challenge prevailing perceptions, while avoiding overt interference, as this will undermine the credibility of internal actors; or, they can engage in a cross-cultural dialogue to exchange insights and strategies of internal discourse.

Cross-cultural dialogue can also seek to promote universality at a theoretical or conceptual level by highlighting moral and philosophical commonalities of human cultures and experiences. For example, the Golden Rule (treating others as one would wish to be treated by them), which is found in some formulation or another in all the major cultural traditions of the world, can be presented as a universal moral foundation of human rights norms. This principle of reciprocity could provide universal rationale for human rights, as those rights that one would claim for oneself must, therefore, be conceded to others. But efforts to articulate shared values and principles must be founded on mutual respect and sensitivity to the integrity of other cultures, especially in view of colonial and postcolonial power relations between the North and South.

The Dynamics of Internal Discourse

As applied to the principle of the best interests of the child, this approach advocates criteria and procedural safeguards for the *process* by which the best interests of the child are identified, challenged, and changed or refined within a specific culture, or between different cultures, at a certain point in time. Given the multiplicity of perspectives regarding the meaning and implications of the best-interest principle within each culture, the main issue is how to regulate the relevant processes of discourse and dialogue in various policy and decision-making settings. The sharing of insights and experiences of such internal discourses will, I suggest, help to mediate over time cultural and contextual differences and thereby produce common standards on the principle of the best interests of the child. In pursuing these processes, the following considerations should be taken into account.

First, the scope and dynamics of the popular participation assumed by the concept of internal discourse are problematic in several respects. For example, while it may appear that there should be no limits on participation, it is unlikely that all segments of a population would have an even relatively equal or proportionate capacity to participate in this discourse in the normal course of events. To maximize participation, discourse should include nonverbal formulations since wide segments of the population are disinclined to verbal articulation of their beliefs and attitudes. The question is, therefore, how to bridge the communication gap between the *words* of the intellectuals and the *world* of their constituencies whose behavior is the central concern of this analysis.

Second, the nature of internal discourse would suggest that the most effective strategy is to promote change through the transformation of existing folk models rather than seek to challenge and replace them immediately. This strategy is successfully applied, for example, by Islamic fundamentalist groups in several Islamic countries today. The fundamentalists are effective because they apparently confirm the existing beliefs and practices of their constituencies while seeking to unite and mobilize them into "radical" action in order to realize effectively what the fundamentalists claim already to be the goals and expectations of those constituencies. Although the fundamentalists are, in my view, actually seeking to transform the beliefs and practices of their constituencies in this process, that objective is skillfully hidden in the rhetoric of a "continuity of tradition" and a "return to the Golden Past."

In contrast, the liberal intellectuals of Islamic societies appear to be, or are presented as, challenging the folk models of their societies and seeking to replace them by alien concepts and norms. This negative perception may be partially due to the rather abstract verbal articulation employed by those intellectuals and their own lifestyle, which is often distant from the daily realities of the population at large. It may well be true that the substance of the message of the liberal intellectuals is not as far removed from the essence of the "tradition" as it is often presented by their fundamentalist opponents. But this fact may not be easily appreciated by the masses of Muslims in the present dynamics of verbal and nonverbal discourse.

The point of this slight digression is to emphasize that the more one is *perceived* to be confirming existing beliefs and practices rather than challenging them, the better are the prospects of wide acceptance and implementation of one's proposals. Since perception is of the essence here, it may be possible, through internal discourse and cross-cultural dialogue as explained above, to achieve the gradual transformation of the same folk models toward greater conformity with international standards. Does this mean that folk models, or elements thereof, can always be reconciled with some minimum standards set by the Child Convention or required by the best interests of the child principle? What should happen when reconciliation is clearly not possible through the proposed methodology?

Process and Purpose

It is certainly true that there is an underlying tension between process and purpose in the proposed approach. The rationale of internal discourse and cross-cultural dialogue presupposes that these processes should freely define their own purpose. If they are allowed to take their full course, however, it is conceivable that these processes may lead to conclusions at variance with international concepts and norms of the rights of the child in general or the best interests principle in particular. Should the processes of internal discourse and cross-cultural dialogue be allowed to define and specify this principle freely, whatever that may lead to in each context, or are these processes only expected to operate within the framework of certain standards already set by the Child Convention?

It may be argued that it is possible to modify or clarify the objectionable aspects of the folk model through internal discourse in order to bring it into greater conformity with the Convention's minimum standards. This argument is premised on the belief that more conformity will in fact be achieved through close analysis and imaginative reinterpretation of the folk models in question and more sensitive presentation of the relevant standards of the Convention. But since there is no way of verifying whether this will actually happen in practice, except through the actual application of this methodology over time, one must admit the possibility of irreconcilable differences between folk models and the standards set by the Child Convention.

Alternatively, it may be argued that folk models should be made the basis for any standards set by the Child Convention because the former is the basis of the legitimacy of the latter. From this point of view, the standards of the Convention should be defined by folk models rather than the reverse. However, one may then wonder about the utility of an international treaty on this or any other human rights subject, if all it can do is conform to existing folk norms and practices. To make folk models the point of reference for international standards is problematic in other respects. For example, those who make such a "folk-centric" claim would readily concede, I suspect, that folk practices should be discontinued if they are shown to be harmful to the physical health of children. The problem, they might respond, is that it is difficult to demonstrate the universal validity of a determination that a folk practice is "harmful" to children when the alleged negative consequences are psychological or sociological rather than physical. This line of thinking is flawed, in my view, for two reasons. First, it draws too sharp a distinction between various types of harm that in fact tend to interact and overlap. How can one distinguish, for instance, between psychological, sociological, and physical consequences of circumcision for the girl child? Second, the folk-centric position assumes that folk models do in fact provide settled and definitive criteria for evaluating international standards, which is unlikely to be the case in practice. What criteria does a practice such as female circumcision set for evaluating international standards and according to which alleged rationale of the practice?

Instead of a simplistic dichotomy between folk models and international standards, which installs one as the definitive norm by which the other is to be judged, I propose a dynamic interaction between the two. On the one hand, international standards should be premised on fundamental global ethical, social, and political values and institutions and thereby have an inspiring, elevating, and informative influence on popular perceptions of existing folk models. These models and their rationale, on the other hand, should be seen as a source of the values and institutions that legitimize the international standards. Both aspects of this dynamic interaction, I suggest, should be mediated through the processes of discourse and dialogue outlined earlier.

The Best Interests Principle in Arab Discourse

It is misleading, especially in view of the premise and analysis of this chapter, to speak of the cultural context of the best interest principle in terms of regional or even national classification. There is very little cultural uniformity in countries like the Sudan or between, for example, Somalia, Syria, and Morocco, which are all said to be parts of the so-called Arab world. Even characterizing these or other countries as "Arab" may be objectionable to some segments of their population. Yet official policies are usually drawn, and purported to be implemented, on national and/or regional basis. The following review may, therefore, be useful but is presented as subject to this caveat and pending more discriminating analysis than I can offer here.

Issues of Description and Characterization

Any intelligent attempt to analyze an issue or to propose a solution for a problem must, of course, begin with a clear and accurate description and characterization of the issue or problem in question. However, such description and characterization would themselves be premised on a certain conceptual framework or influenced by a particular intellectual or cultural orientation. For example, a major Arab League study of the basic needs of the child in the Arab world, by Ismail Sabri Abdalla, is premised on the view that the child is born into an economic, social, and cultural environment that determines to a great extent his or her capabilities at the time of birth. These capabilities develop subsequently in accordance with the same determinants. Thus, Abdalla maintains that the situation of the child should not be discussed in isolation from general economic, social, and cultural backwardness (the term he uses) of the family and society in Arab countries.[3] The study then proceeds to describe, on the basis of twenty country case studies from the region, aspects of the social environment of the child and family in terms of, among other things, rural, nomadic, and urban settings; income levels; physical and cultural environments; social conditions of mothers and the family in general; and questions of basic services for the child.[4]

On the basis of these studies, Abdalla summarizes the state of the Arab child (as of 1980) as being of an environment where children constitute a high percentage of total population but are normally born to illiterate parents and suffer a high rate of mortality. Growing urbanization and modernization are diminishing the role of family in child rearing, and there is a very low degree of social awareness about problems of childhood.[5] He then concludes that Arab development efforts to date have been characterized by the adoption of a Western concept that did not differentiate between development and westernization. Consequently, the concepts and methods for determining the basic needs of the child in the Arab world are drawn in essence from Western societies, despite the clear difference between the conditions of advanced industrialized societies and the actual conditions of underdevelopment of the Arab world, including the oil-rich countries. Westernization exposes children to the shock of conflict between traditional family values and Western modern values, which are encouraged by the mass media and reflect an increasing consumerism. Even if they pretend to do otherwise, Abdalla maintains, the effect of the local media is to instill these Western values.

Following a critique of the methods of delivering basic services to children, Abdalla emphasizes the need for innovative new models of basic services founded on a realistic evaluation of the real needs of society and primarily relying on its own resources.[6] In his view, basic services should be presented in an integrated comprehensive manner and provided through popularly legitimate institutions that are frequented by people in their routine daily lives, such as schools, hospitals, and mosques. He suggests that the assumption that prevailing norms of "under-developed" or poor societies are necessarily archaic and obstacles to development would be valid only if development is completely identified with westernization, a view he rejects.

On the question of child labor, for example, Abdalla notes that, despite the existence of laws that prohibit child labor below a certain age and restrict it at other ages, many children continue to work out of economic and social need. In his view, this discrepancy is due to the fact that official standards are based on Western views, although strict separation between education and work is neither desirable nor realistic in Arab societies. Rather than calling for its total abolition, he suggests that official policies should only be directed at preventing child labor from being exploitative or dangerous to the physical and psychological health of the child. Child labor should be directed toward enhancing the capabilities and skills of children and linked to academic education. Education itself should seek to end the dichotomy between manual and intellectual work.[7]

As clearly shown in another Arab League study by Tahir Labib, however, the very concept of "basic needs of the child" should be clarified. For example, people assume that the needs of the child are obvious, but they are in fact thinking of services (which are the means for satisfying needs) rather than the needs themselves.[8] Some of the needs ascribed to social groups are, in fact, the needs of supervisory bodies. The "establishment," in its various social, economic, and political forms and levels, tends to neglect those needs that it is incapable or unwilling to satisfy while purporting to create needs that it claims to satisfy. It is, therefore, important to distinguish between real needs as perceived by the people concerned and artificial or invented needs identified or specified by others.

Children, and maybe even their parents, have no voice to articulate their own needs, *as perceived by themselves*, and do not constitute pressure groups to demand the satisfaction of those needs. The child does not determine his or her own needs; instead, these needs are defined by the needs of others (parents, school, the state, and so forth). Thus, if the need of others for the child is weak or inadequate, that weakness would be reflected in perceptions and articulations of the "needs of the child," leading to neglect or other adverse effects on the child. The unsatisfactory state of the child in Arab societies might therefore raise questions about the real need of these societies for the child, despite claims that the needs of the child are a first priority.

Labib argues that bureaucracy in the Arab world lacks intellectual initiative and might even be anti-intellectual, on the grounds that its work is administrative and directly practical, not allowing for conceptual thinking. The typical bureaucrat may not therefore appreciate the complexity of the issues involved in making and implementing sound policies on the needs of the child. Moreover, with the persistent political instability of the region, each new government tends to modify priorities and amend lists of needs of, and services for, the child in order to show how different it is from the previous government. In this way, the needs of the child are "modified," while the status quo remains unchanged.

The relationship between the needs of the child and those of others is unavoidable, but one should be aware of the nature and implications of this relationship in evaluating formulations of the needs of the child and their corresponding projects and services. For example, Labib wonders whether child-care facilities are part of the needs of the child or of his or her mother, whether or not she is working regular hours out of the home. I take this question as indicating that a confusion between the two perceptions of "needs," or between need and service, would affect the prospects of satisfaction. Thus, the perception that child-care facilities are a need of mothers who work regular hours outside the home, coupled with a social attitude or policy that mothers should stay at home to take care of children, will probably diminish the prospects of the provision of adequate child-care facilities. In contrast, if child-care facilities are accepted as a genuine need of the child, independently from that of the mother and regardless of whether or not she works regular hours outside the home, the situation might be different.

According to Labib, since needs have a contextual social content, it is important to know who determines that content. Children are not a social sector or a coherent group as such because they have different social origins and relationships. Thus, what is taken to be the needs of children might in fact be class or sectarian needs. While essential needs, such as health and food, appear universal (though they too have their social and political content), the objectives, content, and forms of other needs, such as those relating to education, literature, and arts, cannot be divorced from the social and political structure of society. Since differentiation and its causes or basis are present in all human societies and since the child must bear the consequences of such differentiation within the framework of his or her family and social group, the question arises: the needs of *which* child are we talking about? Unless this question is taken into account and addressed, some social groups would be allowed to determine the needs of the children of other groups in ways that would in fact be for the benefit of the determining group and its own children, rather than of society in general or of all children at large.[9]

In another study, Mahmud Ahmed Musa discusses what he calls the problematic of the negative characteristics of the Arab person and reviews the debate over the desired alternative.[10] According to Musa and the authors he cites, negative Arab characteristics include determinism, excessive submission to authority figures, being backward-looking, emphasizing the form rather than substance, copying rather than creating, close-mindedness, learning by heart rather than understanding, analysis, and discussion. While some authors speculate on ideal alternative models, others emphasize the need for popular participation in the development of appropriate models. All agree that the reconstitution of the Arab person must primarily rely on the nature and objectives of education.

Musa criticizes Arab educational systems as essentially defined by former colonial administrations and expanded after independence without radical change in objectives, structures, and content. Massive quantitative expansion led to the lowering of standards and highly competitive formal academic education. There is also little attention to building character and qualities of organization, discipline, love of knowledge, enjoyment of work, appreciation of art and beauty, independence, and initiative. All this is a reflection of Arab societies and their political regimes, which affects negatively the orientation and character of educated people, for instance, by creating unrealistic and inappropriate work expectations and leading to a tendency to refuse manual labor and migrate to cities to look for office work.[11]

The author links this phenomenon to a critique of social-value systems as reactionary or backward-looking and deterministic, defensive (seeking refuge in the past) rather than evolutionary and forward-looking, and dominated by tribal patriarchal systems based on the values of unquestioning obedience and submission. All this is reflected in the educational system, which emphasizes submission, obedience, and uncritical acceptance of the views of others, without real conviction. What is required, therefore, is reforming the educational system so that it can resist dominant value systems.[12] Musa calls for an independent view of total development that emanates from a unified national perspective and rational methodology. Social transformation should be achieved through socialization processes, either by enhancing the efficacy of existing educational systems or by reforming them.[13] He calls for the intelligentsia to engage the masses and popular institutions in order to challenge "false-consciousness" created by dominant social and political systems to perpetuate their own power. The author reviews several studies on education and false-consciousness in Arab countries (analysis of content of textbooks and school syllabi) and notes both the negative impact of oral traditions in perpetuating stereotypes of male and female—father and mother—role models and the influence of the mass media in creating false consciousness.[14]

The studies by Abdalla and Musa (which are regionally significant and representative) reflect a tension between commitment to indigenous perspectives and self-reliance, on the one hand, and the realities of underdevelopment and dependency of the region on Western intellectual and technical resources and expertise, on the other. For example, while national and regional analysis of Abdalla's study emphasizes contextual and cultural specificity and the need for indigenous solutions and expertise, the "scientific" information on which he relies is Western.[15] This is perhaps why the measures he proposes for satisfying the basic needs of the child sound so abstract and unrealistic.[16] Authors from the region are cited in Musa's critique of Arab educational systems, but when it comes to alternative models and theories, his point of reference becomes the work of Western scholars.[17] One may, therefore, wonder how the reform of educational systems will be achieved in terms of an "independent view of total development," as advocated by Musa, especially in view of his negative characterization of Arab society.

In my view, descriptions and characterizations of issues should take into account the fact that "independence" is, by definition, born out of a state of dependency and can only be achieved through a realistic appreciation of the *possibilities* as well as constraints of the situation. It is also important to appreciate that dependence and independence are relative terms, especially in view of present globalized political, economic, social, cultural, and intellectual relations. The politics of the basic needs of the child discussed by Labib should therefore be seen in international as well as local or national contexts. For example, the consequences of structural adjustments and economic liberalization and their impact on poor families and their children can neither be understood nor redressed at a purely local or national level.[18] This need for a global approach would emphasize the importance of promoting an international overlapping consensus on human rights norms and their implementation through the dynamics of internal discourse and cross-cultural dialogue, as suggested earlier.

I have devoted much space to reviewing these studies because their "basic needs" analysis provides a useful background for developing a tentative model for defining and specifying the principle of the best interests of the child in the region. Many of the "actions concerning children" envisaged by Article 3.1 (where the best interests of the child are required to be a primary consideration), as well as other aspects of the Child Convention and related concerns, can usefully be analyzed in terms of what might be called basic needs of the child.[19] As briefly explained below, the premise and main features of the following tentative model can apply to basic needs analysis in relation to, for example, child labor. The model may also be useful in mediating normative consensus on the issue of corporal punishment and female circumcision, mentioned earlier.

A Tentative Model for Determining What
Constitutes the Best Interests of the Child

It might be helpful to reiterate here that this chapter is concerned with the nature and dynamics of the process by which actions (including norms-setting and decision-making) are taken in relation to, or as rationalized by, best interests of the child considerations. Since, as indicated earlier, there are always different perspectives and options regarding each type of action, the main issue is how to regulate the processes of discourse and dialogue over the interpretation and application of the best interests principle in each case. I therefore recall here my earlier analysis and proposal for promoting genuine normative universality on the best interest principle in relation to the following elements:

1. Clear and accurate description and characterization of the action to which the best interests principle is applicable, whether in terms of a basic needs approach or in some other way. In this regard, as indicated earlier, one should know who is making the description and characterization and according to which framework or orientation.
2. Rigorous analysis of the action in question in order to identify its type or nature, who is taking it, on what basis and for whose benefit, who are the immediate and consequential subjects of the action, and how they are affected.
3. Understanding the nature and dynamics of power relations between and among the various actors and subjects of the action and of the situation in local or broader contexts, as appropriate.
4. Appreciation of the possibilities and constraints of changing or influencing the nature and dynamics of power relations between and among actors and subjects, as well as in the situation at large.
5. In all the above, the fundamental guiding principle should be to maximize opportunities for contesting the nature and rationale of action regarding children from different perspectives and for presenting alternative positions.

Given the integral and dynamic relationship between form and substance, these and related elements should be applied in devising (reforming) and implementing the *procedures and processes* through which action is taken, as appropriate for each type of action. For example, procedure and process

in a private child custody case would be different from those of setting and/
or implementing a policy on basic needs (food, shelter, or health) or with
regard to child labor, and so forth. But the purpose in each case should be
not only to determine (through procedures and processes consistent with the
proposed model) which action is in the best interests of the child under the
circumstances *but also to allow for the subsequent contestation, revision, or
change of the initial action.* The model is applicable to both aspects and with
respect to procedural as well as substantive matters because valid ends cannot
be achieved through invalid means.

The application of this model may be illustrated with respect to the question of child labor. It is not possible to discuss here various causes and consequences of child labor[20] or to review possible explanations and responses to
the serious discrepancy between theory and practice in this regard. Instead, I
wish briefly to discuss how the proposed model might be applied in relation
to Abdalla's suggestion, noted earlier, that, rather than seeking the total abolition of child labor, official policies should be directed at preventing it from
being exploitative or dangerous to the physical and psychological health of
the child.

This proposition reflects the fundamental dilemma of reconciling apparently conflicting basic needs and raises the question of who defines those
needs and for whom. On the one hand, child labor is essential for the child's
immediate and long-term survival in certain situations where such labor also
constitutes a vital educational and socialization institution. The nature and
circumstances of labor, on the other hand, may not only threaten the physical
and mental health of the child but also deprive him or her of the basic needs
of academic education. The very reasons for child labor and conditions under
which it is likely to happen tend to expose children to excessive exploitation
and abuse.

Like all dilemmas, the only solution in situations where child labor is jus-
tifiable or necessary is to seek to achieve its "benefits" while safeguarding
against its dangers and negative consequences. But this sort of simple and obviously reasonable formula is only a broad framework for developing and implementing a resolution of the dilemma. Many questions need to be answered
before specific strategies for action can be devised and implemented, subsequently evaluated, and so forth, in order to resolve the dilemma at any given
point in time. For example, the rationale of the formula seems to suggest that
child labor, or certain types thereof, should be prohibited altogether if it is not
possible to safeguard effectively against its dangers or negative consequences

(or if the risks outweigh the benefits). What does this mean in specific cases? Who makes these determinations and on what basis? How is "mental health" or "exploitation" of the child defined and by whom?

Successful resolutions of the dilemma will probably be too much conditioned by the social, political, cultural, and other circumstances of its context to be readily applied elsewhere. That is to say, the manner in which the formula is specified and implemented (how are terms defined and determinations made and by whom) are unlikely to be transferable to a different setting. It is therefore important to focus on essential prerequisites for and essential features of the *process* by which appropriate resolutions are developed more than on specific solutions—although the latter are no doubt useful in understanding which similar issues might be addressed in other settings.

Since the process through which the dilemma of child labor may be resolved should occur at various official and nonofficial levels and from different perspectives, the proposed model must be specified separately for each level and perspective. In all cases, however, the model calls for maximizing opportunities for contesting prevailing descriptions and characterizations of the action in question, allowing for alternative analysis and so forth. The experiences and insights of such an internal discourse can be influenced and exchanged through cross-cultural dialogue as explained earlier in this analysis.

A similar process can also promote normative universality on the question of corporal punishment. As suggested at the beginning of this chapter, apparent normative universality in the relevant provisions of the Child Convention may in fact hide serious schisms and ambiguity with regard to corporal punishment for children. Nevertheless, I would not recommend that one rule on the admissibility of this form of punishment on the basis of records of preparatory works for the convention or declarations of official positions on the issue. Rather, I call for internal discourse and cross-cultural dialogue in order to develop genuine universal consensus on the normative implications of the relevant provisions of the Convention. The questions to be addressed include the following. Should the Convention's prohibition on "all forms of physical or mental violence" against the child be absolute? Can corporal punishment ever be justified, in some cases or under certain circumstances, "in the best interests of the child"? Do all forms of corporal punishment necessarily violate "the child's human dignity" or constitute "torture or other cruel, inhuman or degrading treatment or punishment"?[21]

In accordance with the proposed model, discourse and dialogue might present alternative descriptions and characterizations of corporal punishment in debating whether to contest or confirm its cultural legitimacy. Rigorous analysis might either substantiate or repudiate the classification of such punishment as physical or mental violence—a necessary stage in prohibiting or exempting it under some formulation of a "best interests" rationale. An appreciation of the nature and dynamics of power relations between proponents and opponents of corporal punishment is necessary for deciding whether to seek to influence and change the situation and how that can be achieved. To the extent that universal consensus on prohibiting corporal punishment cannot be achieved, or until it is realized, the processes of discourse and dialogue can be useful in developing and implementing effective safeguards.

As applied to female circumcision, the proposed model would provide those who oppose this practice with opportunities for contesting prevailing perceptions of the nature, rationale, and consequences of the practice, while presenting alternative ways of responding to sociological, psychological, and other needs that the practice might be believed to satisfy. My concern here is not particularly with reasons for repudiating female circumcision in principle and seeking its total abolition in practice. Rather, I am concerned with the manner in which that determination is made and the consequent action taken, *in the most effective, lasting, and legitimate manner.* Many programs seeking to eradicate this heinous practice, I suggest, have failed to achieve their objective because of the arbitrary, intrusive, and elitist (top-down) manner in which those programs were conceived and implemented.

Conclusion: Toward a Strategy for Substantive Consensus

This chapter is premised on the view that normative universality in human rights should neither be taken for granted nor abandoned in the face of claims of contextual specificity or cultural relativity. Human rights scholars and activists throughout the world must recognize that a universal project, for the rights of the child in this case, cannot be legitimately achieved through the "universalization" of the norms and institutions of dominant cultures, whether at a local, regional, or international level. Such recognition does not mean that one should condone or concede the apologetic or manipulative abuse of contextual specificity or cultural relativity of the type attempted by some governments and elites, especially in certain parts of Africa and Asia today. On the contrary, by challenging its basis in the consciousness of the relevant constituencies, taking cultural diversity seriously is the best way to combat such abuse.

With respect to the principle of the best interests of the child, this chapter proposes the establishment of procedures and processes to ensure not only dynamic diversity of perspectives in taking initial action regarding children but also opportunities for subsequent contestation, revision, and change of such action. Procedural universality, in my view, is both readily achievable and conductive to the realization of genuine normative consensus on the definition and implementation of the principle of the best interests of the child. This approach should be applied to issues of daily implementation as well as the articulation of broad standards regarding the best interest principle.

Chapter 7

Toward an Islamic Hermeneutics
for Human Rights

A central question in the consideration of religion's relation to human rights is whether the various views of what it means to be truly human leave room for a set of *neutrally formulated* common human rights. It is not possible, or desirable, in my view to identify a set of neutrally formulated human rights. Any normative regime, which justifies a set of rights and determines their content, must necessarily represent a commitment to a particular value system. This particularity is especially true of, on the one hand, a regime claiming to justify and formulate a set of human rights because of an organic relationship between the conception and implementation of such rights and, on the other hand, a normative regime, which provides or informs perceptions of human dignity, self-identity, and personal experience.

Nevertheless, I will argue that an "internal" commitment to a normative regime need not and should not be exclusive of the "other" (however he or she is identified) with respect to a set of commonly agreed human rights. In my view, what is at issue is not the possibility of abstract or absolute neutrality from any religious, cultural, or ideological regime; rather, the question is how to reconcile commitments to diverse normative regimes with a commitment to a concept and set of universal human rights. If this reconciliation is achieved, the commitment of some to one regime or another would be, in effect, immaterial from other points of view. In other words, it would be possible to achieve the benefits of neutral formulation without pursuing the illusion of neutrality as such.

It may be argued that excluding the requirement of neutral formulation simply circumvents the question of how to agree on a set of rights accruing universally to all human beings of whatever religious persuasion or lack thereof, irrespective of gender or race (hereinafter referred to as universal human rights). From this point of view, allowing the formulation of a set of rights to reflect a particular value system would impose that system's criteria of entitlement on rights that might *exclude* certain human beings. Judging by the history to date, the argument goes, commitment to a religious value system would almost certainly exclude those who do not adhere to that religion or at least not accord them rights equal to those enjoyed by the adherents of the religion in question. Religious value systems also tend to deny women equality with men. This inequality, it should be added, is true not only of orthodox perceptions of Judaism, Christianity, and Islam but also of other religious traditions, cultures, and even ideologies. In this light, it may be concluded that the only way to achieve consensus on a set of universal human rights is through "neutral formulation."

The difficulty of achieving consensus on universal human rights, however, is not due to commitment to a value system as such, be it religious, cultural, or ideological. What is problematic is the *exclusive* nature of value systems, that is to say, their tendency to define the relationship between the "self" and the "other" in antagonistic or negative terms, thereby diminishing prospects for the acknowledgment of equality and nondiscrimination. I would therefore argue that if and to the extent that it is possible to overcome this feature of the various value systems of the world today, global consensus on universal human rights would be attainable without requiring people to abandon their religious, cultural, or ideological commitments in order to subscribe to such a project.

In any case, it would be counterproductive to require people to choose between their religion, culture, or ideology on the one hand and a supposedly "neutral" universal human rights project on the other. Most people would probably opt for the former for two reasons. First, to the vast majority, no human rights scheme can by itself serve as a substitute for religion, culture, or ideology. Second, most people would maintain that some conception of human rights is integral to their religion, culture, or ideology. To avoid undermining the legitimacy of a universal human rights project by placing it in direct competition with what people hold as their comprehensive fundamental value systems, we must pursue a strategy of *internal transformation* of perceptions of the religion, culture, or ideology in question to achieve a reconciliation between belief systems. Without minimizing the difficulties and risks of this approach, I maintain that such reconciliation is both conceptually possible in general[1] and applicable in the Islamic context.[2] In view of the greater difficulties and risks of trying to establish and implement a supposedly neutral universal human rights scheme, I would recommend attempting to achieve reconciliation as *one of the strategies* for legitimizing and effectuating a universal human rights project.

In this chapter, I will explore the issues and prospects of such internal transformation in relation to Islam and Islamic societies in the present globalized world of diverse religious and other normative systems. To this end, I will define and outline an *Islamic hermeneutics for human rights*. Nevertheless, if the proposed analysis is to be useful for a universal human rights project, it should be applicable to other religions, cultures, and ideologies. I will therefore attempt to extrapolate from the Islamic case some general guidelines on the conceptual and methodological aspects of the process of internal transformation as it may apply to any religion, culture, or ideology.

The Genesis of Exclusion and Inclusion

As suggested earlier, the problem is the exclusive nature of religion, culture, and ideology, rather than these normative systems as such. But it is also clear that some level of exclusivity is integral to the fundamental nature and function of normative systems: the basis of the claim of each system is the commitment of its adherents and the sanction for compliance with its precepts. That is to say, people's commitment to a given normative system is usually premised on the belief that conformity with the precepts of the system in question can bring them specific moral and/or material benefits. Part of this rationale, it seems, is the belief that other normative systems will not achieve those benefits, at least not to the same degree. Thus, the advantage of adhering to one system is appreciated on its own terms as well as in contrast to the disadvantage of adhering to other systems.

The process, however, of achieving the perceived benefits of a normative system is normally protracted, diffuse, and difficult to evaluate in daily life. In the case of some religious normative systems in particular, the most significant benefits, such as becoming a moral person in this life or achieving salvation in the next life, cannot be verified in concrete or immediate terms. Consequently, people need to find ways of sustaining their faith in the ability of their chosen normative system to deliver promised benefits, especially during periods of mounting frustration and helplessness.

One way in which people tend to reinforce their faith in their own normative system is to exaggerate the advantage they have or will have and the disadvantage of those who do not adhere to the same system. In this way, many people come to hold a territorial or proprietary interest in their own system and an adverse view of other systems. This self-vindicating defense mechanism often leads to a "them" versus "us" syndrome that can easily degenerate into hostility and antagonism toward the "them" and absolute solidarity with the "us."

Despite the inevitability of some degree of exclusivity in all normative systems and its tendency to degenerate into hostility and antagonism toward the "other," I contend that commitment to a system at one level can be compatible with a degree of inclusion of the "other" at another level. More specifically, I suggest that one can be fully committed to a certain religion and identify with his or her cobelievers for that purpose while also being fully committed to another normative system and identifying with coadherents of that system. In other words, people can and do have *multiple overlapping identities* and can and do cooperate with the "us" of each of their identities; this cooperation can be achieved without being hostile to the "them" at one level of identity because the latter can be part of the "us" at another level of identity.

For example, I am a Muslim and identify with other Muslims for the purposes of my religion. I am also a Sudanese who belongs to a certain profession and have a variety of interests and concerns I share with other Sudanese and with people from all parts of the world. Ultimately, and most important, I am a human being who is committed to protecting and promoting the values and qualities of being human. The fact that there is a variety of "them" and "us" at the various levels of my overlapping identities indicates to me that my relationship to the "them" of one identity should not frustrate or diminish the prospects of relating to those same people when I need them to be part of the "us" at other levels of identity.

I see the possibility and utility of overlapping identities and cooperation as integral to my faith as a Muslim, in accordance with verse 13 of chapter 49 of the Qur'an (that is, 49:13 as the Qur'an will be quoted in this chapter), which may be translated as follows:

> We [God] have created you [human beings] into [different] peoples and tribes so that you may [all] get to know [understand, and cooperate with] each other; the most honorable among you in the light of God are the pious [righteous] ones.

As I understand it, this verse means that human diversity or pluralism (ethnic, religious, or otherwise) is not only inherent in the divine scheme of things but also deliberately designed to promote understanding and cooperation among various peoples. The last part of the verse emphasizes that the quality of morality and human worth is to be judged by a person's moral conduct, rather than by his or her membership in a particular ethnic, religious, or other group. My choice, however, of this particular verse of the Qur'an, and interpreting it as supporting the principle of overlapping identities and cooperation with the "non-Muslim other," is premised upon a certain orientation that may not be shared by all Muslims today. Muslims of a different orientation may choose to emphasize other, clearly exclusive, verses of the Qur'an such as 3:28, 4:139, 144, and 8:72–73[3] and/or interpret the above-quoted verse as referring to diversity and pluralism not among humanity at large but *within* the global Islamic community (*Umma*). A Muslim of the latter orientation may also interpret the last part of the verse as restricting piety/righteousness to Muslims, so that only a Muslim may qualify for honor in the sight of God in accordance with the quality of his or her personal conduct, as judged by Islamic criteria.

It should be emphasized, however, that choice and/or interpretation of verses of the Qur'an (or any other text for that matter) is *necessarily* informed by the orientation of the person in question. Muslims, for example, have always differed, and will always differ, in their choice of verses to cite in support of their views and also in their understanding of the verses they quote. That interpretive variety is one of the reasons why there are so many schools of Islamic theology and jurisprudence, with a wide variety of views within each school. This feature of Islamic discourse is often cited by Muslims with great pride as conclusive evidence of the flexibility and adaptability of Islam to different circumstances of time and place.

By "orientation" I mean the *conditioning of the existential or material circumstances* of the person reading (or hearing) the Qur'an or another textual source. That is to say, every person interprets the text in question and derives its normative implications in terms of his or her knowledge and experience of the world: perceptions of self-interests in political, economic, and social contexts; realities of intercommunal or international relations; and so forth. A person's orientation may also be influenced by his or her vision for change or improvement in existential or material circumstances. In other words, one need not always feel totality constrained by existing circumstances and may wish to break away from or reform prevailing political, economic, and social conditions. For such a vision to have realistic prospects of fulfillment, however, it must be grounded in existing sociological, political, economic, and intellectual circumstances of the society in question. This requirement is what I will refer to in the next section as the "historical contingency" factor in the hermeneutical process.

In my view, two conclusions can be drawn from an analysis of orientation in relation to the interpretive process. First, there is no such thing as the only possible or valid understanding of the Qur'an, or conception of Islam, since any understanding is informed by the individual and collective orientation of Muslims as they seek to derive normative implications for human behavior. Second, and consequently, a change in the orientation of Muslims will contribute to a transformation of their understanding of the Qur'an and, hence, of their conception of Islam itself.

Before considering whether modern Muslims already have, or are likely to have, an orientation that is conducive to supporting a project of universal human rights, I wish to clarify the concept of hermeneutical discourse in relation to Islam. My goal is to conceptualize what might be called an Islamic hermeneutics, which can be harnessed in promoting and applying a human rights orientation among Muslims today.

Hermeneutics in Context

Hermeneutics is usually defined as the art or science of interpretation, especially of Scripture, and is commonly distinguished from exegesis or explanation and exposition.[4] The need for interpretation as a means of understanding the purpose and normative implications of a text like the Qur'an or the Bible is beyond dispute. But the precise nature and actual practice of hermeneutics, and its relationship to exegesis, would, of course, vary from one religion to another and often within the same religion over time and/or place. I would also emphasize the anthropological dimension of these processes.

For example, according to the 1992 acts of the Christian Reformed Ecumenical Council, hermeneutics is an unavoidable task of the Christian Church in seeking the abiding significance of the Word of God in the constantly changing circumstances of human life and history: "Hermeneutics has to do with the interpretation of the Bible *as it applies to our own time*, taking into account the broad historical, cultural and scientific changes that have taken place, as well as the changes in basic mentality and outlook that characterize the modern world."[5] This document maintains that it is necessary to take into account contextual and cultural factors when applying scriptural ethical directives to concrete life situations.[6] However, it is clear from the argument and conclusions of the document as a whole that the conclusions are cast in terms of a particular tradition within Christianity as distinguished not only from that of the Roman Catholic Church but also from earlier views within the Protestant Church.

Each religion (and each specific tradition within a religion) has its own "framework of interpretation," a set of interpretative rules, techniques, and underlying assumptions that are accepted by its adherents as valid or authoritative. It would therefore seem to follow that there is a "correct" way of understanding and applying the content of scripture (or the Qur'an for Muslims), that is to say, a way that is consistent with the appropriate framework of interpretation.[7] As can be expected, however, participants in the hermeneutical process will claim that their understanding of Scripture is the correct one because it is more consistent with the accepted framework of interpretation. Others may even challenge the authority of a given framework of interpretation and seek to provide an alternative. Such claims underlie differences between, for example, Orthodox, Catholic, and Protestant Christians, Sunni and Shi'a Muslims, Sufi and non-Sufi Muslims, as well as among various factions within each religion.

I would, therefore, emphasize the need to understand how the frame of interpretation is specified, verified, and revised or reformulated, that is, how and by whom it is defined and specified. Does that process provide for reformulation or revision, according to which criteria, and how can that be legitimately done? Ultimately, who is to arbitrate and mediate between competing claims about the frame of interpretation and/or its application?

In my view, the community of believers as a whole should be the living frame of interpretation and ultimate arbiter and mediator of interpretative rules, techniques, and underlying assumptions. This model seems to have been the case during the founding stages of major religions. Over time, however, some factions tended to appropriate and monopolize the process of interpretation and turn it into an exclusive and technical science or art. Thus, the process of religious revival and reformation is often about breaking the monopoly of the clergy or technocrats of hermeneutics and reclaiming the right of the community members to be the living frame of interpretation for their own religion and its normative regime.

In the case of Islam, for example, there is no reference in the early traditions to any special requirements or qualifications for engaging in the interpretation of the Qur'an or exercising *ijtihad* (human reasoning) to derive ethical norms and legal principles. Even the founders of the major *madhahib* (schools of Islamic jurisprudence) simply stated their views for Muslims at large to accept or reject freely without claiming an exclusive right to interpretation or ijtihad. By the end of the third century of Islam, however, the process was rendered so technical and exclusive that the "gate of ijtihad" was said to have been closed, thereby confining subsequent generations of Muslims to be the blind followers of the founding "masters" of Islamic jurisprudence.[8] Since Ibn Taymiyya (fourteenth century), various scholars have tried to break the deadlock of tradition.[9]

A possible reason for this failure is that the sociological, political, economic, and other circumstances of the period were not ripe for a change in the orientation of Muslims, which would have permitted acceptance of the proposed reforms. That is to say, the requirement of historical contingency on their hermeneutical argument was not satisfied at the time of those reform efforts. I would agree that this must have been the case since, and to the extent that, previous reform efforts were not successful as a matter of fact. But I would also emphasize that *historical contingency can only be accurately judged in retrospect.*

It is critical to any reform effort that its proponents should strive to demonstrate that the circumstances of the time are ripe for change. One should also expect the opponents of reform either to dispute the validity of the proposed change as such or to claim that it is premature. Whatever one may think of the hermeneutical argument or other aspects of the case for reform, the historical contingency factor cannot be categorically judged in advance. Only time will tell whether the community in question will eventually accept or reject the proposed reform. Moreover, rejection of a hermeneutical argument for reform at any given point in time should not be seen as final and conclusive, or that its historical contingency will never be satisfied in the future. Subsequent generations of "would-be reformers" may continue to make, refine, and update the argument in their own context and may well succeed when the case for reform is made in the right or appropriate way, time, and place.

An Anthropological Approach to Islam

The above analysis may be described as an "anthropological approach" to the Qur'an and to Islam in general, in the sense that it is premised on an organic relationship between the Qur'an and Islam on the one hand and the nature of human beings (that is, their understanding, imagination, judgment, behavior,

experience, and so forth) on the other. Is such an approach valid from an Islamic religious point of view? If it is valid, what does it mean for the ways in
which Muslims seek to understand Islam and try to conform to its precepts
today?

An anthropological approach to the Qur'an and to Islam in general is
fully justified, indeed imperative, in my view, by virtue of the terms of the
Qur'an itself and the experience of Muslim communities throughout their
history. According to Muslim belief, the text of the Qur'an contains the final
and conclusive message of God to the whole of humanity. This message is
explicitly stated in verses 107:21, 1:25; and is also clear from the many verses
(such as 168:2, 138:3, 31:7 and 49:13, quoted above) in which the Qur'anic
form of address is "Oh, humankind" or "Oh, Children of Adam."

The Qur'anic form of address is also directed mostly to the individual
person, or to a community in some cases, without the intermediacy of clergy
or officials of the state. In so doing, the Qur'an constantly emphasizes that
people should reflect and consider what is being said, should think about this
or that, and so forth, as in verses 219:2, 266:2, 191:3, 3:1–4:13, 44:16, 24:10,
and 8:30. In fact, verses 2:12 and 3:43 declare human reflection and understanding to be the whole purpose of revealing the Qur'an.

Two further points can be added in support of an anthropological approach to the Qur'an and to Islam in general. First, human agency is simply
unavoidable in understanding the Qur'an and the traditions of the Prophet
and in deriving ethical norms and legal principles from those sources to regulate individual behavior and social relations. Ali bin Abi Talib, one of the
leading earliest Muslims and the fourth caliph, is reported to have said, "The
Qur'an does not speak; it is people who speak on its behalf." Second, and as
noted earlier, the actual rich and complex diversity of Islamic theology and
jurisprudence clearly demonstrates the dynamic relationship between the
scriptural sources of Islam on the one hand and the comprehension, imagination, and experience of Muslim peoples on the other.

Thus, there is nothing new about an *Islamic* anthropological approach to
the Qur'an and to Islam in general. What is at issue, in my view, is what this
approach means for the ways in which Muslims seek to understand Islam and
try to conform to its precepts today. Given the fact that the specific historical
context has always affected the perceptions and practice of Islamic principles
by Muslims, how does the modern context affect the perceptions and practice
of present-day Muslims? More importantly, what is the *orientation* through
which Muslims should understand the Qur'an in the modern context?

It is obvious that the orientation of modern Muslims should be different from that of earlier generations because of the radical transformation of the existential and material circumstances of their life today in contrast to those of the past. For better or for worse, Muslims now live in a globalized world of political, economic, and security interdependence, as well as of mutual social/cultural influence. Their conception of Islam, and efforts to live by its precepts, must be conditioned by modern perceptions of individual and collective self-interests in the context of a radically transformed world. Whatever vision Muslims may have for change or improvement in the present realities of the world today must be grounded in the circumstances and conditions of this world. That is, their perceptions of the range of options available to them must take into account the facts of interdependence and mutual influence.

A central issue that modern Muslims have been struggling with over the last two centuries is how to adapt their orientation and transform their conception of Islam in an *authentic and legitimate* manner. Whether in relation to issues of modernity, democracy, human rights, economic development, or some other concern, the central issue has often been legitimizing and rationalizing desired normative or material objectives in terms of the traditions of Islamic societies. Of course, there is more to those traditions than the Islamic dimension, but to the extent that Islam is integral to the circumstances of these societies, there seems to be a spectrum of opinion on issues of political, economic, and social change.

At one end of the spectrum, there is what might be called the traditionalist or "fundamentalist" approach, which insists on strict conformity to Shari'a as a prerequisite for accepting the proposed change. At the other end of the spectrum, there are those who wish to avoid the question of conformity to Shari'a altogether, usually out of a conviction that reconciliation between their objectives and the relevant principles of Shari'a not possible. For example, some advocates of universal human rights in Islamic societies prefer to base their position on the present international standards of human rights, irrespective of the conformity of those standards with principles of Shari'a. Between these two poles of the spectrum, there are many positions that seek to reconcile universal human rights with Shari'a, or with Islam in general, in a variety of ways.

While I agree with those who see Islamic authenticity and legitimacy as imperative for a wide acceptance of universal human rights, I believe that the reconciliation of universal human rights with Shari'a is neither possible nor required. Reconciliation is not possible because Shariʿa is premised on a fundamental distinction between the rights of Muslims and non-Muslims—and those of Muslim men and women, respectively—which totally repudiates the principle of equality and nondiscrimination upon which universal human rights are premised. That is to say, it is simply impossible for Shariʿa to acknowledge any set of rights to which all human beings are entitled by virtue of their humanity, without distinction on grounds of religion or gender. Since what is required is Islamic authenticity and legitimacy, rather than conformity with Shariʿa as such, I believe that this requirement can be satisfied without reconciling universal human rights with Shariʿa. In other words, I argue that it is possible to achieve Islamic authenticity and legitimacy for a set of human rights by distinguishing between Islam and Shariʿa.

The Divinity of Islam and Temporality of Shariʿa

In my view, as a *human* understanding of Islam (hence, necessarily limited by circumstances of time and place), Shariʿa should not be identified with the totality of the religion itself. As explained earlier, any reader of the scriptural sources of Islam would always understand those texts and their normative implications in terms of his or her knowledge and experience of the world. Since that knowledge and experience, and indeed the world itself, tend to change over time, Islam should not be bound by any particular understanding of its scriptural sources. This view is not only consistent with the Muslim belief in the divinity of the Qurʾan and finality of its message but is in fact essential for maintaining the practical relevance of that divinity and finality to the lives of Muslims through successive eras.

One often hears in Islamic discourse the proposition that "Islam is suitable (valid) for all times and places." For this maxim to be true, however, there must be flexibility and change in the understanding and implementation of Islam over time and place. More specifically, given the radical transformation of Islamic societies and the world around them, it is simply impossible for the same principles of Shariʿa formulated by Muslim jurists more than thirteen centuries ago to remain the only valid law of Islam. It follows, therefore, that Shariʿa principles must be reformulated before they can be applied today, whether in themselves or as criteria for accepting and implementing a normative system of universal human rights.

This obviously valid proposition is usually stated in modern Islamic discourse as a critique of what is known as *fiqh* (the juridical and theological opinion of early Muslim jurists) rather than of Shariʿa itself. Moreover, advocates of reform would also call for a modern exercise in ijtihad in order to change those aspects of *fiqh* that they find objectionable or problematic today. Such calls for ijtihad, however, are rarely followed by actual application and concrete derivation of specific new principles of Shariʿa. Space does not permit much elaboration, but I wish to state briefly two objections to this sort of reasoning from the point of view of the advocacy of universal human rights in modern Islamic societies.

First, since universal human rights are untenable in view of some clear and categorical verses of the Qurʾan itself, such as verse 4:34 (often cited as the basis of the inequality of women to men), the problem is one of Shariʿa and not merely of fiqh. Second, since the traditional principle of ijtihad is confined to matters on which there is no clear and categorical text of the Qurʾan, it cannot challenge a principle of inequality based on such a text. In other words, there is a need to reform the principle of ijtihad itself before it can be used to resolve an incompatibility of Shariʿa and universal human rights due to a clear and categorical text of the Qurʾan rather than as fiqh, the opinion of early jurists.

I contend that ijtihad should be reformulated to apply even to matters governed by clear and categorical texts of the Qurʾan, as suggested by the late Sudanese Muslim reformer Ustadh Mahmoud Mohamed Taha. According to Taha's methodology of reform, the Qurʾan itself contains two messages, one intended for immediate application within the historical context of the seventh century and after and another message for subsequent implementation as the circumstances of time and place permit.[10] Such a historical approach to the Qurʾan in general is supported by some of the rulings of Umar ibn al-Khatab, the second caliph, who decided that clear and categorical verses of the Qurʾan should not apply when the objectives intended to be achieved by the revelation are no longer valid.[11] Taha has developed that approach into a comprehensive methodology of Islamic reform that would enable modern Muslim jurists to select and interpret verses of the Qurʾan in order to develop a modern version of Shariʿa.[12]

Taha's methodology may appear to be too radical to many Muslims today, but there appears to be no alternative that will adequately resolve the crisis in modern Islamic reform, especially in relation to universal human rights. Those who wish to achieve Islamic authenticity and legitimacy for universal human rights must overcome both theological objections and political and sociological resistance to an adequate reform methodology, be it that of Taha or any other viable alternative. My own preference to date is the methodology proposed by Taha and explained in the sources cited earlier. I remain open, however, to accepting any alternative methodology that will achieve what I believe to be the necessary degree of Islamic reform.

Moving on from theoretical considerations, in the next section I will offer some reflections on aspects of the political and sociological resistance to approaches that seek to develop and present an Islamic rationale for universal human rights in modern Islamic societies. In my experience, much of the so-called theological or hermeneutical objections to reform methodologies such as that of Taha are, in fact, a product of political and sociological factors. Whatever may be their nature or motivation, I believe that all obstacles to genuine commitment to universal human rights must be identified and overcome by the proponents of universality, each working within his or her own context as well as in collaboration with others.

Prospects of Universality in Global Context

Resistance to an Islamic rationale for universal human rights in Islamic societies today may be traced to several sources, some pertaining to regional and international considerations, while others relate to local dynamics of power relations. It is important to note that this resistance is mostly reactive to perceived threats or other concerns, whether internal or external to the region. It is not possible, of course, to discuss all aspects of this phenomenon, but it may be useful to explore the following aspects with a view to suggesting ways of overcoming resistance to the universality of human rights.

First, there is the perception of universal human rights as yet another element of a "Western" conspiracy to undermine the integrity and independence of Islamic societies. The best defense these societies have against this neocolonial attack, the argument goes, is a strong and uncompromising assertion of a distinctive Islamic identity and culture. Thus, while all Muslim advocates of universal human rights are seen as agents of foreign domination and Western cultural imperialism, those in particular who seek to base their advocacy on an Islamic rationale are even more "dangerous" because they undermine the distinctive Islamic identity and culture.

Second, related to this factor, are popular perceptions of the double standard of Western governments, media, and public at large regarding Muslim concerns, especially in relation to Palestine and, more recently, the former Yugoslavia, in contrast to devastating and decisive action against

Iraq. These perceptions enhance the view that the West is not interested in universal human rights except where they serve its geopolitical and economic interests.

Third, there is the perception that the existing international human rights standards, and mechanisms for their implementation, reflect a Western bias in favor of individual civil and political rights, over against economic and social rights and collective human rights. Besides reinforcing apprehensions of cultural imperialism, this bias is also used to argue that the values and priorities of Islamic societies are not served by the existing international standards.

Fourth, at the local or internal level, there is resistance from those who feel that their vested interests are threatened by universal human rights. These include ruling classes and groups, men, and Muslim majorities in general who would normally tend to resist any threat to their privileged position. The usual argument by these groups is that human rights are alien to the culture and traditions of Islamic societies. Thus, the perceived threat is even more serious when it claims an Islamic rationale, thereby seeking to undermine the rationale of the defense itself.

Strategies for overcoming these and other causes of resistance must be founded on a realistic understanding of the internal logic and perceived basis of opposition to universal human rights. For example, the facts and aftermath of Western colonialism and continuing domination and exploitation must be admitted and confronted, the facts of internal power relations and perceptions of vested interest must be understood and redressed, and so forth.

The key to any effort in this regard, however, is the credibility of advocates of universal human rights in the eyes of their own local constituencies. These advocates must be able to draw on the symbols of their own culture and history, speak the "language" of their own peoples, know and respect their concerns and priorities. In so doing, advocates of universal human rights should appreciate and utilize the "ambivalence and contestability" of their cultures, seek out and explore new options and rationales for advancing the cultural legitimacy of universal human rights. All this will have to be pursued and promoted through what might be called an internal Islamic discourse. Outsiders can assist such an internal discourse by supporting the right of all Muslims insiders to engage in it, as well as by engaging in their own (Christian, Hindu, Buddhist, or other internal religious) discourses to resolve the conflicts and tensions between their respective religions and universal human rights. Universality of human rights can also be enhanced through a cross-cultural dialogue to promote an overlapping consensus on global moral foundations of these rights.[13]

All the major religions of the world agree that there is an organic and dynamic relationship between ends and means, so that legitimate objectives can only be realized through appropriate methods and processes. I would therefore conclude that, in the final analysis, the acknowledgment and implementation of universal human rights should be seen as a cooperative process as well as a common objective—a global joint venture and not an attempt to universalize a particular cultural or religious model.

PART III

Regional and Global Perspectives

Chapter 8

Competing Claims to Religious Freedom and Communal Self-Determination in Africa

This chapter derives from a larger project addressing issues of conflict between competing claims to religious freedom and "communal" self-determination[1] in the context of three regions of the world: Eastern Europe, Latin America, and Africa.[2] This primarily geographical focus of the project as a whole is intended to highlight contextual factors, without underestimating the role of cross-regional dynamics. Those making competing claims to religious freedom and communal self-determination neither perceive their claims in exclusively regional terms, nor do they act or react in isolation of actors and factors in other parts of the world.

Another distinguishing feature of this project is that it seeks to apply a human rights paradigm to the mediation of competing claims over proselytization and its implications. A discussion of how that paradigm might apply and what difference it is likely to make will follow an explanation of the nature, context, and dynamics of proselytization in general, with reference to Africa in particular. It should be noted from the outset, however, that proselytization should not be equated with conversion, as the latter may or may not follow from the former. Conversion may also be an unintended consequence of commercial, social, or other forms of interaction that cannot be characterized as proselytization in the usual sense of the term.

On any given day, one can point to numerous religious conflicts and tensions within and between communities around the world as a major cause of a broader strife that sometimes leads to massive violence and destruction. Regarding each situation, observers will probably disagree about such issues as the underlying causes of the conflict, the role of religion as such, and the identity, motivation, objectives, and relative importance of various internal and external actors. Efforts to explain or understand these situations may recall histories of religious and ethnic rivalries or hostilities, highlight current economic difficulties and political frustrations, emphasize demographic and geopolitical factors, cite the role of charismatic leaders with their complex motivations, and so forth. Prescriptions for resolution will also vary with the analysis and orientation of the parties in relation to particularities of the specific context, as well as pragmatic possibilities of implementation. Proselytization is often an explicit or implicit element of religious conflict in all parts of the world, usually overlapping and interacting with other factors. However, the two phenomena should not be taken as synonymous. This project is concerned with proselytization in particular, not religious conflict and tension in general.

Part of the impetus for this choice arose out of concerns about what Martin Marty, the leading American scholar of religion, has called a "new war for souls" among churches and religious groups competing among themselves over numerical membership and social and political influence, in addition to more conventionally understood forms of proselytization in the sense of seeking new converts. While those initial concerns were confirmed in subsequent studies within the framework of the project as a whole, it also became clear that the concept of proselytization and its manifestations should not be confined to such preconceived notions. In this project, this concept conveys a range of meanings and methods of communication of religious ideas. Similar issues are raised by the numerous possibilities of "conversion" within the same tradition or subtradition in response to internal and/or external stimuli. For example, Muslim proselytizers not only seek to convert non-Muslims to Islam, or from Sunni to Shi'a Islam or from one Sufi group to another, but may also endeavor to motivate and mobilize members of their own subtradition of Islam into a more active mode in support of local political and economic objectives or in response to perceptions of "external" threat, whether identifiable as Islamic or otherwise. Evangelical, Pentecostal, and charismatic forms of Christianity, which have gained momentum in the last two decades in Africa, are also predicated on the spirit of revival within the same religion.

The basic rationale of the project's focus is the paradox of, on the one hand, the greater risks of proselytization in the modern context and, on the other hand, the apparently improved possibilities of peaceful mediation of conflict. On the risks side, recent global and technological developments dramatically enhance the frequency and efficacy of proselytizing initiatives, thereby raising the threat of consequential confrontation and conflict. The ease of international travel and communication and the increased availability of material resources lead to more diverse and potentially conflictual proselytizing initiatives than ever before, thereby raising the political and security stakes for all concerned. What may have been farfetched scenarios of effective proselytization are now easily implemented (from North America and East Asia into Eastern Europe and Russia, from the Middle East and South Asia into central Asia or sub-Saharan Africa) and are therefore more threatening to their opponents. The hold of formally or informally established churches over their membership and territories is fast diminishing in some places, while resurgent religious groups seek to control or influence the state in order to enforce their own models of governance or policy. Massive financial resources, media campaigns, technical expertise, and political influence on powerful states can now easily be mounted in support of cobelievers around the world, whether in support of their right and efforts to proselytize or to "protect" them from proselytization by others. Like many aspects of domestic and international affairs after the Cold War, previously established patterns of religious (sometimes including ethnic) power relations no longer apply, with consequent possibilities of political fragmentation or reorganization of existing states in pursuit of old or new rivalries and alliances. In other words, the same conditions of democratization and economic liberalization often provide the conditions for increased religious pluralization and proselytization activities.

On the mediation side, the same dynamic of increased possibilities of confrontation and conflict may enhance the prospects of negotiations and peaceful settlement precisely because the stakes can become too high for all concerned to pursue hostile means. In other words, the plausibility of violent secession and separate statehood with transnational support and encouragement may force all sides to a conflict to reconsider their options for just and peaceful cooperation within an existing state.[3] That is to say, deadlock or stalemate resulting from relatively matched power and resources of proselytizers and target groups may propel both sides to seek peaceful mediation for their competing claims.[4]

The key question to be addressed later in this chapter is whether the modern human rights paradigm, and the notion of communal self-determination in particular, may provide a theoretical framework for mediation between these competing claims. It is important to note here that such a framework should also be assessed as a possible source of both policy directions and practical guidelines for the mediation of these competing claims. As I will argue later, the possibility of a human rights paradigm should be explored and developed in this context because it is already part of the foundation of freedom of religion, which includes the right to proselytize, on the one hand, and the right to self-determination, which can be the basis of resistance to proselytization efforts, on the other.

Prevailing conceptions of democracy stipulate that the state should foster religious pluralism without undue preference for a particular religion over others. These conceptions of democracy require religions to sustain themselves and thrive on the cogency and validity of their message to believers without coercion or undue advantage over unbelievers and their beliefs or lifestyle.[5] This religious "neutrality" of the state is supposed to be enshrined in the constitution and legal system of the state, which protect religious rights as well as related freedoms of association, assembly, and expression for all, in addition to safeguarding the autonomy of civil society organizations engaged in the provision of educational, health, or social and charitable services. These ideas are also associated with the modern human rights paradigm and the principle of self-determination, though with some conceptual difficulty as discussed later.

Unfortunately, it seems that the emerging democracies of Eastern Europe and the former Soviet Union and the recent wave of democratization in Africa have failed to live up to these ideals. In Eastern Europe and the former Soviet Union, older "established" churches and communities seek to dominate or eliminate local religious and cultural rivals. Yet the same older churches feel threatened by, even besieged by, foreign religious groups deploying vast material resources and human expertise in attempting to attract converts away from their present religious and community affiliations. Unable to match the educational, health, and other advantages of the foreign proselytizers, local religious groups appeal to the state for protection of their traditional status and membership. Yet, the recent veneer of constitutional protection of religious rights and other freedoms is often being subverted by overt state favoritism of some religious groups and oppression of others. Rival local and foreign religious groups in many parts of the world are now locked in a "new war for souls" of mutual defamation, manipulation of political power, and deployment of constitutional norms and legal mechanisms for purported religious advantage, with consequent religious fragmentation and fundamentalism. Before highlighting some aspects of the context and processes of this phenomenon in relation to Africa in particular, it might be helpful to clarify briefly the nature of proselytization in general.

The Dynamics of Proselytization

Perceptions of the nature and role of proselytization are often conditioned or influenced by such factors as personal experience or religious orientation and disciplinary or professional perspectives. Such perceptions can also be affected by the desire to seek or promote pragmatic approaches to resolving acute political or security problems in specific situations. Existing scholarship on the subject in English reflects this diversity of perceptions and perspectives, but mainly in relation to Christianity,[6] with little on Islam, the other proselytizing religion relevant to the African context.[7] Moreover, as observed by Christopher Clark, the largest amount of literature on proselytization is "in house histories," followed in volume by material from a theological and church historical perspective; works that take account of political context and social/cultural factors take third place.[8] Some studies deal with the nature and process of "conversion" and related religious experiences from the perspectives of social-science theory or psychology.[9] The following remarks are not intended to review or discuss this wide variety of literature. Rather, my purpose here is to offer some general reflections on proselytization with a view to addressing the issues in relation to the mediation of competing claims within a human rights framework in particular.

To its proponents, proselytization is about the freedom to propagate one's own religious commitments in an effort to share with others the merits and benefits that the religion is held to provide for the individual and communal life of believers. Proselytization is also represented as a religious imperative for believers to pursue for their own personal salvation and self-realization. The sacred history of Christianity or Islam, for example, is cited to illustrate the transforming power of religious commitment—how the very few powerless and oppressed early believers managed to transform their own lives and to infuse the values and institutions of their religion into many other communities. The underlying claim is that target groups would probably "see the light" if only they were allowed to hear the message or observe the living example of the believers. That is, proselytization is said to be for the "good" of intended target groups as much as it is for the benefit of those who seek to proselytize others.

Such perceptions of proselytization are premised on two claims. First, the members of the target group are free to accept or reject the message of the proselytizer once they have had a chance to hear it from the believers themselves. Second, proselytizers are entitled "as of right" to reach the target group with their religious message, regardless of the declared or presumed response of that group. Both propositions are problematic because, in the majority of cases, the target group is unlikely to be truly free to accept or reject the message of the proselytizer, nor is the demand of access by the proselytizers independent from the material and political interests and concerns of both sides.

Proselytization is hardly ever simply and exclusively about the communication of a religious message, to be accepted or rejected on its own terms. Interaction over a religious message is necessarily embedded in the cultural and ideological context of, on the one hand, the proselytizers and their community of believers and, on the other, the target individuals of proselytization and their community. Throughout human history, religious interaction has always been as much about material interests and power relations as it has been about spiritual insights and moral values. Proselytization is by definition the effort of believers in one religion to change the spiritual and material conditions of perceived unbelievers. Otherwise, the social, economic, and political transformation of convert communities may not occur as claimed in the sacred histories of proselytizing religions.

As a consequence of this dynamic, the opponents of proselytization perceive it as a threat to the political independence, material well-being, and individual and collective self-identity of target groups. From this perspective, proselytization is inherently dangerous and offensive to its actual or potential target group precisely because it seeks to radically change people's identities and lifestyles. This is especially the case when indigenous groups are targeted because their religious beliefs and practices are central to their cultural identity. That is to say, the objection is to the very nature and objectives of the process and is only confirmed by the prospects of its success, regardless of the "fairness" of its methods. At this level, proselytization is rejected for the implicit, if not explicit, assumption of the proselytizer that the target group needs changing and that the religion of the proselytizer offers a better alternative. This implication of religious and cultural superiority is, therefore, integral to the very notion of proselytization, regardless of the methods used or the power relations of the two sides.

Moreover, opponents of proselytization claim that experience everywhere shows that it has been used throughout history to spearhead or legitimize local domination or imperialist expansion by foreign powers. They dispute the facts and implications of the sacred history of Christianity and Islam and challenge claims about the cultural and ideological content of those religions, as well as the material objectives of their proselytizing agents. In so doing, these opponents emphasize that, in the early history or recent experience of their communities, the issue was never simply about spiritual insights or moral values that were to be freely accepted or rejected as such. The objection here is twofold. First, the issue is never simply a matter of a "free market of religious ideas" competing on a "level playing field," where the inherent validity of one set of religious beliefs is seeking to expose the invalidity of the other in order simply to "persuade" believers in the latter religion to freely accept the former. Second, and relatedly, serious and systematic proselytization is unlikely to be attempted, or to be successful, except when the proselytizers are encouraged and supported by extrareligious material advantages over the target group.

This analysis of the all-important *dynamics* of proselytization can be further clarified by highlighting the two aspects of *agency* and *self-determination*. First, advocacy of and opposition to proselytization are usually done by individuals who claim to speak on behalf of their community of believers or the target group, respectively. While the moral and material support of the general public of each community is actively sought by those elites, the community at large is rarely involved in the actual discourse of competing religions, cultures, and ideologies. Second, and regardless of the apparent terms of the debate, these competing claims are necessarily about communal self-determination. On the one hand, the proponents of proselytization demand the possibility of converting others as a matter of exercising their individual freedom of religion in collaboration with other members of their own religious community, but the process also involves an attempt to transform the other community. On the other hand, opponents reject the intrusion in the name of protecting the existing expression of the self-determination of their community, in material as well as ideological terms, often without substantiating their claim to speak for the community or justifying the assumptions they are making about the practical content of self-determination for that community.

In the polemics of proselytization, the proponents tend to avoid acknowledging its wider implications and seek to challenge the right of their opponents to speak on behalf of the target group. That is, the proponents may insist that their objective is purely religious and claim that the target group would be freely willing to listen and perhaps accept the message if only their own elites allowed them to hear it. Paradoxically, that denial of wider political, economic, and cultural agendas is usually coupled with a sense of assertive self-confidence that proselytizers derive from their own material advantage over the target group. In so doing, proselytizers are appropriating the agency of their own religious communities by claiming to discharge its obligation of "a mission of salvation." Since those communities at large are unlikely to agree at least on the wider implications of proselytization, there may be problems of agency between the claims of the individual proselytizers (and their religious organizations), on the one hand, and the wider home communities that fund and support them through the use of (or the threat of the use of) economic and even military power, on the other. Whatever the private motives of proselytizers may be, they are unlikely to be identical to those of the national communities on whose strength and resources they draw in seeking to proselytize others. For example, while missionaries for specific religious communities in the United States draw on the material and diplomatic resources of their country in pursuit of proselytization, other American religious communities and the public at large may not be in agreement with that objective as such, though they may accept the wider material and political benefits of missionary work.

In contrast, opponents tend to emphasize the wider implications of proselytization by believers in another religion and may avoid acknowledging the real nature and internal contradictions of their claim to protect the existing expression of self-determination of the target community. While presenting the proselytizer as simply and purely the agent of an imperial or colonial power, opponents tend to claim that they are only protecting the beliefs or religious identity of their community without admitting the ramifications of that claim. Even to the extent that opponents of proselytization might acknowledge the latter, they are unlikely to recognize that the status quo they are defending may not be a true and valid expression of self-determination by the community at all. In other words, opposition to proselytization is premised on an alleged communal (even national) consensus on the religious beliefs and material conditions of the community (or country at large) that must be defended against external intrusion by the proselytizers and the imperial powers they serve. Internal disagreement about such intrusions, they would assert, must be suppressed in the interest of unity against the allegedly greater external danger of proselytization and its purportedly detrimental consequences.

In my view, a more plausible position between these two polarized claims is to acknowledge the positive aspects of proselytization while trying to guard against its risks and excesses. Notwithstanding the absolutist claims of both proponents and opponents, proselytization initiatives can have positive consequences for both sides of the relationship. The challenge proselytization represents can invigorate the religious, social, and political life of the target group as it attempts to better articulate its own beliefs and enhance the individual and communal life of its members in order more effectively to resist that external threat. The reality of open contestation forces the community to seek to demonstrate to its own members the validity of its claims about their religious and material well-being under the status quo. In the process, significant positive change can occur in practice, if only in an effort to match or do better than the benefits the proselytizers claim to bring to the religious and material life of the community in question. It is also reasonable to expect these processes generally to promote the political awareness and organization of the target community.

Similar consequences can also be expected to occur within the religious community represented by the proselytizers, as it will be challenged to live up to its claims of religious enlightenment and social and personal well-being. The fact that the religious community of the proselytizer is presented as a model for other communities to follow will in itself attract scrutiny and criticism by others, thereby generating internal efforts to address social, political, and economic, as well as religious, problems. In other words, it is true that competition in a free market of religious ideas can be beneficial to all sides, even though this market is hardly ever as free as its proponents claim.

In light of these remarks, I would conclude that, despite its problematic nature and negative associations, proselytization is actually a vital part of the dynamism of spiritual and intellectual development of individual persons, as well as the social, political, material, and artistic life of communities and societies at large. Proselytization is too integral and important to people's lives for it to be suppressed altogether, yet it is too problematic to leave totally unregulated for the powerful to manipulate and exploit at will. Accordingly, the question is not only how proselytization can be practiced subject to appropriate limitations but also how such regulation can be effectively implemented in an orderly and peaceful manner. In order to address this question properly, the issues should be placed in the present African context.

Context and Processes of Proselytization in Africa

Like many other issues of public policy in Africa today, the mediation of competing claims to religious freedom and communal self-determination should be considered against the background of two related phenomena, namely,

European colonialism and globalization. Though African societies were certainly not isolated from each other or insulated from external influence in the past, various types of European colonialism have had the most far-reaching and enduring impact by the sheer scale and magnitude of the changes they introduced in the continent. For the purposes of this chapter in particular, I would emphasize that it was colonialism that primarily determined the nature of the postcolonial states that continue to rule African societies and control their interactions with the rest of the world in this age of growing globalization. What does this mean, and how is it relevant to the mediation of competing claims about proselytization?

Present states in Africa are direct successors of the colonies established by agreements among European powers (especially the Berlin Conference of 1884–85), regardless of the wishes of local groups. The borders of the colonies that African states came to inherit were established by European continental partition and occupation rather than by African political realities or geography. Colonial governments were organized according to European colonial theory and practice, as modified by expediency; their economies were managed with imperial and local colonial considerations primarily in mind; and their legal systems reflected the interests and values of European imperial powers. The vast majority of the African populations of those colonies had little or no constitutional standing in them.[10]

When independence came, it usually signified the transfer of control over authoritarian power structures and processes of government from colonial masters to local elites.[11] With few exceptions, the postcolonial state in Africa, was, as Patrick Chabal observes,

> both overdeveloped and soft. It was overdeveloped because it was erected, artificially, on the foundations of the colonial state. It did not grow organically from within civil society. It was soft because, although in theory all-powerful, it scarcely had the administrative and political means of its dominance. Neither did it have an economic basis on which to rest political power.[12]

Since independence, the preservation of juridical statehood and territorial integrity, rather than promotion of the ability and willingness of the state to live up to the practical requirements of sovereignty, became the primary concern of African states.

To make matters worse, the vast majority of first constitutions were either suspended or radically altered by military usurpers or single-party states within a few years of independence.[13] For decades after independence, successive cycles of civilian and military governments, alike in the majority of African countries, maintained the same colonial legal and institutional mechanisms to suppress political dissent to their policies and to deny accountability for their own actions.[14] Lacking any sense of "ownership," expectation of protection and service, or a general belief in their ability to influence its functioning, African societies often regard the postcolonial state with profound mistrust. They tend to tolerate its existence as an unavoidable evil but prefer to have the least interaction with its institutions and processes.[15] Nevertheless, the postcolonial state is supposed to be firmly in control of the formulation and implementation of public policy at home and the conduct of international relations abroad. In other words, it is the primary framework within which African societies seek to realize their right to self-determination in an increasingly globalized world.

As a working definition, I take *globalization* to refer to the transformation of the relations between states, institutions, groups, and individuals; the universalization of certain practices, identities, and structures; and the global restructuring of economic relations within the modern capitalist framework.[16] Zdravko Mlinar defines the term as "extending the determinative frameworks of social change to the world as a whole" and suggests the following five dimensions of the process: (1) increasing global interdependence whereby the activities of people in specific areas have repercussions that go beyond local, regional, or national borders; (2) the expansion of domination and dependence; (3) homogenization that tends to emphasize uniformity rather than mutual exclusivity; (4) diversification within "territorial communities" as they open to the wealth of diversity of the world as a whole; and (5) overcoming temporal discontinuities by, for example, temporal inclusiveness resulting from the functioning of particular services to global spaces.[17]

In my view, a crucial element of such definitions is the fact that globalization is simply a more effective and comprehensive vehicle or instrument of perpetuating existing power relations within the same country, as well as in its relationship to other countries at the regional and international level. As Tade Akin Aina rightly observes, commonly cited definitions of globalization fail to address "the importance of notions such as coercion, conflict, polarization, domination, inequality, exploitation and injustice. . . . There is little or nothing about monopolies, disruption and dislocation of the labor and other markets, the emergence of a global regulatory chaos and possible anomie and how these are being exploited for gain."[18] Accordingly, one would expect globalization to facilitate and intensify neocolonial relations between African and developed countries,[19] the domination of civil society by the state within African countries themselves, as well as any hegemonic or conflictual relations that may exist within African societies themselves.

Against this background, I will now briefly review available literature on proselytization in Africa. As with the earlier review of literature about proselytization in general, my purpose here is only to highlight aspects that are pertinent to the subject of this chapter, namely, the mediation of competing claims to religious freedom and communal self-determination. For this reason, I am concerned with works that take into account historical and political context, sociocultural factors, and so forth, as opposed to material produced by religious groups for their own internal use or from a theological perspective.[20] Even for this social science type of literature, it is not surprising to find nothing specifically on the subject of mediation of competing claims as such, because this formulation of the issue brings together different disciplinary approaches of scholars who have not been open to possibilities of collaboration. In other words, while scholars of religion rarely consider human rights aspects of their work, lawyers and political scientists who are concerned with human rights issues tend to have a secular perspective.

Available works can be reviewed under the following headings: conversion and related religious experiences, Islamic proselytization, Christian proselytization, and works that consider relations between these two proselytizing religions.

An example of the first type is the dialogue between Robin Horton and Humphrey Fisher regarding the nature and circumstances of conversion from "traditional" to "world" religions. Horton begins (in a book review of John Peel's study of two Aladura or "prayer healing" churches in Nigeria) by asserting that both Islam and Christianity have achieved only conditional acceptance, suggesting that beliefs and practices of the so-called world religions are only accepted where they happen to coincide with the responses of traditional cosmology to other, nonmissionary factors of the modern situation. He sees Islam and Christianity as catalysts that trigger reactions of which they do not always appear among the end products, and he asserts that the success of these two religions as institutions depends on the extent of their willingness to accept these roles.[21] Fisher responds by suggesting that Horton has "overestimated the survival . . . of original African elements of religion; and more important, has under-estimated the willingness and ability of Africans to

make even rigorous Islam and Christianity their own."[22] Following other ex-
changes, Fisher subsequently defines their disagreement as between Horton's
view that "the essential patterns of religious development in black Africa are
determined by the enduring influence of a traditional cosmology which arises
from the ashes of colonialism and conversion," on the one hand, and Fisher's
view that "a genuine religious transference is possible," on the other.[23]

Recent scholarship, however, reflects concern about the analytical utility
of the term *conversion*, even in the framework of a single religion like Christianity. Noting its European connotations, John and Jean Comaroff wonder
whether it oversimplifies the real process it purports to describe: "How does
it grasp the highly variable, usually gradual, often implicit and demonstrably
'syncretic' manner in which social identities, cultural styles, and ritual practices of African peoples were transformed by the evangelical encounter?"[24]
According to K. F. Morrison, "It is a confusion of categories to use the word
conversion as though it were an instrument of critical analysis, equally appropriate to any culture or religion. . . . The word is more properly a subject,
rather than a tool of analysis."[25] Talal Asad comments that "it would be better
to say that in studying conversion, one was dealing with the narratives by
which people apprehend and describe a radical change in the significance of
their lives. Sometimes these narratives employ the notion of divine intervention; at other times the notion of a secular teleology."[26]

On Islamic proselytization, J. Spencer Trimingham provides a historical
analysis in which he divides Africa into seven culture zones and treats each
as a historical unity to provide data on the processes and consequences of
"Islamization" in each region.[27] He discusses factors that affected the spread
of Islam and suggests that it has always followed the routes of traders.[28] A
deeper and more focused historical analysis of the spread of Islam in West
Africa is presented by Mervyn Hiskett, who offers detailed critical examination of proselytization in the context of specific case studies. For example,
he describes the roles of several ethnic groups who differed in their Islamic
emphasis and discusses the role of Islamic education.[29] Reiterating that conversion takes place on a continuum between military conquest and peaceful persuasion, he suggests that, although military means have been labeled
less effective, the change in political and social institutions by the conquerors
often forces ideological change. Distinguishing between "trade" as an institution and "traders" as people using that structure, he insists that it was the
institution that was the most influential factor in spreading Islam in the region.[30] He also further asserts that literacy is often the impetus that propels

The Modern Human Rights Paradigm

Historically, and up to the present time, disputes about proselytization were often settled by the use or threat of force or other form of coercion, rather than through negotiations and agreement as a matter of principle. Proselytizers were sometimes able to compel access to the target group, while at other times they were successfully resisted by their opponents, with religious rationale being used by both sides to legitimate their actions or mobilization of people and resources in support of their cause. The question raised by this chapter is whether it is possible and useful to cast these issues in human rights terms, for both proselytizers and target groups: Why and how is a human rights paradigm relevant? What difference is it likely to make to the mediation of conflicts and tensions over proselytization? How can the potential of a human rights paradigm in this regard be realized?

The realm of what is presently known as human rights can be traced to ancient beginnings of normative attempts to define human relationships in ways that are conducive to peaceful resolution of conflict and tension under the rule of law.[41] The rule of law can also be traced to similar beginnings and long evolution. Those early normative definitions evolved in content and mechanisms of implementation with the development of each community. As European models of states gradually prevailed throughout the world, national governments became responsible for regulating human relationships through the normative systems and mechanisms of implementation of each country. This function continues today under constitutional schemes of rights.

While the modern concept of human rights is supposed to have undergone drastic transformation since the adoption of the Charter of the United Nations in 1945, it remains bound to domestic frameworks for its practical specification and implementation, including questions of competing claims of religious freedom. On the one hand, under the United Nations system,[42] as well as under the regional systems it inspired,[43] normative propositions about human relationships are now made on behalf of all human beings as such, rather than as citizens of particular states. On the other hand, the international law framework that gives binding force to all treaties—including the UN Charter itself and the human rights conventions adopted under its auspices (as well as those adopted under regional systems)—presupposes the sovereignty and exclusive territorial jurisdiction of the state. Not only must a state freely ratify a treaty in order to be bound by its terms but the international legal obligations assumed by a state under such treaties are supposed to be implemented by the state itself through its own domestic jurisdiction.

Moreover, the purported transition of certain norms from domestic civil liberties into universal human rights retains some of the features of that conceptual origin. For example, a key feature of the "universalization" of the domestic civil liberties paradigm is the notion that human rights can only be claimed against the state and its official agents, rather than against whoever might challenge or violate them. Two corollaries of this conception are particularly relevant to the analysis of this chapter: the persistence of the notion that human rights can only be held by individual persons and the realities of a hierarchy of rights despite repeated claims of the interdependence and indivisibility of all human rights. While the first feature tends to frustrate possibilities of articulating and implementing rights for groups or collective entities (herein called collective rights),[44] the second gives priority to civil and political rights over economic, social, and cultural rights, such as the right to food, shelter, health care, and education.

It is true that a people's right to self-determination is recognized under the United Nations system, but this right is generally believed to mean the right of a people to political independence from foreign or colonial rule, rather than the collective right of groups and communities to cultural survival and integrity within an existing state (short of secession and separate statehood). Other examples of what might be called collective rights under international law can be cited,[45] but strong opposition to the concept itself persists among human rights scholars and activists.

Under what has become the established framework after the adoption of the Universal Declaration of 1948, proselytization is generally understood as a matter of freedom of religion of individual persons and their human rights of expression and association as individuals practicing their religion in community with others. While a right to proselytize was taken for granted, the primary concern was with the ability of an individual person to adopt a religion, or change it, according to his or her own free will, without compulsion or coercion. I believe that this conception of individual freedom of religion remains vitally important throughout the world and could certainly be used to achieve some degree of protection for both the proselytizer and individual members of the target group. But I also believe that this conception of individual freedom of religion cannot adequately address the concerns of communities about proselytization and its consequences. Individual religious choices, however freely made, do affect communal interests, especially in view of the dynamic of proselytization as highlighted above. For example, apostasy as a capital crime under traditional Islamic law (Shari'a) should be seen in light of the linkages between religious faith and "citizenship" in early Islamic states and the consequences of individual choices for the community. For a Muslim to abandon belief in Islam, it has been argued by some modern Islamic scholars, was tantamount to treason in the modern sense of the term.[46]

In view of such linkages between individual choices and communal concerns, I suggest that the present human rights paradigm should include a dynamic and creative understanding of *collective rights* in order to address those concerns, as well as individual rights to safeguard freedom of belief. But in suggesting adoption of collective rights, I see them as complementing, not replacing, individual rights. In fact, individual rights will always remain necessary for the definition and implementation of any collective right. For example, the protection of individual freedoms of expression and association is extremely important for the integrity of the process of regulating questions of membership, political representation, equality, and justice within the group. Without valid resolution of such questions, a group cannot be entitled to claim collective human rights.

This thesis will be further explained and substantiated in the next section of this chapter as it applies to issues of proselytization. What I propose to do here by way of introduction is to develop a general argument in support of the *possibility* of the inclusion of collective rights within the human rights framework. I say "possibility" because I am calling for the careful examination of the candidacy of each claim for a collective right, not a blanket inclusion of every assertion of such a right.

My first point is to question the present conceptual opposition to the idea of collective rights as human rights simply because it does not fit the individual human rights paradigm. In my view, this objection not only mocks the universality of human rights but also contributes to the growing isolation and irrelevance of the international human rights movement. Since a collective framework for the realization of rights is essential for the majority of human societies and communities around the world, rejection of any possibility of collective rights undermines the assumption that universal human rights are accepted and applicable everywhere. Moreover, the categorical exclusion of this perspective from the human rights paradigm is making this paradigm less and less relevant to the daily lives of many societies. As emphasized by James Anaya, the Western liberal perspective acknowledges the rights of the individual on the one hand, and the sovereignty of the total social collective on the other, but it is not alive to the rich variety of intermediate or alternative associational group-ings actually found in human cultures, nor is it prepared to ascribe to such groups any rights not reducible either to the liberties of the citizen or to the prerogative of the state.[47]

In my view, the exclusion of any possibility of collective rights is unten-able for two reasons: the actual interdependence of individual and collective rights and the inadequacy of an individual-rights paradigm in certain situa-tions. Regarding the first reason, I suggest that neither can individual rights be fully realized without collective rights nor can the latter be ensured with-out the protection of the former.[48] This is especially true, I believe, because of the need for structural change and long-term solutions, as opposed to the piecemeal, case-by-case approach of individual rights, as explained below. This combination of an acceptance of interdependence of rights and appre-ciation of the need for long-term structural approaches is clearly reflected in Article 5 of the International Convention for the Elimination of All Forms of Discrimination against Women (1979),[49] which provides that "States Parties shall take all appropriate measures: (a) To modify the social and cultural pat-terns of conduct of men and women, with a view to achieving the elimination of prejudices and customary and all other practices which are based on the idea of the inferiority or the superiority of either of the sexes or on stereo-typed roles for men and women." The presumed objective of this Convention is to protect the human rights of individual women, yet it is clear that a more structural approach is needed to eliminate root causes of the violation of these rights. By imposing this obligation under Article 5, the Convention is clearly envisaging men and women as groups, rather than as individual persons.

As to the inadequacy of an individual-rights approach in some situations, we should recall the assumptions and nature of the process by which these rights are supposed to be protected in everyday life. It is commonly asserted that the main advantage of individual human rights from a practical applica-tion perspective is their "justiciability," which signifies the ability of a court of law to identify an individual victim and a violator and to prescribe a remedy for the violation. The way this is supposed to work is that when a person or group of persons believe that one of their individual human rights has been violated by a state policy or administrative action or the behavior of a state official, the aggrieved party or parties can sue for redress (or prosecute if criminal charges are warranted, as in a torture case) before a court of law. If the issue is not settled out of court, a trial may follow whereby the court will determine whether a violation has occurred and direct the implementation of an appropriate remedy.

It is, therefore, clear that this conception of legal protection of individual human rights presupposes that the violation of rights is the exception rather than the rule, because no system for the legal enforcement of rights can have the resources and political will to cope with massive violations. This conception also assumes that potential victims have access to and can afford to pay for legal services, that the judiciary is independent and effective, that government officials will comply with court orders, and so forth. As such, this model is not only limited, exclusive, expensive, and inaccessible to most Africans whose human rights are routinely violated by official and nonofficial actors, but it is also incapable of redressing the type and scope of violations most frequently suffered by Africans. Recent experiences with genocide and ethnic cleansing, massive forced population movements, increasingly unequal economic and political power relations, unpayable national debt, and coercive structural adjustment programs in Africa make an exclusive focus on individual human rights unrealistic, if not counterproductive.

Finally, I believe it is important to recognize the possibility of collective rights as human rights,[50] rather than as part of domestic or constitutional structures or as subject to international law in general.[51] The special value of the modern human rights paradigm is that it provides an external normative frame of reference to which victims can appeal for redress against their own governments in accordance with universal human rights standards—that is, those rights applicable to all human beings without distinction on such grounds as, race, gender, belief, or national origin.

While drawing on previous and existing experiences, the proposed approach to the development of collective rights can be distinguished as follows. Treaty-based regimes for the protection of religious and ethnic minorities can be seen as one of the antecedents of the present human rights paradigm in that they imposed obligations under international law. But those minority-rights regimes offered only specific protections for discrete minorities, rather than as a matter of general principles of international human rights law applicable to all groups throughout the world. In any case, the whole system ended with the collapse of the League of Nations and was deliberately rejected at the time of the drafting of the Universal Declaration of Human Rights.[52] Domestic constitutional regimes not only vary with the peculiar historical, economic, and political context of each country but are also supposed to operate only within the domestic constitutional framework of the country in question.[53] In other words, domestic regimes as such do not permit the possibility of challenging their own scope and/or implementation in terms of internationally established norms and institutions. My point here is that, while constitutional regimes of rights should certainly be maintained and improved, they should not be seen as an adequate substitute for the development of an internationally recognized regime of collective human rights that offers the benefits of the above-mentioned external, international frame of reference.

It is true that the notion of collectivities as bearers of rights is problematic because of ambiguities in the nature and dynamics of membership, as well as in agency and representation. But it should be noted that the notion of individual human rights—as entitlement of all human beings by virtue of their humanity and without distinction on such grounds as race, gender, belief, or national origin—also has had its problems. That is, the present concept of individual human rights is the product of a long historical process of contestation and negotiation. The practical implementation of individual human rights continues to be hampered by entrenched notions of sovereignty and exclusive territorial jurisdiction; weak acceptance of economic, social, and cultural rights; and so forth. In addition to facing similar difficulties of implementation, the notion of collective rights remains conceptually problematic precisely because it has not yet received serious consideration by human rights scholars and activists. What is important is that when collective rights are considered, they should not be expected to fit the same conceptual framework and implementation strategies of individual rights.[54]

In conclusion of this section, I suggest that the same dynamics that have transformed the rights of citizens into universal rights of all human beings will probably continue to propel further evolution of the concept, as well as its content and implementation mechanisms. The initial transformation of the concept of domestic constitutional rights into the paradigm adopted by the Universal Declaration of Human Rights of 1948 was produced by a sequence of local and global developments culminating in the catastrophic events leading to and including the Second World War, which exposed the drastic inadequacy of exclusive national jurisdictions for the protection of civil liberties. The political will to combat a state's oppression of its own citizens generated the modern conceptual and institutional instruments for the promotion and protection of universal human rights. While much needs to be done to realize that vision, significant progress in the protection of individual civil and political rights has already been achieved around the world. The same drive must continue today, I suggest, to expand the conceptual and institutional limits of the present framework in response to new threats to the protection of human rights arising from local and global developments. This possibility is particularly important for the application of a human rights paradigm to issues of proselytization.

The Mediation of Competing Claims of Proselytization and Self-Determination

In the section above on the dynamics of proselytization, I have attempted to highlight the basic dilemma presented by such activities, especially in the present African context. For one thing, the issue is hardly ever simply and exclusively a matter of communicating a religious message to be accepted or rejected on its own terms. As a deliberate effort to change the spiritual and material conditions of target groups, proselytization is by definition offensive and hegemonic—that is, it is premised on the assumption of proselytizers that the belief systems and institutions of target groups need to change and that those of the proselytizer offer a better alternative. Moreover, the claims of proselytizers that they have a "right" to propagate their beliefs, while their target groups have the "freedom" to accept or reject the message, overlook the role of power relations. Without a power differential in their favor, proselytizers would not have the self-confidence and resources needed in seeking to convert others. Yet, without redressing that differential, the freedom of the target community to accept or reject the message cannot be realized. Nevertheless, proselytization is too integral to people's lives to be suppressed altogether, yet it is too problematic to leave totally unregulated.

In response, I suggested that a human rights paradigm should be applied to mediate competing claims about proselytization and its consequences. Given the communal nature and implications of the interaction, however, especially in the African context, the proposed human rights paradigm should include collective or group rights as well as the rights of individual persons. The primary reason for the need for collective rights is that communal concerns are necessarily those of the community at large, rather than of some of their specific individual members. Otherwise, certain self-appointed elites will claim to speak on behalf of the whole community without credible accountability to that community. That misappropriation is precisely what the human rights paradigm is supposed to prevent. In other words, for the human rights paradigm to play its mediatory role, it has to include collective rights as well as individual rights. Without the former, communal concerns cannot be properly formulated, and without the latter, there is the risk of elite appropriation of the voice of the community.

How, then, will these rights operate in practice without violating the rights of individual persons in the community? In particular, how will questions of membership, agency, and representation be resolved and by whom? For example, who is to decide on the existence and termination of the membership of a person in a specific community? To address these questions in proper context, it might be helpful to specify briefly some of the problems raised by the competing claims of proselytization and self-determination.

If the conclusions made earlier about the context and process of proselytization in Africa are to be formulated as problems to be overcome, they may read as follows:

1. How does one reduce, and eventually eliminate, the hegemonic, unilateral nature of proselytization in Africa? What is that rationale, as agreed upon by all parties? Moreover, since that presupposes that all sides must understand and appreciate the concerns of one another, how can this prerequisite be realized?

2. If the validity of the assumptions of well-informed freedom of choice and fair play of matched protagonists on a "level playing field" is part of the answer to the above question, how can that be achieved and verified in practice? Would a voluntary code of conduct be sufficient without independent verification of compliance? If such verification is entrusted to a judicial or quasi-judicial institution of the state, what will safeguard against other forms of state interference for ulterior motives?

3. If another part of the answer is for proselytizers to respect the apprehensions of communities about the profound communal conditions of presumably autonomous individual action, how can that be achieved? Can proselytizers accept the proposition that individual decisions to convert, even if they were well-informed and freely made, undermine and erode communal identity and institutions, and yet still maintain the vigor of their mission? Does not such vigor require disrespect, if not contempt, for the communal identity and institutions of the communities they seek to convert, which are probably based on the religion the proselytizers wish to replace with their own?

The approach I propose for addressing these questions in the African context is the process of mediation of competing claims rather than an attempt to prescribe specific solutions in advance. It is in this context that I see a vital role for the state not only as mediator of competing claims of proselytizers according to some basic "ground rules" but also as protector of the interests of the target groups. As noted earlier, given the inability or unwillingness of the state in Africa to perform this regulatory function, the so-called right to proselytize would be open to serious abuse without the prospects of redress. It was also noted above that since globalization simply intensifies existing power relations, it is likely to exacerbate any hegemonic or conflictual relations that may exist within the same African society, both among competing proselytizers and between them and their subjects.

But despite the importance of its role, the state is only one party to the process of mediation I am proposing. Other parties include existing religious institutions within the communities, other civil society organizations (whatever form of operation they may actually take in the community), as well as representatives of proselytizing groups. Moreover, the external constituencies of those non-state actors also have their role. One of the consequences of globalization is that the increasing ease of communication and expanding reach of the media enable groups and communities throughout the world to cooperate in pursuit of shared objectives. As shown by the cases of the Ogoni of Nigeria and Sabbistas of Mexico, apparently isolated local communities can now attract much attention and support for their cause among human rights organizations, environmental groups, and other constituencies from around the world.

Much of the success of the proposed process of mediation will depend, in my view, on the effectiveness of educating all parties about the concerns of the others. A related but slightly different requirement is the need to inspire or persuade all sides to respond positively to the concerns of the others. But first of all, there has to be an appreciation of the need for the mediation of competing claims. If the proselytizers are true to their claims of moral commitment, they should understand and appreciate the concerns of the communities about the survival of their identity and institutions. Should that happen, then the communities would have no justification for refusing to allow proselytizing activities. But if either or both parties fail to live up to these mutual expectations, then the state should act as arbiter. The state, in turn, should be held accountable to civil society institutions for its performance of its role as arbiter. In this way, the mediation process acts as its own guardian.

Chapter 9

Globalization and Jurisprudence:
An Islamic Perspective

Professor Harold J. Berman has argued since the 1980s that the three traditional (and here we can read Western) schools of jurisprudence—positivism, naturalism, and historicism—should be integrated or that an integrative jurisprudence would draw on elements of all three schools.[1] Although I agree with the vision and rationale of Professor Berman's approach to an integrative jurisprudence, I maintain an overriding concern about its ability to incorporate different historical experiences and conceptions of law. As I understand it, the basic thrust of his approach is to revive the historical school of legal theory and to reintegrate it with its two rivals, positivism and natural law theory. The premise and rationale of this proposal owe much to the dynamics of an increasingly multifaceted globalization, which underpin Berman's call for the clarification and institutionalization of what he terms "world law."[2] It is to be expected that Berman would explain and illustrate his proposal with references to the historical experiences and conceptions of law most familiar to him—what he calls the "Western legal tradition."[3] But the questions remain. Can the concepts and methodologies of an integrative jurisprudence incorporate significantly different legal traditions from other parts of the world, even at a theoretical or conceptual level? Is such a project possible at all, and, if so, in what sense?

Since Berman's approach draws primarily on preexisting conceptions of Western schools of legal theory, the philosophical and political scope of such constituent elements, when integrated into a global school of jurisprudence, becomes uncertain. The fact that shared legal and philosophical principles operate through different national jurisdictions does not necessarily preclude the formulation of a more inclusive, integrative jurisprudence. The scope of the proposed jurisprudence can, of course, be limited to so-called national legal traditions, like that of the United States of America or what Berman calls the Western legal tradition. It seems to me that such limited claims, however, raise serious questions about the concept and methodology of the proposed integrative jurisprudence. At the national level, one may wonder about whose history or vision of history and whose conceptions of law are taken seriously in the formulation of this approach. Does it include minority or marginalized perspectives, like those of Native Americans or Hispanic communities? Indeed, are notions like "positivism" and "natural law" meaningful for such minority or marginal perspectives?

If the scope of an integrative jurisprudence is supposed to be broader than a specific national jurisdiction, the determination of that scope becomes problematic. To take a geographic criterion for the Western legal tradition would require accounting for the experiences of Spain under Francisco Franco, Nazi Germany, and Soviet Russia, which requires some ideological and political analysis. A geographic criterion would also leave out Latin America, Australia, and other parts of the world that are generally considered to be part of a Western legal tradition. Founding the determination on some normative or ideological ground is similarly problematic. For instance, how does the Western legal tradition account for socially conservative and economically capitalist perspectives, as well as liberal, socialist, or welfare ideologies that do not share the same ideological or philosophical assumptions? However conceived, it seems to me, such broad categories like the Western legal tradition raise corresponding questions of inclusion and exclusion in defining law and elaborating its jurisprudential framework.

Moreover, Berman's use of the term "world law" and emphasis on multifaceted globalization may indicate that he is speaking of a global scope for his proposed integrative jurisprudence. At that level, the same questions arise even more strongly when one considers the meaning of underlying notions of positivism and natural law and how such views of law and jurisprudence can be integrated. It is not clear, for example, how this approach applies to drastically different concepts of law, such as Islamic or Jewish law, which claim a divine source for legal authority, or to other significantly different legal traditions like those of China. How and to what extent can one speak of law and jurisprudence in the various legal traditions of the world in comparative terms that make an integrative jurisprudence possible at all?

In this light, it seems that Berman's call for an integrative jurisprudence raises similar questions at whatever level it is applied. For the purpose of this chapter, I take his proposal to be applicable at various levels according to the degree of integration of the legal system in question. This position does not mean that any legal system must be totally integrated, since there can be variations within even the same national system, as can be observed among federal and state jurisdictions in the United States. Rather, it is a matter of a sufficient degree of integration according to certain foundational principles that make it a coherent system. From my perspective, whether that is supposed to happen in a national, regional, normative, or ideological system—or at a global level as Berman suggests for world law—the basic question is whether, and to what extent, the analysis is inclusive of competing perspectives within the scope of the system.

It is not possible in this brief response to enumerate or closely examine the variety of possible factors that can limit or constrain the scope of analysis, which warrants some degree of generalization about law and its jurisprudential framework. At one level, such analysis can reflect differentials in power relations within and between various societies, whereby some conceptions of law and jurisprudence prevail over others. That ideological dominance, in turn, can be seen as representing concrete economic and political conditions or reflecting some normative ideological or cultural superiority of some models. In my view, the latter type of reasoning is illustrated by the ideology of European colonialism during the mid-nineteenth to mid-twentieth centuries that asserted the superiority of Western legal traditions over those of colonized societies in Africa and Asia.[4] Similar reasoning apparently asserted the irreversible triumph of Western economic liberalism on the collapse of Soviet Marxism by the early 1990s.[5] I am not concerned here with an assessment of such claims or their theoretical underpinnings.

Instead, I wish to explore the possibility of constructing a theoretical framework that can inform a more inclusive cross-cultural dialogue about an integrative jurisprudence. In my view, this line of thinking can contribute to advancing Berman's proposal in the present global context and its implications for different types of legal systems at the national, regional, and global levels. From this perspective, it seems clear to me that Berman's analysis indicates the need for an integrative jurisprudence but does not address the limitations of legal imagination and political will that can frustrate this initiative. A more inclusive, systematic, and creative approach to comparative legal studies than what prevails at present can improve the imagination of scholars and opinion leaders about the theoretical possibilities and practical benefits of the sort of integrative jurisprudence I would support. But this approach will have little sustainable impact unless it is accompanied by the necessary political will to overcome apprehensions about its policy implications at home and abroad.

In the last section, I will briefly examine the possibility of applying Berman's proposal to Islamic law, in light of the concerns and suggestions I make below. Both aspects of my response, however, are premised on my strong rejection of Samuel Huntington's simplistic and dangerous notion of the "clash of civilizations" that Berman seems to accept.[6] As already indicated regarding the Western legal tradition, purported dichotomies of civilizations or cultures are both simplistic and problematic. By any reasonable definition of the term, a so-called Western civilization would not only include the brutal conquest and colonization of the Americas, Africa, and much of Asia by European powers—and the United States, in a few cases—but also Nazi Germany and Fascist Spain and Italy only a few decades ago. These substantial, recent experiences of Western societies are hardly consistent with the enlightened liberal values that are supposed to distinguish Western civilization from African, Islamic, or Chinese civilizations. My stronger objection to Huntington's thesis is that it can easily be turned into a self-fulfilling prophecy, when each tradition conceives its relationship to others in terms of confrontational clash, instead of cooperation and mutual respect.

In my view, each civilization or culture contains competing values that correspond to similar values existing within other cultures. There are those who thrive on hostility and violent confrontation in Islamic as well as Western societies and those who seek cooperation and peaceful coexistence among both groups of societies. To take Huntington's thesis seriously would promote hostile and confrontational elements on both sides of his purported divide, while rejecting this dangerous view would support cooperative elements among them. From this perspective, I am suggesting that if lawyers and policymakers of different societies study each other's legal traditions in a constructive and respectful manner, they will find many more grounds for cooperation than for confrontation.

Globalization and Cosmopolitan Justice

A compelling and critical part of Berman's proposal is the argument that increasing economic, cultural, and demographic globalization makes it impossible to maintain isolationist or parochial views of law and jurisprudence.[7] The realities of the mobility of capital and labor, the decentralization of production, the intensification of trade, and the increase of population movements are now affecting the social and economic relations within societies, as well as in their relations with other societies. This dynamic is particularly true of the complex societies of Western Europe and North America, with their highly developed economies and global trade links throughout the world, but it can also be seen to a less drastic degree in developing African and Asian countries. These realities call for legal and jurisprudential responses that are genuinely inclusive of the wide variety of cultural and social composition of national populations and their global interactions. National as well as international law and jurisprudence must, therefore, take into account the requirements of global economic and security interdependence within and among all countries, regardless of their level of economic and social development, political stability, and military power. For our purposes here, the particular challenge facing American lawyers is to respond appropriately to the increasing ethnic and cultural diversity of the United States.[8] This view of legal and jurisprudential reflection is what I refer to in this section as "cosmopolitan justice."

This view may sound naïve or misguided in light of current international relations and the domestic environment in the United States in particular, which seem to be moving in the opposite direction. From my perspective, however, the atrocities of 9/11 emphasize even more the need for an integrative jurisprudence in support of international legality and the rule of law on a global scale. The fact that a small group of determined fanatics were able to inflict such massive loss of life and suffering—with far-reaching economic, political, security, and other consequences within the most powerful and developed country in the world—emphasizes what I call our shared human vulnerability. This interdependence is also underscored by the fact that atrocious terrorist attacks continue to occur in all parts of the world, in the name of all sorts of alleged causes or justifications. Moreover, since we cannot morally condemn and effectively combat these serious threats if we descend to the same level of barbarity, the nature and methods of international terrorism clearly confirm the need to uphold and promote the norms, institutions, and processes of lawful protection of security and effective accountability in accordance with the rule of law.

Yet the United States is doing the exact opposite by undermining, indeed repudiating in my view, the existing norms, institutions, and processes of international legality through its global military campaign and related activities.[9] For instance, it is ironic that the United States continues to resist and actively undermine the broad international initiative to establish the International Criminal Court in The Hague, which would have had jurisdiction over crimes against humanity, such as the 9/11 attacks, if it were operational at the time.[10] Despite opposition by the United States, the court was formally inaugurated on July 1, 2002, and, one hopes, will make useful contributions to the credibility of international legality and accountability, thereby rendering self-help and unilateral retaliation even more unnecessary.

Nevertheless, and perhaps because of the threat of international terrorism and the counterproductive militant response of the United States, I suggest that it is becoming clear that there is no alternative to peaceful cooperation within and among human societies everywhere. Regarding Berman's analysis in particular, the constituent elements of the integrative jurisprudence he proposes should reflect the historical, cultural, and legal diversity of national populations and their global interdependence. On a basic existential level, this view is premised on the reality of our cosmopolitan existence, as we are continually crossing borders and sharing identities throughout the world. Even for those who are physically confined to specific places, the realities of mounting globalization mean that their economic and security interests, as well as social relations and cultural identities, are not determined exclusively by their respective locations. But the notion of crossing borders and relating to different geographies is only a metaphor for reframing the same basic questions. Consciousness of this global cosmopolitanism of crossing borders and belonging to new geographies does not mean that it is possible to evade the fundamental questions of politics, identity, and justice, wherever one happens to be located. Whenever we cross boundaries, we are forming new boundaries or redefining old ones, rather than extinguishing all boundaries, and we must respond accordingly to the challenges of our new or modified location.

Thus, cosmopolitanism cannot mean complete detachment from time and place. As no human being can exist in suspended animation, he or she is always *somewhere* and constituted as *someone*, socially and politically, in relation to other human beings. In this light, the question is one of social and political location, that is, of which boundaries of inclusion and exclusion apply or need to be negotiated in one's specific location in time and place. The question is also one of power relations within these processes of shifting boundaries of inclusion and exclusion. Wherever the boundaries may be, and whatever membership or identity applies, such notions and their policy and legal implications must be negotiated through a specific set of power relations. If one talks about justice, then what is the measure of justice? Who defines it? How, in relation to which frame of reference and context, is it defined?

What are its policy and practical implications, and for whom? These questions should lead to reflection on a normative and institutional framework for achieving and sustaining cosmopolitan justice, whereby law and jurisprudence are responsive to the needs and aspirations of increasingly diverse populations and their national and global interdependence.

The notion of cosmopolitan justice can, of course, be invoked in a wide variety of settings and in relation to an extensive range of issues and concerns. Consequently, an equally wide variety of actors, speaking of a correspondingly extensive range of experiences and priorities, should continue to negotiate the meaning and implications of justice in each case. This negotiation can be in relation to problems of terrorism and retaliatory violence, as in the 9/11 attack and its aftermath, or over issues of race, health, development, the environment, and so forth. Instead of speculating about what the principle of cosmopolitan justice means in such a wide range of settings, I wish to propose a sufficiently broad framework where the concept and its implications can be negotiated and mediated among competing claims and perspectives. That is, what are the underlying guiding principles or standards for assessing success or failure in achieving a measure of justice that is responsive to the needs and aspirations of the wide variety of national populations in their global interaction with other populations? Regarding 9/11 and its aftermath, for instance, what is the frame of reference for determining what the United States is entitled to do at home and abroad, and what should it expect from other governments and societies?

From this perspective, I propose that international human rights law provides a practical set of safeguards to ensure sufficient "space" for all perspectives to emerge and be considered, as well as an institutional framework for realizing specific objectives. In my view, however, all human rights, whether classified as civil and political; economic, social, and cultural; or individual or collective, contribute to this combined framework for cosmopolitan justice. For example, civil and political rights like freedom of expression and association are obviously necessary to ensure the space for the articulation of claims, but the right to education, commonly regarded as a social right, is equally necessary to ensure such a space. That is, education is critical in enabling people effectively to exercise their freedoms of expression and association.[11] Furthermore, while both sets of rights belong to individual persons, they can only be realized in a meaningful and sustainable manner in group or collective settings, as no individual person exists in isolation from other persons and groups, such as families and communities.[12]

It is equally clear to me, moreover, that the success of human rights in this role is contingent on a variety of factors, especially the possibility of the universality of these rights, which is the fundamental and essential prerequisite of the concept itself. The universality of human rights means that they are the rights of every human being, everywhere, without any requirements of membership or location other than being human. As such, human rights cannot be defined or implemented except through constant and dynamic inclusion of all perspectives, experiences, and priorities. In other words, the universality of human rights can only be defined and realized, in practice, through the most globally inclusive, multilateral process. In view of shared human vulnerability, as emphasized earlier, we need to invest in human rights as a normative system that can protect all of us, whoever we are and wherever we happen to be. This view of human rights also requires them to be evolving constantly because, as new constituencies emerge and new identities are framed, formed, or negotiated, more or different priorities and concerns also need to be addressed. This is not to say that every claim of a new right has to be conceded, but for the concept to retain its universal quality, new claims must be taken seriously and judged through the widest possible multilateral process.

Normative and Institutional Framework

In promoting the candidacy of human rights as a framework for cosmopolitan justice, due consideration must be given to the normative and institutional sides of the equation, as well as the dialectic between the two. On the one hand, the content of internationally recognized human rights standards must be inclusive of all priorities and concerns, as already emphasized. On the other hand, the mechanisms and processes for their implementation must be multilateral in an institutional manner and not just through ad hoc coalitions of convenience, as happened with the unilateral military campaign of the United States in retaliation for the terrorist attacks of 9/11. In fact, such unilateral or extra-institutional actions undermine the very possibility of cosmopolitan justice. This plea for universality of human rights as a normative and institutional framework for cosmopolitan justice must also challenge several dominant assumptions about economic and political relations at the national, as well as international, level.

For example, the universality of human rights must transcend its liberal antecedent in Western political history and philosophy, in relation to economic, social, and cultural rights (ESCR), as well as claims of collective or group rights. On the first count, ESCR must be fully accepted as fundamental human rights and not just benefits or outcomes of fair and open political processes that are dependent on the protection of civil and political rights. At present, the human rights standing of ESCR is more acknowledged than it used to be, but not at the same level of immediate obligation as civil and political rights; moreover, the idea of collective or group rights is resisted as incoherent and dangerous. These traditional views must be challenged because of their serious implications for the possibility of the universality of human rights itself as well as for the practical implementation of any of these rights.

In comparison to individual rights, which are more familiar and better developed, the notion of collective rights is problematic, but that does not deny any possibility of at least some collective rights. In fact, the collective right to self-determination is already enshrined in Article 1 of the International Covenant on Civil and Political Rights[13] and the International Covenant on Economic, Social and Cultural Rights,[14] both of 1966. This principle can be interpreted to authorize some collective-rights claims, like rights to cultural or ethnic identity or, more broadly, a right to development. But the possibility of collective rights should extend beyond this to give serious consideration to such claims regardless of whether they fit any specific understanding of the right to self-determination as such. Since not every collective or group right claim can or should be conceded, the question is how to agree on the nature, rationale, and scope of this category of human rights. In particular, it is necessary to address concerns about the risk of abuse of collective or group rights, as when elites appropriate the collective voice of a community to promote a fascist agenda or justify the suppression of dissidents within the same community. But the main point, for our purposes here, is that challenging the liberal bias against the very idea of a collective right, as well as its reticence fully to endorse ESCR as human rights, is critical for the universality of human rights. To allow any cultural, philosophical, or religious tradition to dominate the determination of what constitutes human rights for all humanity is by definition a negation of the universality of these rights. In the same way that the Islamic tradition is challenged on the rights of women, for example, the liberal tradition should be challenged on collective rights, the Hindu tradition on discrimination on grounds of caste, and so forth.

Another sort of challenge to the universality of human rights comes from a double paradox in the idea that any set of rights that are due to all human beings everywhere are due simply because of their humanity. First, since human rights standards are contained in international treaties that are negotiated, ratified, and supposedly enforced or implemented by states, there is a paradox in expecting a state effectively to regulate itself to protect human rights against violation by its own officials and organs. The second paradox is that, while human rights are for all human beings everywhere, both the domestic and international law principles we rely on for practical implementation of these rights are premised on the sovereignty of states over their own territory and citizens. Since, as clearly affirmed by the Charter of the United Nations,[15] sovereignty means noninterference in the internal affairs of states, how can one redress a state's failure to respect the rights of persons who are subject to its territorial jurisdiction? Moreover, since there are legitimate grounds for distinguishing between citizens and other persons living within the territory of a state, what are the implications of that distinction for the human rights of noncitizens?

To mediate the first paradox of self-regulation by the state, we need to expand the concept and relevance of human rights beyond its present state-centric, legalistic, and reactive focus. While it is important to strive to expand the legal obligation of states to respect and promote these rights under international treaties, as many may not be willing to assume such obligations under their national constitutional systems, we should appreciate the profoundly political nature of the whole system. Given the organic and dialectic relationship between state and society, respect for and protection of human rights must be seen as a high priority for the whole society, rather than being left to state officials and institutions. However clear and categorical a legal obligation may be, it is unlikely to be respected in practice without a political constituency that is willing and able to push for enforcement. The broader implementation of human rights—in ways that preempt actual violations, instead of reacting to them after they happen—requires the political will to allocate human and material resources and to adopt and implement necessary policies and legislation. The sustainable realization of human rights in any setting would, therefore, require an interdisciplinary approach to human rights education and scholarship, as well as action at the political, social, and economic level.

The second paradox of universal human rights in a world of national sovereignty and citizenship can be mediated by viewing respect for these rights as integral to the definition of sovereignty itself, coupled with a more effective implementation of these rights everywhere as "a common standard of achievement for all peoples and all nations," as proclaimed in the Preamble of the Universal Declaration of Human Rights in 1948.[16] When viewed as such and equally applied to all countries, none would have reason to complain that its sovereignty is compromised more than anybody else. The common human resistance to being judged by others is mitigated by the knowledge that all are being judged by the same standard, equally and consistently. That is why the conduct of the United States—having one of the poorest records of ratification of human rights treaties and resisting the establishment of the International Criminal Court as noted earlier—so seriously undermines the principle of universality of these rights. While thereby implying that its own sovereignty is superior to that of other countries, the United States claims the right to judge others for their human rights violations, but only when that suits its own foreign policy objectives. The United States is willing to overlook the horrendously poor human rights records of its allies in "the war against terrorism," while justifying its policy of isolation and harassment of Cuba for more than four decades as designed to improve respect for civil and political rights in that country.

Regarding the distinction between citizen and alien, it should first be noted that all rights are always violated or protected *on the ground*, so to speak, within the territorial jurisdiction of some country or another. The antecedents of human rights are often traced to the English Magna Carta, the American Declaration of Independence, and the French Declaration of the Rights of Man and the Citizen; but all those documents were concerned exclusively with the rights of citizens, and on a very limited understanding of citizenship at that. The idea of universal rights for all human beings only emerged after World War II and the establishment of the United Nations. Still, this revolutionary idea does not seek to equate human rights with the rights of citizens but only to set a minimum standard of universal human rights for all human beings everywhere. For example, freedom from torture and the right to due process of law are due to all human beings, but citizens have additional rights, like the right to vote and hold public office in their own country. The human rights doctrine requires the territorial state to respect the human rights of all persons who are subject to its jurisdiction, while recognizing that the citizens of the state in question have additional rights that are not due to aliens.

We should also note that current models of the nation-state, and the notions of citizenship on which they are premised, are the products of specific historical developments in Europe since the seventeenth century. Since these ideas are products of a historical process, they can change over time. Indeed, they are already changing through the dialectic of regional integration that is most clearly illustrated by the European Union and by globalization in general. But such changes are likely to happen through a gradual diminishing of the supremacy of sovereignty and a relaxation of the exclusivity of citizenship into regional, and eventually global, inclusion, rather than through a sudden and categorical change. The recent economic drive, globally, for trade liberalization and the work of World Trade Organization and, regionally, the European Union and the North American Free Trade Agreement, are all contributing to diminishing preexisting notions of sovereignty and exclusive citizenship. Yet, these same developments also have negative economic and social consequences that have to be confronted and mediated, especially in relation to developing countries.

Mediating Differentials in Power Relations

The idea of universal human rights is yet to be fully realized, but there are good beginnings in the impressive set of international standards adopted since the Universal Declaration of 1948, as well as various implementation mechanisms at the international, regional, and national levels.[17] This standard-setting and implementation process has also been accompanied by certain favorable political developments, with rapid decolonization resulting in the membership in the United Nations tripling, thereby bringing many new voices and concerns to the international level. This expansion and diversity in the membership of the United Nations gradually transformed the composition of its relevant organs, like the Human Rights Commission, and agencies like UNESCO. Technological advances in communications, travel, and a series of United Nations conferences on the environment, development, human rights, and women's rights have also facilitated the development of global networks of NGOs and groups cooperating on these issues at the local as well as global level.[18] The development of regional systems in Europe, the Americas, and Africa have also fostered a stronger sense of relevance and legitimacy for human rights standards and reduced charges of Western cultural imperialism in the field. For example, the provision of the same rights under the African Charter of Human and Peoples' Rights of 1981[19] cannot be dismissed within the continent itself as a neocolonial imposition of Western values. At the same time, the African Charter, and its limited implementation system, has enabled African governments, scholars, and activists to express their concerns about collective rights to development, peace, and the protection of the environment, while confronting them with the difficulty of the practical implementation of these rights.

While these developments have certainly enhanced the prospects for a more truly universal notion of human rights, and of more inclusive processes of implementation, the question remains whether real and sustainable advances have been made since the adoption of the Universal Declaration. It is of course difficult and misleading to generalize about the actual protection of human rights around the world not only because of the lack of systematic and comprehensive monitoring but also because of the difficulty of assessing the positive success of these rights, as distinguished from other factors. On the first count, the model of human rights monitoring and advocacy by NGOs set by Amnesty International in the 1960s, and adopted by national and international NGOs since, tends to focus on limited instances of violation of the civil and political rights of elites, rather than general assessment of compliance with human rights standards. The "Human Development Index" of the United Nations Development Programme is the closest we have to a systematic and comprehensive assessment of the development of various populations around the world according to a wide range of indicators. However, and perhaps because of the clear connections between development and human rights, it is difficult to identify the causes of human rights violations as such, as opposed to a wide range of historical and contextual factors that affect the human development of a society in general.[20] Subject to these and related conceptual and methodological difficulties, one can still recognize the clear association between low levels of respect for human rights standards and such factors as political instability, poverty, economic underdevelopment, and weakness or corruption of institutional structures and resources, like the civil service, judiciary, and police.

A realistic assessment of what has been achieved and what remains to be done should therefore lead to the question of how to mediate differentials in power within and among countries and societies. To say that poverty and underdevelopment should end through more investment and development assistance or through better trade terms between rich and poor countries only invites the question of how that is going to happen. Decrying bad planning and mismanagement of the economy by corrupt local elites or the weakness of national structures and institutions, does not address how or why any of this will change. My earlier critique of the United States for undermining international legality as the basis of the universality of human rights similarly invites the question of how that is going to change.

The key to significant and sustainable change, in my view, is in framing the issue in terms of what needs to be done, rather than simply what needs to happen. That is, the question is about what people do or fail to do, the role of the human agency of all us, everywhere, in realizing sustainable change in practice. To move away from the symptoms to the underlying causes, we need to focus on the human beings whose actions can create resources, re-form weak or corrupt national and international institutions, or change the foreign policies of countries like the United States. In terms of the proposed framework, the question is how to motivate and empower people to address the conceptual and practical difficulties of realizing the universality of human rights as the normative and institutional framework of cosmopolitan justice.

It should first be acknowledged that the universality of any normative system, like human rights, is profoundly problematic because it goes against the grain of our inherent relativity, which is the inevitable product of the in-dividual and collective conditioning of our social and material location. We can only understand the world and relate to notions of right and wrong, just and unjust—in other words, locate our entitlements and responsibilities in the web of human relations—in terms of who we are and where we live. Con-sidering, from the perspective of cosmopolitan justice that I am suggesting, the presumably established paradigms of modernity and rationality that are implicit in Berman's proposal, questions arise about whose understanding of modernity and whose measure of rationality should be preferenced—as there are no abstract definitions or criteria of these notions independent of the social and material context of the people making the claim or asserting the value in question. As experiences of colonialism by post-Enlightenment Europe and of postcolonial Islamic fundamentalism in the Middle East and South Asia clearly show, neither the claims of rationality and secularism as universal values by the former, nor of religious piety and divine guidance by the latter, guarantee against inflicting pain and suffering on others.

Nevertheless, this universal difficulty of escaping our respective relativi-ties can be mediated through an overlapping consensus on commonly agreed principles, even despite disagreement on our respective reasons for that shared commitment.[21] However, to establish genuine universality of human rights, as explained earlier, this process must be fully inclusive and genuinely open-ended in order for all of us to be both appreciative of other perspectives and critical of our own. The more we are sensitive to our own ethnocentric-ity and the tendency to project our assumptions and perceptions on other people, the more we can challenge ourselves about assumptions, values, and practices that are closer to home. The more we can manifest that sensitivity everywhere in practice, and not only in theoretical assertions or rhetorical proclamations, the closer we get to the universality of human rights. As I emphasized earlier, the more multilateral and globally inclusive the standards for judging each other are, with a willingness to apply the same standards to our own actions, the more our judgment will be acceptable to others and will motivate them to change objectionable practices. There is no doubt that a quandary exists in this, but it is one that we should negotiate over time through promoting an overlapping consensus, instead of the illusion that we can overcome it by universalizing our own relativities.

In light of the preceding analysis and reflections, I suggest that the mediation of power relations for the sustainable promotion of cosmopolitan justice has to be done by all of us, in our own lives, before it can materialize in the world around us. This will entail taking many serious risks and require sustained political action that may also attract a harsh response from those who feel threatened by it. Belief in cosmopolitanism as a global existential condition requires us to "step out of our skin" to perceive critically the limitations of our own ethnocentricity and to empathize with other human beings, especially when they are culturally different or physically far removed from us. We must also accept judgment by the same universal standards in order to have the moral credibility to judge others. This will entail many real and serious difficulties, but it is clearly better than the alternative, which is certain loss of freedom and human dignity for all of us—not only for those we deem to be "at risk" of drastic violation of their human rights. Recalling earlier remarks about our shared vulnerability, none of us is secure in the pretense that human rights violations happen to other people in different places than our own. Human dignity and freedom are at risk more when the democratic will of our societies is undermined by deliberately cultivated ignorance and public indifference than from foreign invasion: the former negates our human agency, while the latter can unite us in resistance.

An Integrative Jurisprudence of Islamic Law

In this final section, I will briefly highlight the nature and sources of Islamic law and its relevance in the modern context in order to consider the possibility and implications of an integrative jurisprudence for that extremely diverse tradition. As emphasized earlier in the chapter, however, constructive engagement with the different legal traditions of the world is premised on mutually respectful acceptance of difference and on a rejection of Huntington's notion of the "clash of civilizations," which can be a dangerous self-fulfilling prophecy of doom.

To begin with a caveat: the term Islamic law is misleading in that Shari'a, the normative system of Islam, is both more than and less than "law" in the modern sense of this term. It is more than law in that it encompasses doctrinal matters of belief and religious rituals, ethical and social norms of behavior, as well as strictly legal principles and rules. Shari'a is also less than law in the sense that it can be enforced only as positive law through the political will of the state, which would normally require statutory enactment or codification as well as practical arrangements for the administration of justice. When these two features are taken together, it becomes clear that the corpus of Shari'a includes aspects that are supposed to be observed voluntarily by Muslims, individually and collectively, independent of state institutions, and other aspects that require state intervention to enact and enforce them in practice. In this light, I prefer to use the term Shari'a, rather than Islamic law.

The primary sources of Shari'a are the Qur'an (which Muslims believe to be the final and conclusive divine revelation) and Sunna (traditions of the Prophet) as well as the general traditions of the first Muslim community of Medina, the town in western Arabia where the Prophet established a state in 622.[22] Other sources of Shari'a include *ijma* (consensus), *qiyas* (reasoning by analogy), and *ijtihad* (juridical reasoning when there is no applicable text of Qur'an or Sunna).[23] But these were matters of juridical methodology for developing principles of Shari'a, rather than substantive sources as such. The early generations of Muslims are believed to have applied those techniques to interpreting and supplementing the original sources (Qur'an and Sunna) in regulating their individual and communal lives. But that process was entirely based on the understanding of individual scholars of these sources and the willingness of specific communities to seek and follow the advice of those scholars. Some general principles also began to emerge at that stage, through a gradually evolving tradition of leading scholars, which constituted early models of the schools of thought that emerged during subsequent stages of Islamic legal history.

The more systemic development of Shari'a began with the early Abbasid era (after 750). This view of the relatively late evolution of Shari'a, as a coherent and self-contained system in Islamic history, is clear from the timeline of the emergence of the major schools of thoughts (*madhabib*, singular *madhhab*), the systematic collection of Sunna as the second and more detailed source of Shari'a, and the development of a methodology (*usul al-fiqh*). All these developments took place about 150 to 250 years after the Prophet's death. In other words, the first several generations of Muslims did not know and apply Shari'a in the way that this term came to be accepted by the majority of Muslims during the last one thousand years.

The early Abbasid era witnessed the emergence of the main schools of Islamic jurisprudence, including the main schools that survive to the present day, which are attributed to Abu Hanifah (d. 767), Malik (d. 795), al-Shafi'i (d. 820), Ibn Hanbal (d. 855), and Ja'far al-Sadiq (d. 765—the founder of the main school of Shi'a jurisprudence). The subsequent development and spread of these schools, however, have been influenced by a variety of political, social, and demographic factors. These factors sometimes resulted in shifting the influence of some schools from one region to another, confining them to certain parts—as is the case with Shi'a schools at present—or even the total extinction of some schools, like those of al-Thawri and al-Tabari in the Sunni tradition. Another factor of note is that Muslim rulers tended to favor some schools over others throughout Islamic history. But until the late Ottoman Empire, as noted below, state sponsorship of certain schools traditionally happened through the appointment of judges trained in the chosen school and specification of their geographical and subject-matter jurisdiction, rather than legislation or codification in the modern sense of these terms. For example, having originated in Iraq, the center of power of the Abbasid dynasty, the Hanafi school enjoyed the important advantage of official support of the state and was subsequently brought to Afghanistan and later to the Indian subcontinent, from where emigrants from India brought it to East Africa. This connection with the ruling authority was to remain a characteristic of the Hanafi school down to the Ottoman Empire.[24]

The timing of the emergence and the early dynamics of each school also seem to have influenced the content and orientation of their views on Shari'a. For instance, the Hanafi and Maliki schools drew more on preexisting practice than the Shafi'i and Hanbali schools, which insisted that juridical elaborations must have more direct textual basis in the Qur'an or Sunna. These differences reflect the historical and intellectual context in which each school emerged and developed—which partly explains the similarities in the views of the latter two schools, in contrast to the stronger influence of reasoning and social and economic experience on the Hanafi and Maliki schools. However, the principle of consensus (*ijma*) apparently acted as a unifying force that tended to draw the substantive content of all four Sunni schools together through the use of juristic reasoning (ijtihad). Moreover, the consensus of all the main schools has always been that if there are two or more differing opinions on an issue, they should all be accepted as equally legitimate attempts to express the particular rule.[25]

But a negative subsequent consequence of the strong emphasis on consensus is the notion that creative possibilities of ijtihad drastically diminished in the tenth century on the assumption that Shari'a had already been fully and exhaustively elaborated by that time. This rigidity was probably necessary for maintaining the stability of the system during the decline, sometimes breakdown, of the social and political institutions of Islamic societies. Some historians question this commonly held view,[26] but the point is, of course, relative. It is true that there were some subsequent developments and adaptations of Shari'a through legal opinions and judicial developments after the tenth century. But it is also clear that these took place firmly within the already established framework and methodology of *usul al-fiqh*, rather than through significant innovation outside that framework and methodology. In other words, there has not been any change in the basic structure and methodology of Shari'a since the tenth century, although practical adaptations continue in limited scope and location. While our understanding of how Shari'a worked in practice at different stages of its history will continue to improve,[27] the fact remains that the traditional nature and core content of the system continue to reflect the social, political, and economic conditions of the eighth to tenth centuries, thereby growing increasingly out of touch with subsequent developments and realities of society and state, especially in the modern context.

Moreover, the essentially religious nature of Shari'a and its focus on regulating the relationship between God and human beings were probably one of the main reasons for the persistence and growth of secular courts to adjudicate a wide range of practical matters in the administration of justice and government in general. The distinction between the jurisdiction of the various state and Shari'a courts under different imperial states came very close to the philosophy of a division between secular and religious courts.[28] This early acceptance of a "division of labor" between different kinds of courts has probably contributed to the eventual confinement of Shari'a jurisdiction to family law matters in the modern era. Another aspect of the legal history of Islamic societies that is associated with the religious nature of Shari'a is the development of private legal consultation (*ifta*). Scholars who were independent of the state issued legal opinions (*fatwa*) at the request of provincial governors and state judges, in addition to providing advice for individual persons from the very beginning of Islam.[29] This type of private advice persisted through subsequent stages of Islamic history and became institutionalized in the mid-Ottoman period,[30] but there is a significant difference between this sort of moral and social influence of independent scholars and the enforcement of Shari'a by the state as such.

It is not possible or necessary here to examine the variety of mechanisms to negotiate the relationship between Shari'a and secular administration of justice over the centuries. The main point for our purposes is that varying degrees of practical adaptability did not succeed in preventing the encroachment of European codes from the mid-nineteenth century on. As openly secular state courts applying those codes began to take over civil and criminal matters during the colonial era, and from independence in the vast majority of Islamic countries, the domain of Shari'a was progressively limited to the family law field.[31] But even in this field, the state continued to regulate the relevance of Shari'a as part of broader legal and political systems of government and social organization.[32] A related development during the Ottoman Empire, which dominated much of the Muslim world for more than five centuries, was the patronage of the Hanafi school by the Ottoman dynasty, which eventually resulted in the codification of that school by the mid-nineteenth century.[33]

However, there was a tension between state sponsorship of a particular school and the need to maintain the traditional independence of Shari'a, as rulers are supposed to safeguard and promote Shari'a without claiming or appearing to create or control it.[34] This tension continues into the modern era, in which Shari'a remains the religious law of the community of believers, independently of the authority of the state, while the state seeks to enlist the legitimizing power of Shari'a in support of its political authority. This ambivalence persists as Muslims are neither able to repudiate the religious authority of Shari'a nor willing to give it complete control over their lives because it does not provide for all the substantive and procedural requirements of a comprehensive and sustainable modern legal system.[35] This came to be more effectively provided for by European colonial administrations throughout the Muslim world by the late nineteenth century. The concessions made by the Ottoman Empire to European powers set the model for the adoption of Western codes and systems of administration of justice. Moreover, Ottoman imperial edicts justified the changes not only in the name of strengthening the state and preserving Islam but also in an effort to ensure equality among Ottoman subjects, thereby laying the foundation for the adoption of the European model of the nation-state and its legally equal citizens.

These reforms introduced into Ottoman law a Commercial Code of 1850, a Penal Code of 1858, a Code of Maritime Commerce of 1863, a Commercial Procedure of 1879, and a Code of Civil Procedure of 1880, following the European civil law model of attempting a comprehensive enactment of all relevant rules. Although Shariʿa jurisdiction was significantly displaced in these fields, an attempt was still made to retain some elements of it. The Majallah, which came to be known as the Civil Code of 1876, though it was not devised as such, was promulgated over a ten-year period (1867–77) to codify the rules of contract and tort according to the Hanafi school, combining European form with Shariʿa content. This major codification of Shariʿa principles simplified a huge part of the relevant laws and made them more easily accessible to litigants, jurists, and lawyers.

The Majallah acquired a position of supreme authority soon after its enactment, partly because it represented the earliest and most politically authoritative example of an official promulgation of large parts of Shariʿa by the authority of a modern state, thereby transforming Shariʿa into positive law in the modern sense of the term.[36] Moreover, that legislation was immediately applied in a wide range of Islamic societies throughout the Ottoman Empire and continued to be applied in some areas into the second half of the twentieth century. The success of the Majallah was also due to the fact that it included some provisions drawn from sources other than the Hanafi school, thereby expanding possibilities of "acceptable" selectivity from within the Islamic tradition. The principle of selectivity (*takhayur*) among equally legitimate doctrines of Shariʿa was already acceptable in theory, as noted earlier, but not done in practice. By applying it through the institutions of the state, the Majallah opened the door for more wide-reaching subsequent reforms, despite its initially limited purpose.[37]

This trend toward increased eclecticism in the selection of sources and toward the synthesis of Islamic and Western legal concepts and institutions not only became irreversible but also was carried further, especially through the work of the French-educated Egyptian jurist Abd al-Razzaq al-Sanhuri (d. 1971). The pragmatic approach of al-Sanhuri was premised on the view that Shariʿa cannot be reintroduced in its totality and could not be applied without strong adaptation to the needs of modern Islamic societies. He used this approach in drafting the Egyptian Civil Code of 1948, the Iraqi Code of

1951, the Libyan Code of 1953, and the Kuwait Code and Commercial law of 1960–61. In all cases, al-Sanhuri was brought in by an autocratic ruler to draft a comprehensive code that was "enacted" into law without public debate. In other words, such reforms would not have been possible if those countries were democratic at the time, as public opinion would not have permitted the formal and conclusive displacement of Shariʿa by what were believed to be secular, Western principles of law.

Paradoxically, those reforms also made the entire corpus of Shariʿa principles more accessible to judges and policymakers in the process of selecting and adapting those aspects that could be incorporated into modern legislation. Moreover, in that process, the synthesis of the Islamic and European legal traditions exposed the impossibility of the direct and systematic application of traditional Shariʿa principles in the modern context. The main reason for the impossibility was (and continues to be) the complexity and diversity of Shariʿa itself, as it has evolved through the centuries. In addition to strong disagreements among and within Sunni and Shiʿa communities, which sometimes coexist within the same country—as in Iraq, Lebanon, Saudi Arabia, Syria, and Pakistan—different schools or scholarly opinions may be followed by the Muslim community within the same country, though not formally applied by the courts. In addition, judicial practice may not necessarily be in accordance with the school (*madhhab*) followed by the majority of the Muslim population in the country, as in North African countries that inherited the official Ottoman preference for the Hanafi school, while popular practice follows the Maliki school. Since the modern state can only operate on officially established principles of law of general application, Shariʿa principles can be influential politically and sociologically but not automatically enforced as positive law without state intervention.

The legal and political consequences of these recent developments were intensified by the significant impact of European colonialism and global Western influence in the fields of general education and professional training of state officials. Curricular changes in educational institutions meant that Shariʿa was no longer the focus of advanced instruction in Islamic knowledge and was displaced by a spectrum of secular subjects, many derived from Western models. In contrast to the extremely limited degree of literacy in traditional Islamic societies of the past, where scholars of Shariʿa (*ulama*) monopolized the intellectual leadership of their communities, mass basic literacy is growing fast throughout the Muslim world, thereby opening the door for a much more "democratic" access to knowledge. Thus, the ulama not only lost their historical monopoly on knowledge of the "sacred" sources of Shariʿa, but traditional interpretations of those sources are no longer viewed as sacred or unquestionable by ordinary "lay" Muslims. Regarding legal education in particular, the first generations of lawyers and jurists took advanced training in European and North American universities and returned to teach subsequent generations or hold senior judicial office.

Another extremely significant transformation of Islamic societies, for our purposes here, relates to the nature of the state itself in its local and global context. Although there are serious objections to the manner in which it happened under colonial auspices, the establishment of European-model nation-states for all Islamic societies, as part of a global system based on the same model, has radically transformed political, economic, and social relations throughout the region.[38] By retaining this specific form of political and social organization after independence from colonial rule, Islamic societies have freely chosen to be bound by a minimum set of national and international obligations of membership in a world community of nation states. While there are clear differences in the level of their social development and political stability, all Islamic societies today live under national constitutional regimes—including countries that have no written constitution such as Saudi Arabia and the Gulf states—and legal systems that require respect for certain minimum rights of equality and nondiscrimination for all citizens. Even where national constitutions and legal systems fail to acknowledge expressly and provide effectively for these obligations, a minimum degree of practical compliance is ensured by the present realities of international relations. The fact that countries where Muslims constitute the predominant majority of the population have acknowledged these principles as binding on them is used by foreign governments and global civil society to pressure for compliance. These changes are simply irreversible, though stronger and more systematic conformity with the requirements of democratic governance and international human rights remains uncertain and problematic for some of these countries. The same is true for Muslim minorities living in other countries, including Western Europe and North America, as noted below.

Conclusion

Reflecting on Berman's analysis against the preceding background, I wish to conclude with the following remarks. First, the sort of transformations of what he calls the Western legal tradition also happened in the Islamic legal tradition over a long period of time. In fact, there are many parallels between the two legal traditions, as they each have negotiated the relationships between religion, state, and society over the last millennium. As to be expected, however, each legal tradition, or set of traditions to be more precise, has been negotiating those relationships according to its own normative and institutional foundations, as well as the specific political, economic, and social context of each society within the broader tradition. Consequently, there is not only a basic similarity in the notion of "natural law" in the Islamic and Western traditions but also significant differences due to the various theological and legal resources that were deployed in support of that idea. Moreover, there are also similarities and differences in the relationship between natural law and positivism within and among these two main legal traditions. I am therefore in agreement with Berman's strong emphasis on the critical role of history in understanding these developments and their jurisprudential implications in the Islamic as well as Western legal traditions.

Regarding the role of history, one should consider the internal history of each society as well as the history of its relationship with other societies. This is not to say, of course, that the internal history of a society is completely independent of external influences but rather to indicate two sides of the same coin. For instance, the history of the Islamic societies in the Middle East of the twelfth and thirteenth centuries had a primarily internal dimension, as well as an external dimension, particularly in relation to the Christian Crusades of that period. A similar process is also true of the relationship of more recent Islamic societies with European colonialism and postcolonial Western hegemony. Yet, it can be argued that the features of these recent relations between Islamic societies and Western countries are more the consequence than the cause of the internal weakness and stagnation of Islamic societies. At the same time, the nature of the power relations among both groups has had profound effects on the dynamics of internal transformation within Islamic societies, as outlined earlier.

I would therefore recall here my earlier emphasis on international human rights law, and international legality in general, as a framework for cosmopolitan justice among and within both Western and Islamic societies. Failure to adhere to that framework for mediating differentials in power relations raises the atrocious prospect of international terrorism, as well as unilateral military retaliation that can only succeed in promoting more terrorism and arbitrary political violence. Berman's proposal, subject to the concerns and suggestions I made earlier, is also necessary for the proper development and operation of international human rights law and international legality in general. There is a critical need for an integrative jurisprudence in these legal fields and for history to mediate and supplement natural law and positivist theories of international law as well as its domestic application within national jurisdictions.

Finally, there is the question of the relevance of Shari'a to Muslims living in Western societies. Why is it important to consider the possibility of an integrative jurisprudence of Shari'a when it is no longer applicable as positive law for Muslims living in the United States or France, for instance? There are many ways or levels of responding to this question, but the one I would emphasize here is that these Muslim citizens are as entitled as citizens of Christian background, for example, to their legal tradition being taken seriously in the future development and application of American or French law. For the millions of American Muslims, Shari'a principles should and can be relevant to the legal tradition of their adopted country. The question of what practical difference that will make to law and jurisprudence in the United States today cannot be addressed intelligently when American lawyers have such little interest in comparative law, indeed even international law, as I believe to be the case now. This is, therefore, a plea for taking these critical fields of legal education seriously. as well as an endorsement of Berman's call for an integrative jurisprudence.

Chapter 10

The Politics of Religion and
the Morality of Globalization

The thesis I wish to examine in this chapter is that globalization can facilitate the politics of religion. This facilitation, I would add, can be done in ways that enable the politics of religion to instill some moral restraints on the dynamics of economic globalization in the interest of social justice. Because such synergy and mediation would need to be initiated and promoted by human agency, as explained later, I propose that an emerging global civil society can play this role. This thesis is premised on three propositions:

1. Religious doctrine and practice are influenced by dynamic processes of change and adaptation within and among communities of believers, in response to a variety of internal and external factors.
2. The forces and processes of economic globalization are unlikely to be responsive to social justice concerns without the influence of some moral frame of reference.
3. There is an emerging global civil society that is partly motivated by religion and facilitated by globalization. This global civil society can both promote the transformation of exclusive tendencies of religious communities and, thereby, enable them to infuse moral constraints on economic globalization through transreligious solidarity and consensus in the interest of social justice.

I will begin with brief working definitions of "religion," "globalization," and "global civil society," which address aspects of each paradigm that are problematic for my thesis. Through further elaboration on my working definitions and the tripartite premise of my analysis, I will argue that those problematic aspects can be transformed through synergy and mediation among all three paradigms.

For our present purposes, religion can be defined as a system of belief, practices, institutions, and relationships that provides the primary source of moral guidance for believers. Religion also commonly serves as an effective framework for political and social motivation and mobilization among believers. If the necessary interreligious and intrareligious consensus and solidarity can be generated and sustained, these general features of at least the major religious traditions make them good candidates for instilling moral restraints on economic globalization.

But religion is unlikely to play this role insofar as religious communities perceive the doctrine of their faith in orthodox and exclusive terms that suppress dissent within the tradition and undermine solidarity and cooperation with those deemed to be nonbelievers or heretics. Such hegemonic and exclusive tendencies will impede the emergence of a dynamic global consensus on social policy that is capable of checking the excesses of economic globalization.

However, as I will argue later, this tendency toward hegemony and exclusivity can and should be resisted within the context of each religious community, which is almost always more heterogeneous and pluralistic than claimed by the advocates of religious exclusivity. As I attempt to illustrate with reference to Hinduism and Islam later in this chapter, it is possible and desirable to interpret religious traditions in more inclusive ways that enhance possibilities of interreligious solidarity and cooperation. This development is particularly attainable, I suggest, under current conditions of accelerated and intensified globalization. But the possibility of contesting dominant religious doctrine, through the proposal of alternative understandings of each tradition, is contingent on a variety of factors, both internal and external to the religion in question. This process of contestation is what I call the "politics of religion," which can have different outcomes, including the possibility of bringing moral restraints to bear on economic globalization.

By "economic globalization" I refer to an increasing assimilation of economies through international integration of investment, production, and consumption that is driven by market values. The primary purpose of globalization in this sense is the achievement of rapid and endless corporate growth, fueled by the search for access to natural resources, new and cheaper labor, and new markets. From this perspective, economic globalization is a means of reducing barriers to corporate activity, without regard for social justice, environmental, or public health concerns (International Forum on Globalization, IFG, 2).[1] The question therefore is whether it is possible to adjust the operation of economic globalization in favor of greater social justice. By making this definition specific to "economic" globalization, I mean to suggest that there is a "social" dimension to the concept that can be used to promote the social responsibility of economic actors. This is what I call the *morality of globalization*. The question is, however, who is going to moderate the harsh social consequences of economic globalization and how that moderation can be realized.

It appears that there is an emerging global civil society (GCS) that is manifest in underlying social networks of transnational, national, and local actors who are engaged in negotiations about civil matters with governmental, intergovernmental, and transnational business actors at various levels. This network has become "thicker," stronger, more durable, and more effective over the last decade of the twentieth century.[2] GCS feeds on and reacts to economic globalization, while seeking to expand its scope to include interconnectedness in political, social, and cultural spheres. These additional dimensions of globalization tend to promote and enhance a growing global consciousness of shared human vulnerability to political violence, poverty, and disease. The question, then, for the purposes of this chapter is this: under which conditions can GCS effectively check the exclusivity of religion and promote social concern in economic globalization?

Upon incorporating these tentative working definitions, the thesis of this chapter is that global civil society offers possibilities of synergy and mediation, whereby the exclusivity and intolerance of some religious communities can be moderated by the impact of economic globalization, while the latter's lack of concern for social justice can be redressed through the moral guidance of religion. In other words, GCS can play a mediatory role within and among religious traditions, as well as in relation to economic globalization. Moreover, GCS can stimulate the internal transformation of religious communities to promote consensus on universal values of social justice and pluralism, as well as influence the forces of economic globalization in favor of these values. In short, I am calling for a tripartite process of mutual influence and transformation within and among all three paradigms.

As already indicated, this thesis and analysis are dependent on the critical role of *human agency* in realizing and sustaining the transformative possibilities of each of these paradigms. By "human agency" I mean that human actors can conceive and realize the sort of religious transformation that can promote among various actors in economic globalization an accountability for the social consequences of their actions. The term is also intended to emphasize that *only* human actors can achieve the mediatory potential of GCS. In other words, all aspects of the tripartite processes of mutual influence and transformation depend on both the choices people make and how they act on those choices.

In emphasizing the centrality of human agency in this context, however, I am not assuming that it would necessarily work in favor of the transformations, synergy, and mediation I am proposing. Indeed, my analysis is premised on the expectation that the agency of some actors will surely be opposed to such objectives but that it can be countered by those in favor of the proposed synergy and mediation. Accordingly, the question is how to secure the best possible conditions for human agency to operate within and among religion, globalization, and GCS in favor of synergy, mediation, and social justice. Before discussing this and related questions in the last section of this chapter, it may be helpful to further elaborate on each of these three paradigms.

Politics of Religion

The premise of what I call the *politics of religion* is that religion everywhere is *socially constructed*, dynamic, and embedded in socioeconomic and political power relations, always in the particular context of specific religious communities. This premise is clearly indicated by the variety both of interpretations within each religious tradition and of their local adaptations at various stages of history or in different settings during the same historical period. The reality of competing interpretations and the contingent nature of prevailing views will be illustrated with a brief examination of two contrasting views of Hinduism, its role in politics, and its relationship to the state in India. I will also attempt to make the same point by a similar contrast between Islamic fundamentalism and liberal interpretations of Islam. The experience of liberation theology in Latin America will be presented in the last section of this chapter to illustrate the possibilities of an integrated religious and civil-society response to the inequities of economic globalization.

Hinduism Between Gandhi and Religious Nationalism

One view of religion that clearly illustrates the thesis of this chapter is the one Gandhi articulated and sought to implement during the struggle for the independence of India. For him, religion was a source of possibilities of social, political, and cultural identity and expression that were neither restricted to a set of practices or personal beliefs nor ultimately delimited by scripture.[3] The way he understood and applied his conception of religion drew on his reading of Hinduism, but in the sense of "the peculiar mix of classical and folk Hinduism and the unselfconscious Hinduism by which most Indians, Hindus as well as non-Hindus, live."[4] This flexible and unsystematic framework allowed Gandhi to incorporate insights from diverse perspectives to define religion as an expression of social, cultural, and political values.

As Robert Young observes, Gandhi's "thinking was always inherently anti-systematic, and operated as a kind of radical cultural eclecticism. . . . [He] freely borrowed ideas from different religions, particularly Christianity, Buddhism, and more strategically from Islam, [and produced] creative synthesis of different aspects of different religious."[5] Gandhi's notion of religion offers those for whom religion is an important dimension of their worldview and normative frame of reference the possibility of full membership in, and engagement with, pluralistic civil society at the local, national, and global level. To him, the spiritual was the foundation that orients *all* aspects of life, and religious expression is entwined with cultural, political, and social values, whereby religious identity is neither the sole province of the individual nor the only basis for political or social action. Religion provides the individual an ethic to live by (*swaraj*, or self-rule), a mode and medium of political action and expression, and a basis for political independence.[6]

Gandhi saw tradition, politics, economics, social relations, and autonomy as tightly linked to what is currently referred to as "development," but he was critical and suspicious of modernization (which today would be called economic globalization) because it undermines harmony.[7] He believed that the danger of modernization is that it diminishes the sense of duty individuals once carried for one another by enmeshing them in interlocking dependencies as consumers and producers who are strangers to each other and, therefore, do not care much for one another. Instead, he sought "a society of mutuality among people who know and care about each other and who recognize the many debts they owe one another."[8]

In relation to issues of religion and social justice in particular, Gandhi regarded as problematic the distinction between the public and the private sphere, whereby morality belongs in the private sphere and economic choice and political freedom in the public sphere. He questioned the notion of autonomy associated with modernization when it constricts and diminishes the lives of any segment of the population. For him, the moral costs of modernization *must be part of the calculation* about any supposed increase in autonomy that modernization delivers. Since institutions alone cannot ensure autonomy and freedom, Gandhi sought to hold them accountable to moral autonomy and equality.[9] He also insisted that "any new technology must be *primarily judged* by its effects on the present generation, particularly its *most vulnerable members*, and not by some future good."[10] Gandhi also "reminds us that people have multiple needs that are affected by the economy, not just economic ones."[11]

As if to confirm Gandhi's apprehensions about modernization and traditional understandings of religion, a drastically different view of religion and politics was advanced by the Hindu fundamentalism of the Bharatiya Janat Party (BJP) in India during the 1990s. Relevant to our purposes here in particular, there seems to be a strong association between religious radicalism and economic globalization in the rise of the BJP to national power. The distinct subset of the Indian population that can be identified as the core of the support for the movement comprised the same groups who have been most threatened by the new economic liberalization initiatives aimed at greater privatization and increased global competitiveness.[12]

There were, of course, other factors contributing to the rise of Hindu fundamentalism. For example, a major sequence of events in this process was the destruction of the Babri mosque on December 6, 1992, at Ayodhya that led to widespread communal tension and Hindu–Muslim riots. Claiming that this mosque had been built on the site of the destroyed Ram temple (birthplace of the god Ram), Hindu nationalists launched a political protest movement that seeks to erect a Ram temple on the site of the Babri mosque.

Thus, as often happens in a variety of settings, religious symbols and discourse were used by disadvantaged groups at the local and national level to mobilize politically in face of the harsh economic consequences of globalization. In the case of India, religion and fears about the impact of globalization combined in propelling a right-wing party with a strong religious agenda into controlling the national government of one of the most religiously and ethnically diverse countries in the world. In terms of the thesis of this chapter, does this mean the permanent loss of the Gandhian view of religion and politics, or is it a setback that can be reversed under certain favorable conditions?

Islamic Fundamentalism and Liberal Islam

A similar politics of religion can be observed in postcolonial Islamic societies in different parts of the world. For our purposes here, the problem with fundamentalists, whether associated with religious, secular, nationalistic, or other forms of ideology, is their determination to mobilize all the resources of their societies for the realization of their own specific vision of the public good. Each form of fundamentalism, nevertheless, will probably have its own characteristic features and particular forms of discourse in relation to its own frame of reference. With this caveat in mind, I use the term here as a shorthand reference to a complex and controversial ideological and political manifestation of the politics of religion; moreover, I focus primarily on its Islamic expression because of my familiarity with the subject and concern about its implications.

What is commonly known today as Islamic fundamentalism can be found at different stages of history of various societies, always as an exceptional response to severe crisis rather than the normal state of affairs among Islamic societies or continuously in any one of them. This is true for the first Islamic civil war of the mid-seventh century, the jihad movements of eighteenth and nineteenth century West Africa and Sudan, to the current movements in various parts of the Muslim world.[13] In other words, Islamic fundamentalism should be understood as an indigenous response to profound social, political, and economic crises, *not* as the inevitable outcome of Islamic religious scripture or history.

As both a product and an agent of social change in Islamic societies, emerging as a result of certain configurations of factors in each case, and seeking to influence the course of events in favor of its own social and political objectives, each movement is best understood in its own specific context.[14] Whatever one may think of such movements, their declared hostility to other religious communities and repression of internal dissent seriously undermine the prospects of interreligious and intrareligious consensus and solidarity that are needed for a GCS effectively to check the excesses of economic globalization.

Islamic fundamentalist movements tend to claim legitimacy and seek political power in various postcolonial Islamic societies in the name of the right of Muslim peoples to self-determination through the strict observance of Shari'a. Accordingly, I suggest, they should be judged by the validity of their claim to represent and exercise genuine national self-determination and by their ability to deliver on that promise. The question arises, however, of how the claim of Islamic fundamentalists that they represent the totality of national population at home can be verified, especially when they suppress all political dissent or opposition as religious heresy. Another question is whether such movements really understand, and operate under, the realities of global relations, through which the right to self-determination can be realized today.

Regarding the issues of dissent and representation, Islamic fundamentalists must maintain a total and credible commitment to democracy at home so that Muslims can continue to express their support or opposition freely and without fear of violent retaliation. These movements must also respect the equal citizenship of non-Muslim nationals of the state, because that is the only possible basis of peace, political stability, and economic development at home, as well as of acceptance by and cooperation with the international community abroad. Regarding the issue of global relations, fundamentalists must accept the principles of the rule of law in international relations because that is also essential for peace, political stability, and economic development of their own country.

It therefore seems clear that Islamic fundamentalism is unacceptable as a legitimate expression of the collective right of Muslims to self-determination; that is, its ideology is inherently inconsistent with the conditions under which Islamic societies may exercise this right today, both within those societies and in their relations with the non-Muslim world. Regardless of the apparent appeal of fundamentalism to many Muslims today, it is clear that the internal and external context in which Islamic identity and self-determination can be realized is radically different from what it was in the precolonial era. A primary underlying cause of this transformation of local context in each case is the reality that all Islamic societies are now constituted into nation-states, which are part of global political, economic, and security systems. They are all members of the United Nations and subject to international law, including universal human rights standards. None of these states is religiously homogeneous, politically insulated, or economically independent from the non-Muslim world.

It is therefore clear that the right to self-determination cannot mean that Muslims are completely free to do as they please in their own country, let alone in relation to other countries, because their right to self-determination is limited by the rights of others. In other words, it is neither legally permissible nor practically viable for fundamentalists to force other citizens of the state (whether Muslim or non-Muslim) to accept and implement their view of Shari'a as a matter of state policy. As I have argued elsewhere, the idea of an Islamic state is not only unprecedented in Islamic history but also morally and politically untenable, as well as practically unviable in the modern context.[15] That is, in addition to the fact that the idea of an Islamic state, as presently advocated by fundamentalist movements, has no precedent in more than fifteen centuries of Islamic history, recent experience in countries like Iran, Pakistan, and Sudan illustrates that this idea is also practically unviable today. The idea is morally untenable because whatever views of Shariʿa are enforced by those who control the state will violate the freedom of religion of those Muslims who disagree with those views, as well as the human rights of women and non-Muslims.[16]

Islamic fundamentalism is problematic for the thesis I am exploring in this chapter because of its violent intolerance of all differences, both within the same tradition and in relation to other religious and ideological perspectives. Movements that subscribe to this view tend to drastically repress internal dissent through intimidation and charges of heresy, which seriously inhibits any possibility for internal contestation of their exclusionary interpretation of Islam. The intolerance among Islamic fundamentalists toward other religious communities and their commitment to an expansive view of jihad not only obstructs the development of interreligious alliances in GCS but also constitutes a serious threat to international peace and security.[17] As already emphasized, however, it is also part of the thesis of this chapter that religious traditions must remain open to change and transformation in favor of global solidarity for social justice.

The question is, therefore, how to achieve the necessary transformation within each religious tradition, Islam in this case, that would enable GCS to organize across religious and cultural divides to mobilize and pressure agents of economic globalization to integrate social-justice concerns into their calculations. Such transformation obviously requires a combination of elements, including theological arguments about different interpretations of the religion in question and an appreciation of conditions under which some of them may prevail over others. This process is also affected by factors that facilitate free debate and dissent at home and the rule of law in international relations abroad. As to be expected, these necessary conditions are neither completely lacking nor sufficiently secured.

For instance, while some Islamic countries are better than others in securing the necessary domestic conditions, it is clear that the "space" for free debate and dissent is seriously lacking in many of them. While the idea of GCS raises expectations of collaboration in promoting such conditions for favorable change, a positive role for religion in the democratization of Islamic societies does not appear to be supported by GCS because of the fear that, given the choice, Muslims will choose fundamentalist Islam. Ironically, this lack of support may turn into a self-fulfilling prophecy, whereby Islamic fundamentalism prevails because genuine and sustainable democratization is not given a chance.

Like other societies, moreover, Muslims tend to become defensive and conservative when they perceive themselves to be under attack, especially when they see that their personal safety and national sovereignty are not protected by international law. That is, Islamic fundamentalist notions of jihad are legitimized by the prevalence of similar notions of lawlessness and self-help by major powers. It is from this perspective that I believe that the manner and scale of the military retaliation by the United States against the terrorist attacks of September 11, in its unilateral use of force abroad and denial of due process of law for foreign captives, are tantamount to a fundamental repudiation of the premise of peaceful coexistence.[18] The proponents of jihad as aggressive war are more likely to gain legitimacy among the majority of Muslims in a world where military force and self-help prevail over the rule of law in international relations.

In my view, there is an alternative, more liberal, understanding of Islam that is capable of challenging the theological and ideological basis of Islamic fundamentalists and denying them the moral and political force of Islam in many parts of Africa and Asia. To speak of liberal Islam raises the question of whether it has to conform to a particular Western understanding of liberalism and secularism. An underlying tension regarding this question relates to the meaning of secularism and its implications for liberalism—that is, whether a commitment to liberalism would necessarily entail a commitment to a "secular" view of the relationship between religion and the state and what that means in practice in different contexts. Another pertinent inquiry relates to the conditions that are likely to facilitate and promote the development of liberal Islam. For instance, what is the role of the nation-state and of transnational movements in generating or sustaining liberal understandings of Islam in different parts of the world?

It is not possible to examine all these questions here, but a sampling of how they might be addressed may be helpful. For instance, there is a general aversion, at times even hostility, to secularism, which is seen as an antireligious Western ideology. The Indonesian scholar Nurcholish Madjid calls for a revitalization and liberalization of Islamic thought and understanding through what he calls "secularization." He insists, however, that secularization does not mean the application of secularism, because "secularism" is the name for an ideology, a new closed worldview that functions very much like a new religion.[19]

This common aversion to what is perceived to be a "Western-imposed conception of secularism" is probably due to associating it with colonialism and militant antireligious attitudes. To dispel this apprehension, secularism should be understood as a doctrine of public policy that is necessary for freedom of religion, rather than antagonistic to religion, as well as being indigenous to Islamic history, instead of being imposed by colonialism.

As a general principle, the separation of religion and the state simply means that the state should not impose one view of Islam that would deny Muslims themselves freedom of choice among competing interpretations of their religion that are all equally valid and legitimate.[20] Keeping the state neutral regarding the wide variety of views about the position of Shariʿa on issues of public policy and law would enable Muslims to freely debate which view should prevail at any given point in time. Instead, state law of general application should be based on "public reason," that is, justifications that all citizens can share, reject, or accept without fear of charges of heresy or intercommunal hostility. In contrast, claiming that any proposed legislation becomes law *because* it is Shariʿa (the will of God) means that it is beyond criticism or amendment. Whatever the source, the policy and law enforced by the state must always respect the equal fundamental constitutional and human rights of the totality of the population, Muslims and non-Muslims, men and women.

This rehabilitation of secularism in modern Islamic societies is integral to conceptualizations of liberal Islam as an interpretive approach that contrasts the historical context of the original formulation of religious doctrine by early Muslim scholars with the modern context in which Islam is to be understood and applied today. In general, the proponents of this approach tend to distinguish between one aspect of Islam as a religion with its sacred, unchanging, eternally determined body of rules for believers and another aspect that is capable of development and transformation through time. The need for reinterpretation requires the use of fresh and creative ijtihad (independent reasoning and interpretation of the scripture). The proponents of a liberal interpretation of Islam also hold that, since the law must have the purpose of serving humankind, it must be adaptable to its needs.[21]

Although the terms in which the discussion of Islamic liberal thought must be framed, as well as the content and tensions of that discussion, may be different from those of debates about liberalism in other parts of the world, such differences should not be exaggerated either. For example, Islamic liberal thought cannot assume or presuppose Western conceptions of secularism, the nation-state, or a well-organized and active civil society. But such conceptions and institutions are evolving in different parts of the Muslim world, though necessarily in local terms, as should be expected. Moreover, since liberal Islam has to tackle these issues in the specific history and context of each Islamic society, one should expect a diversity of perspectives on Islamic liberalism, reflecting such factors as the nature of the nation-state and the dynamics of its relationship with civil society.[22]

The tentative conclusion of this section is that religious traditions are constantly being contested by competing interpretations of the scripture in the specific context of each community of believers, which is more conducive for religious pluralism and interreligious consensus in some settings than in others. This space for contestation raises the possibility of more inclusive conceptions of religion that can facilitate solidarity around shared concerns among different religious communities, as discussed in the final section of this chapter. I will now turn to a brief elaboration on the moral deficit of economic globalization, which I am proposing can be redressed through an overlapping consensus among different religious traditions, as mediated by an emerging global civil society.

Morality of Globalization

The antecedents of what is presently known as globalization as a conduit of trade, culture, travel, economics, knowledge, science, and technology go back thousands of years in human history.[23] What is new is a fundamental change in the scale, intensity, and speed of these processes due to enormous advances in the technology of travel and communication that have also had far-reaching social and political consequences. As indicated earlier, the problem with the economic dimensions of globalization is their indifference to the social consequences of this unrelenting drive for rapid growth and profits, at the cost of making the poor poorer or at least denying them their fair share of the global economic pie.[24] For example, in the midst of rising wealth generated through globalization, nearly a billion people struggle to live on less than one U.S. dollar a day, the same as in the mid-1980s.[25] There is also a gross widening of the gap between the wealthy and the poor, even within the rich developed countries. For instance, the chief executive officers of American corporations were paid on average 458 times more than production workers in 2000, up from 104 times in 1991.[26]

These negative consequences of economic globalization are neither inevitable nor irreversible because the same processes have resulted in a rapid intensification of the integration of ideas, knowledge, norms, values, and consciousness that can be conducive to the promotion of social justice and universal human rights on a global scale. The possibility of using the same processes and dynamics of globalization to redress economic, social, and political problems is critical for what I am referring to here as the "morality of globalization." Relevant questions in this regard include whether it is possible to transform the values underlying economic globalization to make it more morally responsible to human suffering everywhere. This transformation in turn requires appreciation of ways to influence primary actors in the sphere of economic globalization.

The main actors of economic globalization are major transnational corporations whose primary motivation is maximizing profits through free trade and corporate deregulation.[27] As corporations become less regulated, it becomes very difficult for national governments to protect local jobs and resources or to influence how the market works. The same developments tend to favor a global monoculture that will maximize potential markets and facilitate better production, more cost-effectiveness, and greater profit. But these features of economic globalization are challenged on the ground by competing ideas and values within and among different segments of society, as well as at the transnational and global level. Mediation among these competing values and interests requires a combination of the political dynamism of democratic governance and the normative guidance of international human rights standards within the framework of a legitimate international legal order. While democracy can facilitate the functioning of the market, it should also serve to correct the market's negative effect on social justice. However, democratic structures are unlikely effectively to regulate economic globalization without the support of agreed standards that are accepted as binding on the actors.

In principle, governments should be allowed to set policies on the development and welfare of their people, provided that they are politically and legally accountable to local and national constituencies. Both aspects of this proposition are integral to the international law principle and the collective human right to self-determination, including the right to determine the terms under which governments enter into trade with others or invite others to invest in their economies.[28] However, this principle and right will be undermined without effective transparency and accountability of governments to civil society. In other words, the legitimacy of economic globalization depends on the transparency of economic institutions and processes and their accessibility to civil society actors who can ensure their accountability to generally agreed-on objectives of social policy.

Economic globalization is also pushing toward privatization of elements that have always been out of the reach of the trading system. For instance, aspects of life that have been accepted as the collective and inalienable property of all peoples, the common heritage of humankind, are now being marketed as commodities in the global markets.[29] It is now possible to gain property rights to genetic structures of human life through rules on intellectual property. Lifesaving medication, healing herbs that have been known and used by local communities since time immemorial, even lakes and streams are being monopolized by corporations through patent laws, to be sold at prohibitively high prices. Patent holders have the ability to exclude the whole world from making, duplicating, or selling what is deemed to be patented property, without regard to collective human investment in the development of these resources in the first place.

As new markets tend to reward existing markets that already have productive resources, such as land, financial and physical assets, and human capital, economic globalization offers a high return to countries that have stable political systems, secure property rights, and adequate human services because they are better able to cope with market changes. Conversely, countries stricken with poverty, unstable political systems, and insufficient human services are disadvantaged by increased globalization because they are unlikely to have the resources to protect themselves in ruthlessly "free markets." Global entrepreneurs are thereby enabled to withdraw their investment and transfer it elsewhere when an enterprise fails to maximize the return, even if it functions well in social terms.

The inability of poor countries to participate in economic globalization and all its devices—ironically because they lack the freedom to do so—has become the sure means of keeping most of the population of the world in bondage.[30] The market values that are the driving force behind globalization should include mechanisms and processes for combating corruption and promoting trust in economic, social, or political relationships that enable all aspects of global society to flourish.[31] Globalization must therefore be conceived in a way that mandates the removal of major sources of restriction and limitation of freedom, such as poor economic opportunities, poverty, systematic social deprivation, and neglect of public facilities.

A possible and viable framework for this conception is the universality of international standards of human rights, provided this paradigm is taken to include affirmative obligations of the state to promote social and economic rights, like the human rights to education and health care, as well as political and civil rights, such as the liberty to participate in public discussion and scrutiny.[32] Article 22 of the Universal Declaration of Human Rights refers to the economic, social, and cultural rights as "indispensable for [one's] dignity and free development of [one's] personality" and to "the right to social security," which entitles everyone to access to welfare provisions.[33] At the core of social rights is the enjoyment of an adequate standard of living, which requires, at a minimum, that everyone shall enjoy the necessary subsistence rights—adequate food and nutrition, clothing, housing, and the necessary conditions of care and health services. Closely related to these rights is the right of families (mothers and children) to special assistance.

The enjoyment of these social rights also requires certain *economic* rights, like the right to property, the right to work and other work-related rights, and the right to social security. Most of the people in the world ensure the livelihood of their families through work outside the formal sector.[34] The majority of indigenous people work in areas that are not often integrated into the national or global market. Small-scale entrepreneurial activities and subsistence agriculture can be found in rural areas; these activities, however, often do not offer regular income. People living in the urban areas of poor countries sometimes have to survive without regular jobs or incomes. In most countries around the world, economic globalization is depriving greater numbers of people of the essential means of human dignity. The right to social security is essential when a person does not own sufficient property or is not able to secure an adequate standard of living through work, due to unemployment, old age, or disability.[35]

Education is both a social and a cultural right. The right to education obligates states to develop and maintain a system of schools and other educational institutions to provide education to everybody—free of charge, if possible. The obligations of states to promote equality of opportunity and treatment in education are laid down in greater detail in the UNESCO Convention Against Discrimination in Education of 1960.[36] Since it enhances the human capital of society at large, education is one of the few human rights where the individual has a corresponding duty to exercise the right.

Moreover, there is clear interdependence between such economic and social rights, on the one hand, and what is commonly known as civil and political rights, on the other, such as freedom of opinion, expression, and association; protection against arbitrary arrest or detention; equality before the law; and the right to effective remedy for any violation of one's rights. For example, freedom of association is an enabling right that facilitates the development and realignment of power and the space for other elements of civil society. This freedom includes the right to form and participate in trade unions without state interference. Freedom of association allows local communities to be empowered through bargaining and choice, to participate in economic activities that enhance their political power and ability to pursue effective remedies for the violation of their rights.[37] This human right enables workers to challenge unjust and discriminatory practices such as the failure of employers to provide equal pay for equal work, as happens routinely to women around the world.

For our purposes here, civil and political rights are particularly important for enabling one to participate effectively in the political process of electing government and holding it accountable for its policies. This participation would enable disadvantaged segments of the population to have a voice in the direction of their country's social and economic development, including such matters as increasing the minimum wage, protecting union activists from retaliation, enforcing prohibitions on discrimination, regulating industries, or ensuring that investments are made with social values in mind. But the practical utility of such civil and political rights can be seriously diminished by the policies of liberalization and withdrawal of subsidies, which are the conditions imposed by the International Monetary Fund (IMF) and the World Bank. In curtailing the ability of the state to determine its own economic and social policies in this way, these global actors tend to undermine the relevance and efficacy of democratic and constitutional governance in developing countries. Thus, the populations of developing countries are struggling for constitutionalism and democratic governance at a time when the state they seek to control and hold accountable is losing control over its own economic and social policies.

This loss of control is particularly serious because, as noted earlier, when religious communities feel threatened by external forces, like economic globalization, they are likely to drift into fundamentalism as an apparently easy and categorical answer to all their problems. As is to be expected, fundamentalists take advantage of the situation to dominate public discourse and eventually control the state. A frequent response from those threatened by the rise of religious fundamentalism, whether ruling elites or liberal intellectuals, is to insist that religion must be relegated to the purely private domain, thereby denying it a role in promoting the social responsibility of economic actors.

The tentative conclusion of this section is that the human rights paradigm seems to offer the possibility of a comprehensive and systematic response to the challenges of economic globalization. In terms of the thesis of this chapter, this paradigm is a good candidate for being the basis of the sort of interreligious solidarity and consensus that is needed for infusing moral values into the processes of economic globalization in the interest of social justice. Although there are good reasons for viewing the process of globalization with apprehension, it clearly has many potentially positive aspects if it is pursued for the common good, not just for the benefit of a few. Globalization has opened up profound possibilities for human development and enhanced the quality of life for many people around the world. Information technology has collapsed time and space for far-off events, making them easily accessible to people everywhere and promoting the exchange of ideas and customs between peoples of different countries. Live communications enable people to participate instantaneously in the historical development of different societies and to create and promote global concern over social concerns, human security, and environmental issues. Ways of thinking and behaving are now challenged beyond accepted traditional patterns, thereby enhancing possibilities of solidarity across political, social, cultural, and religious boundaries. These aspects of globalization can be particularly helpful in creating and sustaining interreligious understanding, solidarity, and consensus building. They can also facilitate the development of a global civil society and enable it to mediate more effectively the excesses of economic globalization.

Global Civil Society and Human Rights

The question here is whether there is, or can be, a GCS with such a degree of consensus and solidarity among groups with similar or shared concerns that enables it to act collectively in moderating the exclusivity of religion and excesses of economic globalization. Relevant questions include whether local civil society, *as it exists on the ground* in different parts of the world, is organized and motivated in ways that facilitate or hinder the sort of consensus and solidarity that promotes and sustains GSC as envisioned here. Assuming or to the extent that that is the case, we should also note how differentials in power relations among various actors in GCS affect the agenda, strategies, and outcomes of their solidarity. In relation to the subject of this chapter in particular, for millions of people around the world, social, political, and cultural issues are inextricably tied to perceptions of religious identity in a local context, as well as religious rationale of social institutions and behavior. Questions raised by this focus include how to account for that dimension of religion in the lives of individuals and communities in theorizing about economics, development, nationalism, and the nature and dynamics of the public sphere where GCS is supposed to operate. Indeed, are different religious conceptions or formations of local civil society compatible with any uniform understanding of a global civil society?

The term "civil society" can be understood as signifying particular types of social processes that relate to an intermediary participatory realm between the private and the public sphere, a network of institutions mediating between an administrative source of power and the political-social actions and practices of peoples. As Dipankar Gupta observes, *"civil society is not a thing*, but a set of conditions within which individuals interact collectively with the state."[38] As such, civil society can be found to *exist, in and of itself*, throughout the world, and not only in Western or developed stable countries. Thus, we are concerned here with the nature of the social processes and intermediary participatory realm that signify "civil society," whatever that may be in each setting. In other words, it is a matter of whether one is looking for the concept in one place as it has been conceived in another or in terms of the place where one is looking. That is, as Rajni Kothari argues, civil society needs to draw "upon available and still surviving traditions of togetherness, mutuality and resolution of differences and conflict—in short, traditions of a democratic collective that are our own and what we need to build in a changed historical context."[39]

But how does this view of civil society deal with the question of which normative content the concept should have for it to be a useful medium of analysis or comparison? That is, does opening the concept to different possibilities of meaning than what it has had in its so-called countries of origin raise the risk of rendering it meaningless? If whatever *intermediary participatory realm between the private and the public sphere* happens to be on the ground would qualify as "civil society," the term would be meaningless. But if some social processes qualify as civil society and others do not, the question becomes one of the difference between the two types of the intermediary realm. In other words, how do the descriptive and prescriptive aspects of any definition of civil society operate in relation to each other? How can the realities of civil society on the ground be reconciled with what they ought to be for the institution to serve its purposes?

Some scholars define civil society in terms of civility, associability, and citizenship, understood as follows. Civility is tolerance of the other so that groups and individuals with very different ideas can live together in peace, working within a representative and participant system for their individual goals. Associability is a spirit of cooperation for citizens to organize peacefully and openly around political issues, professions, or any common interest. Citizenship is a crucial component that underpins civil society.[40] While these ideas are certainly critical, I believe that each of these terms can take on a range of meanings that cannot be separated and distilled from the contexts in which they are lived and practiced. For instance, instead of limiting the definition of civility to what has been elucidated in the tradition of Western liberal political thought, the term should also include notions about civic association that exist in other cultural traditions.

For the purposes of this chapter in particular, a central question is how religion can provide a basis for these normative components in many regions and cultures of the world. In response, I would first question the underlying dichotomy between religious and secular conceptions of the self in the discourse on civil society. The issue is not whether there can be a "religious civil society" as opposed to a "secular civil society," for that merely reproduces the dichotomy. Rather, it is how to develop a normative definition of civil society with due regard to an understanding of religion, without forfeiting the normative premise of civil society. Since religion is a necessary form of associational life for most people around the world, it is imperative to include it in any understanding of the normative elements of civil society.

Indeed, where it provides the basis for a powerful critique of those aspects of the state that are inimical to civil society, religion may provide the impetus that civil society needs. Thus, for instance, Islam was the most feasible and practical ideology and language available to Iranians in the 1970s. It was a rallying point for the political aim of ridding themselves of the shah and American hegemony, since, as Mary Elaine Hegland writes, "In uniting under the leadership of Ayatollah Khomaini and the progressive ideology of Ali Shariati, Iranians were taking self-assertive, constructive steps forward to deal with the political realities of today's world. . . . [Islam] was the more effective as a revolutionary ideology and ethos because it does not recognize a distinction between political and religious effort, nor does it regard politics as outside the realm of religious concern."[41] For Iran itself and other situations like those in Pakistan and Sudan, however, carrying that motivating link between religion and politics into a formal and institutional unification of religion and the state has been profoundly problematic for any coherent sense of civil society.

Thus, assuming that one accepts the need to incorporate the role of religion in different societies into conceptions of GCS, the next question is how that can be done in ways that are consistent with the nature and dynamics of both sides of this process. That is, how can religion be included without compromising the authenticity of religious experience, on the one hand, or undermining the core meaning and function of global civil society, on the other? While each society must struggle with these issues on its own terms and in its specific context, there is need for an overarching framework that can facilitate the process of internal transformation within each religious tradition, as well as the sort of transreligious consensus and solidarity necessary for GCS to emerge and operate effectively.

In my view, the human rights paradigm, as explained earlier, provides the means for such consensus and solidarity to materialize, as well as the nonnative content of social justice and individual freedom for which GCS should strive. But the human rights paradigm itself is constantly being both challenged as a form of "cultural imperialism" that is seeking to impose Western values on other societies and undermined by charges of practical inefficacy and irrelevance. The first issue relates to the universality of the human rights, while the second refers to their realistic efficacy on the ground.

As I have argued elsewhere,[42] the universality of human rights has to be constructed through an internal discourse within and among different cultural and religious traditions, rather than simply proclaimed through international declarations and treaties. The objective of internal discourse is to transform people's attitudes in favor of acceptance of a diversity of perspectives within and among traditions and the deliberate promotion of cross-cultural consensus and solidarity on universal values. Moreover, the mere fact that this process is taking place in one setting can be cited by proponents of universal human rights in another setting to enhance the legitimacy and efficacy of the process in their own situation. Thus, it would enhance the credibility and efficacy of Muslim advocates of the universality of human rights to be able point to such efforts taking place in European and North American settings. Conversely, Muslim advocates may be dismissed as romantic fools, if not agents of hostile foreign powers, if they are unable to point to similar efforts by other advocates in their respective situations.

Moreover, there is synergy between the theoretical legitimacy and practical efficacy of human rights standards, whereby each side of this formula influences the other, whether positively or negatively. Thus, successful internal discourse and cross-cultural dialogue in favor of the universality of human rights would lead to greater commitment to the practical implementation of these rights, which will, in turn, promote the local legitimacy of human rights. That is, as human rights norms become better observed in practice as a product of the indigenous values and policy objectives of each society, the practical relevance and efficacy of these norms will be enhanced, thereby leading to more observance, and so forth. The reverse is also probably true: the lack or failure of internal discourse and cross-cultural dialogue means less commitment to the practical implementation of human rights norms, which will then be taken as evidence of their inefficacy and irrelevance. That perception may then reinforce earlier negative attitudes about the whole paradigm and therefore diminish political commitment to their implementation.[43]

In this light, human rights norms can be an effective framework for challenging the negative consequences of economic globalization to the extent that they are accepted by different societies as culturally legitimate, as well as practically effective in achieving that objective. Yet these norms are unlikely to be accepted and implemented unless they deliver on their promise. The way out of this apparent paradox, I suggest, is to see the process as an incremental synergy of cultural legitimacy and practical efficacy in the following logical sequence: the negative social and human consequences of economic globalization can lead to calls for a global framework and strategy to mobilize the political will to redress those problems. Taking the human rights paradigm as a possible candidate for that role, local actors can then seek to promote the legitimacy of these rights. As they are able to point to the ways in which this paradigm can in effect redress the problems of economic globalization, its practical implementation will begin to increase, thereby initiating the synergy between theory and practice envisaged here.

Since this process must be undertaken by human actors, the question becomes how to motivate people to act in this way and to encourage their communities to give this approach a chance. Thus, in accordance with the thesis of this chapter, GCS can be the medium for this process, and religion can play a critical role in motivating and mobilizing people in this direction. At the same time, the technical and material benefits of globalization can facilitate the development of interreligious and transcultural consensus and solidarity in support of human rights as a framework for redressing the negative consequences of economic globalization.

Possibilities of Mediation

To illustrate the proposition that religion can enable GCS actors to bring moral constraints to bear on purely economic globalization in the interest of social justice, I will review in this final section the experience of liberation theology in Latin America as an example of efforts to infuse moral values into economic globalization.

Liberation theology is best known for its Latin American context, where it emerged around 1968–71 as a radical religiously motivated challenge to oppressive structures in various parts of the continent.[44] To its founders, the fundamental tenets of liberation theology combined the love of God with the urgency of solidarity with the poor[45] and emphasized human agency in taking direct action to help the poor. The movement used Marxist ideology in pursuit of a socialist system for sharing wealth.[46] Its ideology is based on the assumption that oppressed peoples and classes are fundamentally in conflict with the wealthy nations and oppressive classes.[47] Subsequent developments sought to expand the scope of the movement in the 1980s and 1990s to include race, gender, culture, and ecological issues,[48] though it remained primarily an ecclesiastic movement with a focus on the liberation of the poor.[49]

While the movement was by no means uniform, its various currents shared the same three assumptions: (1) that the majority of individuals live in a state of underdevelopment and unjust dependence, (2) that this state is sinful as viewed in Christian terms, and (3) that it is the responsibility of the members of the church to work to overcome this sinful state.[50] The same fundamental theme was defined by Gutiérrez[51] in terms of "solidarity with the poor and rejection of poverty as something contrary to the will of God." This fundamental underlying theme of the whole movement was linked to the work of grassroots Christian communities and the evangelical mission of the church.[52]

In a paradigm shift from classical doctrine, liberation theology focused on putting God's will into practice in solidarity with the poor, in contrast to the "detachment and reflection" of traditional theology.[53] The movement also preferred social science analysis over the philosophical reflection of classical theology in its effort to link action with thinking.[54] Leading theologians of the movement also stressed the importance of the communitarian experience as essential to liberation practice and saw that methodology as manifest in spirituality and in one's life as a Christian. Liberation theologians distinguished between material poverty, as "the lack of economic goods necessary for a human life worthy of the name," and spiritual poverty, as "an interior attitude of unattachment to the goods of this world."[55] They also maintained that, from a Christian perspective, poverty is contrary to human dignity and against the will of God.[56]

Applying a social science approach, liberation theology viewed the cause of poverty in Latin America as inequality in the system of power and ownership that inhibits access of the masses to participation in society.[57] Instead of the prevalent view that Third World countries only need to "catch up" with developed industrialized countries, liberation theologians argue that massive poverty is "the result of *structures of exploitation and domination*; it derives from centuries of *colonial domination* and is reinforced by the present international *economic system*."[58]

However, the movement always had an ambivalent relationship with the Vatican. The Vatican's response has been consistently wary of the political role of liberation theology, especially its use of Marxism as a tool of social analysis, while at the same time apparently supporting the movement's agenda of social justice. To the Vatican, liberation theology's advocacy of an alternative church (the *iglesia popular*) was an affront to the official church.[59] Leading liberation theologians like Gutiérrez and Boff continued to insist that Marxism is used only as a conduit to understanding societal forms of oppression. But the Vatican and other critics held that Marxism cannot be used for empirical analysis without regard for its critique of religion itself.[60]

Liberation theology continues to be practiced at the grassroots level, and those who spearheaded efforts to further the movement during its inception continue to be prolific in their writings. However, new strains have emerged, and although the underlying theme remains that of liberation from oppression, diverse perspectives within the movement have their own strong, new agendas. Liberation theology has also lost large numbers of supporters due to changes in political, social, and religious circumstances throughout Latin America. Commentators mention several factors as contributing to the decline of liberation theology in recent years, such as the failure of Marxism, conflict with the Vatican, and the rise of Pentecostalism. Adding issues of race, gender, culture, and sexuality, as well ecological and indigenous people's concerns, to its agenda is necessary for the movement's relevance but also diminishes the clarity of its original focus.[61] Another factor in the decline of the movement is the rise of Pentecostal churches that are posing a serious challenge to Catholicism as the underlying doctrine of liberation theology.[62] The focus of liberation theology on a purely socioeconomic analysis of conflict without addressing the dynamics of culture and religion may have contributed to Latin Americans turning to other religious movements.[63] Recent more sustainable and thoroughgoing democratization in the main Latin American countries where liberation theology had its strongest following may have also diminished the need for this particular avenue of political resistance and economic protest.

On the other hand, the strong focus on poverty and development linked liberation theology to other intellectual and political currents in the region, as well as to global trends. For example, Paulo Freire criticized the churches for failing to exercise the true prophetic function and called on them to take sides in struggles for political liberation or they will end up supporting repressive regimes. Freire also sees a relationship between black theology and Latin American liberation theology in that both have a political nature, aligned with the struggle of the oppressed, and emphasize revolutionary praxis.[64] Black North American liberation theology parallels liberation theology in that its leaders also deviated from the traditional theological paradigm.

Other parallel Christian theological trends in Africa, in Asia, and among feminists have also emerged as reactions against the European and North American theological establishment that tended to assume that its theology was the only model of "Christian" theology. Each of these emerging theologies has its own focus and priorities, which do not necessarily coincide with those of Latin American liberation theology. African theology, for instance, tends to focus on the problem of "indigenization and the role of native African religions."[65] While each strain of theology is uniquely suited for its context, they are all linked by the preferential option for the poor.

I am not in a position to assess the scale and scope of the successes and failures of liberation theology or to predict its future prospects in Latin America or elsewhere. All I am suggesting here is that it seems to have been (and may continue to be) a good example of a religious challenge to the negative consequences of economic globalization, especially in its local and national manifestations. However, the main question for the thesis of this chapter is whether the highly contextual nature of this Christian liberation theology and similar trends in other religious traditions, like liberal Islam or Gandhian Hinduism, would permit the forging of transreligious consensus and solidarity of GCS. The main challenge here, as explained earlier, is how to transcend the exclusivity of religious traditions to subscribe to a shared normative content and collaborative strategies in infusing moral constraints on economic globalization. In particular, are such diverse religious movements likely to agree on the universality of human rights as an overarching framework for infusing moral values into the institutions and processes of economic globalization in the interest of social justice?

I believe that this is possible through the processes of internal discourse and cross-cultural dialogue, as explained earlier. The idea of overlapping consensus requires unity of purpose and mutual respect for difference, not ideological and associational uniformity. But this consensus building must also take account of the unevenness of political and institutional power relations between different regions of the world. The process of inclusion and incorporation of local or regional participants, like liberal Islam and Christian liberation theology, should also be sensitive to the risks of serious cross-cultural misunderstandings, which can be compounded by religious and cultural normative differences among all participants in GCS.

Chapter 11

Global Citizenship and Human Rights: From Muslims in Europe to European Muslims

My objective in this chapter is to link two enlightened and humane ideas of our time, human rights and citizenship, in order to invite scholars, opinion leaders, and the general public to explore how the synergy and mutual support of these two concepts can contribute to protecting human dignity and social justice at home and abroad. The main premise of my argument is that the universality of human rights assumes, or presupposes, the possibility of "global citizenship" as the basis of the entitlement to rights and the ability to enforce them. Despite their different antecedents in the intellectual and political histories of various societies, the concepts of citizenship and fundamental rights have also been joined in mutual support and synergy in the development of the human rights paradigm. Accordingly, my thesis proposes that the idea of global citizenship as the basis of the universality of human rights not only can clarify the meaning and implications of national citizenship but can also support human rights claims by noncitizens. Since human rights are due to all human beings by virtue of their humanity, enjoyment of these rights should not be limited to the citizens of the state where a person happens to be.

Moreover, while rethinking citizenship at the conceptual level as simultaneously national and global, the proposed approach is also supported at the pragmatic level by the present historical moment. At present, there is an increasing convergence of opinion and developments around the basic idea of global citizenship as a complement to national citizenship—despite disagreement regarding precise definitions, feasibility, and strategies for realizing that shared vision. There are also sound policy reasons for the proposed approach, such as the dependency of European economies on migrant labor and consequent need for their social accommodation—including provision of education, health and other services—which can be appreciated without reference to human rights principles as such.

This approach, however, does not mean abolishing all legal and political distinctions between citizens and noncitizens of a state, which are indeed necessary and justified from a human rights point of view.[1] It is already established that the universality of human rights requires certain minimum standards in the treatment of noncitizens by the authorities of the state, regardless of their legal status. That is, the idea of universality guarantees human rights to every person, everywhere all the time, whatever his or her status may be, whether he or she is in a country legally or illegally, lawfully subject to deportation or not. That does not eliminate the need to consider the rationale and implications of distinctions among citizens and noncitizens, as well as among different categories of noncitizens, in relation to particular claims of rights. But such determinations should not be based on broad categories of civil and political rights versus economic, social, and cultural rights, because that is neither an accurate classification—since each right can contain both elements—nor can granting or denying each right be justified in relation to all groups of persons. In other words, each right should be considered in relation to each group of claimants, instead of lumping together different rights or groups of claimants.

For example, human rights such as protection against torture or inhuman degrading treatment or punishment and the requirement of fair trial and due process of law must be secured on a universal basis. In contrast, the right to vote or be elected to public office are clearly due only to citizens, though limited voting rights may be accorded to long-term residents of a country or municipality in proportion to their contribution to the well-being of the community. It is also possible to justify a higher level of entitlement to education, health services, and employment opportunities for citizens than it is for noncitizens; a lower level of some of these benefits for permanent residents; and none for transient visitors to a country who do not pay taxes or fulfill other obligations of citizenship or legal residence. While such questions should clearly be considered in relation to specific claims and individual conditions of claimants, my plea is that this should be done with due regard to the underlying rationale of universality of human rights, which does not exclude other valid and relevant factors in determining policy.

Moreover, I am suggesting that the linkage of universality of human rights and global citizenship should facilitate the granting of citizenship at the national level while gradually diminishing any distinction between citizens and noncitizens that cannot be justified in human rights terms. To illustrate the point, a human rights approach would require more liberal grounds for granting legal citizenship to Muslims who came to various European countries as guest workers or students or for family reunification or other reasons. The same approach would also require securing the human rights of those who do not qualify for legal citizenship. In other words, the Muslims in Europe should neither be disadvantaged nor privileged for being Muslims, and the same applies to all other adherents of any religion or belief.

To be clear and categorical on this point from the outset, the application of this human rights approach to Muslims does not imply that the Muslims in Europe are either an undifferentiated monolithic entity or helpless, "innocent" victims of racism and xenophobia. Indeed, those commonly collectively referred to as "Muslims" in Europe often have much more in common with other Europeans than with each other. Moreover, for most Muslims, especially second- and third-generation immigrants, whether citizens or not, the European country they now live in is the only home they have. They are as European as their neighbors, and no longer people from another place who can somehow "go home." In my view, the construction of "European" as a cultural category that excludes Islam, or that being Muslim is incompatible with being European, is inconsistent with the principle of the universality of human rights. At the same time, Muslims should not take such entitlements for granted without affirming their commitment to the universality of human rights and obligations of citizenship of their country and of the world at large.

The urgent need to challenge such simplistic claims by all sides is at the core of my call for promoting a human rights approach to citizenship in social policies, in educational programs, through the media, and through other civil society activities. In all these activities, it is necessary to maintain a balance between competing rights or claims, rather than pretend that there is no tension or conflict among them. On the one hand, it is necessary to respect the cultural and religious right to self-determination, for example, to avoid requiring Muslims (or other immigrants) to abandon or renounce their own identity in order to be accepted as citizens or noncitizen residents of the country. On the other hand, all communities must also be willing and able to question and transform their own traditions in response to the requirements of their own internal and broader contexts.

The challenge of rethinking citizenship from a human rights perspective is profoundly "global" in the sense that it faces adherents of all religions and belief systems, state and non-state actors, national and transnational entities, scholars, civil society actors, and businesses. I am calling here on European states and societies to take the lead in responding to this global challenge not only because this region is the home of the concept of the "territorial" state that has come to define national citizenship throughout the world[2] but also because of the normative and institutional strength of the universality of human rights among Europeans.

The establishment and development of human rights as due to all human beings by virtue of their humanity and without any kind of distinction under the Charter of the United Nations of 1945 and the Universal Declaration of Human Rights (UDHR) seek to achieve the benefits of constitutional entrenchment of certain rights beyond the contingencies of national politics. That is, these founding documents initiated the process of internationalization of the principle of a constitutional bill of rights on a global scale, as rights that are protected against abrogation by the government of the day, even with the support of the strong majority of the population. The significant difference is that constitutional rights at the national level are due only to the citizens of the particular state, whereas human rights are due to all human beings everywhere. Yet, while set as the "common standard of achievement for all peoples and nations," according to the Preamble of the UDHR, universal human rights can only be implemented in practice through national constitutional and legal systems. Human rights treaties and institutions that have evolved since 1945 seek to implement the universality of human rights, but they can only do so through national systems. It may be helpful at this stage to explain briefly the dual paradox of the idea of universality and the present system of its implementation.

The first paradox is that, while it is imperative to uphold and protect human rights throughout the world, the universality of these rights cannot be assumed or simply proclaimed. Since all human societies adhere to their own normative systems, which are necessarily shaped by their particular context and experiences, any universal concept is by definition a *construct* or *hypothesis* that cannot be simply proclaimed or taken as given. Human beings know and experience the world as themselves, men or women, African or European, Christian, Muslim or Hindu, rich or poor. The consciousness, values, and behavior of human beings everywhere are partly shaped by their local cultural and religious traditions. The quality of being a universal norm can, therefore, only be achieved through a global consensus-building process and neither assumed nor imposed through the hegemony of universalizing claims from one relativist perspective or another.

As I have argued elsewhere,[3] this paradox can and should be *mediated and negotiated* through practice over time, rather than expected to be resolved once and for all. The notion of mediation is used here to emphasize that the tension remains, while the idea of negotiation indicates the multiplicity of authorship and contributions from a variety of perspectives. The underlying principle of equality and nondiscrimination includes the right to be different, as people do not abandon their distinctive identity and religious or philosophical beliefs in order to qualify for human rights but claim these rights as the persons they are and through their own experiences.[4] The challenge is, therefore, how to promote and sustain consensus on universal human rights norms despite the permanence of difference among persons and cultures. To avoid misunderstanding, my purpose in raising this challenge is to affirm and realize the universality of human rights as a practical principle of policy for all societies, rather than question its validity.

The present system and processes by which human rights are supposed to be implemented are premised on the traditional view that rights are to be understood and realized under a specific political or legal system and understood within a particular religious or cultural frame of reference. The tension between the universality of human rights and citizenship stems from their complex relationship with the European model of the territorial state with exclusive sovereignty and jurisdiction, which came to prevail throughout the world through colonialism.[5] This model of the state has also been incorporated into international law, which is the legal framework for the protection of human rights under the UN and other regional systems. Universal human rights are legally binding on states because they are provided for in treaties under international law, yet these obligations are supposed to be implemented by sovereign states within their own exclusive territorial jurisdiction. In other words, human rights are the standard by which the performance of every state must be judged, regardless of what its own constitution, legal system, or policies provide for or implement. But since territorial sovereignty precludes intervention in the "internal affairs of states" (Article 2(7) of the UN Charter), the paradoxical result is that states are entrusted with the implementation of international standards within their own borders. As a framework for international cooperation in the protection of human rights, the present system also relies on the willingness of states to hold each other accountable for their human rights failures, often at some economic, political, security, or other risk to their own national interests.

This paradox is real because the violation or protection of human rights necessarily happens within the geographical and legal jurisdiction of one state or another, yet the principle of sovereignty and the territorial integrity of the state preclude external intervention to protect human rights without the consent and cooperation of the state itself. Moreover, since pressure by external actors is difficult to sustain, and is often counterproductive, it is ultimately up to citizens to hold officials of the state accountable for any violation that may occur. It is also citizens who can ensure the adoption of appropriate policies and the provision of necessary resources by the state for broader implementation of human rights norms. The ultimate measure of success is for human rights to be respected and protected routinely in the first place, as well as ensuring that effective accountability immediately follows whenever a violation occurs. In both aspects, in the final analysis, it is citizens acting through a variety of strategies and levels, who can ensure systematic and sustainable protection of human rights.

To explain briefly, official human rights practitioners at the governmental and intergovernmental level, as well as civil society advocates, tend to do their work in a piecemeal and reactive manner, responding to human rights violations after they occur, rather than preventing their occurrence in the first place. Monitoring and advocacy systems also tend to focus on specific cases, or at best limited issues, in order to be effective in the short term, without attempting to address structural causes of human rights violations or creating institutional mechanisms for the protection and promotion of rights.

When violations are publicized, the assumption is that other governments are not only willing to risk their national interests in pressuring offending governments but also have an effective way to exert such pressure. The contingency of foreign policy objectives and shifting priorities of all governments often preclude reliable prediction of whether any government will act, when, and how. It is also difficult to achieve sustainable change without the willingness of other governments to stay focused on the specific situation long enough for results to be achieved.

In light of these reflections, it is clear that the mediation of the two paradoxes of universality and self-regulation by the state is ultimately founded on the legitimacy and coherence of human rights standards among the general population of each country. Without such legitimacy and coherence, citizens are unlikely to take the necessary political and legal action to ensure compliance by the state. This is the reason for emphasizing the inherent connection between citizenship and human rights. As I continue to clarify this approach in subsequent sections, I would recall that I am using the case of Muslims in Europe only to illustrate the challenge facing all societies and communities, religious, and cultural traditions throughout the world. As applied to this illustration, this "universal" challenge can be stated as follows. On the one hand, if Muslims are to found their citizenship claims on human rights grounds, they should have no hesitation in upholding the universality of these rights. On the other hand, European policymakers and opinion leaders should also be clear about the sense in which the relationship between Islam and human rights is or is not relevant to the situation of European Muslims. I am deliberately introducing this issue here to anticipate the assumption that Muslims find it difficult to accept the universality of human rights just because they are Muslims.

Islam, Muslims, and Human Rights

In taking the relationship between Islam and human rights seriously, I am asserting that this is an important issue, without implying or suggesting that there is either compatibility or incompatibility between the two. Given the very recent origins and radical nature of the universality of the human rights paradigm, it would be unrealistic to expect this idea to be in full accord, or in total discordance, with vastly complex and varied Islamic traditions. Yet, if human rights are indeed universal, that universality cannot be claimed without taking into account religious perspectives and experiences. The idea of universal human rights would be incoherent if it did not take Islam into consideration. Muslims constitute 21.01 percent of the total world population, living in every continent and region, predominantly in Africa and Asia.[6] They are the majority of the population in forty-four states, and one-quarter of the membership of the United Nations. While Islam is not the only determining factor of the attitudes of Muslims regarding the universality of human rights, engaging this and other world religions is critical for the validity and efficacy of the concept.

The issue I am raising here is how being a Muslim is relevant to one's view of, or commitment to, human rights. Since Islam, or any other religion for that matter, cannot be the sole source or cause of the behavior of believers, Muslims may accept or reject human rights norms regardless of what they believe to be the "Islamic" view on the subject. The level of compliance with human rights norms is more likely to be associated with such conditions as political stability and economic and social development than with Islam as such. To the extent that Islam is a relevant factor, its impact or influence cannot be understood in isolation from those broader conditions, nor from the specific interpretation of Islamic principles that are prevalent in the particular country or region. It is not possible, therefore, to predict or explain the degree or quality of human rights compliance as the logical consequence of the relationship between Islam and human rights, in an abstract theoretical sense.

In fact, the vast majority of countries where Muslims constitute the majority of the population have ratified the major human rights treaties, and their record of compliance is similar or comparable to that of other countries in their regions. Moreover, the human rights record of those countries in East or West Africa and South or Southeast Asia is similar to that of other countries in their regions, presumably because that is shaped or influenced by similar political and economic factors, legal systems, and institutional capacity. Many Muslims, whether part of a majority or minority of the population of the country, have also expressed their acceptance of human rights by struggling for the protection of those rights locally and in collaboration and solidarity with other persons and civil society organizations throughout the world. To my knowledge, there are no studies showing a correlation between Muslims constituting the majority or significant minority of the population and level of human rights observance. On the contrary, studies show that Muslims share commitment to these values.[7]

In other words, there are no factual bases for any negative perception about Islam and Muslims in relation to human rights in general. It can be easily demonstrated that the Islamic tradition at large is basically consistent with most human rights norms, except for some specific, albeit very serious, aspects of the rights of women and freedom of religion and belief. It is not possible to discuss these problematic aspects here, and I have presented elsewhere an Islamic reform methodology for addressing those questions at the theoretical level.[8] The main point I want to emphasize is that the validity and efficacy of human rights among Muslims must be promoted through an internal transformation of their attitudes about Shari'a in general, and the interpretation of particular principles, especially regarding the rights of women and non-Muslims.[9] What would be counterproductive and constitute a human rights violation in itself is to attempt to force Muslims to make a choice between Islam and human rights. If issues are presented in such terms, there is no doubt that Muslims will uphold Islam over human rights every time, as this limited and largely procedural paradigm cannot be a substitute for religion or rival its transformative power in their lives.

I find that framing the issue in terms of seeking to transform attitudes and values is more constructive than simply asserting the compatibility or incompatibility of Islam and human rights. Such binary positions tend to overlook the diversity and flexibility of interpretations of Islam, on the one hand, and the dynamism and pragmatism of human rights, on the other. In contrast, the transformative approach is necessary for mediating the paradox of the idea of universal human rights in a world of profound and permanent cultural and contextual difference. As emphasized earlier, since all human beings are entitled to these rights by virtue of their humanity, without any distinction on such grounds as race, sex, religion, language, or national origin, no person should be required to give up any of these essential aspects of identity in order to qualify for these rights. The revolutionary idea of universal human rights remains challenging for all human societies because we all tend either to discriminate among people in terms of such attributes as religion and sex or to expect them to conform to our own ethnocentric and uniform notions of a universal human being. Muslims should neither discriminate against people on any of those grounds nor be required to abandon their religion in order to qualify for these rights. To justify their own human rights claims without distinction on such grounds as race, sex, or religion, Muslims must accept the right of others to be entitled to the same rights and without distinction on such grounds.

The UDHR avoided identifying religious justifications for these rights in an effort to find common grounds among believers and nonbelievers. But this does not mean that human rights can only be founded on secular justifications because that does not address the need of believers to relate their moral and political actions to their religious beliefs. The underlying rationale of the human rights doctrine itself would entitle believers to found their commitment to these norms on their own religious beliefs, in the same way that others may seek to affirm their commitment on secular philosophy. We are all entitled to expect equal commitment to the human rights doctrine from others in our communities and societies, at the national and international level. But this does not mean that any of us can prescribe the grounds on which others may wish to found their commitment. In any case, I find that the dichotomy between the religious and the secular is often exaggerated when it is taken to mean an inherent incompatibility of the two, though they are, in fact, interdependent with human rights.[10]

Another point I wish to emphasize regarding the relationship between religion and human rights is that human interpretation and action are unavoidable in rendering any religious text relevant to the lives of believers. Muslims believe that the Qur'an is the literal and final word of God and that Sunna (traditions of the Prophet) is the second divinely inspired source of Islam. But both sources have no meaning and relevance in the daily lives of believers and their communities except through human understanding and experience. The Qur'an was revealed in Arabic, which is a language that evolved in its own specific historical context, and many verses of the Qur'an were addressing specific situations in the daily lives of early Muslims at that time (610–632) in their local context of western Arabia. Sunna also had to respond to the immediate concerns arising in that local reality in its broader context.[11] Thus, *human agency* was integral to the process of revelation, interpretation, and daily practice since the time of the Prophet, as it was integral to subsequent generations of Muslims who adhered to the Qur'an and Sunna according to their own understanding in their respective historical context and daily experiences. But it should also be noted that acknowledging this fact does not necessarily mean accepting or rejecting any particular interpretation of Islamic sources. Rather, my point is that, since any understanding of Islam is unavoidably human, the ability of believers to challenge or modify any interpretations, however established or orthodox it may seem, is, in fact, integral to being a believer.

It should also be noted that the human agency of all human beings, Muslims and non-Muslims alike, is interactive with that of other people and influenced by relevant events, whether local or further away. Thus, our choices and responses are often conditioned or influenced by what others do or say, and the outcomes of our agency are contingent on what else is happening in the world around us. The role of Muslims in contributing to the global joint-venture of protecting and promoting human rights at home and abroad includes their collaboration with others in that regard. Since human rights are by definition universal in concept and application, each society must take this paradigm seriously before it can demand the same from others. While ideally our commitments to human rights principles should be independent of how other people feel or what they do, in practice people tend to relate their own attitudes and actions to that of others. So charges of the double standards and hypocrisy of others are often made to justify our own actions, as if to say, if you fail to uphold my human rights, I will retaliate by refusing to uphold yours.

It is, therefore, appropriate to speak of Muslims not Islam, Christians not Christianity, Hindus not Hinduism, and so forth, because these religions do not act as autonomous entities, but rather through the attitudes and actions of believers. Posing the question in terms of believers, and not the abstract beliefs they are presumed to hold, makes it clear that it is the same general question of how human beings everywhere negotiate the relationships between their religious beliefs and human rights. That is, the question is always about people's understanding and practice of their religion, whatever it may be, and not the religion itself as an abstract notion. This does not deny the communal dimension of religious experience or collective identity of believers but emphasizes that this aspect is also the product of human agency, even when organized as religious authority or social institution.

Commitment to human rights should also be related to these rights as a living and evolving body of principles and rules, and not as purely theoretical concepts. Whether regarding religion or human rights, the reference to states, countries, or international organizations like the United Nations is really to the people who control the state apparatus, inhabit a country, or work through international institutions. The human rights action of such entities is always about how people negotiate power, justice, and pragmatic self-interest, at home and abroad. Such negotiations always take place in specific historical contexts and in response to the particular experiences of believers and unbelievers living together. Each religion, culture, or philosophy is relevant to those who believe in it in the specific meaning and context of their daily lives and not in an abstract, decontextualized sense.

Issues regarding Muslims, whether constituting the majority of a country's population or living as a small minority, should be framed on the basis of a clear appreciation of the permanent social, cultural, and political diversity among Muslims, particularly in relation to their understanding and practice of Islam. That diversity testifies to the impact of contextual and historical factors in the theological and legal development of the Islamic traditions. Being Muslim did not, in fact, have the same meaning in different places or over time. From an Islamic perspective, the reality and permanence of difference among all human beings, Muslims and non-Muslims alike, are expressly and repeatedly affirmed in the Qur'an.[12] This permanent reality is one reason why the protection of such human rights as freedom of belief, opinion, and expression is imperative from an Islamic point of view in order to protect the rights of Muslims to be believers in their own way, without risks to life and livelihood. After all, without the existence of the right to disbelieve, there is no possibility of genuine belief.

It may also be helpful to consider the implications of this reality of Islamic diversity for the nature or basis of religious beliefs. The fact that specific verses in the Qur'an are taken to authorize or require certain actions does not explain why some Muslims choose to act on one understanding of such verses, while others act on a different understanding or have a different relationship to the text altogether. Such choices are the product of the human agency of believers, not the inherent or eternal meaning of Islam as such, independent of all material conditions under which Muslims live and interact with others. If beliefs regarding the rights of women are the direct meaning of Islamic texts, there would not be so much disagreement among Muslims on these issues.

The existence of disagreement, however, does not mean that any of the established schools of Islamic jurisprudence (*madhahib*) already accept equality for women because that is simply not true. In fact, it would be an unrealistic expectation since those schools were established more than a thousand years ago, which means that their interpretations of relevant texts reflected the historical context of those scholars. By the same token, alternative interpretations are possible and are being developed by many Muslims in terms of their present context.[13] Since any formulation of Shari'a is the product of human interpretation in a specific time and place, it can change through the same process, over time.

It is clear, then, that the manner in which Muslims are likely to interact with human rights will be conditioned by such factors as what other societies are doing about the same issues and the orientation, motivation, or objectives of various actors on all sides. For instance, many Muslims may become entrenched in conservative or defensive positions in response to perceptions that that they are required to "prove" their allegiance to the human rights paradigm while others are not expected or required to do the same. Some Muslims may also resent the constant propaganda that their tradition is inherently regressive or authoritarian, with little understanding of the rich diversity and enlightened aspects of that tradition.

Another set of factors that can influence positions has to do with power relations and institutions: how inclusive is the international law that is supposed to provide the legal framework for human rights? Does it sufficiently respect the sovereignty of Muslims, with due regard for their concerns about security and development? Are Muslims accepted as genuine *subjects* of international law or merely "objects" of a system that is defined and applied by powerful Western countries to control other peoples and exploit their resources? When vivid memories of European colonialism are reinforced by the illegal invasion and occupation of Iraq by the United States and United Kingdom, the latter having been the previous colonial power throughout the Muslim world until a few decades ago, is it really surprising that many Muslims find it difficult to accept the credibility and legitimacy of international law, which is the basis of the binding force of international human rights norms?

I am not, of course, suggesting that Muslims reject the universality of human rights as a religious imperative. Rather, my point is that the attitudes or views of Muslims should be understood in a broader historical context and through the application of socioeconomic and political analysis, as with any other human beings and their communities. While many Muslims do indeed uphold this principle and others reject or oppose it, the reasons or rationale of their positions is not Islam as such. This is not to suggest that Islam is totally and completely irrelevant but only to emphasize that its relevance or role is not different from that of other religions among their believers. In other words, I am calling for applying a historical and social scientific analysis to understanding the role of Islam among Muslims, as should be done with other believers and their societies.

Rights and Citizenship

Turning now to an elaboration on the second human rights paradox of self-regulation by the state indicated earlier, I would first note that this tension has always been true of the protection of constitutional rights in national settings. Whenever national constitutions provide for entrenched fundamental rights against abuse or excess of power by the state, the authority and power to enforce those rights remain with the state. That paradox has traditionally been mediated at the national level by the emergence of strong local civil society organizations that are willing and able to use domestic legal institutions and political processes to force governments to comply. Domestic civil society organizations and public opinion at large must also be willing and able to act in a similar manner in relation to these universal norms. Since external human rights defenders cannot be at the sites of violations long enough, with sufficient resources, understanding of the local situation, and ability to achieve sustainable change, the most viable strategy in my view is to invest in empowering local actors to protect their own rights.

This view does not prescribe a particular set of activities for all human rights actors in every situation or necessarily proscribe other strategies. My point is that the degree and quality of empowering local actors to protect their own human rights should be the underlying criterion for evaluating all activities and strategies because this is consistent with the rationale of human rights in the first place. The human dignity of every person should be upheld by his or her own agency, instead of being dependent on the goodwill of others, which is often doubtful or mixed with their own interests. This means that the focus of human rights implementation should be more people-centered and less dependent on the ambiguities and contingencies of intergovernmental relations.[14] Realistically, it will remain necessary for all governmental and nongovernmental actors to maintain the highest possible level of monitoring and advocacy for the protection of the human rights of all, everywhere, because victims are usually unable to assert their own rights effectively. But the objective must be to gradually diminish such dependency on external protection.[15]

From this perspective, one connection between citizenship and rights in general is the critical role of citizens in protecting their own rights. This approach was first applied to fundamental constitutional rights in national settings and then extended to human rights since the UN Charter and UDHR, which sought to internationalize the idea of an entrenched bill of rights to a global scale. It is from this perspective that I would emphasize the importance of the mutual support and synergy of human rights and global citizenship. That is, global citizenship is needed to play the role for universal human rights that is played by national citizenship for national constitutional rights. Since both paradoxes of universality and self-regulation by the state can only be mediated through the agency of human beings everywhere, global citizenship is a critically important status and institution that enables and safeguards that agency in practice. The mutual support and synergy of the two concepts is that human rights provide the normative content of citizenship, which is the practical framework for people to organize to enforce and protect these rights on the ground. This interconnectedness is facilitated by the dynamic and evolving nature of both human rights and citizenship,[16] but I am concerned here with the dynamism and evolution of citizenship through theoretical reflection, as well as through political and legal developments.

As indicated at the beginning, the need for the evolution of the concept of citizenship from its traditional national scope to a global scale is inherent to the idea of the universality of human rights as the rights of every human being and not only of the citizens of a particular state. National citizens are entitled to civil rights provided for by their own national constitutional and legal system, but aliens are not entitled to those rights unless they are able to assert them as human rights under the jurisdiction of a state without being its citizens. This is the most significant difference between national civil rights and universal human rights, which is that human rights are due to all human beings by virtue of their humanity, while national civil rights are due to citizens by virtue of their citizenship. This basic tension can be illustrated by the clear distinction made by the United States government between citizens and aliens in the aftermath of the terrorist attacks of September 11, 2001.[17] For example, aliens who are held in the custody of the United States under the ambiguous category "enemy combatants" (instead of prisoners of war entitled to protection under international humanitarian law) are denied basic due process and fair trial rights under international human rights law.[18] This policy is in clear violation of international human rights law because the trial rights that are denied to these aliens by the United States government are provided for by Article 14 of the International Covenant on Civil and Political Rights of 1976, which is one of the few human rights treaties actually ratified by the United States.

This situation in the United States is particularly disturbing because of the wider global consequences of that policy. But the underlying tension between the civil rights of citizens and human rights of all human beings is a complex and difficult issue in many parts of the world. The apparent difficulty, as noted earlier, is that it is neither realistic nor desirable to expect states to grant the civil rights of citizens to foreigners, who do not owe allegiance to the state or fulfill obvious obligations of its citizens like paying taxes, voting, or otherwise participating in the political process of the country. The approach I am proposing for mediating this tension is the development and application of the concept of global citizenship as the basis of the human rights claims of all human beings, as distinguished from national citizenship as the basis of the civil rights of citizens and possibly permanent residents.

As shown in the next section, the idea of citizenship as we know it today is very recent in human history in general and has remained contested almost throughout the world well into the twentieth century. This point can be illustrated with reference to the status of African Americans in the United States, Turks in Germany, and North Africans in France, in addition to more obvious cases in Africa, Asia, and Latin America. But these situations also demonstrate that the concept and reality of citizenship are being gradually realized through cultural understandings and theoretical reflections, as well as through the development of appropriate political and legal institutions. Considering this historical evolution of the basic concept of citizenship, is it possible to imagine how the concept might work at multiple levels, from the local to the regional and global? The idea of global citizenship I am arguing for here is neither inconsistent with nor exclusive of traditional conceptions and experiences of national citizenship. As indicated above, global citizenship relates to universal human rights, while national citizenship applies to national civil rights. The conceptual and practical challenge is in trying to apply both concepts simultaneously within the territory and under the jurisdiction of the same state.

It seems to me that the present situation of Muslims in Europe provides a good opportunity for clarifying and testing these ideas for at least three sets of factors. First, the various countries of this region already enjoy a high level of economic and social development, political stability, and institutional capacity, as well as strong commitment to the universality of human rights. This combination of factors promises both the capacity to clarify and apply the two overlapping conceptions of citizenship and a high level of development of the underlying values and necessary political and legal institutions of constitutionalism and democratic governance.

A second set of factors relates to the tensions and dilemmas presented by the situation of Muslims in Europe. As I will briefly outline later, the majority of European societies are torn between concerns about the stability and security of their own countries, on the one hand, and a humane commitment to the universality of human rights, on the other. Consequently, European societies are neither able to ignore their immediate concerns with stability and security nor willing simply to violate the civil rights of Muslims citizens or human rights of noncitizens. Recalling the point made earlier about the interplay of the right to be the same and the right to be different, European societies are struggling in good faith to accept the Muslims in Europe as citizens who happen to be Muslims, rather than Muslims who happen to be in Europe.

The third set of factors relates to the concept of transnational European citizenship that has evolved under various regional institutions, especially the Council of Europe and what is commonly known as the European Union. In other words, Europeans have already come to accept a regional conception of citizenship that can be a logical step toward global citizenship. The governmental authorities and civil society actors have already learned how to work with a transnational system that enjoys a high degree of legitimacy and efficacy among the various societies of Europe.

In emphasizing the strong promise of these and other factors, I am not suggesting that positive outcomes for the synergy and mutual support of global citizenship and universality of human rights are secure or irreversible in the European context. All I am saying and hope to substantiate in this chapter is that the situation of the Muslims in Europe offers realistically strong prospects for the approach I am proposing, but only time will tell whether my optimism is justified. It is all a matter of the moral and political choices Europeans make and the action they take. Surely, every effort must be made to clarify concepts, cultivate political support, design and implement strategies, and so forth. But one should not wait for guarantees of success before taking the necessary action because that situation will never arise. I now turn to some clarification of concepts as a prerequisite for all other tasks in this process, in relation to Europe in particular. Similar analysis may be applied to other parts of the world, but with due regard to local historical and philosophical context.

The Evolution of Citizenship

The antecedents of the European concept and practice of citizenship can be traced all the way back to ancient Greece, when the citizen was defined as a member of the *polis*, a city-state such as Athens.[19] Aristotle, whose view of Athenian citizenship represented the accepted paradigm, "felt that the performance of citizenship was a core element of humanity."[20] Citizenship in that context was not merely an identity affording certain rights and responsibilities but a framework within which to live life. The governmental, militaristic, and religious values of citizenship were internalized from birth. The ancient Greek term *atimos*, which was used to describe those stripped of such functions of their citizenship as attending assembly meetings and jury duty, literally meant being without honor and value, which emphasizes the moral and communitarian sense of citizenship. But the honor and value of citizenship were limited and exclusive, as the citizen had to be a male of known genealogy, a patriarch, a warrior, and the master of the labor of others (normally slaves). To qualify as a citizen, the individual had to be the patriarch of a household (*oikos*), where the labor of slaves and women satisfied his needs and left him free to engage in political relationships with his equals.

That principle of limited and exclusive citizenship was continued by the

Romans, but the concept differed from its Greek meaning. Initially, during the Roman Republic government (500 B.C.E.–27 C.E.), the *civis Romanus* corresponded to the ancient Greek paradigm in which citizenship was rooted in the social and political community, but it eventually came to denote solely legal status. As the Romans viewed most actions as revolving around property or things, a person came to be "defined and represented through his actions upon things. . . . The individual thus became a citizen through the possession of things and the practice of jurisprudence."[21] Thus, a Roman citizen came to mean someone who was free to act by law, free to ask for and expect the protection of the law, who enjoyed legal standing within the Roman legal community. That paradigm shift reflected changes in the structure of government, from the republican Rome sense of being a citizen as "to rule and to be ruled" to the imperial centralized government started by Julius Caesar and perfected by Augustus, in which "citizenship became little more than an expression of the rule of law."[22] Under the Roman imperial government, citizenship was increasingly used as a bureaucratic organizational and administrative tool, rather than signifying a privileged legal identity. During that stage, the Romans found that granting citizenship to the peoples of the empire was expedient for collecting taxes and improving military functions. The edict of Emperor Caracalla that granted citizenship to all of the peoples of the Roman Empire signified the evolution of the concept of citizenship into a pragmatic and extensible sense, away from the earlier "ideal" notion.[23]

With the increasing Christianization of the late Roman Empire, membership in the church replaced citizenship in satisfying the social, political, and legal needs of the people. That period brought a "new localism" in which religious bonds counted more than civic responsibilities.[24] But, with the revival of commerce and civic competition, a demand to look for the ancient legal, philosophical, and political underpinnings of citizenship emerged. Thus, the increased commercialism and the protection-support model it precipitated resulted in a new civic consciousness. The status of the citizen in the medieval period, however, was acquired only by a quasi-aristocratic minority who had exclusive access to certain privileges, immunities, and resources, with the honorable recognition of independence as a *civitates* countering feudal forms of dependency.

The Renaissance brought the concept of citizenship into the forefront of political thought and practice. In the Italian city-states during the fifteenth century, there was a return to the democratic or active conception of citizenship that had ceased to exist since the fall of the Roman Republic. However, the Renaissance not only looked to ancient Greece and republican Rome for a sense of the active-political citizen but also sought to reaffirm the legal implications of citizenship developed by imperial Rome. The city-states of Italy based their citizenship regulations upon the Roman law presented in the *Corpus juris civilis* of Justinian, which also indicated the legal dynamism of citizenship, as it formed the basis of constant litigation.[25] The Italian Renaissance's renewed use of citizenship influenced other European territories to adopt and adapt the concept to their own sociopolitical situations. Scholars who came to Italy to study Roman law carried the concept of citizenship back to their homelands where it was subsequently grafted onto feudal practices.

With the increasing centralization of power in the royal monarch in France and other territories, the powers and rights of individuals against the monarchy came to be asserted in terms of a citizenship that signified rights that the king could not legally deny if the citizen continued to be obedient. By the early sixteenth century, Italian ideas had fused with French legal and legislative practices to produce principles of national citizenship. Those principles were clarified and organized into coherent theories during the sixteenth century by jurists and political thinkers, like Jean Bodin who conceived citizenship as signifying a personal relationship between the individual and the king.[26] During the absolutist period of the seventeenth century, the state was considered to be the person of the monarch, and devotion to the king was the most important duty of a citizen, who was thus transformed into a royal subject. Thus, the Renaissance tradition of active citizenship was transformed during that period into a more passive practice of service for the monarch.[27]

The Christian Reformation expedited the replacement of the king by the state as the focal point of power and allegiance as well as the source of rights. With the establishment of what came to be known as the nation-state (territorial state) after the Peace of Westphalia in 1648, the early modern concept of national citizenship emerged. Political philosophers like Thomas Hobbes developed theories of a direct relationship between the individual and the state.[28] John Locke built on Hobbes's conceptualization of the direct relationship of the individual to the state to construct a rights-based theory of citizenship, which became the characteristic feature of European political philosophy in the eighteenth century. As the state grew more powerful, it increasingly became the focal point for demands for the extension of rights.[29] The growing complex and bureaucratic structure of government also increased possibilities of interaction and communication between citizens and the state, thereby promoting the democratic principle of rule-by-consent.

The idea of territorial (national) citizenship was firmly established through the 1689 British Declaration of the Rights and Liberties of the Subject, as well as the French and American Revolutions.[30] The conception of citizenship in the French Revolution was not only linked to the Declaration of the Rights of Man and the Citizen, promising universal and egalitarian potential of status, but also the obligation of civic and military service to the nation. The view that emerged from the French Revolution of citizenship as a collective national identity, and not only an individual political, social, and legal status, was inspired by the idea of Jean-Jacques Rousseau that "a community could be united by a 'general will' that transcended social conflict."[31] Rousseau also promoted the concept of *popular sovereignty*, whereby sovereign individual citizens enter into a social contract with the state. This view was also adopted by the American Revolution in the Declaration of Independence, which explicitly vested sovereignty in the people.

While I have my own reservations about the fiction of "social contract," I also find the underlying rationale of democratic national citizenship that was promoted on those terms applicable to entities other than the immediate state, hence the possibility of regional and global citizenship I am proposing here. But those European conceptions of citizenship in the eighteenth century had to struggle with the question of the demographic scope of citizenship. For instance, while in the beginning foreigners could claim French citizenship, there was an increasing trend toward narrower scope of citizenship as France's wars with other countries militarized the idea of the nation and therefore citizenship. Thus, Western states gradually extended citizenship within the boundaries of each state, while at the same time excluding those who were not accepted as sharing the same national identity.

The next significant development in the European concept of citizenship, which came to prevail globally through colonialism (the United States itself is a product of colonialism), may be found in the welfare state paradigm of T. H. Marshall.[32] According to Marshall, citizenship is essentially a matter of ensuring that everyone is treated as a full and equal member of society. For him, the fullest expression of citizenship requires a liberal democratic welfare state that guarantees civil, political, and social rights to all. In this way, the welfare state ensures that all citizens are full members of society, able to participate in and enjoy its common life of society. If any of these rights are violated, people will be marginalized and feel unable to participate.[33] While Marshall seems to take the European notion of national citizenship for granted, that paradigm has been increasingly challenged by the realities of economic globalization and political interdependence. While this view appears to be receding by the end of the twentieth century, it may well regain currency in the near future.

Global Citizenship from a Historical Perspective

Though it may sound idealistic or futuristic, the idea of a global or world citizenship has in fact been discussed for the last 2,500 years. The philosophical antecedents of this idea may be found in the fourth century B.C.E., when Diogenes the Cynic (412–323) called himself a "citizen of the world."

The Stoics of Greece and Rome had universalistic and cosmopolitan visions of a city of the world in which "all human beings could live in peace with each other under a universal natural law."[34] The Stoics argued in favor of having dual civic rights, duties, and identities as both a citizen of the state and a citizen of the world. This is the concept of layered citizenship I hope to draw on later in this chapter. Zeno is reported to have said, "Our life should not be based on cities or people each with its own view of right or wrong, but we should regard all men as our fellow-country men and there should be one life and one order, like that of a single flock on a common pasture feeding together a common law."[35] The discourse on global citizenship and ideals of universalism and cosmopolitanism was continued during the Enlightenment. Such thinkers as Erasmus based their sense of global citizenship and cosmopolitanism on Christian-moral lines. In *Complaint of Peace*, Erasmus said, "The English despise the French, for no other reasons than that they are French, the Scots are disliked because they are Scots. . . . Why as men are they not benevolent to man, as Christians well-disposed towards fellow Christians?"[36]

The gradual establishment and consolidation of state sovereignty in the sixteenth and seventeenth centuries raised issues of the limits of sovereignty in global politics and how far cosmopolitan values should influence law and practice, which continue to be discussed today. Hugo Grotius, for instance, argued for limiting the sovereignty of the state according to the "law of nature" because all persons are members of a world society.[37] He also drew examples from the non-Western world, including Muslim practices and the cultures of South America.[38] One of the first known proposals to establish a political institution to enforce the cosmopolitan ethos and global citizenship ideal was submitted by Emeric Cruce (1590–1648). In *The New Cyneas* (1623), he proposed a global association, including non-Western nations like Persia, China, and Ethiopia. All would send ambassadors to an assembly where decisions would be made by majority to vote on policies and rules, with the goal of not only cultivating peace but of "religious toleration, freedom of trade, and reduction of poverty."[39]

Perhaps the culmination of early modern Enlightenment discourse on cosmopolitanism and global citizenship was found in the thought of Immanuel Kant. In his essay *Perpetual Peace* (1795), Kant proposed three constitutional principles for the promotion of peace: (1) a republican civil constitution for every state based on principles of freedom and legal equality of all citizens subject to a representative system of common legislation and separation of powers; (2) the rights of nations to be based on a federation of states that would protect the equal rights of constitutional democracies and form a gradually expanding alliance to prevent war; and (3) the cosmopolitan rights of foreigners in their relations with foreign states.[40] Kant envisioned a universal community that has "developed to the point where a violation of the laws in one part of the world is felt everywhere."[41]

Ancient antecedents of the idea of global citizenship can also be found in non-Western traditions. For example, ancient Indian texts like the *Mahabharata* (200 B.C.E.?) laid down universal principles of tolerance, respect for the individual, peace, and cooperation such as *vasudheva kutumbakam*—that we are all one family—that propounded universal equality and *ahimsa*, or nonviolence, toward all creation in word and deed. The concept of *chakravarti* in political theory advocated a one-world government to establish peace, and the code of law, *Dharmashastra*, was written (by Manu) "for the entire human race, not for any particular nation." Being universal in its reach, its legal concepts were especially emphasized.[42] Similar ideas of universal human connection are also found in the writings of Confucius, like the *Analects*.[43] Such earlier antecedence in various non-Western traditions did not directly contribute to recent debates and developments regarding global citizenship. Without digressing into a discussion of possible reasons for that, it is still important to note such intercultural religious and philosophical foundations for the idea of global citizenship today because, by definition, the concept and practice must integrate the widest possible range of human experiences.

It is also relevant to note, regarding Muslims in particular, that the notion of global *Umma*, in the sense of shared identity and tradition, is as old as Islam itself. It is therefore to be expected that Muslims in Europe, like European Christians, Hindus, and Jews, can claim multiple intellectual and cultural legacies and heritages that are consistent with antecedent ideas of global citizenship. Those experiences can be seen in sub-regional and interregional settings, as in North and West Africa or the Indian Ocean communities of southern Arabia, East Africa, and India, all the way to Southeast Asia. In other words, Muslims have always negotiated overlapping identities and cultural solidarities across borders of local, regional, and global *Umma*. The "local" and the "global" have always coexisted and complemented each other in the lived reality and the experience of Muslim communities. While that history has been complicated by the "national" during the twentieth century, it is sufficiently present in the consciousness of present generations of Muslims to be mobilized in support of overlapping national and global citizenship. But this possibility also raises the challenge of reimagining the *Umma* in relation to other forms of national and regional identities in the European context.

Despite this wide-ranging intellectual history of, and practical experiences with, the idea of global citizenship, practice has tended to lag behind, especially in the present world of territorial states. The development of the political worldview that is capable of sustaining the idea of global citizenship has been overcome by perception of interstate relations in Europe since the nineteenth century "in terms of conflicting interests moderated by the balance of power."[44] Despite increased cooperation between governments that was enhanced by easier global communication and economic exchange during the nineteenth century, law and citizenship remained focused on state sovereignty and territorial jurisdiction. It is also important to emphasize that all intergovernment discourse and interaction was strictly limited to the Western powers to the exclusion of the rest of the world during the nineteenth and early twentieth centuries, when traditional international law was developed.[45] Any practice of global citizenship during that period was necessarily imperialistic and hegemonic, which defeats its purpose.

Theoretical reflection and political developments continued during the first half of the twentieth century around such issues as "the possibility of a federal world structure" and "the role of the individual *qua* world citizen."[46] For example, in a 1918 article, Orrin McMurray argued that the mobility of people from one nation to another required that a "citizenship in a world state" be cultivated that had a federal-like relationship to the nation-state, analogous to the relationship of a state with the union of the United States.[47] Drawing on a sense of the weakening of the traditional relation between the sovereign and subject and the declining relevance of national citizenship due to an increasing global mobility, it was debated almost a century ago whether the world was entering into a post-national age, raising the possibility of layered citizenship.[48]

With renewed determination to establish and secure a peaceful and stable world order after the Second World War, a wide range of politicians, educators, scientists, and other opinion leaders participated in the global citizenship discourse.[49] For example, Mary E. Woolley argued for world citizenship to be cultivated through education to enlist the power of thought and spirit to "inspire human attitudes."[50] In 1944, Julio Álvarez del Vayo, who was also the foreign minister of republican Spain, appealed to the concept of global citizenship and the rights and responsibilities it entails.[51] A group of scientists that included Albert Einstein and J. Robert Oppenheimer made similar appeals out of concern for the threat of the atomic bomb.[52] Therefore, although due more to pragmatic global security issues than to a sense of universal human rights or similar virtuous ideals, World War II engendered an unprecedented discourse on global citizenship. Although the UN was seen as a step in the right direction, it was not believed to be enough.

By 1950, the World Movement for World Federal Government had member groups in twenty-two countries and an estimated 156,000 members.[53] While such initiatives and efforts declined with the onset of the Cold War, the end of that era also reinvigorated the discourse on cultivating both a moral, social, and political sense of global citizenship. In this most recent phase, there was a paradigm shift away from a world government (likely federal in form) toward "the concept of global governance and the proposals for reform of existing institutions to promote greater accountability to the people of the world."[54] Global governance consists of the multiplicity of international and regional bodies, business corporations, nongovernmental organizations, and social movements. Another theme that is leading to linking calls for global citizenship to demands for global governance has been an increased consciousness of global environmental problems.[55]

Global Citizenship in Current Discourse

The contemporary discourse on global citizenship is approached by scholars and politicians from widely divergent perspectives. For instance, one approach seeks to cultivate global citizenship through "a global market, run in accordance with rules set by global bodies, in which individuals act primarily as entrepreneurs and consumers."[56] Proponents of this view argue that the economy is becoming increasingly denationalized and more global through such mechanisms as the World Trade Organization. They cite concrete evidence in support of this approach, advocating an increased

liberalization of trade, thus minimizing the role of nation-states in economic relations.[57]

Another aspect of the current debate relates to the role of the nation-state
as both an obstacle and a vehicle for the realization of a legal conception
of global citizenship. Some point to the paradox of state self-regulation to
argue for defining citizenship through a clearer statement of the individual's
relationship to supra-state machinery. In other words, this view calls for moving away from the present community of states acting in their own interests
as states, instead of fulfilling their role as protector and guarantor of global
citizenship rights.[58] It is also noted that the growing importance of the supra-
national authority on human rights treaties and institutions is paradoxical in
relying on state agencies to control and guide themselves in the absence of an
international agency that has the right to "interfere in internal affairs."[59]

Rather than seek to realize global citizenship rights through a global governmental body, some scholars argue for shared sovereignty, whereby a legal
conception of global citizenship can coexist with the nation-state as long as
nation-states cooperate in sharing collective sovereignty through institutions
like the United Nations. From this perspective, it may be possible to determine an alternative to totally integrated shared sovereignty that has proven
elusive so far. It may then be possible to get closer to a legal and political
global citizenship through a layered structure of multiple or overlapping citi-
zenships. One possibility is "regional" citizenship, which would foster social
development and civil rights as well as security by linking states together into
"core (prosperous), intermediate, peripheral (developing) regions."[60] As noted
earlier, the European Union seems to be heading in this direction of regional
citizenship that coexists with traditional national citizenship.

This sense of layered citizenship is linked to the widespread entry of
transnational migrant communities into the public sphere, long-distance
nationalism, the rise of dual national identities, and the emergence of cross-
border civic and political communities, as well as multilateral institutions
and regional integration in Europe. From a theoretical point of view, a broad
approach to transnational or layered citizenship ascribes citizenship to any
of the multilevel processes through which social, civic, and political actors
claim rights in the transnational public sphere. This view is consistent with an
understanding of citizenship as allowing for a plurality of identities beyond
the nation-state. Through a broad approach to citizenship, people's membership in a state and their rights and responsibilities there are mediated by their
membership in other collectivities and polities, within, across, or beyond a

state, as well as by other identities such as class, gender, age, and sexuality. In contrast, a narrow approach would limit the definition of transnational citizenship to those migrants who manage to sustain or create dual or multiple national identities. It is true, of course, that this is not the same as being a citizen,[61] but the question I am raising is *why not?*

Along with the Kantian cosmopolitan view, some scholars have argued for an approach to global citizenship that is based much more on morality and education than on legality or international governmental institutions.[62] The underlying tenets of this cosmopolitan educational approach to global citizenship are individualism, universality, and generality. According to this view, the first tenet is that the primary unit of concern is the individual rather than families, ethnic, cultural, or any other subgroupings of nations or states. Proponents of this view also see that the tenet of universality requires that the primacy of the individual, as the central unit of concern, be afforded to all human individuals without exception. The third tenet of generality, or the Golden Rule principle, is the belief that the primary concern for every individual extends to all humanity. One's concerns for others does not stop at the border, nor is it a privilege of only those who share one's own race, religion, or other features held in common.[63]

Human rights as well as global environmental concerns have also been used to cultivate an abstract, psychological sense of world citizenship through liberal education, which makes students "citizens of the world" who can interact competently and respectfully with people and cultures from around the globe.[64] This educational model requires the individual's capacity to cultivate a shared sense of humanity, and thus global citizenship, through critical reflection on oneself and one's traditions. Moreover, it requires one to look beyond local identity, as a citizen of a particular country, to becoming a human being who is bound to all other human beings by ties of recognition and concern, which requires the ability to understand the world from the point of view of others.[65]

As to be expected, the idea of global citizenship, as well as the various approaches to realizing it, has been subject to considerable criticism. One line of criticism argues that true citizenship entails not only rights but political duties and responsibilities such as participation in "lawmaking" or engagement in political debate at some level.[66] Since citizenship implies a "determinate relationship to a political community," the idea of being a "citizen pilgrim" or perhaps a person who can *identify* with a variety of nation-states should not be considered citizenship. From this perspective, while a global civil society can be cultivated through transnational interaction and a shared sense of human rights as well as through global economic interdependence, to call this global citizenship would dilute an "immensely valuable achievement."[67]

Another criticism of the above-mentioned theories and approaches to global citizenship is that they presume a shared cultural, social, and moral compass. Given the rich and enduring diversity of human cultures and traditions, whose conception of justice and reason is to be the standard? Since the consciousness of a global citizen cannot be the sum total of all the existing ethnic, national, and cultural identities, how is that consciousness to be imagined? Why should it be assumed that such questions are to be answered from a liberal-democratic Western perspective, as if it were the ideal model to which all others aspire or the center toward which they were drawn?[68] To another critic, global citizenship in terms of cosmopolitanism is necessarily based on such a generalized concern for an abstract humanity that it is not sufficient for inspiring true human solidarity.[69] Another argument against the cosmopolitan-moral underpinnings of global citizenship is their lack of specificity: "if an individual has obligations to everyone, which are impossible to fulfill, then this may suggest a lack of specific obligation to anyone."[70]

While accepting the value of such criticisms in clarifying and developing the meaning and implications of global citizenship, I do not find them sufficient for discarding this powerful concept. For instance, it is indeed possible and desirable to insist on the mutuality of rights and duties of global citizenship or to devise mechanisms of accountability at regional and global levels. In other words, the need for "law making" and political participation is no longer limited to so-called national territorial entities, and the practical means for doing so can be devised. The challenge is to our imagination and political will to realize this, as it has been realized in the transition from city to "national" citizenship, rather than an inherent inability of the concept to operate beyond those historical boundaries.

Drawing on the earlier framing of the relevance of Islam to human rights and the preceding discussion of citizenship in historical and current discourse, I now turn to considering the present situation of Muslims in Europe. As indicated earlier, I will use this case to illustrate the argument I attempted to develop earlier about the synergy and mutual support of the universality of human rights and global citizenship. Once again, however, I recall the caveat from the outset that the situation of Muslims in Europe is used to illustrate my argument without implying uniformity among Muslims or ascribing guilt to European societies or segments thereof.

Demographic Profiles and Public Perceptions
of Muslims in Europe

There are over sixteen million Muslims who live in Europe, as citizens, legal residents, and migrant workers. Islam is the second largest religion in almost every European state.[71] Except in the Balkans, most Muslims have immigrated to European cities. But because of different immigration patterns, the Muslim population in European states reflects different demographic features, including varieties of ethnicities, languages, and cultures. While I am unable to discuss here underlying issues of immigration in the situation of Muslims in Europe, this connection can be appreciated from the following brief review of the demographics of Muslim populations in a small sample of European countries, in alphabetical order.[72]

There are approximately 400,000 Muslims in Belgium, out of a total population of 10.3 million. Although Belgium had virtually no connection with the Muslim world during the colonial period, Muslims have emigrated to Belgium since the 1960s under labor migration agreements first with Morocco and Turkey and later with Algeria and Tunisia. In 1974, Belgium imposed strict conditions on the entry of foreign labor but continued to have one of the most liberal policies in Europe for family reunion. Currently, there are about 125,000 individuals of Moroccan descent in Belgium, 70,000 of Turkish descent, 8,500 from Algeria, and 4,000 Tunisian. There are also small numbers of Muslims from Bosnia-Herzegovina, Pakistan, Lebanon, Iran, Syria, and Egypt. Since approximately 35 percent of the Turkish and Moroccan communities are under the age of eighteen, compared to 18 percent of the native Belgian population, there is a high proportion of Muslim youths in certain areas. It is estimated, for example, that 25 percent of individuals under the age of twenty in Brussels are Muslims.

Between 1985 and 1997, approximately 113,842 Muslim immigrants acquired Belgian citizenship. Belgian immigration laws were liberalized in 2000, so that anyone born in Belgium or anyone with at least one Belgian parent or anyone who had resided in Belgium for at least seven years could become a citizen. Those who have been in the country for over three years must fulfill a language and cultural requirement to qualify for citizenship. Islam is one of seven recognized religions in Belgium, which entitles Muslim religious organizations to a number of subsidies and resources from the government. Unemployment and poor housing, however, have been causes of concern for Belgian Muslims.

With a total population of 62.3 million, France is home to approximately 5 to 6 million Muslims, representing 8–9.6 percent of the population, making it the largest Muslim population in Western Europe. French Muslims are largely of North African descent from the former French colonies of Algeria (approximately 1.5 million), Morocco (approximately 1 million) and Tunisia (about 350,000). There are also about 100,000 Muslims from various Arab countries, 315,000 from Turkey, 250,000 from sub-Saharan Africa, 100,000 from Asia, and approximately 40,000 French converts. According to government statistics, the bulk of Muslims in France are citizens.

French immigration policies are based ideally on the principles of equality for all backgrounds and the expectation that immigrants will integrate into French society. From World War II through the 1970s, French immigration policies were more liberal, accepting immigrant workers to support the national economy. But with the widespread economic difficulties of the 1970s, immigration policies became more restrictive in the belief that immigrants were partly to blame for employment problems in France. In an attempt to address these issues, France entered into agreements with the main countries of origin of immigrants to provide social and political services and develop policies to encourage immigrants to return to their native countries. As those policies failed to produce the desired results, more restrictive laws were passed in the 1980s and 1990s to reduce and reverse immigrant flow. In accordance with European Union policies, many of these restrictive policies were softened and revised to prevent discrimination. But after the terrorist attacks of September 11, 2001, in the United States, France again returned to more restrictive immigration laws, including a law that makes it easier to deport individuals who "have committed acts justifying a criminal trial" or whose behavior "threatens public order."

It is perhaps relevant to note here the French conception of secularism (laïcité), which limits religious freedom with an active pursuit of secular orientation in all state activities. This concept has had a particularly significant impact on Muslims in France, as seen in the ban on religious symbols, including the Muslim headscarf (hijab), in public schools, which led to rioting and protests from French Muslims. This debate, of course, highlights the tension between public policy and private choices, between the concept of laïcité and the aspirations of Muslim students and their families to express their Islamic identity as French citizens.

There are more than three million Muslims in Germany, constituting about 3.6 percent in the country's total population of 82.5 million. The majority of Muslims (about 70 percent) in Germany are of Turkish origin, and most of them continue to maintain strong links to Turkey. A number of Muslims, who were relatively secular, also emigrated to Germany from Iran in the beginning of the 1980s. In addition, during the Balkan wars of the 1990s, which followed the breakup of the former Yugoslavia, approximately 300,000 Muslims from Bosnia-Herzegovina, Albania, and Kosovo have fled to Germany. The majority (65 percent) of German Muslims are Sunni, but there are also notable populations of Alevites, Imamites, and Turkish Shiʿa. The pattern of immigration of Muslims to Germany can be traced back to the country's serious need for labor after World War II. As a result, large numbers of immigrants, including Muslims, were allowed to enter Germany for temporary stays as "guest workers" who were expected to return to their homelands.

The founding of German nationhood in the nineteenth century on German decent (*jus sanguinis*) on the premise of *Volksgeist*, or spirit of the people as an organic cultural and racial entity marked by a common language, reflected strong opposition to the social integration of culturally different individuals and groups. This principle was embodied in the first codification of the law of national citizenship in 1913, which was affirmed by the Basic Law (constitution) of the Federal Republic in 1948 and remained in force until 1999. The clear contrast between the German *Volk*-centered and the French state-centered conception of citizenship reflects the different historical context in which the concept emerged and evolved in each country.[73] For our purposes here, this difference confirms the historical and contextual contingency of conceptions of citizenship among European societies. Another indication of this fact is the recent change in the German conception, as embodied in the new citizenship law (*Staatsangehörigkeitsrecht*) of May 1999, which came into force on January 1, 2000. This law retains the old basis of citizenship on ancestral origin but adds two more grounds, namely, birth in the country (*jus soli* or "right of soil") and naturalization. The requirements of naturalization include legal residence for eight years, ability to support self and family, not having been convicted of a major felony, and renouncing previous citizenship. This last requirement is subject to a good range of exceptions.[74] The point for us here is that the definition of citizenship can change in response to changing demographic, social, and economic circumstances.

Germany allows for freedom of religion but does not officially recognize some faiths, including Islam. Consequently, Muslims are not entitled to the privileges granted to believers in a recognized religion, like full independence in matters of employment, recognition of religious oath in a court of law, freedom to organize councils with religious hierarchy of authority, fiscal protection and exemption from real estate taxes on property designated as belonging to the public domain, or the right to receive a percentage of the national revenue based on a taxpayers' declaration of membership.

The Netherlands is home to about 945,000 Muslims, comprising 5.8 percent of the total population of 16.3 million. The first wave of Muslim immigrants came in the 1950s from the former Dutch colonies of Suriname and Indonesia. The Netherlands also has a substantial Somali minority, as well as labor immigrants from Turkey and Morocco who immigrated in the 1960s. Traditionally, the Netherlands has had a very liberal immigration policy, but the government enacted new antiterrorism laws and restrictive immigration laws after the 2004 murder of Theo Van Gogh. But even before September 11, 2001, there were concerns in the Netherlands about the failure of foreigners to integrate into Dutch society. There have been many efforts to teach Dutch language and culture to immigrants.

The Moroccan and Turkish governments exercise substantial control over religious matters in the Netherlands through an official Turkish organization and a network of Moroccan social organizations. In contrast, there were no relations between Muslim communities and the Dutch state. That is consistent with the general severance of formal ties between state and religion in the Netherlands since 1983, where the constitutional principles of freedom of religion and nondiscrimination are supposed to apply to ensure equal treatment for different religious groups. But this general policy seems to be changing for Muslims since the murder of Van Gogh, which resulted in calls for the creation of a union of Dutch imams to negotiate important issues with the state. Two new organizations were recently recognized by the state, Contact Groep Islam (CGI), which represents some 115,000 Muslims, and Contactorgaan Moslims en de Overheid (CMO), which represents 500,000 Muslims and is attempting to represent the entire Muslim population in the Netherlands.

Despite the general policy of no formal recognition of religious communities since the 1980s, the Dutch state continued to facilitate social or cultural activities of religious communities, such as schools, broadcasting, and spiritual care in prisons and the army. There is generally no difficulty for Muslims to qualify for this status. For example, there are thirty-seven Islamic primary schools and one secondary school in Rotterdam that started in August 2000, which are recognized and financed by the state. The courses offered must follow a national curriculum that fills most of the available time, while a few hours per week are allotted to weekly religious lessons and ceremonies. In public schools, which are governed by the municipalities, parents can organize religious lessons, which will fall outside the school's responsibility. This means that the parents have to find and pay the teacher. Muslim parents use this legal opportunity only in exceptional cases. Some municipalities (like Rotterdam), however, subsidize this activity. There are also some private institutions of higher education, like the Islamic University of Rotterdam (IUR) and an Islamic University of Europe in Schiedam, as well as some smaller training institutes. There is also a four-year program in the Education Faculty of Amsterdam to train teachers for secondary schools.

The 43.1 million total population of Spain includes approximately one million Muslims (about 2.3 percent). After the long legacy of Islamic rule of much of Spain faded over time, Muslims began to arrive in significant numbers in the 1970s, mostly from the Spanish protectorate areas of northern Morocco, and settled in Catalonia, working mainly in the tourism industry. At that time, many other European countries were instituting more restrictive immigration policies, leading many immigrants to settle in Spain. It is estimated that, by the end of the 1970's, there were approximately 100,000 Moroccans in Barcelona. Immigrants from Syria, Lebanon, Jordan, and Iraq, who came as students and entrepreneurs, also accounted for the rising numbers of Spanish Muslims in the 1970s. By 1977, Spain was also home to Palestinian refugees and Iranian refugees after 1979. The 1970s also saw an increase in the number of converts to Islam, and there are currently about 6,000 Muslim converts in Spain. During the 1980's, the numbers of Spanish Muslims grew due to family reunification.

Spain provided to immigrants a set of rights and privileges that conformed to European standards. However, since 9/11, there has been a trend toward more restrictive immigration laws, as well as tightened security at borders, airports, bases, and embassies. In addition, individuals may be expelled for actions that are considered to be threatening to Spain's external relations or public order, even if there are no concurrent criminal charges.

The United Kingdom has a long history of contact with Muslims since the European Crusades in the Middle East of the twelfth and thirteenth centuries, but the large current Muslim presence in the country is associated with British colonialism. In the late 1960s and early 1970s, "Africanization" policies in Kenya and Tanzania and forced expulsion from Uganda promoted an influx of highly skilled, middle-class professionals from East Africa. Estimates indicate that of the 150,000 East African immigrants, 20,000 were Muslim, with roots in South Asia.

In April 2001, the British government conducted a decennial census, which included a voluntary question regarding religious affiliation. Based on the answers of about 92 percent of the population, there are currently approximately 1.6 million individuals practicing Islam in the UK, 2.7 percent of the total population of the country.[75] According to government statistics, British Muslims are the clear majority (52 percent) of non-Christian communities in the UK. The statistics also indicate that approximately 75 percent of British Muslims are of South Asian descent, primarily from Pakistan. About 11 percent of British Muslims are of a white ethnic group, with 6 percent of black African descent, the majority from North and West Africa, especially Somalia. The April 2001 survey also indicates that 93 percent of Muslims in the UK are British citizens, the clear majority (about 46 percent) being born within the UK.[76] It is estimated that there are approximately 5,000–10,000 Muslim converts, mostly from the Afro-Caribbean communities. The survey also shows that immigrants from outside the South Asia region are from Turkey (3 percent), Somalia (2 percent), Kenya (1 percent), and the former Yugoslavia (1 percent).

Traditionally, British political discourse has been inclusive and strongly supportive of multiculturalism, but that has been questioned by some, including prominent Muslim leaders, after the London bombings of July 7, 2005. There have also been some concerns about race relations and possible discrimination against British Muslims. Although the British government and media attempted to stay balanced, 500 suspected extremists were deported in the weeks following the attacks, and a sudden increase in hate crimes against Muslims immediately followed the attacks.

As this brief review shows, despite the different origins and dynamics of Muslim immigration to various countries of Western Europe, there are also some common features. For example, the main underlying causes of Muslim immigration have either been colonial history, mainly in the cases of France and the United Kingdom, or the need for foreign labor for countries like Germany and the Netherlands. Political asylum has also been a common basis of immigration. Another common feature to note is how the immigration policies of different countries have responded to cultural tensions, security concerns, and changing economic conditions. But there are two main features that are particularly relevant to our discussion. First, for most Muslims, especially second- and third-generation immigrants, whether citizens or not, the European country they now live in is the only home they have. They are as European as their neighbors and no longer people from another place who can "go home." The second important feature is that these Europeans commonly referred to as "Muslims" have much more in common with other Europeans than with each other. They are divided by ethnicity and race, culture, country or region of origin, and even in their beliefs as Muslims. It is, therefore, extremely misleading and unproductive to call them Muslims, as if that defines who they are as a coherent monolithic group or sets them apart from their non-Muslim neighbors.

Yet this irrational and grossly misleading perception not only continues but seems to be rising as shown in the following review of public perception of Muslims in Europe, which would be particularly relevant to the theme of citizenship and human rights I am arguing for in this chapter. One caveat to note here is that, while the significant diversity of Muslims in Europe defies generalizations, it seems that they share some of the realities and experiences of other immigrants. For instance, unemployment rates for foreign-born individuals are more than twice as high as those for natives in virtually every European state. Thus, Muslims (and other immigrants) in most European states tend to remain toward the lower end of the socioeconomic spectrum. It may, therefore, be helpful to consider the situation of Muslims in the wider context of the situation of minorities and immigrants in general.

The European Monitoring Centre on Racism and Xenophobia (EUMC) issued a report in 2003 on the attitudes of the majority populations toward immigrants and minorities.[77] According to the report, about half of the Eastern and Western European populations were resistant to immigrants, while resistance to asylum seekers was supported by less than 33 percent of the general population.[78] Approximately 25 percent of the general population were resistant to multiculturalism—concerns here relate to the existence of different religions and cultures, which would eventually affect the stability of the majority culture. About 50 percent of the population were resistant to diversity, and about 65 percent favored limits to multicultural society by limiting constant immigration and societal acceptance of minority groups. Preference for ethnic distance, that the majority should try to keep its distance from minority groups and try to avoid interethnic contact, was expressed by 20 percent of the general population. A growing minority of 20 percent in member states of the European Union favored repatriation policies for legal migrants, who were actually entitled to stay in the country.

Within this broader framework, it seems that negative public attitudes toward Muslims in particular have been growing since the 1990s. The underlying causes of such attitudes are complex, often reflecting specific local or national dynamics. But it is also reasonable to assume that current public perceptions of Islam and Muslims in Western Europe are influenced by the terrorist attacks of 9/11 in New York and Washington, D.C., March 11, 2004, in Madrid, and July 7 and July 21, 2005, in London. Other incidents that may have contributed to such public perceptions also include the murder of Theo Van Gogh in the Netherlands. Despite the large number of Muslims living in Europe for decades, the implication of this recent trend is that Muslims are outside the Western realm and incompatible with the Western way of life.

In the Netherlands, for example, anti-Muslim sentiment became apparent with the rise of Pim Fortuyn, a populist who characterized Islam as too socially conservative to integrate with traditionally liberal Dutch culture. Although Fortuyn was killed by an animal rights activist, not a Muslim, the anti-Muslim sentiment he generated has become a powerful force in Dutch politics. These attitudes did not seem to lead to a great deal of discrimination until the murder of provocative filmmaker Theo Van Gogh in 2004. Prior to his murder, Theo Van Gogh turned a high profile lens on the issue of the treatment of women in traditional Islamic society. His film *Submission* (2004) told the story of a Muslim woman forced into an arranged marriage in which she is seriously abused. The film was made with the help of Ayaan Hirsi Ali, a liberal Dutch-Somalian politician who escaped from an arranged marriage herself. Particularly controversial in the film were scenes of a semi-naked woman with marks from beating and verses from the Qur'an inscribed on her body. Similar simplistic charges of the purportedly "inherent" contradiction between Islam and Western civilization emerged most recently in the controversy over the publication of cartoons of the Prophet Muhammad in a Danish newspaper in September 2005.

This hardening of European public attitudes toward Muslims is documented, for example, in a report issued in November 2005 by the EUMC on the impact on Muslim communities in the EU of the July 7, 2005, London bomb attacks. According to the report, although media outlets and government agencies attempted to remain neutral during initial reports of the attacks, "there was a distinct change in the kind of reporting, shifting to issues of integration and the radicalization of members of the Muslim community in Britain" after it became clear that the attackers were all British nationals.[79] This trend then broadened into a debate on immigration, residency status, and human rights legislation. In a Mori poll for the BBC, a notable 32 percent of the individuals interviewed thought that multiculturalism "threatens the British way of life" and 54 percent said that "parts of the country don't feel like Britain anymore because of immigration."[80] There was also an immediate increase in hate crimes against Muslims and other communities such as Sikhs.[81]

It should be noted, however, that the British government has attempted to maintain a balanced position. On the one hand, it reacted to the London attacks, in part, by deporting 500 individuals, and British law has seen a stricter emphasis on security and immigration, with an eye toward preventing and rooting out terrorism. On the other hand, the British government also has begun programs to encourage Muslim communities in Britain to confront and root out extremism. According to Home Secretary Charles Clarke, "Tackling extremism is not something that can be done by Government alone. . . . We look forward to continuing the dialogue with Muslim communities and supporting the work that they are undertaking."[82]

Outside the United Kingdom, reactions were varied, but there are indications of rising Islamophobic and xenophobic rhetoric in various European countries. For example, in the Czech Republic, the non-parliamentary National Party issued a declaration in which it demanded the expulsion of all Muslims and closing of the borders.[83] The Danish People's Party also warned that there was a large group of Muslim fanatics in Denmark and demanded more surveillance and tighter border controls.[84] On July 16, 2005, Philippe de Villiers, president of the Mouvement pour la France, spoke against the "progressive Islamization of French Society," urging for stricter border control, checks on mosques, and more investment in Muslim areas.[85] The Christian Democratic Union in Germany also has called for stricter regulation of Muslim immigration, calling for policies that make it easier to deport Muslims and withdraw their German citizenship if they have been naturalized.[86] Ján Slota, chairman of the opposition party Slovak National Party (SNS), claimed that the London bombings gave "clear evidence that there was an undeclared war of civilizations between Christian European culture and Islamic extremism."[87] In Poland, articles such as "They Want Our Destruction," "Throw Muslims out of Poland?" and "New York, Madrid, London. Genocide of the 21st Century" appeared after the second bomb attacks in London (July 21, 2005).[88]

Muslims in Europe or European Muslims?

The variation in the title of this chapter is intended to raise a question: are Muslims in Europe accepted as citizens who happen to be Muslims, or is their religious affiliation emphasized to imply denying or diminishing their citizenship? In terms of the thesis I am attempting to advance here, I am suggesting that the concept of global citizenship can, in fact, promote and enhance traditional national citizenship. I also find that this conception of citizenship can benefit from the universality of human rights because the enjoyment of these rights should not be limited to the citizens of the country where a person happens to be. While legitimate legal and political distinctions between citizens and noncitizens should be maintained, that does not justify any violation of human rights norms, regardless of the citizenship status of the person. Indeed, the universality of human rights requires specific minimum standards in the treatment of noncitizens precisely because they are more vulnerable to the violation of their rights than citizens tend to be. Beyond these commonly accepted principles, the additional argument I try to advance here is that emphasizing the linkage of universality of human rights and global citizenship should facilitate the granting of national citizenship while gradually diminishing the distinction between citizens and noncitizens. I will now highlight and reflect on the interaction or dialectic of national and European Union citizenship as part of the process of evolution toward global citizenship in accordance with the universality of human rights.

The idea of a "nation," as a people joined by common ties of shared descent, culture, religion, language, and territory is an ancient concept.[89] It is also reasonable to assume that an association with permanent residence in a certain territory may well have been the rationale of emphasizing membership in that community. But this does not mean that the nation is an inherent attribute of humanity, although "it has now come to appear as such."[90] Since it is "an imagined political community" in which members will never know most of their fellow members except in their minds,[91] the nation in the present usage of the term is necessarily a construction of human imagination. Moreover, the coincidence of a nation and the exclusive territory and jurisdiction of a "nation-state" is primarily the product of late eighteenth- and nineteenth-century Europe. In other words, the idea of allocating a specific territory for members of a particular nation (defined by race, color, religion, etc.) to the exclusion of all other persons and groups is much more recent in comparison to earlier conceptions of nation as social identity. It may, therefore, be helpful to consider the current progression from national to regional citizenship in the European Union as a step toward broader, overlapping conceptions, including a sense of global citizenship as an underlying principle that informs and guides practice at all levels.

The notion of a substantive form of "European citizenship" can be traced back to the Treaty Establishing the European Community (Treaty of Rome), which devoted its entire second part to this subject. But it was not until the Treaty on European Union (Maastricht) of 1992 that citizenship of the Union was formally established within the legal context of the community. As of 2006, every citizen of the Union has the following rights: to circulate and remain and live freely on the territory of all member states; to take part in elections to the European Parliament and in municipal elections in his or her place of residence; to benefit from diplomatic and consular protection by the authorities of all states of the European Union, and have access to extrajudicial recourse through a mediator; and to petition the European Parliament.[92] Still, this concept has been criticized for a "striking absence of rights that could trigger a more active concept of citizenship."[93] On the one hand, the weak representation of citizens in European Union institutions undermines the democratic legitimacy of the EU.[94] On the other hand, the lack of active citizenship is probably a reflection of the dependence of the EU on its nation-state members, including determination of who is an EU citizen and what that entails. Article 17 of the EC Treaty provides that EU citizenship is due only to persons holding the nationality of a Member State, which means that EU citizenship is "completely determined by rules outside the legislative procedures of the EU."[95]

This emerging concept seems disappointing because our purposes here include its failure to provide a framework for universal rights for a welfare state.[96] The Social Charter, for instance, was adopted only as a nonbinding "social declaration" of the European Council, and "references to *citizens* were replaced with references to *workers* to avoid the appearance of an expanded social policy mandate for the Community."[97] Integration was identified with deregulation and political disengagement from the economy, and the intergovernmental character of the community was confirmed by the Single European Act. "A free European market, if this is all that is to be, does not 'require' a 'Europe of the citizen'; in fact, citizenship makes the market less 'free.'"[98] Another tension relates to the significant differences among member states of the EU in terms of geographic extension, population size, economic strength, religious and sociocultural factors, and the geopolitical role of states beyond Europe. These and other factors, like strong diversity in political attitudes and citizenship tradition, can make it harder to achieve agreement on expanding the rights and responsibilities of EU citizenship, as illustrated earlier regarding French and German conceptions of citizenship.[99]

Another instructive and relevant development relates to the proposed Constitution for Europe, which, although rejected in both France and the Netherlands, is now under reconsideration, has the motto "united in its diversity." The draft explicitly addresses the dilemma of citizens belonging both to their member states and to the Union. Optimistically, the authors of the draft affirm their conviction that "while remaining proud of their own national identities and histories, the peoples of Europe are determined to transcend their ancient divisions and, united ever more closely, to forge a common destiny."[100] In reality, the concept of EU citizenship has proven a challenge to the political imagination of Europeans, including questions of transnational democracy, social policy, language, and cultural relations. The whole EU process may have created the preconditions necessary for a relaxation of sovereignty, and the EU citizenship was never presented as a substitute for national citizenship, yet popular and institutional resistance to the idea of post-national politics remains strong throughout the region.[101]

The human rights approach to citizenship I am proposing may be more appropriate for the "territorial state" of the twenty-first century in its global context, as opposed to the "nation-state" of the nineteenth and twentieth centuries. The notion of national uniformity on the basis of ethnic, racial, cultural, or religious identity is probably factually unfounded, especially under present conditions of demographic diversity and mobility of populations. That traditional notion of national uniformity can easily be manipulated to oppress minorities and dissident individuals in the name of unity and stability. European examples of this problem range from issues of long-term language and culture in sub-national politics to genocide of European Jews and other minorities in the mid-twentieth century in Nazi Germany and in Bosnia half a century later. It seems clear to me that such difficulties will probably persist as long as the notion of the "heterogeneous nation" is maintained as the primary basis of citizenship of the territorial state.

Another dimension that is particularly relevant to the situation of Muslims in Europe is that the legacy of nationhood and citizenship does not seriously consider immigration as a basis of citizenship. The more serious consequences of this lack of consideration of immigration as a factor in population policies underlies some of the bigoted stereotypical policies and attitudes, ranging from apathy to antagonism.[102] For example, in the federal state Baden-Wurtenberg, the ruling Christian Democratic Union party recently administered a thirty-topic loyalty test for applicants to become naturalized citizens. The questions, which range from domestic issues, such as women's rights and female attire, to political issues, such as 9/11, religious freedom, and terrorism, apparently target Muslim applicants in particular.[103]

Concluding Remarks

As indicated at the beginning, the limited primary focus of this chapter is to clarify the relationship between the universality of human rights and the concept and institutions of citizenship. The main premise of my analysis of synergy and mutual support between the universality of human rights and global citizenship is that citizenship is the basis of entitlement to rights, while rights secure the meaningful content of citizenship. The idea of conceptual and practical synergy and mutual support is necessary to mediate the apparent paradox that citizenship is both the means for protecting human rights and a limitation on the universality of those rights. If only citizens are entitled to rights like freedom of expression, opinion, and belief, health care, and education, how can these rights also be due to all human beings? The solution I propose for mediating this paradox is to think of two sets of overlapping entitlements: civil rights based on national citizenship and human rights based on global citizenship. The progression of the analysis I presented can be summarized as follows.

I began by outlining how the revolutionary idea of universal human rights was first declared in the Charter of the UN, elaborated in the Universal Declaration of Human Rights, and finally rendered binding under international law through a series of subsequent treaties. That is a good starting point to emphasize the significant difference between civil rights, which are due only to the citizens of the particular state, and human rights, which are due to all human beings everywhere. Yet, while supposed to be the standard for judging the protection of rights in every state or country, universal human rights can only be implemented in practice through the national constitutional and legal systems of states. This is what I referred to as the paradox of self-regulation by the state, namely, that the state is the legal entity bound to protect human rights against the excess or abuse of power by officials of the same state.

Given the critical and complex relationship of the two concepts, I have offered some general discussion of citizenship and rights, followed by a review of the historical and current debates about citizenship and global citizenship. One point to draw from that review in support of the thesis of this chapter is that, while the idea of global citizenship is as old as the idea of citizenship itself, the restriction of this status to the territorial or nation-state is very recent. In fact, the evolution from the citizenship of the Renaissance city-state to that of the nation-state can logically lead to broader conceptions of citizenship in this age of global interdependence and diminishing territorial sovereignty. One difficulty with this possibility is the correspondence of the rights and obligations of territorial citizenship, whereby the entitlement to civil rights and social benefits is reciprocal to the obligations to pay taxes, serve in the national defense of the country, and other public civic duties. This correspondence can also be seen in the organic relationship between territorial sovereignty and democratic constitutional governance.

It may be possible to negotiate these issues, as shown by the recent experience of the Western European societies with citizenship of the European Union. But that same process also demonstrates the difficulties of progression from national to regional identity and democratic self-governance. One way of easing these tensions is to suggest that, instead of seeing the issues in terms of drastic choice among various levels of citizenship, progress can be made for intermediate ideas of shared or overlapping sovereignty, whereby a moral and political conception of global citizenship can coexist with legal national citizenship, each applicable to its domain of rights and obligations.

In the final analysis, the dynamic role of the citizen in self-governance and other civic functions clearly indicates that citizenship in a democratic polity should be earned and not granted by an autocratic sovereign. Since this means that the Muslims in Europe must demonstrate their commitment to this concept of citizenship, it is important to clarify the sense in which Islam is relevant to this process by discussing the relationship between Islam and human rights. Recalling that human rights are about the right to be the same and the right to be different, the Muslims in Europe should be entitled to citizenship without having to abandon their religious identity. The demographic profile and inter-communal experiences of Muslims and other immigrant groups in Europe confirm the need to facilitate greater inclusion and recognition as citizens. But Muslims and other immigrants must also be able and willing to accord the same entitlement to others. This is not to say that Islam as such is problematic from a human rights and citizenship perspective but that Muslims need to confront the challenges of Islamic reform to avoid historical difficulties in this regard.

I hope that I have raised enough interest in the possibilities of mutual support and synergy between the universality of human rights and global citizenship to encourage scholars and social activists to take this subject seriously, despite its present conceptual ambiguities and political and social difficulties.

This must also be done with a clear understanding of the protracted nature of social change, where regression is always part of progression. As we have seen in the intellectual history of the concept of citizenship in general, ideas can play a powerful leading role in the processes of social translation, but it is social movements and political organizations that eventually realize the promise of visionary ideas.

Notes

Chapter 1. Islamic Ambivalence to Political Violence:
Islamic Law and International Terrorism

An earlier version of this chapter was published in *German Yearbook of International Law* 31 (1988): 307–36.

1. Arnold, *The Violence Formula*, 1.

2. See generally Falk, Kratochwil, and Mendlovitz, eds., *International Law: A Contemporary Perspective* (Boulder, 1985), but especially Grenville and Sohn, chap. 5, "Introduction to World Peace Through World Law," 73–99, and Young, chap. 6, "Compliance in the International System," 99–111; and Detter Delupis, *The Law of War*, chap. 2.

3. Bibliographic volumes on the subject indicate that over 99 percent of the works cited have been published after 1968. See Norton and Greenberg, *International Terrorism* and Mickolus, *The Literature of Terrorism*.

4. See generally Bassiouni, "Perspectives on the Origins and Causes of Terrorism," 5–10.

5. Rapoport, "Fear and Trembling."

6. See the entry on terrorism in *Webster's New Collegiate Dictionary*, 1951.

7. Arnold, *The Violence Formula*, 3.

8. Arnold, *The Violence Formula*, 3, 4.

9. Schmid, *Political Terrorism*, 73–75.

10. Schmid, *Political Terrorism*, 76, 77.

11. Provizer, "Defining Terrorism," 5.

12. Arnold, *The Violence Formula*, 8, 9.

13. Arnold, *The Violence Formula*, 9.

14. Wardlaw, *Political Terrorism*, 4.

15. Arnold, *The Violence Formula*, 5.

16. Provizer, "Defining Terrorism," 8.

17. Johnson, *Can Modern War Be Just?* 61.

18. A distinction has been suggested between international terrorism, involving activity wherein the perpetrators are controlled by states, and transnational terrorism,

where the perpetrators are essentially autonomous private actors. See Schmid, *Political Terrorism*, 258.

19. Vesey-Fitzgerald, "Nature and Sources of the Shari'a," 85. For an analysis of the development of the concept of Shari'a, see Rahman, *Islam*, 101–9; Hasan, *The Early Development of Islamic Jurisprudence*.

20. Coulson, *A History of Islamic Law*, 11, 12, 17; Rahman, *Islam*, 33–37; Vesey-Fitzgerald, "Nature and Sources of the Shari'a," 87.

21. Coulson, *A History of Islamic Law*, 12; Rahman, *Islam*, 69; Vesey-Fitzgerald, "Nature and Sources of the Shari'a," 87.

22. See generally Burton, *The Collection of the Qur'an*, on the processes by which the present text of the Qur'an, *al-Mushaf*, came to be accepted as the authentic and full text of the final and literal word of God.

23. Rahman, *Islam*, 63–65; Schacht, *Origins of Muhammadan Jurisprudence*, 3, 4.

24. Schacht, *Origins of Muhammadan Jurisprudence*, 36–39.

25. Coulson, *A History of Islamic Law*, 42; Vesey-Fitzgerald, "Nature and Sources of the Shari'a," 93.

26. Coulson, *A History of Islamic Law*, 63; Vesey-Fitzgerald, "Nature and Sources of the Shari'a," 94.

27. Hasan, *The Early Development of Islamic Jurisprudence*, chap. 7; Schacht, *Origins of Muhammadan Jurisprudence*, 82–99.

28. MacDonald, *Development of Muslim Theology, Jurisprudence and Constitutional Theory*, 86; Vesey-Fitzgerald, "Nature and Sources of the Shari'a," 93.

29. Coulson, *A History of Islamic Law*, 80, 81; Schacht, *An Introduction to Islamic Law*, 69–75.

30. See generally Adams, *Islam and Modernism in Egypt*; Gibb, *Modern Trends in Islam*; Kerr, *Islamic Reform*.

31. Hallaq, "Was the Gate of Ijtihad Closed?"

32. Coulson, *A History of Islamic Law*, chaps. 2–5, provides a most concise statement of the development of Shari'a.

33. Mahmassani, *Falsafat al-Tashri fi al-Islam*, 32–35, lists the names of the founding jurists of the surviving as well as the extinct schools of Islamic jurisprudence, and the dates of their deaths.

34. Coulson, *A History of Islamic Law*, 106.

35. Mahmassani, *Falsafat al-Tashri fi al-Islam*, 38; Fyzee, "Shi'a Legal Theories," 117.

36. For detailed explanations of Shi'a sects, see Watt, *Islamic Philosophy and Theology*, 20–26, 50–56, 99–104. Reference may also be made to the numerous detailed works on the Shi'a, such as Arjomand, *The Shadow of God and the Hidden Iman*; Momen, *Introduction to Shi'a Islam*.

37. Eliash, "The Ithna 'ashari Shi'a Juristic Theory of Political and Legal Authority," 29.

38. Coulson, *A History of Islamic Law*, 105.

39. Fyzee, " Shi'a Legal Theories," 123.

40. Fyzee, "Shi'a Legal Theories," 114–21.

41. Fyzee, "Shi'a Legal Theories," 121, 122.

42. Coulson, *A History of Islamic Law*, 120.

43. Coulson, *A History of Islamic Law*, 82, 83.

44. Coulson, *A History of Islamic Law*, 83, 84. Individual jurists preferred different variations of these basic categories; see Hasan, *The Early Development of Islamic Jurisprudence*, 34–39; Rahman, *Islam*, 83, 84.

45. Faruki, *Islamic Jurisprudence*, 166–94; Coulson, *A History of Islamic Law*, 47–51.

46. Schacht, *An Introduction to Islamic Law*, 68.

47. Schacht, *An Introduction to Islamic Law*, 76.

48. Coulson, *A History of Islamic Law*, 120.

49. Vesey-Fitzgerald, "Nature and Sources of the Shari'a," 91.

50. Schacht, *Origins of Muhammadan Jurisprudence*, 84.

51. Rahman, *Islam*, 79; Coulson, *A History of Islamic Law*, 23–27.

52. Schacht, *An Introduction to Islamic Law*, 23; Coulson, *A History of Islamic Law*, 27.

53. Rahman, *Islam*, 79.

54. Goldziher, *Introduction to Islamic Theology and Law*, 45; Schacht, *An Introduction to Islamic Law*, 49; Rahman, *Islam*, 93.

55. Coulson, *A History of Islamic Law*, 121.

56. Anderson, *Law Reform in the Muslim World*, 1, 2.

57. Anderson, *Law Reform in the Muslim World*, 14–32; Liebesny, *Law of the Near & Middle East*, 56; Coulson, *A History of Islamic Law*, 161.

58. Anderson, *Law Reform in the Muslim World*, 36.

59. This phenomenon has been documented and discussed in numerous scholarly works; see, for example, Esposito, ed., *Islam and Development*; Ayoob, ed., *The Politics of Islamic Reassertion*; Voll, *Islam: Continuity and Change*; Piscatori, ed., *Islam in the Political Process*; Pipes, *In the Path of God*; Esposito, ed., *Voices of Resurgent Islam*; Esposito, ed., *Islam in Asia*.

60. Khadduri, *The Islamic Law of Nations*, "Introduction."

61. See, for example, Ibn Taimiyya, *Public and Private Law in Islam*.

62. Haykal, *The Life of Muhammad*, 115–30; Hamidullah, *The Muslim Conduct of State*, 48–61.

63. Haykal, *The Life of Muhammad*, 15, 16; Donner, *The Early Islamic Conquests*, 20ff.

64. Hamidullah, *The Muslim Conduct of State*, 51.

65. Donner, *The Early Islamic Conquests*, 37ff.

66. Khadduri and Liebesny, *Law in the Middle East*, 353ff.

67. Khadduri and Liebesny, *Law in the Middle East*, 3.

68. Khadduri and Liebesny, *Law in the Middle East*, 10ff.; Khadduri, *War and Peace in the Law of Islam*, 42–58.

69. Khadduri, "Islam and the Modern Law of Nations," 359.

70. The term *ijtihad*, or independent juristic reasoning in developing principles and rules where the Qur'an and Sunna were silent, is derived from the same root as *jihad*, namely *jahd*, to make strenuous and sincere effort. Thus, exerting juristic effort in developing legal principles and rules is a form of *jilhad*.

71. Al-Kaya al-Harasiy, *Ahkam al-Qur'an*, vol. 1, 89.

72. *Mukhtasar Tafsir ibn Kathir* (Islamic calendar, corresponding to 1979).

73. Zayd, *AI-Nasikh wa al-Mansukh*, 289–501; Zayd, *AI-Nasikh wa al-Mansukh*, vol. 2, 503–83; Hasan, *The Early Development of Islamic Jurisprudence*, 67, 68.

74. Mohammad, "The Doctrine of Jihad," 385.

75. See, for example, Abu Zahrah, "Nazariayt al-Harb fi al-Islam," 6; Shaltut, *Al Islam wa al-'alaqat al-Dawliya*, 38. This claim was made by Ibn Taymiyya in the fourteenth century; see Ibn Taymiyya, *Qa'ida fi Qital al-Kuffar*, 115–46.

76. For an English translation of an early account by a Muslim historian, see Hitti, trans., *The Origins of the Islamic State*.

77. Khadduri, *War and Peace in the Law of Islam*, 59.

78. For a translation and references to many other records of similar instructions by the Prophet, see Hamidullah, *The Muslim Conduct of State*, 305–6; Khadduri and Liebesny, *Law in the Middle East*, 75–77.

79. Hamidullah, *The Muslim Conduct of State*, 167–69.

80. Mohammad, "The Doctrine of Jihad," 389.

81. Khadduri, *War and Peace in the Law of Islam*, 94–137; Khadduri, *The Islamic Law of Nations*, 95–105.

82. Hamidullah, *The Muslim Conduct of State*, 190–92.

83. *Mukhtasar Tafsir ibn Kathir*, vol. 1, 170.

84. For translations and references to their original sources, see Hamidullah, *The Muslim Conduct of State*, 305–9.

85. Khadduri, *The Islamic Law of Nations*, 106–29; Khadduri, *War and Peace in the Law of Islam*, 118–32.

86. Khadduri and Liebesny, *Law in the Middle East*, chap. 15; Khadduri, "Islam and the Modern Law of Nations," 358–60; Shihata, "Islamic Law and the World Community," 107; Kruse, "The Islamic Doctrine of International Treaties."

87. Khadduri and Liebesny, *Law in the Middle East*, 354, 358.

88. Khadduri, *War and Peace*, 56, 57; Khadduri, *The Islamic Law of Nations*, 15.

89. See note 78 and accompanying text.

90. Hitti, trans., *The Origins of the Islamic State*, 64.

91. Hamidullah, *The Muslim Conduct of State*, 171–88.

92. Khadduri, *The Islamic Law of Nations*, 39–49.

93. Khadduri, *War and Peace in the Law of Islam*, 76–80.

94. This point was in fact appreciated by some early Muslim scholars such as al-Mawardiy who said that these classes come under international law only when they

are of sufficient power or have acquired territory and rule over it. See Hamidullah, *The Muslim Conduct of State*, 170.

95. For the events of that period, see Hodgson, *The Venture of Islam*, vol. 1, 212–23.

96. Hodgson, *The Venture of Islam*, 220; see Momen, *Introduction to Shi'i Islam*, 239, for a table of Shi'a religious commemorations.

97. See, for example, verses 3:104, 3:110, 3:114, 4:114; 9:71, 9:112, 22:41 of the Qur'an.

98. The term "fundamentalist" was first used with reference to a movement in American Protestantism in the early twentieth century. See generally George Marsden, *Fundamentalism and American Culture*. However, insofar as this term implies a commitment to the "fundamentals," most Muslims would claim such a commitment. It may not, therefore, be appropriate to confine its use in the Muslim context to militant and literalist proponents of the modern application of Shari'a, as seems to be the common practice, especially in news media reports of the activities of these groups.

99. For an example, see the translation of the basic text of the group who assassinated President Sadat of Egypt in Jansen, *The Neglected Duty*, 160–230.

100. Qur'an, 6:164, 17:15, 35:18, 39:7, 53:38.

101. The Qur'an condemns this attitude in many verses such as 2:170, 5:104, 40:78, 31:21, and 43:22. Although these verses apparently refer to previous peoples and to polytheists who rejected Islam, they are equally applicable to similar attitudes of Muslims themselves.

102. Schmid, *Political Terrorism*, see note 20 and accompanying text.

103. Taha, *The Second Message of Islam*. *Ustadh* means "revered teacher."

Chapter 2. Problems of Universal Cultural Legitimacy for Human Rights

This chapter was first published in *Human Rights in Africa: Cross-Cultural Perspectives*, ed. Abdullahi An-Na'im and F. M. Deng (Washington, D.C.: The Brookings Institution, 1990), 331–67.

1. Preiswerk, "The Place of Intercultural Relations," 251. On the different senses in which the term *culture* is used, see Eliot, *Notes Towards the Definition of Culture*; and Williams, *Keywords*, 76–82.

2. For a critique of some of these anthropological definitions, see Cafagna, "A Formal Analysis of Definitions of 'Culture'" and Kroeber and Kluckhohn, *Culture*.

3. Malinowski, "Culture."

4. See generally Shweder and LeVine, eds., *Theory*.

5. Geertz, *The Interpretation of Cultures*, 89.

6. D'Andrade, "Cultural Meaning Systems," 89.

7. Preiswerk, "Place of Intercultural Relations," 252.

8. The term "third generation rights" was coined to refer to these collective or solidarity rights; civil and political rights are considered "first generation rights," and

economic, social, and cultural rights are "second generation rights." See, for example, Marks, "Emerging Human Rights."

9. Benedict, *Patterns of Culture,* 253. Alexander Goldenweiser expresses the same notion in *History, Psychology, and Culture*, 59.

10. See Benedict, *Patterns of Culture,* 254–78.

11. Spiro, "Some Reflections on Cultural Determinism," 323. See the assumptions underlying cross-cultural studies summarized later in this essay.

12. See Renteln, "Relativism and the Search for Human Rights," 59.

13. Stocking, *Race, Culture, and Evolution*, 115–17; and Spiro, "Culture and Human Nature," 336.

14. Renteln, "Relativism and the Search for Human Rights," 58–62.

15. J. Cook, "Cultural Relativism as an Ethnocentric Notion," 294.

16. Herskovits, *Man and His Works*, 76.

17. Barnes and Bloor, "Relativism, Rationalism and the Sociology of Knowledge," 21, 47; Hatch, *Culture and Morality*, 12.

18. Hartung, "Cultural Relativity and Moral Judgments," 122–23.

19. Redfield, *The Primitive World and Its Transformations*, 146–47.

20. Renteln, "Relativism and the Search for Human Rights," 63.

21. Bidney, "The Concept of Value in Modern Anthropology," 698.

22. Renteln, "Relativism and the Search for Human Rights," 64.

23. Donnelly, "Cultural Relativism and Universal Human Rights," 410.

24. Donnelly, "Cultural Relativism and Universal Human Rights," 408.

25. Donnelly, "Cultural Relativism and Universal Human Rights," 414–18. The two covenants are the Covenant on Economic, Social and Cultural Rights and the Covenant on Civil and Political Rights. Donnelly quotes the "right of free and full consent of intending spouses" under the declaration, and the requirement of segregation of juvenile defendants under the civil and political rights covenant. Since the first right reflects a specific cultural interpretation of marriage and since the very notion of a juvenile criminal defendant does not exist in many cultures, his version of weak relativism would exclude these rights from the universal scope of human rights.

26. Donnelly, "Cultural Relativism and Universal Human Rights," 417.

27. An-Na'im, "Religious Minorities Under Islamic Law and the Limits of Cultural Relativism," 1–18.

28. Bozeman, *The Future of Law in a Multicultural World*, 14. Bozeman's heavy bias against non-Western traditions is revealed very early in her book.

29. Bozeman, *The Future of Law in a Multicultural World*, 27

30. Bozeman, *The Future of Law in a Multicultural World*, 183, 184

31. Bozeman, *The Future of Law in a Multicultural World*, xv.

32. UN Commission on Human Rights, Second Sess., ElCN 4130, November 12, 1947.

33. See generally, Tucker, *The Inequality of Nations*; Beitz, *Political Theory and International Relations*; Donelan, ed., *The Reason of States*; Hoffman, *Duties Beyond Borders*.

34. Higgins, "Conceptual Thinking About the Individual in International Law," has argued convincingly that there is no conceptual reason to prevent individuals from being subjects of international law. Nevertheless, it is still correct to say that individuals are not subjects of international law in the traditional sense of the term.

35. International nongovernmental organizations, such as the International Committee of the Red Cross and Amnesty International, operate through contacts with government officials.

36. Gottlieb, "Global Bargaining," 210–35.

37. On the stages of the expansion of the membership of the United Nations, see Jenks, *The World Beyond the Charter in Historical Perspective*, 92, 93.

38. Peter Berger of Boston College, as quoted in Meron, ed., "A Report on the N.Y.U. Conference on Teaching International Protection of Human Rights," 901.

39. As far as non-Western cultural perspectives are concerned, the Soviet Union was a Western country, though not a liberal one.

40. Meyer, "The International Bill."

41. Malik represented Lebanon in twelve out of the first thirteen sessions of the United Nations. Karem Azkoul, another prominent representative of Lebanon, was educated at St. Joseph's University, Beirut; at the Sorbonne; and at Munich and Berlin universities. He was acting representative of the drafting committee of Human Rights and acting representative of the Commission of Human Rights. "United Nations General Assembly, Official Records," Third Session, First Part, Plenary Meeting 98 (1948–49), 113.

42. UNGA Official Records, Third Session, First Part, Plenary Meeting 98, 114.

43. UNGA Official Records, Third Session, First Part, Plenary Meeting 181 (1948–49), 875–934.

44. Morsink, "The Philosophy of the Universal Declaration."

45. See, for example, Vasak, *Birthright of Man*; Vasak, ed., *The International Dimensions of Human Rights*; Diemer, *Philosophical Foundations of Human Rights*.

46. See, for example, three publications by the International Commission of Jurists, *Human Rights in a One-Party State*; *Development, Human Rights and the Rule of Law*; and *Seminar on Human Rights in Islam*. See also De Bary et al., eds., *Sources of Indian Tradition*; Luard, ed., *The International Protection of Human Rights*; Eide and Schou, eds., *International Protection of Human Rights*; Pollis and Schwab, eds., *Human Rights*; Thompson, ed., *The Moral Imperatives of Human Rights*; Nelson and Green, eds., *International Human Rights*; Nanda, et al., *Global Human Rights*; Hennelly and Langan, eds., *Human Rights in the Americas*.

47. This criticism is particularly true of works such as Wafi, "Human Rights in Islam," 64–75; Ishaque, "Human Rights in Islamic Law," 30–39; ICJ, *Seminar on Human Rights in Islam*; and Al Faruqi, "Islam and Human Rights," 12–30.

48. For the view that analysis of the debates at the Third Committee of the UN in the fall of 1948 reveal that the philosophy of the Universal Declaration was perceived by many delegates to be emanating from eighteenth-century philosophy of natural rights, with some significant modifications, see Morsink, "The Philosophy of the Universal Declaration."

49. There are many good books on Islam available in English; for example, Rahman, *Islam*; and Hodgson, *The Venture of Islam*.

50. See generally, Burton, *The Collection of the Qur'an*; and Schacht, *The Origins of Muhammadan Jurisprudence*.

51. An-Naʿim, *Toward an Islamic Reformation*, 57–60.

52. See, for example, Hassan, "On Human Rights and the Qur'anic Perspective."

53. See generally, Taha, *The Second Message of Islam*. See also, for example, the following works by An-Naʿim: "Religious Freedom in Egypt," 43; "The Islamic Law of Apostasy and Its Modern Applicability," 197–224; "Islamic Law, International Relations and Human Rights," 317–35; and "Mahmud Muhammad Taha and the Crisis in Islamic Law Reform," 1–21.

54. On the conception and organization of the Yale survey, see Murdock, "The Cross-Cultural Survey."

55. The seven assumptions I list closely follow Murdock, "The Cross-Cultural Survey," 48–52. The basic premise and some of its consequent assumptions are further explained and supported in other essays in Moore, ed., *Readings in Cross-Cultural Methodology*, such as Kluckhohn, "Universal Categories of Culture." The assumptions are also eloquently explained and emphasized by Ruth Benedict in *Patterns of Culture*.

56. Shils, *Tradition*, chaps. 5–7.

57. See, for example, Herskovits, *Cultural Dynamics*; and Opler, "Cultural Evolution and the Psychology of Peoples."

58. See, for example, Ottenberg, "Ibo Receptivity to Change," 130, and Schneider, "Pakot Resistance to Change," 144.

59. On that "experiment," see Masselt, "Law as an Instrument of Revolutionary Change."

60. Renteln, "Relativism and the Search for Human Rights," 65, 66. She adopts this definition from the distinction made by Herskovits between universals and absolutes, which he defines as fixed and not admitted to have variation, to differ from culture to culture, from epoch to epoch.

61. Renteln, "Relativism and the Search for Human Rights," 66.

Chapter 3. Toward a Cross-Cultural Approach
to Defining International Standards of Human Rights

This chapter was first published in *Human Rights in Cross-Cultural Perspectives: A Quest for Consensus*, ed. Abdullahi A. An-Naʿim (Philadelphia: University of Pennsylvania Press, 1992), 19–43. I am grateful to Prof. Wanda Wiegers and Dr. Tore Lindholm for their helpful comments and suggestions, and to Shelley-Anne Cooper-Stephenson for editorial assistance.

1. See generally An-Naʿim, "Problems and Prospects of Universal Cultural Legitimacy."

2. For the results of this questionnaire, see UNESCO, *Human Rights*, Appendix I.

3. See, for example, Executive Board of the American Anthropological Association, "Statement on Human Rights."

4. See, for example, Donnelly, "Human Rights and Human Dignity," 303; Howard and Donnelly, "Human Dignity, Human Rights and Political Regimes," 801.

5. Nickel, "Cultural Diversity and Human Rights," 43.

6. Milne, *Human Rights and Human Diversity*.

7. Renteln, "The Unanswered Challenge of Relativism" and "A Cross-Cultural Approach to Validating International Human Rights," 7. See generally her *International Human Rights*.

8. See, for example, Eliot, *Notes Towards the Definition of Culture*; Williams, *Keywords*, 76–82.

9. See generally, for example, Kroeber and Kluckhohn, eds., *Culture*.

10. Preiswerk, "The Place of Intercultural Relations," 251.

11. Geertz, *The Interpretation of Cultures*, 89.

12. I am grateful to Tore Lindholm for suggesting this useful analogy.

13. Herskovits, *Cultural Dynamics*, 54.

14. See generally, Benedict, *Patterns of Culture*; and Herskovits, *Cultural Dynamics*, chap. 4.

15. Herskovits, *Man and His Works*, 76.

16. Hatch, *Culture and Morality*, 12.

17. Jarvie, "Rationalism and Relativism," 46.

18. Howard and Donnelly, "Introduction," in *International Handbook of Human Rights*, 20.

19. Ladd, "The Poverty of Absolutism," 158, 161.

20. Geertz, "Distinguished Lecture," 265.

21. Geertz, "Distinguished Lecture," 276.

22. Herskovits, *Cultural Dynamics*, 62.

23. Renteln, "Relativism and the Search for Human Rights," 64.

24. I find Jack Donnelly's classification of radical relativism and universalism as extreme positions in a continuum, with varying mixes of (strong or weak) relativism and universalism in between, useful in this connection. While a radical (extreme) relativist would hold that culture is the sole source of validity of a moral right or rule, a radical universalist would hold that culture is irrelevant to the validity of moral rights or rules that are universally valid. See his article "Cultural Relativism and Universal Human Rights," 400, 401. He argues that "weak" cultural relativism is acceptable and even necessary for the implementation of human rights.

For a critique of Donnelly's position, see Renteln, "The Unanswered Challenge of Relativism," 529–31.

25. Edmund Burke as quoted in Vincent, "The Factor of Culture," 256.

26. Herskovits, *Cultural Dynamics*, 4, 6.

27. Herskovits, *Cultural Dynamics*, 49–50.

28. In his Introduction to UNESCO, *Human Rights*, 10–11.

29. Article 5 of the Universal Declaration of Human Rights of 1948 and Article 7 of the International Covenant on Civil and Political Rights of 1966. The latter adds that "In particular, no one shall be subjected without his free consent to medical or scientific experimentation." For the texts of these instruments, see Brownlie, ed., *Basic Documents*, 21 and 128 respectively.

30. Article 1.2 of the 1975 Declaration on the Protection of All Persons from Being Subjected to Torture and Other Cruel, Inhuman or Degrading Treatment or Punishment. UNGA Res. 3452 (XXX), 30 U.N. GAOR, Supp. (No. 34) 91, U.N. Doc. A/100 (1975).

31. Article 1.1 and Article 1 of the Convention against Torture and Other Cruel, Inhuman or Degrading Treatment or Punishment, UNGA Res. 3946 (1984). This convention came into force in June 1987. For the text, see *International Commission of Jurists Review* 39 (1987): 51. It is interesting to note that, whereas the 1975 Declaration requires such pain and suffering to be consistent with the United Nations Standard Minimum Rules for the Treatment of Prisoners, the 1984 Convention omitted this requirement. This was probably done in order to encourage countries that do not comply with the Standard Minimum Rules to ratify the Convention.

32. Bossuyt, *Guide to the "Travaux Préparatoires"*, 151. See the review of early work of the Drafting Committee, 1947–48; Bossuyt, *Guide*, 147–49; and discussions at meetings of the Commission on Human Rights, 1949–52, 151–54.

33. U.N. Doc. E/CN.4/SR.312, 13.

34. Bossuyt, *Guide*, 155.

35. Bossuyt, *Guide*, 155–58. In its final version, the sentence ends with the word "experimentation" and does not include the phrase "involving risk."

36. The 5th and 6th Sessions of the Commission on Human Rights, 1949, 1950. Bossuyt, *Guide*, 150.

37. Bossuyt, *Guide*, 151.

38. UNGA Res. 3469 (1979), cited in Amnesty International, *Human Rights*, 27.

39. By virtue of Article 1 of the Optional Protocol to the 1966 International Covenant of Civil and Political Rights, a State-Party to the Covenant may recognize the competence of the Human Rights Committee established under the Covenant to receive and consider communications from individuals subject to the state's jurisdiction who claim to be victims of a violation by that state. The protocol provides for the admissibility and processing of such communications, which may culminate in the communication of the committee's views to the state-party concerned and to the individual and the inclusion of those views in the annual report of the committee. Thus, this procedure may bring moral and political pressure to bear on a state that elected to ratify the Optional Protocol by publicizing its human rights violations, but it does not provide for direct enforcement. For the text of the protocol, see Brownlie, ed., *Basic Documents*, 146.

40. In the context of the Optional Protocol, the Human Rights Committee is restricted by its terms of reference to making specific findings on the case rather than stating general principles and guidelines. See CCPR/C/OP/1, *International Covenant on*

Civil and Political Rights: Human Rights Committee, Selected Decisions Under the Optional Protocol (Second to Sixteenth Sessions) (New York: United Nations, 1985), for examples of the sort of treatment that, according to the committee, constituted violations of Article 7 of the Covenant: see 40, 45, 49, 57, 72, 132, 136. All the communications relating to Article 7 published in this report involve very similar situations in a single country, Uruguay, over a short period of time, between 1976 and 1980. It would have been more helpful if the report had covered a wider variety of situations from more countries.

41. U.N. Doc. A/3740 (1982), 94, 95.

42. On the sources and development of Shariʿa, see generally, An-Naʿim, *Toward an Islamic Reformation*, chap. 2.

43. For fuller explanations, see generally An-Naʿim, *Toward an Islamic Reformation*, chap. 5; El-Awa, *Punishment in Islamic Law*; Safwat, "Offenses and Penalties in Islamic Law," 149.

44. An-Naʿim, *Toward an Islamic Reformation*, 114–18, 131–33.

45. Rationality is also relative to the belief system or frame of reference. What may be accepted as rational to a believer may not be accepted as such by an unbeliever, and vice versa.

46. Taha, *The Second Message of Islam*, 74, 75.

47. *Encyclopedia Judaica*, 5: 142–47, 6: 991–93.

Chapter 4. State Responsibility Under International Human Rights Law to Change Religious and Customary Laws

This chapter was first published in *Human Rights of Women: National and International Perspectives*, ed. Rebecca J. Cook (Philadelphia: University of Pennsylvania Press, 1994), chap. 7. I am grateful to Tore Lindholm and Shelley Cooper-Stephenson for their very helpful comments and suggestions on an earlier draft.

1. As explained below, religious and customary laws come in a wide variety of forms and operate in many different ways. It might, therefore, be inappropriate or misleading to describe all of them as "law" in a coherent jurisprudential sense. They are referred to here as "laws" in the plural because there is usually more than one religious or customary law "system" in a country and also to distinguish them from the formal or official state law.

2. Some of the problems of custom as a source of international human rights standards are highlighted below. Articles 1.3, 55, and 56 of the UN Charter impose an obligation of respect for, and observance of, "human rights and fundamental freedoms." But since that treaty does not define this clause, it is necessary to find another source for any particular or specific human right that states parties to the Charter are obliged to respect and protect.

3. For a brief review of the requirements and qualifications of custom as a source of international law, see Brownlie, *Principles of Public International Law*, 4–12.

4. See, for example, Henkin et al., *International Law: Cases and Materials*, 998; and Harris, *Cases and Materials on International Law*, 696. Cf. Gunning, "Modernizing Customary International Law."

5. G.A. Res. 34/180 U.N. GAOR, 34th Sess., Supp. No. 46, 193, U.N. Doc. A/34/46 (1979). As of January 1992, 131 states have ratified this Convention; see App. A, 585.

6. For the text of Egypt's reservations, see Lillich, ed., *International Human Rights Instruments*, 11. Other Islamic countries have entered similar reservations. See Sullivan, "Gender Equality and Religious Freedom." On the question of reservations to this Convention in general, see R. Cook, "Reservations to the Convention on the Elimination of All Forms of Discrimination Against Women."

7. On the issues that might arise in this connection, see generally O'Connell, *International Law* 1: 246–80; or Harris, *Cases and Materials on International Law*, 729–816.

8. For such an argument, see Jenefsky, "Permissibility of Egypt's Reservations," 208–13, 226–31.

9. See generally Hannum, ed., *Guide to International Human Rights Practice*.

10. For studies from a variety of perspectives, see Koskenniemi, ed., *International Law*, 3–60.

11. The fact that changing religious and customary laws is made the subject of "state responsibility" raises issues of sovereignty and indicates the limitations on direct enforcement in international law. On the nature and scope of state responsibility in international law, see Brownlie, *Principles of Public International Law*, 431–35. For a more comprehensive treatment of relevant issues see Harris, *Cases and Materials on International Law*, 460–93.

12. On land tenure issues in Africa, see generally Lowe, *Agricultural Revolution in Africa*; Davison, ed., *Agriculture, Women, and Land*; Downs and Reyna, eds., *Land and Society in Contemporary Africa*; Riddell and Dickerman, *Country Profiles of Land Tenure*; and Dickerman, *Security of Tenure and Land Registration*. On female genital mutilation, see generally Hosken, *The Hosken Report* and Hosken, *Female Sexual Mutilation*. These two sources contain useful bibliographies.

13. See generally An-Na'im and Deng, eds., *Human Rights in Africa*; and An-Na'im, ed., *Human Rights in Cross-Cultural Perspectives*. The question of the legitimacy of internationally recognized standards of human rights should be seen in the context of the broader issue of the legitimacy of international law itself. On this broader issue, see Franck, "Legitimacy in the International System"; Koskenniemi, "The Normative Force of Habit"; and Sathirathai, "An Understanding of the Between."

14. See, for example, Leary, "The Effect of Western Perspectives."

15. For an elaboration on these remarks, see An-Na'im, "Problems of Universal Cultural Legitimacy."

16. For an elaboration see An-Na'im, "Toward a Cross-Cultural Approach," 27–28.

17. The concept of global overlapping consensus is similar to that proposed by John Rawls for social justice at the domestic level. See Lindholm, "Prospects for Research on

the Cultural Legitimacy of Human Rights," 400; and Rawls, "The Idea of an Overlapping Consensus."

18. Falk, "Cultural Foundations," 45–46.

19. For further explanation of the proposed approach, see Falk, "Cultural Foundations," and An-Na'im, "Problems of Universal Cultural Legitimacy," 339–45, 361–66.

20. See, for example, Sullivan, "Gender Equality and Religious Freedom," especially 848–54.

21. For a general explanation of what are known as African traditional religions and a critique of terms and classifications applied to them in earlier Western scholarship, see, Sharevskaya, *The Religious Traditions of Tropical Africa*, 13–66. See generally Ranger and Kmambo, eds., *The Historical Study of African Religions*; Fuller, "Native and Missionary Religions"; Schoffeleers and Van Binsbergen, eds., *Theoretical and Methodological Explorations*; Blakely et al., *Religion in Africa*.

22. On the case of the Sudan, see Hosken, *The Hosken Report*, 95–119.

23. In this case, a native (Indian or Aboriginal) woman challenged before the UN Human Rights Committee a Canadian statute that discriminated against female members of native bands in Canada. See *Lovelace v. Canada*, 1983; Pentney, "*Lovelace v. Canada*: A Case Comment," 259.

24. For brief comments on the *Shah Bano Begum* case, see An-Na'im, "Islam, Islamic Law and the Dilemma of Cultural Legitimacy," 43–46; and Sullivan, "Gender Equality and Religious Freedom," 849–52.

25. See, for example, McChesney, "Aboriginal Communities, Aboriginal Rights and the Human Rights System in Canada."

26. I have discussed these and related matters in detail in *Toward an Islamic Reformation*.

27. For a general discussion of Shari'a and the human rights of women, see An-Na'im, "The Rights of Women and International Law in the Muslim Context." A more empirical discussion of the process of changing Shari'a law from a human rights point of view can be found in my "Human Rights in the Muslim World."

28. An-Na'im, "Islam, Islamic Law, and the Dilemma of Cultural Legitimacy," 43–46.

29. There are some theoretical exceptions. For instance, according to some jurists of Shari'a, a woman can stipulate in the contract of marriage that the man may not take another wife while married to her and can "persuade" her husband to divorce her on the payment of monetary compensation known as *khul'*. However, in practice few women know about these exceptions or can afford to exercise them. Moreover, the terms of the exceptions themselves are premised on male guardianship of women and the inferior status of women in the relationship, rather than as a challenge or repudiation of those principles of Shari'a.

30. On this point and the following methodology of Islamic law reform, see An-Na'im, *Toward an Islamic Reformation*, esp. chaps. 2, 3.

31. See my translation of his major work, Taha, *The Second Message of Islam*. It is

important to note that Taha's methodology does not affect the devotional and ritual aspects of Shari'a *'ibadat*.

32. See my "Toward a Cross-Cultural Approach," 29–39.

33. It is not possible to discuss here the question of when and how international human rights law might be subjected to critical examination and reformulation. In any case, it is too early for me to express definite views on this aspect of the intermediatory or cross-cultural approach to human rights. For a brief review of my tentative thinking, and proposals for research, on this and other relevant issues, see "Toward a Cross-Cultural Approach," 20–29.

Chapter 5. Islamic Foundations of Religious Human Rights

This chapter was first published in *Religious Human Rights in Global Perspectives: Religious Perspectives*, ed. John Witte, Jr., and Johan D. van der Vyver (The Hague: Martinus Nijhoff, 1996), 337–59.

1. For analysis of the development of the concept of Shari'a, see Rahman, *Islam*, 101–9.

2. Human rights are those claims to which every human being is entitled by virtue of his or her humanity, without distinction as to race, color, sex, religion, language, or national origin. The current formulation of these rights is to be found in the 1948 Universal Declaration of Human Rights and subsequent international instruments, but I do not take these sources to be either definitive or exhaustive. New formulations can and should emerge, and old ones should remain open to revision, elaboration, and reformulation.

3. On various aspects of this necessary but problematic relationship, see generally An-Na'im et al., eds., *Human Rights and Religious Values* and Swidler, ed., *Religious Liberty and Human Rights*. For some of the issues in relation to the subject matter of this book, see, generally Ashburn, ed., *The State of Religious Human Rights in the World*.

4. The basis of universality of human rights and practical criterion for their identification are in the Golden Rule, or the principle of reciprocity, that is, these are rights I claim for myself as a human being, not by virtue of any legal or other status, and must, therefore, concede to others by the same token because that is the basis of my claim. See An-Na'im, *Toward an Islamic Reformation*, 162–63.

5. Taken as a set of fundamental beliefs or principles, human rights can certainly be described as a creed, but I use the term here for a short-hand reference, without necessarily implying or rejecting the validity of its application to human rights.

6. The fundamental fact and legitimacy of necessary and permanent plurality are emphasized by the Qur'an itself, in verse 13 of chapter 49, which I would translate as follows: "We [God] have made you [all human beings] into peoples and tribes so that you may get to know each other and cooperate. Those who are most honored by God are the pious and righteous ones."

7. An-Na'im, *Toward an Islamic Reformation*, 52–62.

8. The Qur'an is the written text of what Muslims believe to be the final and conclusive record of divine revelation. The Qur'an was delivered by the Prophet and memorized by the first generation of Muslims until it was collected in a written text about two decades after the Prophet's death. Except for minor differences in the style of recitation, that text of the Qur'an, known as *Al-Mushaf Al-Uihmani*, is acknowledged by all Sunni Muslims as the only valid text of the Qur'an. The version of the text accepted by Shi'a Muslims is slightly different, but not in ways significant for purposes of this chapter. See generally Burton, *The Collection of the Qur'an*.

Sunna of the Prophet are oral traditions of his verbal utterances and living example that were collected in written compilations for the first time during the second and third centuries of Islam, the eighth and ninth centuries. The authenticity and relative authority of some texts of Sunna continue to create controversy among Sunni as well as Shi'a Muslims to the present day. On the concept and process of collection of Sunna and sources of controversy, see Rahman, *Islam*, chap. 3; and Hasan, *The Early Development of Islamic Jurisprudence*, chap. 5.

9. Rahman, *Islam*, 81–83.

10. Thus, each of the surviving four Sunni schools (Maliki, Hanafi, Shafi'i, and Hanbali, named after their founding scholars of the eighth and ninth centuries), tends to have a certain territorial sphere of influence within the Islamic world. Whereas the Maliki school, for example, is now generally more prevalent in North and West Africa, the Hanbali school is followed in Saudi Arabia, at least as the "official" doctrine of the kingdom. But in the Saudi Arabian case, it is the Wahabi interpretation of the Hanbali school that prevails, rather than that of the other scholars of the school as a whole. Shi'a schools have a similar territorial spread: the Ja'fari school in Iran, Zaiydi in southern Arabia, the Isma'ili among the Shi'a of the Indian subcontinent, and so forth.

11. With the spread of Islam east into Persia and India and west through North Africa to Spain, the diverse peoples who embraced the faith or came under the domain of its political power did not know the Arabic language or the history of early Islamic communities. Moreover, those peoples had their own pre-Islamic cultures; some had ancient and highly developed civilizations, including their distinctive legal and theological systems, as well as social, political, and economic institutions. The interaction and cross-fertilization of Islamic principles and rules with pre-Islamic norms and institutions of the newly Islamized communities were expected, as indeed had already happened in Arabia and the Middle East, but that had to be in accordance with Islamic criteria as developed by the early more authoritative scholars and model communities..

12. On the formative stages of Islamic jurisprudence and methodological developments, see Schacht, *An Introduction to Islamic Law*, 45–48, 58ff.; Khadduri, trans., *Islamic Jurisprudence*, 40–84; Hasan, *The Early Development of Islamic Jurisprudence*, chap. 8; Coulson, *A History of Islamic Law*, chap. 4; Makdisi, "The Juridical Theology of Shafi'i," 5–47.

13. An-Na'im, *Toward an Islamic Reformation*, chap. 3.

14. Coulson, *A History of Islamic Law*, 80–81; Schacht, *An Introduction to Islamic*

Law, 69ff.; An-Na'im, *Toward an Islamic Reformation*, 27–29. Cf. Hallaq, "Was the Gate of Ijtihad Closed?" 3.

15. Schacht, *The Origins of Muhammadan Jurisprudence*, 84.

16. On the process of displacement of Shari'a by Western laws during the colonial period, see Liebesny, *The Law of the Near & Middle East*, 56; Anderson, *Law Reform in the Muslim World*, 1–2, 33.

17. Anderson, *Law Reform in the Muslim World*, 36.

18. For a critique of the theoretical model of a Shari'a state in the modern context, see generally An-Na'im, *Toward an Islamic Reformation*, chaps. 4–7.

19. These two groups are certainly too diverse to be subsumed under single terms, even within the same country at a given time. While noting the variety of discourses and diversity of participants and contexts, the following analysis will focus on discourse about the role of Islam as political ideology and the definitive framework of constitutional and legal systems. In this light, I will use the term Islamists to refer to those who present themselves as such and deliberately employ Islamic concepts and terminology in their discourse. Since those who do not present themselves as Islamists and do not use Islamic concepts and terminology as a matter of preference are united in their opposition to the Islamists, I will refer to them as such.

20. For elaboration and documentation of the Shari'a scheme, see An-Na'im, *Toward an Islamic Reformation*; An-Na'im, "Religious Minorities Under Islamic Law," 1–18.

21. For a recent example of this, see An-Na'im, "The Islamic Law of Apostasy and Its Modern Applicability," 197–223.

22. For an elaboration on this point and the following remarks, see An-Na'im, "Toward an Islamic Hermeneutics for Human Rights."

23. See, e.g., *Tafeiral-Tabari*, 9, 314–18 (*Daral-Ma'arif bi-Masr*, not dated).

24. See An-Na'im, *Toward an Islamic Reformation*, 86–87.

25. For a concise clarification prompted by the needs of an Islamic discourse without being part of it, see Hoibraaten, "Secular Society."

26. I see this process as integral to the project of promoting universal cross-cultural legitimacy of human rights. See generally An-Na'im and Deng, eds., *Human Rights in Africa*; An-Na'im, ed., *Human Rights in Cross-Cultural Perspectives*.

Chapter 6. Cultural Transformation and Normative Consensus
on the Best Interest of the Child

This chapter was first published in *International Journal of Law and the Family* 8 (1994): 62–81.

1. The terms North and South are used here subject to the observation made by Clarence Dias (of the International Center for Law in Development, New York) at various conference presentations that these terms refer to concepts rather than geographical regions. There are pockets of the North within the South and of the South within the North.

2. See generally An-Naʿim and Deng, eds., *Human Rights in Africa*; and An-Naʿim, ed., *Human Rights in Cross-Cultural Perspectives*.

3. Abdalla, "Elements of a Strategy for the Development of the Arab Child," 22–28.

4. Abdalla, "Elements of a Strategy," 22–35.

5. Abdalla, "Elements of a Strategy," 37–38. For more recent information on these indexes, see, for example, Miladi and El Din, eds., *The State of the Child in the Arab World 1990*; and the UNICEF/Oxford University Press annual series on *The State of the World's Children*.

6. Abdalla, "Elements of a Strategy," 39–40.

7. Abdalla, "Elements of a Strategy," 40.

8. Labib, "The Arab Child," 375–79.

9. While Labib's analysis generally supports the rationale of child self-determinism, it would also raise valid concerns regarding the diversity of the "self" of the child, the circumstances under which it is supposed to exercise "self-determinism," and the process by which that might be articulated and implemented.

10. Musa, "Arabic," 215–19.

11. Musa, "Arabic," 224–29.

12. Musa, "Arabic," 229–31.

13. Musa, "Arabic," 233–37.

14. Musa, "Arabic," 238–45.

15. Abdalla, "Elements of a Strategy," 2–3 and 14.

16. Abdalla, "Elements of a Strategy," 16–18.

17. Musa, "Arabic," 227–29.

18. See generally UNICEF, *The State of the World's Children 1992*. For a discussion in relation to Egypt, see Kuriym, "Athar Siyasat al-Islah al-Iqtisady ala al-Usar Mahdudat al-Dakhl wa al-Atfal bi-Masr" (The effects of the policy of economic reform on limited-income familities in Egypt).

19. See, for example, UNICEF, *The State of the World's Children 1993*, 37–49.

20. See generally, for example, Azer and Ramzy, *Child Labor in Egypt*.

21. Cf. An-Naʿim, "Toward a Cross-Cultural Perspective," 19–43.

Chapter 7. Toward an Islamic Hermeneutics for Human Rights

This chapter was first published in *Human Rights and Religious Values*, ed. Abdullahi A. An-Naʿim, Jerald D. Gort, Henry Jansen, and Hendrik M. Vroom (Grand Rapids, Mich.: Eerdmans, 1995), 229–42.

1. See An-Naʿim and Deng, eds., *Human Rights in Africa*.

2. An-Naʿim, *Toward an Islamic Reformation*.

3. These verses speak about "believers" as *awliya'* (allies and supporters of) one another and "non-believers" as *awliya'* of one another. I will address the question of criteria and rationale of reconciling apparently conflicting verses of the Qur'an below, especially in the last section.

4. *Oxford Universal Dictionary*, 3rd ed., 1955.

5. Reformed Ecumenical Council, *Acts of the Reformed Ecumenical Council*, 28, 29 (emphasis mine).

6. Reformed Ecumenical Council, *Acts of the Reformed Ecumenical Council*, 49–51.

7. Vroom, "Scripture Read and Interpreted."

8. Hallaq, "Was the Gate of Ijtihad Closed?" 341.

9. Kerr, *Islamic Reform*.

10. Taha, *The Second Message of Islam*.

11. An-Na'im, *Toward an Islamic Reformation*, 28.

12. See, generally, An-Na'im, *Toward an Islamic Reformation*.

13. An-Na'im, *Toward an Islamic Reformation*; An-Na'im and Deng, *Human Rights in Africa*.

Chapter 8. Competing Claims to Religious Freedom and Communal Self-Determination in Africa

This chapter was first published in *Proselytization and Communal Self-Determination in Africa*, ed. Abdullahi Ahmed An-Na'im (Maryknoll, N.Y.: Orbis, 1999), 1–28.

1. The term *communal* here indicates, as elaborated below, that the right to self-determination should not be confined to achieving political independence and separate statehood.

2. This project builds directly on two preceding projects of the Law and Religion Program of Emory University: "Christianity and Democracy" (1989–92) and "Religious Human Rights" (1992–95). The themes of the extensive program of discussion and publication generated by those two projects clearly indicated that issues of proselytization and its implications are intimately connected to conceptions, institutions, and processes of democratization, as well as to the definition and protection of religious human rights in all parts of the world.

3. An-Na'im and Deng, "Self-Determination and Unity: The Case of Sudan."

4. While proselytization efforts usually target individuals, rather than a whole group all at once, I am here using the notion "target group" as the operational term to indicate the strategic use of individuals in transforming the status of the community as a whole. Reference to groups is also appropriate for the purposes of this chapter in particular because conflicts generally occur between communities (whether religiously, culturally, or politically conceived), rather than isolated and autonomous individuals.

5. The term *beliefs* is used instead of *faith* throughout because the latter term is normally used to refer to so-called world religions to the exclusion of indigenous traditions, which are particularly important in the African context.

6. Macmullen, *Christianizing the Roman Empire*; Marty and Greenspan, eds., *Pushing the Faith*.

7. Goodman, *Mission and Conversion*.

8. Clark, *The Politics of Conversion*, 5.

9. For example, as a cognitive psychologist, Leon Festinger sought to develop a theory of why and how proselytization occurred. Goodman draws on variations of this theory in arguing that the early Christians could not agree on certain important theological questions, so they focused on proselytizing new members to calm the movement's internal disagreement. For social-science analysis, see Rambo, *Understanding Religious Conversion*; and Hefner, *Conversion to Christianity*. See also Festinger, *A Theory of Cognitive Dissonance*; Goodman, *Mission and Conversion*.

10. Jackson and Rosberg, "Sovereignty and Underdevelopment," 5–6.

11. Ayoade, "States Without Citizens," 104.

12. Chabal, "Introduction: Thinking About Politics in Africa," 13. On the crisis of the postcolonial state and the search for explanation, see Young, *The African Colonial State in Comparative Perspective*, 2–12.

13. Okoth-Ogendo, "Constitutions Without Constitutionalism; Shivji, "State and Constitutionalism."

14. Young calls the postcolonial state in Africa the "integral state," which he defines as "a design of perfected hegemony, whereby the state seeks to achieve unrestricted domination over civil society." See Young, *The African Colonial State*, 287.

15. Young, *The African Colonial State*, 5.

16. Falk, "Regionalism and World Order," 71.

17. Mlinar, "Individuation and Globalization," 20–22.

18. Aina, *Globalization and Social Policy in Africa*, 11.

19. Bach, "Reappraising Postcolonial Geopolitics"; Othman, "Postscript."

20. I am referring here to the classification made by Clark, *The Politics of Conversion*, 5.

21. Horton, "African Conversion," 104–5.

22. Fisher, "Conversion Reconsidered," 27.

23. On 170 of this article, Fisher characterized his disagreement with Horton as a matter of focal point in the consideration of religious development. See also Hackett's discussion of different types of conversion. Fisher, "The Juggernaut's Apology," 153; Horton, "On the Rationality of Conversion"; and Hackett, *Religion in Calabar*.

24. Comaroff and Comaroff, *Of Revelation and Revolution*, 250.

25. Morrison, *Understanding Conversion*, xiv.

26. Asad, "Comments on Conversion," 266.

27. This book is useful as a historical overview, though somewhat dated. For example, he does not address Islamic political movements, and his use of the term "Islamization" is not nuanced in the modern sense of the term. Trimingham, *The Influence of Islam upon Africa*, 5.

28. Trimingham, *The Influence of Islam upon Africa*, 38, 39.

29. Hiskett, *The Development of Islam in Western Africa*, 44, 55–58 respectively.

30. Hiskett, *The Development of Islam in Western Africa*, 303–5.

31. Hiskett supports Humphrey Fisher's three stages of conversion to Islam—quarantine, mixing, and reform—but stresses that they cannot be applied rigidly; see

Hiskett, *The Development of Islam in Western Africa*, 305, 319. For another example of specific case studies on the spread of Islam, see Banwo, "The Nineteenth Century Ilorin Wars."

32. Rouse, "The Missionary Motive."

33. Beidelman, "Social Theory and the Study of Christian Missions in Africa," 235; "Contradictions Between the Sacred and the Secular Life"; *Colonial Evangelism*, 9.

34. Isichei, *A History of Christianity in Africa*, esp. chap. 3.

35. Sanneh, *Encountering the West*, 19.

36. Yates, *Christian Mission in the Twentieth Century*; Isichei, "Seven Varieties of Ambiguity," 209–27; McCracken, *Politics and Christianity in Malawi*.

37. King, *Christians and Muslims in Africa*.

38. This second source includes a statistical table of Muslims and Christians in Africa. See Haafkins, *Claiming the Promise*; "The Christian Muslim Encounter in Sub-Saharan Africa."

39. Bartholomew, "The Challenge of Islam in Africa."

40. Sanneh, *The Crown and the Turban*, 1997.

41. Steiner and Alston, *International Human Rights in Context*, 117–65.

42. When the Universal Declaration of Human Rights was adopted in 1948, it was envisaged that binding treaties would follow. In due course, the two main human rights treaties—the International Covenant on Economic, Social and Cultural Rights, and the International Covenant on Civil and Political Rights—were adopted in 1966. The International Convention on the Elimination of All Forms of Racial Discrimination already had been adopted in 1965. Others followed, such as the Convention on the Elimination of All Forms of Discrimination against Women of 1979; Convention against Torture and Other Cruel, Inhuman or Degrading Treatment or Punishment of 1984; and Convention on the Rights of the Child of 1989. On the UN human rights system, see Steiner and Alston, *International Human Rights in Context*, 347–455.

43. Namely, the European Convention for the Protection of Human Rights and Fundamental Freedoms of 1950; the American Convention on Human Rights of 1969; and the African Charter on Human and Peoples' Rights of 1981. There is no regional system for Asia yet. On these regional systems, see Steiner and Alston, *International Human Rights in Context*, 563–705.

44. On the concept "collective rights" and its relation to ideas of individual rights, see, for example, Van Dyke, "Collective Rights and Moral Rights", 21–40; Garet, "Communality and Existence", 1001–1075; MacDonald, "Group Rights," 117–36; Sanders, "Collective Rights."

45. See, for example, the International Labour Organization Convention concerning the Protection and Integration of Indigenous and Other Tribal and Semi-Tribal Populations in Independent Countries (ILO, No. 107) of 1957 and the Convention concerning Indigenous and Tribal Peoples in Independent Countries (ILO, No. 169) of 1989. The European regional system is also beginning to tentatively explore the possibility of collective rights, as can be seen in the 1994 document "Framework Convention for the

Protection of National Minorities." However, the most far-reaching formulations of collective rights so far are under the African Charter.

46. Al-Mubarak, *Nizam al-Islam fi al-Hukm wa al-Dawla* (The Islamic Order for Governance and the State), 24–28; An-Na'im, *Toward an Islamic Reformation*, 86–87, 109.

47. Anaya, "The Capacity of International Law to Advance Ethnic or Nationality Rights Claims," 326.

48. Shepherd, "Transnational Development of Human Rights," 215.

49. This Convention was adopted December 18, 1979, entered into force September 3, 1981. As of April 2010, 186 countries have ratified the Convention. Curiously, the U.S. is the only country that has signed but not ratified it. See http://treaties.un.org/Pages/ViewDetails.aspx?src=TREATY&mtdsg_no=IV-8&chapter=4&lang=en.

50. Van Dyke, *Human Rights, Ethnicity and Discrimination*.

51. Thornberry, *International Law and the Rights of Minorities*; Kymlicka, ed., *The Rights of Minority Cultures*; Anaya, *Indigenous Peoples in International Law*.

52. Steiner, and Alston, *International Human Rights in Context*, 86–89.

53. McDonald, ed., *Collective Rights*.

54. Abi Sab, "The Legal Formulation of a Right to Development," 163.

Chapter 9. Globalization and Jurisprudence: An Islamic Perspective

This chapter was first published in *Emory Law Journal* 54 (2005): 25–51.

1. See, for example, Berman, *Toward an Integrative Jurisprudence*, 779, 800–801.

2. Berman, "Integrative Jurisprudence and World Law."

3. See generally Berman, *Law and Revolution*.

4. See Collins et al., *Historical Problems of Imperial Africa*; Fage and Tordoff, *A History of Africa*; and Strawson, "Islamic Law and English Texts." Charles Hamilton's 1791 translation of *al-hidaya al-marghiniani* is "the earliest complete Islamic legal text in English" (Strawson, 113). In discussing Hamilton's translation, Strawson observes that "orientalism is not necessarily a crude science" (115). The Orientalist scholar Hamilton did convey some of the intricacies and core methodology of Islamic law. But, ultimately, "the Orientalist discourse establishes the superiority of European values." Strawson points out that, for Hamilton, "Whatever the value of a particular norm of Islamic law, the whole system is invalid" (119). He also maintains that this legal Orientalism can be seen in more recent works. See, e.g., Schacht, *An Introduction to Islamic Law*; see also Mann, "Dealing with Oriental Despotism."

5. See generally Fukuyama, *The End of History*.

6. Berman, "Integrative Jurisprudence and World Law," 10–11. See generally Huntington, *The Clash of Civilizations and the Remaking of World Order*.

7. Berman, "The Historical Foundations of Law," 20–24.

8. For example, there are now an estimated five to six million Muslim citizens in the United States. See Woodrow Wilson International Center for Scholars, *Event*

Summary, Conference: Muslims in the United States: Demography, Beliefs, Institutions, and Political Participation (June 18, 2003), http:// www.wilsoncenter.org/index .cfm?fuseaction=events.event_summary&event_ id=15883. There is no accurate count of the number of Muslims in the United States because theCensus Bureau does not collect data on religious identification.

9. See, e.g., Paust, "Antiterrorism Military Commissions," and "Post-9/11 Overreaction."

10. See generally R. Arnold, *The ICC as a New Instrument for Repressing Terrorism*; Schabas, *An Introduction to the International Criminal Court*; Sewall and Kaysen, eds., *The United States and the International Criminal Court*.

11. An-Naʿim, "The Contingent Universality of Human Rights," 29, 63.

12. An-Naʿim, "Human Rights and the Challenge of Relevance."

13. March 23, 1976, 21 U.N. GAOR Supp. (no. 16), 52; U.N. Doc. A/6316 (1966), 999 U.N.T.S. 171.

14. Jan. 3, 1976, G.A. Res. 2000A (XXI); 21 U.N. GAOR Supp. (No. 16), 49; U.N. Doc. A/6316 (1966), 993 U.N.T.S. 3.

15. UN Charter, Article 2, paragraph 7.

16. G.A. Res. 217A, U.N. Doc. A/810, 1948, 71.

17. Reisman et al, eds., *International Law in Contemporary Perspective*, 520.

18. Reference here is to such international events as the United Nations World Summit on Sustainable Development in Johannesburg, South Africa, 2002; the United Nations World Conference Against Racism, Racial Discrimination, Xenophobia, and Related Intolerance in Durban, South Africa, 2001; and the Thirteenth International Aids Conference in Durban, South Africa, 2000.

19. African Charter on Human and Peoples' Rights, June 27, 1981, 21 I.L.M. 58.

20. As Mahbub ul Haq, author of the concept of "human development," of the United Nations Development Programme, said, "The basic purpose of development is to enlarge people's choices. In principle, these choices can be infinite and can change over time. People often value achievements that do not show up at all, or not immediately, in income or growth figures: greater access to knowledge, better nutrition and health services, more secure livelihoods, security against crime and physical violence, satisfying leisure hours, political and cultural freedoms and sense of participation in community activities. The objective of development is to create an enabling environment for people to enjoy long, healthy and creative lives." UNDP, *The Human Development concept*, http://hdr.undp.org/en/humandev/ (visited April 5, 2010); see also *Human Development and Human Rights Report on the Oslo Symposium*, 2000; *Human Development and Human Rights Report on the Oslo Symposium*, 1998.

21. An-Naʿim, "Introduction," in *Human Rights in Cross-Cultural Perspectives*, 2–6.

22. Rahman, *Islam*, 11–29.

23. Hallaq, *A History of Islamic Legal Theories*, 1–35.

24. Weiss and Green, *A Survey of Arab History*.

25. Pearl and Menski, *Muslim Family Law*, 14–17.

26. See, e.g., Gerber, *Islamic Law and Culture*; Hallaq, "Was the Gate of Ijtihad Closed?"

27. See, e.g., Hallaq, *A History of Islamic Legal Theories*; Al-azmeh, "Islamic Legal Theory and the Appropriation of Reality."

28. See Coulson, *A History of Islamic Law*, 122.

29. Masud et al., "Muftis, Fatwas, and Islamic Legal Interpretation," 3, 8–9.

30. Hallaq, *A History of Islamic Legal Theories*, 123, 143.

31. Coulson, *A History of Islamic Law*, 149–55.

32. Coulson, *A History of Islamic Law*, 218–25.

33. Coulson, *A History of Islamic Law*, 151.

34. Imber, *Ebu's-Su'ud*.

35. Gerber, *Islamic Law and Culture*, 29.

36. Messick, *The Calligraphic State*, 57.

37. Pearl and Menski, *Muslim Family Law*, 19–20.

38. See generally Piscatori, *Islam in a World of Nation-States*.

Chapter 10. The Politics of Religion and the Morality of Globalization

This chapter was first published in *Religion and Global Civil Society*, ed. Mark Juergensmeyer (Oxford: Oxford University Press, 2005), 23–48.

1. IFG, *Alternatives to Economic Globalization*, 19, 20.

2. Anheier, Glasius, and Kaldor, "Introducing Global Civil Society," 4.

3. Parekh, *Gandhi*, 37.

4. Nandy, *The Intimate Enemy*, 104.

5. R. Young, *Postcolonialism*.

6. R. Young, *Postcolonialism*, 338.

7. Terchek, *Gandhi*, 119

8. Terchek, *Gandhi*, 110.

9. Terchek, *Gandhi*, 111.

10. Terchek, *Gandhi*, 108, emphasis added.

11. Terchek, *Gandhi*, 109

12. Freitag, "Contesting in Public," 226–27.

13. Al-Azm, "Islamic Fundamentalism Reconsidered"; Lapidus, *A History of Islamic Societies*, 416–28.

14. An-Na'im, "Muslim Fundamentalism and Social Change."

15. An-Na'im, "*Shari'a* and Positive Legislation."

16. An-Na'im, *Toward an Islamic Reformation*.

17. An-Na'im, "Islamic Ambivalence to Political Violence."

18. An-Na'im, "Upholding International Legality Against Islamic and American *Jihad*."

19. Madjid, "The Necessity of Renewing Islamic Thought," 286.

20. An-Naʿim, " *Shariʿa* and Positive Legislation."

21. Dalacoura, *Islam, Liberalism and Human Rights*, 63, 64

22. Hermassi, "Notes on Civil Society in Tunisia," 77–78.

23. Sen, "How to Judge Globalism," A2.

24. Sen, "How to Judge Globalism," A5.

25. Oxfam 2002, 5.

26. IFG, *Alternatives* to *Economic Globalization*, 30.

27. IFG, *Alternatives* to *Economic Globalization*, 20.

28. IFG, *Alternatives* to *Economic Globalization*, 78.

29. IFG, *Alternatives* to *Economic Globalization*, 22, 81.

30. Sen, *Development as Freedom*, 7.

31. Sen, *Development as Freedom*, 9.

32. Sen, *Development as Freedom*, 3.

33. Eide, "Making Human Rights Universal," 9

34. IFG, *Alternatives* to *Economic Globalization*, 73.

35. Eide, "Making Human Rights Universal," 10.

36. Eide, "Making Human Rights Universal," 10.

37. Eide, "Making Human Rights Universal," 10.

38. Gupta, *Culture, Space and the Nation-State*, 159; emphasis in original.

39. Kothari, "Human Rights," 29.

40. Schwedler, "Introduction: Society and the Study of Middle East Politics Civil," 10, 11.

41. Hegland, "Islamic Revival or Political and Cultural Revolution?"

42. An-Naʿim, "Introduction," in *Human Rights in Cross-Cultural Perspectives*, 1–18.

43. An-Naʿim, "The Contingent Universality of Human Rights."

44. MacLean, *Opting for Democracy*, 123; Turner, *An Introduction* to *Liberation Theology*, 3, 9.

45. Gutiérrez, "The Task and Content of Liberation Theology," 27.

46. Fitzgerald, "The Economics of Liberation Theology," 229; Turner, *An Introduction* to *Liberation Theology*, 4.

47. Gutiérrez, *A Theology of Liberation*, 36.

48. Turner, *An Introduction* to *Liberation Theology*, 5; Tombs, "Latin American Liberation Theology Faces the Future," 46–48.

49. Berryman, *Liberation Theology*, 157; Duque, ed., *Por una sociedad donde quepan todos*, 54.

50. Galilea, "Liberation Theology and New Tasks Facing Christians," 167.

51. Gutiérrez, "The Task and Content of Liberation Theology," 27.

52. Gutiérrez, "The Task and Content of Liberation Theology," 19.

53. Gutiérrez, "The Task and Content of Liberation Theology," 28, 29; Rowland, ed., *The Cambridge Companion* to *Liberation Theology*, 4.

54. Richard, "La Teología de la Liberación en la nueva coyuntura," 2; D. T. Williams, *Capitalism, Socialism, Christianity and Poverty*, 199.

55. Gutiérrez, *A Theology of Liberation*, 204.

56. Gutiérrez, G. *A Theology of Liberation*, 291.

57. Boff, "Christ's Liberation via Oppression," 129.

58. Dussel, "Theologies of the 'Periphery' and the 'Centre,'" 89; emphasis in original.

59. Gibelleni, *The Liberation Theology Debate*, 46.

60. Turner, "Marxism and Liberation Theology," 203.

61. Tombs, "Latin American Liberation Theology Faces the Future, 53–56.

62. Tombs, "Latin American Liberation Theology Faces the Future, 55.

63. Moltmann, "Political Theology and Theology of Liberation," 74.

64. Elias, *Paulo Freire*, 145.

65. Fenn, "Third-World Liberation Theology," 3.

Chapter 11. Global Citizenship and Human Rights:
From Muslims in Europe to European Muslims

This chapter was first published in *Religious Pluralism and Human Rights in Europe: Where to Draw the Line?* ed. M. L. P. Loenen and J. E. Goldschmidt (Antwerp: Intersentia, 2007), 13–55.

1. This point will be indicated hereinafter by the term "national citizenship" as a legal and political quality of being a citizen of a specific state, as distinguished from the broader concept of regional or global citizenship that I am trying to develop here.

2. By "national" citizenship I mean political and legal citizenship of a specific state or country, as distinguished from regional and global citizenship, which are not yet widely accepted or sufficiently established. I prefer the term "territorial state" because the idea of the "nation" is often used to exclude or suppress religious and other minorities.

3. See, for example, An-Na'im, *Human Rights in Cross-Cultural Perspectives*, "Cultural Transformation and Normative Consensus," and "The Contingent Universality of Human Rights."

4. Sachs, *Advancing Human Rights in South Africa*, ix.

5. Anghie, *Imperialism, Sovereignty and the Making of International Law*, 199–204.

6. CIA, *The World Fact Book*, https://www.cia.gov/library/publications/the-world-factbook/geos/xx.html, viewed April 5, 2010.

7. Iinglehart and Norris, "The True Clash of Civilizations."

8. See, for example, An-Na'im, *Toward an Islamic Reformation*.

9. An-Na'im, "State Responsibility Under International Human Rights Law to Change Religious and Customary Law" and "Islamic Foundations of Religious Human Rights."

10. An-Na'im, "The Interdependence of Religion, Secularism, and Human Rights."

11. See, for example, Hallaq, *A History of Islamic Legal Theories*, 1–15.

12. See, for example, 10:93; 11:118–19; 32:25; and 45:17 (cited here by chapter and verse).

13. See, for example, Mernissi, *Women in Islam*, 49–81; Mernissi, *The Veil and the Male Elite*; Karam, *Women, Islamisms, and the State*; Wadud, *Qur'an and Woman*; Cooke, *Women Claim Islam*; Barlas, *Believing Women in Islam*; Barazangi, *Woman's Identity and the Qur'an*; and Mahmood, *Politics of Piety*.

14. An-Na'im, "Expanding the Limits of Imagination."

15. An-Na'im, "Introduction: Expanding Legal Protection of Human Rights in African Context"; "Human Rights in the Arab World: A Regional Perspective."

16. An-Na'im, "Human Rights and the Challenge of Relevance."

17. Elsea, "Detention of American Citizens as Enemy Combatants," CRS, Report for Congress, www.fas.org/sgp/crs/natsec/RL31724.pdf, viewed March 10, 2010.

18. For a comprehensive discussion, including most recent cases before U.S. courts, see Abrams, *Anti-Terrorism and Criminal Enforcement*, 295–380.

19. Pocock, "The Ideal of Citizenship." I am referring here to *written* records in the European context, without excluding other antecedents, as may be found in ancient Chinese or Hindu civilizations or in oral traditions of different peoples around the world.

20. Faulks, *Citizenship*, 14.

21. Pocock, "The Ideal of Citizenship," 40.

22. Faulks, *Citizenship*, 20.

23. Heater, *Citizenship*, 16.

24. Riesenberg, *Citizenship in the Western Tradition*, 99.

25. Wells, *Law and Citizenship*, xv.

26. Wells, *Law and Citizenship*, 80.

27. Wells, *Law and Citizenship*, 103; Wolfe, "Review of Law and Citizenship in Early Modern France," 292.

28. Faulks, *Citizenship*, 23.

29. Faulks, *Citizenship*, 25.

30. Shaw, "The Enlightenment Concept of Citizenship, Rights and Governance in Modern and Postmodern States," http://www.porirua.net/CitizenshipShawpdf.pdf, 8, viewed April 5, 2010.

31. Faulks, *Citizenship*, 32.

32. Marshall, "Citizenship and Social Class."

33. Kymlicka and Norman, "Return of the Citizen."

34. Carter, *The Political Theory of Global Citizenship*, 12.

35. Carter, *The Political Theory*, 12.

36. Carter, *The Political Theory*, 20.

37. Carter, *The Political Theory*, 26.

38. Carter, *The Political Theory*, 28. See also Bull, Kingsbury, and Roberts, *Hugo Grotius and International Relations*, 36–48.

39. Hinsley, *Power and the Pursuit of Peace*, 18.

40. *Kant: Political Writings*, 93–130.

41. *Kant: Political Writings*, 107–108.

42. Sundara, "Awakening of Human Rights," 3.

43. Crane, "Confucian Cosmopolitanism," http://uselesstree.typepad.com/ useless_tree/2006/01/confucian_cosmo.html, viewed March 10, 2010.

44. Carter, *The Political Theory*, 5l.

45. Carter, *The Political Theory*, 69.

46. Heater, *World Citizenship and Government*, 139.

47. McMurray, "Inter-Citizenship," 313.

48. McMurray, "Inter-Citizenship, 306.

49. Heater, *World Citizenship and Government*, 139.

50. Woolley, "Progress, Man's Distinctive Mark Alone," 656.

51. Alvarez del Vayo, "The Duties of World Citizenship," 500.

52. Federation of American (Atomic) Scientists, *One World or None*.

53. "World Government," Wikipedia, March 10, 2010.

54. Carter, *The Political Theory*, 145.

55. Heater, *A Brief History of Citizenship*, 110.

56. Carter, *The Political Theory*, 150.

57. Juris International, *General Agreement on Trade in Services*, http://www.jurisint .org/pub/06/en/doc/25.htm, viewed March 10, 2010.

58. Bowden, "The Perils of Global Citizenship," 130.

59. Yuval-Davis, "The Multi-Layered Citizen," 128.

60. Hettne, "The Fate of Citizenship in Post-Westphalia," 44.

61. Fox, "Unpacking Transnational Citizenship," 175–76.

62. Pfister, "Citizenship and Globalization."

63. Bowden, "The Perils of Global Citizenship," 354.

64. Friedman, "Educating for World Citizenship," 586–601.

65. Nussbaum, *Cultivating Humanity*, 9–11.

66. Miller, "Citizenship and Pluralism," 448.

67. Dower, "The Idea of Global Citizenship," 556; Miller, "Bounded Citizenship," 79.

68. Bowden, "The Perils of Global Citizenship," 358.

69. Pinsky, "Eros Against Esperanto," 85.

70. Carter, *The Political Theory*, 171.

71. "Muslim Population Statistics," compiled by Canadian Society of Muslims, available at http://muslim-canada.org/muslimstats.html (March 10, 2010).

72. These figures were current at the time of writing in 2007. This information is taken from http://bbc.co.uk/l/h/world/europe/4385768.stm at the time of original writing and publication, but the webpage was no longer available to re-verify at the time of this re-publication.

73. Brubaker, *Citizenship and Nationhood in France and Germany*.

74. Joppke and Morawska, "Integrating Immigrants in Liberal Nation-States."

75. Robinson, "Religion in the United Kingdom," http://www.religioustolerance .org/uk_rel.htm, viewed April 5, 2010.

76. National Statistics Online, based on April 2001 Census by the Office of National

Statistics and General Register Office for Scotland; National Identity is based on the Labour Force Survey from June 2003 to May 2004; Religious Identity based on the Home Office Citizenship Survey 2001, all available at http://www.statistics.gov.uk/hub/index .html, viewed April 5, 2010.

77. "Majority Populations" Attitudes Towards Migrants and Minorities, Report for the European Monitoring Centre on Racism and Xenophobia (April 1, 2003) (hereinafter "EUMC Report on Attitudes").

78. EUMC Report on Attitudes, Report 1 at section 1.6.

79. EUMC Report on the Impact of 7 July 2005 London Bomb Attacks on Muslim Communities in the EU, Section 1.2, 10 (November 2005) (hereinafter EUMC Report on Impact of Bomb Attacks).

80. The poll's results were published by the BBC on their website at http://news.bbc .co.uk/1/hi/uk/4137990.stm on December 8, 2005. Currently the page is not available

81. EUMC Report on Impact of Bomb Attacks, Section 1.3.1., 13–26

82. At http://www.homeoffice.gov.uk/about-us/new/tacklilng-extremism, viewed July 10, 2005. This link was available at the time of first publication of this chapter. Other efforts by the British government to tackle extremism together can be found at: http://www .homeoffice.gov.uk/documents/cons-prev-extreme/, viewed April 6, 2010.

83. EUMC Report on Impact of Bomb Attacks, 36. See also http://www.narodni-strana. cz/clanek.php?id_clanku=1349, viewed April 10, 2005. The link is no longer available.

84. EUMC Report on Impact of Bomb Attacks, 37. See also http://www.dansk-folkeparti.dk/sw/frontend/newsletterpreview.asp?id=236&template_id=3&mbid= 19123 (January 8, 2005). The party's homepage is not in English, thus I could not do further research on it to find similar information. See also or instead, http://www.npr .org/templates/story/story.php?storyId=124351545.

85. EUMC Report on Impact of Bomb Attacks, 37–38.

86. *Financial Times Deutschland* (July 17, 2005) and *Welt am Sonntag* (July 17, 2005).

87. See EUMC Report on Impact of Bomb Attacks, 38. See also *SME*, "SNS vyzýva na prehodnotenie liberálnej migracnej politiky," http://www.sme.sk/clanok .asp?c1=2289723, viewed July 25, 2005.

88. See EUMC Report on Impact of Bomb Attacks, 46. See also *Newsweek* (July 31, 2005); *Polityka* (July 23, 2005); and *Wprost. Special Edition* (July 17, 2005).

89. Kedourie, *Nationalism*.

90. Gellner, *Nations and Nationalism*, 6.

91. B. Anderson, *Imagined Communities*.

92. Official European Union Web site: http://europa.eu/eu-life/rights-advice/index_ en.htm, viewed on April 6, 2010

93. Prentoulis, "On the Technology of Collective Identity" 198.

94. Borja, "The Citizenship Question and the Challenge of Globalization."

95. Pruess et al., "Traditions of Citizenship," 5.

96. Leibfried, "Towards a European Welfare State?," 150–51.

97. Streeck, "From Market Making to State Building?," 402–3.

98. Streeck, "From Market Making to State Building?" 413.

99. Preuss, "Traditions of Citizenship," 10.

100. Giscard d'Estaing, V. G. Amato and J. L. Dehaene, "Draft Treaty Establishing a Constitution for Europe," 2004, http://europa.eu.int/futurum/constitution/preamble/index_en.htm. Cannot access that page, but can see http://europa.eu/scadplus/constitution/index_en.htm.

101. Beasley, "Public Discourse and Cosmopolitan Political identity," 133–45.

102. Fijalkowski, "Aggressive Nationalism, Immigration Pressure and Asylum Policy," 861.

103. Polat, "Baden-Wurtternberg's Conscience Test Zeitgeist of Fear and Prejudice," trans. M. Lawton, Qantara, February 16, 2006; http://www.qantara.de/webcom/show_article.php/_c- 478/_nr- 402/i.html.

Bibliography

Abdalla, I. S. "Elements of a Strategy for the Development of the Arab Child." In *Al-ihtiyajat al-Assasiya lil- Tiftfi al-Watan al-Araby* (The Basic Needs of the Child in the Arab Homeland), ed. General Secretariat of the Arab League, Social Affairs Administration. Tunis: Arab League, 1982.

Abi Sab, Georges. "The Legal Formulation of a Right to Development." In *Le droit au developpement au plan international: colloque*, La Haye, 16–18 October 1979. The Hague: Hague Academy of International Law, 1980.

Abrams, Norman. *Anti-Terrorism and Criminal Enforcement*. 2nd ed. St. Paul, Minn.: Thomson/ West, 2005.

Abu Zahrah, Muhammad. "Nazariayt al-Harb fi al-Islam (The Theory of War in Islam)." *Revue Égyptienne du Droit International* 14 (1958):

Adams, Charles C. *Islam and Modernism in Egypt: A Study of the Modern Reform Movement Inaugurated by Muhammad 'Abduh*. London: Oxford University Press, 1933.

Aina, Tade Akin. *Globalization and Social Policy in Africa: Issues and Research Directions*. CODESRIA Working Paper 6. Dakar: CODESRIA, 1997.

Al-Azm, Sadik J. "Islamic Fundamentalism Reconsidered: A Critical Outline of Problems, Ideas and Approaches." Pts. 1 and 2. *South Asia Bulletin* 13/14 (1993–94): 93–121; 73–98.

Al-Azmeh, Aziz. "Islamic Legal Theory and the Appropriation of Reality." In *Islamic Law: Social and Historical Contexts*, ed. Aziz Al-azmeh. London: Routledge, 1988.

Al Faruqi, Isma'il R. "Islam and Human Rights." *Islamic Quarterly* 27 (1983).

Al-Kaya Al-Harasiy. *Ahkam al-Qur'an*. Vol. 1. Beirut: Dar al-Kutub al-'Ilmiyah, 1983.

Al-Mubarak. *Nizam al-Islam fi al-Hukm wa al-Dawla* (The Islamic Order for Governance and the State). Beirut: Da al-Fikr, 1981.

Álvarez del Vayo, Julio. "The Duties of World Citizenship." *Nation* 159, 17 (October 21, 1944)

Amnesty International. *Human Rights: Selected International Standards*. London: Amnesty International Publications, 1985.

Anaya, S. James. "The Capacity of International Law to Advance Ethnic or Nationality Rights Claims." In *Rights of Minority Cultures*, ed. Kymlicka.

———. *Indigenous Peoples in International Law*. Oxford: Oxford University Press, 1996.

Anderson, Benedict. *Imagined Communities: Reflections on the Origin and Spread of Nationalism*. New York: Verso, 1991.

Anderson, James Norman D. *Law Reform in the Muslim World*. London: Athlone, 1976.

Anghie, Antony. *Imperialism, Sovereignty and the Making of International Law*. Cambridge: Cambridge University Press, 2004.

Anheier, Helmut K., Marlies Glasius, and Mary Kaldor. "Introducing Global Civil Society." In *Global Civil Society 2001*, ed. H. K. Anheier, M. Glasius, and M. Kaldor. Oxford: Oxford University Press, 2001. 3–22.

An-Naʿim, Abdulahi Ahmed. "The Contingent Universality of Human Rights: The Case of Freedom of Expression in African and Islamic Contexts." *Emory International Law Review* 11 (1997): 29–66.

———. "Cultural Transformation and Normative Consensus on the Best Interest of the Child." *International Journal of Law and the Family* 8 (1994): 62–81.

———. "Expanding the Limits of Imagination: Human Rights from a Participatory Approach to New Multilateralism." In *Innovation in Multilateralism*, ed. Michael G. Schecter. Tokyo: United Nations University Press, 1998: 205–222.

———. "Human Rights and the Challenge of Relevance: The Case of Collective Rights." In *The Role of the Nation-State in the 21st Century: Human Rights, International Organizations and Foreign Policy: Essays in Honour of Peter Baehr*, ed. Monique Castermans-Holleman, Fried van Hoof, and Jacqueline Smith. The Hague: Kluwer, 1998 3–16.

———, ed. *Human Rights in Cross-Cultural Perspectives: A Quest for Consensus*. Philadelphia, University of Pennsylvania Press, 1992.

———. "Human Rights in the Arab World: A Regional Perspective." *Human Rights Quarterly* 23, 3 (2001): 701–32.

———. "Human Rights in the Muslim World: Socio-Political Conditions and Scriptural Imperatives." *Harvard Human Rights Journal* 3 (1990): 13–52.

———. "The Interdependence of Religion, Secularism, and Human Rights." Symposium Talking Peace with Gods, *Common Knowledge* 11, 1 (2005): 56–80 .

———. "Introduction." In *Human Rights in Cross-Cultural Perspectives*, ed. An-Naʿim.

———. "Introduction: Expanding Legal Protection of Human Rights in African Context." In *Human Rights Under African Constitutions: Realizing the Promise for Ourselves*, ed. Abdulahi Ahmed An-Naʿim. Philadelphia: University of Pennsylvania Press, 2002. 1–28.

———. "Islam and Human Rights in Sahilian Africa." in *African Islam and Islam in Africa*, ed. Eva Evers Rosander and David Westerlund. Uppsala: Nordic Africa Institute and Uppsala University, 1997. 79–94.

———. "Islam, Islamic Law and the Dilemma of Cultural Legitimacy for Universal Human Rights." In *Asian Perspectives on Human Rights*, ed. Welch and Leary.

———. "Islamic Ambivalence to Political Violence: Islamic Law and International Terrorism." *German Yearbook of International Law* 31 (1988): 307–36.

———. "Islamic Foundations of Religious Human Rights." In *Religious Human Rights in Global Perspective: Religious Perspectives*, ed. John Witte, Jr., and Johan van der Vyver. The Hague: Nijhoff, 1996. 337–59.

———. "Islamic Law, International Relations and Human Rights: Challenge and Response," *Cornell International Law Journal* 20, 2 (1987): 317–35.

———. "The Islamic Law of Apostasy and Its Modern Applicability: A Case from the Sudan," *Religion* 16 (1986): 197–223.

———. "Mahmud Muhammad Taha and the Crisis in Islamic Law Reform: Implications for Interreligious Relations." *Journal of Ecumenical Studies* 25, 1 (1988): 1–21.

———. "Muslim Fundamentalism and Social Change." In *The Freedom to Do God's Will: Religious Fundamentalism and Social Change*, ed. Gerrie ter Haar and James J. Busuttil. London, Routledge, 2002. 25–48.

———. "Problems and Prospects of Universal Cultural Legitimacy for Human Rights." In *Human Rights in Africa*, ed. An-Naʿim and Deng. 331–67.

———, ed. *Proselytization and Communal Self-Determination in Africa*. Maryknoll, N.Y.: Orbis, 1999.

———. "Religion and Global Civil Society: Tactical Co-operation or Reluctant Partnership?" In *Global Civil Society Yearbook 2002*, ed. Helmut K. Anheier, Marlies Glasius, and Mary Kaldor. Oxford: Oxford University Press, 2002. 55–76.

———. "Religious Freedom in Egypt: Under the Shadow of the Islamic *Dhimma* System." In *Religious Liberty and Human Rights*, ed. Swidler.

———. "Religious Minorities Under Islamic Law and the Limits of Cultural Relativism." *Human Rights Quarterly* 9, 1 (February 1987): 1–18.

———. "The Rights of Women and International Law in the Muslim Context." *Whittier Law Review* 9 (1987): 265–76.

———. "*Shariʿa* and Positive Legislation: Is an Islamic State Possible or Viable?" In *Yearbook of Islamic and Middle Eastern Law* 5, ed. Eugene Cotran and Chibli Mallat. The Hague: Kluwer, 2000. 29–42.

———. "State Responsibility Under International Human Rights Law to Change Religious and Customary Law." In *Human Rights of Women: National and International Perspectives*, ed. Rebecca J. Cook. Philadelphia: University of Pennsylvania Press, 1994.

———. "Synergy and Interdependence of Human Rights, Religion, and Secularism." *Polylog: Forum for Intercultural Philosophizing.* http://them.polylog.org/3/faa-en.htm. March 13, 2009.

———. "Toward a Cross-Cultural Approach to Defining International Standards of Human Rights: The Meaning of Cruel, Inhuman or Degrading Treatment or Punishment." In *Human Rights in Cross-Cultural Perspectives*, ed. An Naʿim and Deng.

———. "Toward an Islamic Hermeneutics for Human Rights." In *Human Rights and Religious Values*, ed. An-Naʿim et al.

———. *Toward an Islamic Reformation: Civil Liberties, Human Rights and International Law*. Syracuse, N.Y.: Syracuse University Press, 1990.

———. "Upholding International Legality Against Islamic and American *Jihad.*" In *Worlds in Collision: Terror and the Future of Global Order*, ed. Ken Booth and Timothy Dunne. London: Palgrave, 2002. 162–71.

An-Naʿim, Abdullahi, and Francis M. Deng, eds. *Human Rights in Africa: Cross-Cultural Perspectives*. Washington, D.C.: Brookings Institution, 1990.

———. "Self-Determination and Unity: The Case of Sudan." *Law & Society* 18 (1997): 199–223.

An-Naʿim, Abdullahi Ahmed, Jerald D. Gort, Henry Jansen, and Hendrik M. Vroom, eds. *Human Rights and Religious Values: An Uneasy Relationship?* Grand Rapids, Mich.: Eerdmans, 1995.

Arjomand, Said Amir. *The Shadow of God and the Hidden Iman: Religion, Political Order, and Societal Change in Shiʿite Iran from the Beginning to 1890*. Chicago: University of Chicago Press, 1984.

Arnold, Roberta. *The ICC as a New Instrument for Repressing Terrorism*. Ardsley, N.Y.: Transnational Publishers, 2004.

Arnold, Terrell E. *The Violence Formula: Why People Lend Sympathy and Support to Terrorism*. Lexington, Mass.: Lexington Books, 1988.

Asad, Talal. "Comments on Conversion." In *Conversion to Modernities: The Globalization of Christianity*, ed. Peter van der Veer. New York: Routledge, 1996.

Ashburn, Daniel G., ed. *The State of Religious Human Rights in the World: Preliminary Consultation*. Preliminary Documents of [Pew Foundation] Religious Human Rights Project 2 (1993).

Ayoade, John A. A. "States Without Citizens: An Emerging African Phenomenon." In *The Precarious Balance: State and Society in Africa*, ed. Donald Rothchild and Naomi Chazan. Boulder, Colo.: Westview Press, 1988.

Ayoob, Mohammad, ed. *The Politics of Islamic Reassertion*. New York: St. Martin's, 1981.

Azer, Adil, and Nahed Ramzy. *Child Labor in Egypt*. Cairo: National Center for Social and Criminological Research and UNICEF Egypt, 1992.

Bach, Daniel C. "Reappraising Postcolonial Geopolitics: Europe, Africa and the End of the Cold War." In *Legitimacy and the State in Twentieth-Century Africa: Essays in Honour of A. H. Kirk-Greene*, ed. Terence Ranger and Olufemi Vaughan. London: Macmillan, 1993.

Baladhur I, Ahmad ibn Ya-hyá. *The Origins of the Islamic State: being a translation from the Arabic, accompanied with annotations, geographic and historic notes of the Kitâb futû h al-buldân of al-Imâm Abul Abbâs, Ahmad ibn-Jâbir al Balâdhuri*. Trans. Philip Khuri Hitti. Studies in History, Economics and Public Law, edited by the Faculty of Political Science of Columbia University 68, number 163. New York: AMS Press, 1968.

Banwo, Adeyinka. "The Nineteenth Century Ilorin Wars and the Growth of Islam in Yorubaland: A Re-Assessment." *Hamdard Islamicus* 18 (1995): 85–97.

Barazangi, Nimat Hafez. *Woman's Identity and the Qur'an: A New Reading*. Gainesville: University Press of Florida, 2005.

Barlas, Asma. *Believing Women in Islam: Unreading Patriarchal Interpretations of the Qur'an.* Austin: University of Texas Press, 2002.

Barnes, Barry, and David Bloor. "Relativism, Rationalism and the Sociology of Knowledge." In *Rationality and Relativism*, ed. Martin Hollis and Steven Lukes, Cambridge, Mass.: MIT Press, 1982.

Bartholomew, Craig. "The Challenge of Islam in Africa." *Journal of Interdisciplinary Studies* 6 (1994): 129–146.

Bascom, William R., and Melville J. Herskovits, eds. *Continuity and Change in African Cultures.* Chicago: University of Chicago Press, 1959.

Bassiouni, M. Cherif. "Perspectives on the Origins and Causes of Terrorism." In *International Terrorism and Political Crimes*, ed. Bassiouni. Third Conference on Terrorism and Political Crimes, Syracuse, Sicily, 1973. Springfield, Ill.: Thomas, 2005.

Beasley, Alessandra. "Public Discourse and Cosmopolitan Political Identity: Imagining the European Union Citizen." *Futures* 38, 2 (2006): 133–45.

Beidelman, Thomas O. *Colonial Evangelism: A Socio-Historical Study of an East African Mission at the Grassroots.* Bloomington: Indiana University Press, 1982.

———. "Contradictions Between the Sacred and the Secular Life: The Church Missionary Society in Ukaguru, Tanzania, East Africa, 1876–1914." *Comparative Studies in Sociology and History* 23 (1981): 73–95

———. "Social Theory and the Study of Christian Missions in Africa." *Africa* 44 (1974): 235–49.

Beitz, Charles R. *Political Theory and International Relations.* Princeton, N.J.: Princeton University Press, 1979.

Benedict, Ruth. *Patterns of Culture.* Boston: Houghton Mifflin, 1959.

Berman, Harold J. "The Historical Foundations of Law." *Emory Law Journal* 13 (2005): 13–24.

———. "Integrative Jurisprudence and World Law." In *Theorie des Rechts und der Gesellschaft: Festschrift für Werner Krawietz zum 70. Geburtstag*, ed. Manuel Atienza et al. Berlin: Duncker and Humblot, 2003.

———. *Law and Revolution: The Formation of the Western Legal Tradition.* Cambridge, Mass.: Harvard University Press, 1983.

———. *Toward an Integrative Jurisprudence: Politics, Morality, History,* California Law Review, vol. 76, No. 4 (July 1988): 779–801

Berryman, Phillip. *Liberation Theology: The Essential Facts About the Revolutionary Movement in Latin America and Beyond.* New York: Pantheon, 1987.

Bidney, David. "The Concept of Value in Modern Anthropology." In *Anthropology Today: An Encyclopedic Inventory*, ed. A. L. Kroeber. Chicago: University of Chicago Press, 1953.

Blakely, Thomas D., W. E. A. van Beek, and Dennis L. Thomson, eds. *Religion in Africa: Experience and Expression.* London, James Currey, 1991.

Boff, Leonardo. "Christ's Liberation via Oppression: An Attempt at Theological Construction from the Standpoint of Latin America." In *Frontiers of Theology in Latin America*, ed. Gibellini. 100–32.

Borja, Jordi. "The Citizenship Question and the Challenge of Globalization: The European Context." *City* 4, 1 (April 2000): 43–52.

Bossuyt, Marc J. *Guide to the "Travaux Préparatoires" of the International Covenant on Civil and Political Rights*. Dordrecht: Nijhoff, 1987.

Bowden, Brett. "The Perils of Global Citizenship." *Citizenship Studies* 7, 2 (2003): 349–62.

Bozeman, Adda B. *The Future of Law in a Multicultural World*. Princeton, N.J.: Princeton University Press, 1971.

Brownlie, Ian, ed. *Basic Documents on Human Rights*. 2nd ed. Oxford: Clarendon Press, 1981.

———. *Principles of Public International Law*. 3rd ed. Oxford: Clarendon Press, 1979.

Brubaker, Rogers. *Citizenship and Nationhood in France and Germany*. Cambridge, Mass.: Harvard University Press, 1992.

Bull, Hedley, Benedict Kingsbury, and Adam Roberts. *Hugo Grotius and International Relations*. Oxford: Clarendon Press, 1990.

Burton, John. *The Collection of the Qur'an*. Cambridge: Cambridge University Press, 1977.

Cafagna, Albert Carl. "A Formal Analysis of Definitions of 'Culture.'" In *Essays in the Science of Culture*, ed. Dole and Carneiro.

Canadian Society of Muslims. "Muslim Population Statistics." http://muslim-canada.org/muslimstats.html.

Carter, April. *The Political Theory of Global Citizenship*. New York: Routledge, 2002.

Chabal, Patrick. "Introduction: Thinking About Politics in Africa." In *Political Domination in Africa: Reflections on the Limits of Power*, ed. Patrick Chabal. Cambridge: Cambridge University Press, 1986.

CIA. *The World Fact Book*. https://www.cia.gov/library/publications/the-world-factbook/geos/xx.html

Cingranelli, David Louis. "A Cross-Cultural Approach to Validating International Human Rights: The Case of Retribution Tied to Proportionality." In *Human Right: Theory and Measurement*, ed. Cingranelli. Basingstoke: Macmillan, 1988.

———. *International Human Rights: Universalism Versus Relativism*. Newbury Park, Calif.: Sage, 1990.

Clark, Christopher. *The Politics of Conversion: Missionary Protestantism and the Jews in Prussia 1728–1941*. Oxford: Clarendon Press, 1995.

Collins, Robert O., James McDonald Burns, and Erik Kristofer Ching, eds. *Historical Problems of Imperial Africa*. Topics in World History. Princeton, N.J.: Wiener, 1994.

Comaroff, Jean, and John Comaroff. *Of Revelation and Revolution*. 2 vols. Chicago: University of Chicago Press, 1991.

Cook, John. "Cultural Relativism as an Ethnocentric Notion." In *The Philosophy of Society*, ed. Rodger Beehler and Alan R. Drengson. London: Methuen, 1978.

Cook, Rebecca J. "Reservations to the Convention on the Elimination of All Forms of

Discrimination Against Women." *Virginia Journal of International Law* 30 (1990): 643–663.

Cooke, Miriam. *Women Claim Islam: Creating Islamic Feminism Through Literature.* New York: Routledge, 2000.

Coulson, Noel J. *A History of Islamic Law.* Edinburgh: University Press, 1964.

Crane, Sam. "Confucian Cosmopolitanism." In Crane, blog, *The Useless Tree: Ancient Chinese Thought in Modern American Life*; http://uselesstree.typepad.com/useless_tree/2006/01/ confucian_cosmo.html.

Dalacoura, Katerina. *Islam, Liberalism and Human Rights: Implications for International Relations.* London: Tauris, 1998.

D'Andrade, Roy G. "Cultural Meaning Systems." In *Culture Theory*, ed. Shweder and LeVine.

Davison, Jean, ed. *Agriculture, Women, and Land: The African Experience.* Boulder, Colo.: Westview, 1988.

De Bary, William Theodore et al., eds. *Sources of Indian Tradition.* New York: Columbia University Press, 1958.

Detter Delupis, Ingrid. *The Law of War.* Cambridge: Cambridge University Press, 1987.

Dickerman, Carol W. *Security of Tenure and Land Registration in Africa: Literature Review and Synthesis.* Madison: University of Wisconsin-Madison Land Tenure Center, 1989.

Diemer, Alwin. *Philosophical Foundations of Human Rights.* Paris: UNESCO, 1986.

Dole, Gertrude E., and Robert L. Carneiro, eds. *Essays in the Science of Culture: In Honor of Leslie A. White.* New York: Crowell, 1960.

Donelan, Michael D., ed. *The Reason of States: A Study in International Political Theory.* London: Allen and Unwin, 1979.

Donnelly, Jack. "Cultural Relativism and Universal Human Rights." *Human Rights Quarterly* 6 (November 1984): 400–419.

———. "Human Rights and Human Dignity: An Analytic Critique of Non-Western Conceptions of Human Rights," *American Political Science Review* 76 (1982): 303–16.

Donner, Fred McGraw. *The Early Islamic Conquests.* Princeton, N.J.: Princeton University Press, 1981.

Dower, Nigel. "The Idea of Global Citizenship: A Sympathetic Assessment." *Global Society: Journal of Interdisciplinary International Relations* 14, 4 (2000): 553–67.

Downs, R. E., and Stephen P. Reyna, eds. *Land and Society in Contemporary Africa.* Hanover, N.H.: University Press of New England, 1988.

Duque, José, ed. *Por una sociedad donde quepan todos.* San José: Departamento Ecuménico de Investigaciones, 1995.

Dussel, Enrique. "Theologies of the 'Periphery' and the 'Centre': Encounter or Confrontation?" In *Different Theologies, Common Responsibility: Babel or Pentecost?* ed. Claude Geffro, Gustavo Gutiérrez, and Virgilio Elizondo. Edinburgh: T & T Clark, 1984. 87–97.

Eide, Asbjørn. "Making Human Rights Universal in an Age of Economic Globalisation."

In *Praxis-Handbuch UNO: Die Vereinten Nationen im Lichte globaler Herausforderungen*, ed. Sabine Von Schlorlemer. Berlin: Springer, 2003. 241–62.

Eide, Asbjørn, and August Schou, eds. *International Protection of Human Rights: Proceedings*. Seventh Nobel Symposium, Oslo, September 25–27, 1967. New York: Wiley, 1968.

El-Awa, Mohamed S. *Punishment in Islamic Law*. Indianapolis: American Trust Publications, 1982.

Elias, John L. *Paulo Freire: Pedagogue of Liberation*. Malabar, Fl.: Krieger, 1994.

Eliash, Joseph. "The Ithna ʿashari Shiʿi Juristic Theory of Political and Legal Authority." *Studia Islamica* 24 (1969): 17–30.

Eliot, T. S. *Notes Towards the Definition of Culture*. London: Faber and Faber, 1948.

Elsea, Jennifer K. *Detention of American Citizens as Enemy Combatants*. CRS Report for Congress. New York: Nova Science, 2008.

Encyclopedia Judaica. Vols. 5 and 6. Jerusalem: Keter, 1971.

Esposito, John, ed. *Islam and Development: Religion and Sociopolitical Change*, Syracuse, N.Y.: Syracuse University Press, 1980.

——, ed. *Islam in Asia: Religion, Politics, and Society*. New York: Oxford University Press, 1987.

——, ed. *Voices of Resurgent Islam*. New York: Oxford University Press, 1983.

European Monitoring Centre on Racism and Xenophobia (EUMC). *Attitudes Towards Migrants and Minorities in Europe*, by ERCOMER Faculty on Utrecht: Universiteit Utrecht, ERCOMER Faculty of Social Scientes, April 1 2003.

Executive Board of the American Anthropological Association. "Statement on Human Rights." *American Anthropologist* 49, 4 (1947): 539–43.

Fage, J. D., and William Tordoff. *A History of Africa*. 4th ed. London: Routledge, 2002

Falk, Richard. "Cultural Foundations for the International Protection of Human Rights." In *Human Rights in Cross-Cultural Perspectives*, ed. An-Naʿim.

——. "Regionalism and World Order After the Cold War." *St. Louis Warsaw Transatlantic Law Journal* 9 (1995): 71–88.

Falk, Richard, Friedrich V. Kratochwil, and Saul H. Mendlovitz, eds. *International Law: A Contemporary Perspective*. Studies on a Just World Order 2. Boulder, Colo.: Westview, 1985.

Faruki, Kemal, *Islamic Jurisprudence*. Karachi: Pakistan Publishing House, 1975.

Faulks, Keith. *Citizenship*. New York: Routledge, 2000.

Federation of American (Atomic) Scientists. *One World or None: A Report to the Public on the Full Meaning of the Atomic Bomb*. Ed. Dexter Masters and Katharine Way. 1946; reprint New York: New Press, 2007.

Fenn, Deane William. "Third-World Liberation Theology." In *World Religions and Human Liberation*, ed. Dan Cohn-Sherbok. Maryknoll: Orbis, 1992. 1–20.

Festinger, Leon. *A Theory of Cognitive Dissonance*. Stanford, Calif.: Stanford University Press, 1957.

Fijalkowski, Jürgen. "Aggressive Nationalism, Immigration Pressure and Asylum Policy

Disputes in Contemporary Germany." *International Migration Review* 27, 4 (Winter 1993): 850–69.

Fisher, Humphrey. "Conversion Reconsidered." *Africa* 43 (1973): 27–40.

———. "The Juggernaut's Apology: Conversion to Islam in Black Africa." *Africa* 55(2) (1986): 153–173.

Fitzgerald, Valpy. "The Economics of Liberation Theology." In *The Cambridge Companion to Liberation Theology*, ed. Christopher Rowland. Cambridge: Cambridge University Press, 1999. 218–34.

Fox, Jonathan. "Unpacking Transnational Citizenship." *Annual Review of Political Science* 8 (2005): 171–202.

Franck, Thomas M. "Legitimacy in the International System." In *International Law*, ed. Koskenniemi.

Freitag, Sandria B. "Contesting in Public: Colonial Legacies and Contemporary Communalism." In *Contesting the Nation: Religion, Community, and the Politics of Democracy in India*, ed. David Ludden, Philadelphia: University of Pennsylvania Press, 1996. 211–35.

Friedman, Marilyn. "Educating for World Citizenship." *Ethics* 110, 3 (2000): 586–601.

Fukuyama, Francis. *The End of History and the Last Man*. New York: Free Press, 1992.

Fuller, Charles E. "Native and Missionary Religions." In *The Transformation of East Africa*, ed. Stanley Diamond and Fred G. Burke. New York: Basic Books, 1966.

Fyzee, Asaf Ali Asghar. "Shi'a Legal Theories." In *Law in the Middle East*, vol. 1, ed. Khadduri and Liebesny.

Galilea, Segundo. "Liberation Theology and New Tasks Facing Christians." In *Frontiers of Theology in Latin America*, ed. Gibellini. 163–83.

Garet, Ronald. "Communality and Existence: The Rights of Groups." *Southern California Law Review* 56 (1983):

Geertz, Clifford. "Distinguished Lecture: Anti Anti-Relativism," *American Anthropologist* 86, 1984: 263–78.

———. *The Interpretation of Cultures: Selected Essays*. New York: Basic Books, 1973.

Gellner, Ernest. *Nations and Nationalism*. Ithaca, N.Y.: Cornell University Press, 1983.

Gerber, Haim. *Islamic Law and Culture, 1600–1840*. Ed. Ruud Peters and Bernard Weiss. Leiden: Brill, 1999.

Gibb, H. A. R. *Modern Trends in Islam*. Chicago: University of Chicago Press, 1947.

Gibellini, Rosino, ed. *Frontiers of Theology in Latin America*. Maryknoll, N.Y.: Orbis, 1979.

———. *The Liberation Theology Debate*. Maryknoll, N.Y.: Orbis, 1988.

Goldenweiser, Alexander. *History, Psychology, and Culture*. Gloucester, Mass., Peter Smith, 1968.

Goldziher, Ignaz. *Introduction to Islamic Theology and Law*. Trans. Andras and Ruth Hamori. Princeton, N.J.: Princeton University Press, 1981.

Goodman, Martin. *Mission and Conversion: Proselytization in the Religious History of the Roman Empire*. Oxford: Clarendon Press, 1994.

Gottlieb, Gidon. "Global Bargaining: The Legal and Diplomatic Framework." In *International Law*, ed. Falk, Kratochwil, and Mendlovitz.

Grenville, Clark and Louis B. Sohn. "Introduction to World Peace Through World Law." In *International Law: A Contemporary Perspective*, Falk, Richard, Friedrich V. Kratochwil, and Saul H. Mendlovitz, eds. Studies on a Just World Order 2. Boulder, Colo.: Westview, 1985:,73–99

Gunning, Isabelle R. "Modernizing Customary International Law and the Challenge of Human Rights." *Virginia Journal of International Law* 31 (1991): 227–234

Gupta, Dipankar. *Culture, Space and the Nation-State: From Sentiment to Structure*. New Delhi: Sage, 2000.

Gutiérrez, Gustavo. "Liberation Praxis and Christian Faith." In *Frontiers of Theology in Latin America*, ed. Gibellini. 1–16.

———. *The Poor and the Church in Latin America*. Sydney: Catholic Institute for International Relations, 1984.

———. "The Task and Content of Liberation Theology." In *The Cambridge Companion to Liberation Theology*, ed. C. Rowland, Cambridge: Cambridge University Press: 1–16.

———. *A Theology of Liberation: History, Politics, and Salvation*. Maryknoll, N.Y.: Orbis, 1973.

Haafkens, Johannes. "The Christian Muslim Encounter in Sub-Saharan Africa." *Church and Society* (March/April 1995): 66–78.

———. *Claiming the Promise: African Churches Speak*. New York: Friendship Press, 1994.

Hackett, Rosalind I. J. *Religion in Calabar*. New York: Mouton, 1989.

Hallaq, Wael B. *A History of Islamic Legal Theories: An Introduction to Sunni Usul Al-Fiqh*. Cambridge: Cambridge University Press, 1997.

———. "Was the Gate of Ijtihad Closed?" *International Journal of Middle East Studies* 16 (1984): 3–41. Reprint in *Law and Legal Theory in Classical and Medieval Islam* 3 (1994).

Hamidullah, Muhammad. *Muslim Conduct of State*. Lahore: Ashraf, 1966.

Hannum, Hurst, ed. *Guide to International Human Rights Practice*. 2nd ed. Philadelphia: University of Pennsylvania Press, 1992.

Harris, David J. *Cases and Materials on International Law*. 4th ed. London, Sweet & Maxwell, 1991.

Hartung, Frank E. "Cultural Relativity and Moral Judgments." *Philosophy of Science* 21 (1954): 118–26.

Hasan, Ahmad. *The Early Development of Islamic Jurisprudence*. Islamabad: Islamic Research Institute, 1970.

Hassan, Riffat. "On Human Rights and the Qur'anic Perspective." *Journal of Ecumenical Studies* 19, 3 (1982): 51–65.

Hatch, Elvin. *Culture and Morality: The Relativity of Values in Anthropology*. New York: Columbia University Press, 1983.

Haykal, Muhammad Husayn. *The Life of Muhammad*. Trans. Isma'il A. al Faruqi. Indianapolis: North American Trust, 1976.

Heater, Derek Benjamin. *A Brief History of Citizenship*. Edinburgh: University Press, 2004.

———. *Citizenship*. London: Longman, 1990.

———. *World Citizenship and Government: Cosmopolitan Ideas in the History of Western Political Thought*. New York: St. Martin's, 1996.

Hefner, Robert, ed. *Conversion to Christianity: Historical and Anthropological Perspectives on a Great Transformation*. Berkeley: University of California Press, 1993.

Hegland, Mary Elaine. "Islamic Revival or Political and Cultural Revolution? An Iranian Case Study." In *Religious Resurgence: Contemporary Case Studies in Islam, Christianity and Judaism*, ed. Richard T. Antoun and Mary Elaine Hegland. Syracuse, N.Y.: Syracuse University Press, 1987. 194–219.

Henkin, Louis et al., eds. *International Law: Cases and Materials*. St. Paul, Minn.: West Group, 1987.

Hennelly, Alfred, and John Langan, eds. *Human Rights in the Americas: The Struggle for Consensus*. Washington, D.C.: Georgetown University Press, 1982.

Hermassi, Abdelbaki. "Notes on Civil Society in Tunisia." In *Toward Civil Society in the Middle East? A Primer*, ed. Jillian Schwedler. Boulder, Colo.: Lynne Rienner, 1995.

Herskovits, Melville J. *Cultural Dynamics*. New York: Knopf, 1964.

———. *Man and His Works: The Science of Cultural Anthropology*. New York: Knopf, 1948.

Hettne, Björn. "The Fate of Citizenship in Post-Westphalia." *Citizenship Studies* 4, 1 (2000): 35–46.

Higgins, Rosalyn. "Conceptual Thinking About the Individual in International Law." In *International Law*, ed. Falk, Kratochwil, and Mendlovitz. 476–94.

Hinsley, F. H. *Power and the Pursuit of Peace: Theory and the Practice in the History of Relations Between States*. Cambridge: Cambridge University Press, 1967.

Hiskett, Mervyn. *The Development of Islam in Western Africa*. New York: Longman, 1984.

Hodgson, Marshall G. S. *The Venture of Islam*. Vol. 1. Chicago: University of Chicago Press, 1974.

Hoffman, Stanley. *Duties Beyond Borders: On the Limits and Possibilities of Ethical International Politics*. Syracuse, N.Y.: Syracuse University Press, 1981.

Hoibraaten, Helge. "Secular Society: An Attempt at Initiation." In *Islamic Law Reform and Human Rights: Challenges and Rejoinders*, ed. Tore Lindholm and Karl Vogt. Oslo: Nordic Human Rights Publications, 1993.

Horton, Robin. "African Conversion." *Africa* 41 (1971): 85–108.

———. "On the Rationality of Conversion." *Africa* 45 (1975): 373–99.

Hosken, Fran P. *Female Sexual Mutilation: The Facts and Proposals for Action*. Lexington, Mass.: Women's International Network News, 1980.

————. *The Hosken Report.* 3rd rev. ed. Lexington, Mass.: Women's International Network News, 1982.

Howard, Rhoda E., and Jack Donnelly, "Human Dignity, Human Rights and Political Regimes." *American Political Science Review* 80 (1986): 801–17.

————. "Introduction." In *International Handbook of Human Rights*, ed. Howard and Donnelly. Westport, Conn.; Greenwood Press, 1988.

Huntington, Samuel P. *The Clash of Civilizations and the Remaking of World Order.* New York: Simon and Schuster, 1996.

Ibn Taymiyya, Ahmad. *Public and Private Law in Islam or Public Policy in Islamic Jurisprudence.* Trans. Omar A. Farrukh. Beirut: Khayyats, 1966.

————. *Qaʿida fi Qital al-Kuffar* (A Principle in Fighting Unbelievers). Cairo, 1949.

Iinglehart, Ronald, and Patricia Norris. "The True Clash of Civilizations." *Foreign Policy* (March/April 2003): 62–70.

Imber, Colin. *Ebuʾs-Suʿud: The Islamic Legal Tradition.* Stanford, Calif.: Stanford University Press, 1997.

International Commission of Jurists (ICJ). *Development, Human Rights and the Rule of Law: Report of a Conference Held in The Hague 27 April–1 May 1981.* Elmsford, N.Y., Pergamon Press, 1981.

————. *Human Rights in a One-Party State.* International Seminar on Human Rights, Their Protection and the Rule of Law in a One-Party State. London: Search Press with ICJ, 1978.

————. *Seminar on Human Rights in Islam.* Papers presented at Seminar, Kuwait, December 1980, organized by ICJ, University of Kuwait, and Union of Arab Lawyers. Geneva: ICJ: 1982.International Forum on Globalization. *Alternatives to Economic Globalization.* San Francisco: Berrett-Koehler, 2002.

Ishaque, Khalid M. "Human Rights in Islamic Law." *International Commission of Jurists Review* 12 (1974): 30–39.

Isichei, Elizabeth. *A History of Christianity in Africa.* London: Society for Publishing Christian Knowledge, 1995.

————. "Seven Varieties of Ambiguity: Some Patterns of Igbo Response to Christian Missions." *Journal of Religion in Africa* 3 (1970): 209–27.

Jackson, Robert H., and Carl G. Rosberg. "Sovereignty and Underdevelopment: Juridical Statehood in the African Crisis." *Journal of Modern African Studies* 24 (1986): 1–31.

Jansen, Johannes J. G. *The Neglected Duty: The Creed of Sadat Assassins and Islamic Resurgence in the Middle East.* New York: Macmillan, 1986.

Jarvie, Ian Charles. "Rationalism and Relativism." *British Journal of Sociology* 34 (1983): 44–60.

Jenefsky, Anna. "Permissibility of Egypt's Reservations to the Convention on the Elimination of All Forms of Discrimination Against Women." *Maryland Journal of International Law and Trade* 15 (1991): 199–233.

Jenks, C. Wilfred. *The World Beyond the Charter in Historical Perspective: A Tentative Synthesis of Four Stages of World Organization*. London, Allen and Unwin, 1969.

Johnson, James Turner. *Can Modern War Be Just?* New Haven, Conn.: Yale University Press, 1984.

Johnston, Darlene M. "Native Rights as Collective Rights: A Question of Group Self Preservation." In *Rights of Minority Culture*, ed. Kymlicka.

Joppke, Christian, and Ewa T. Morawska. "Integrating Immigrants in Liberal Nation-States: Policies and Practices." In *Toward Assimilation and Citizenship: Immigrants in Liberal Nation-States*, ed. Joppke and Morawska. London: Palgrave Macmillan, 2003.

Juergensmeyer, Mark, ed. *Terror in the Mind of God: The Global Rise of Religious Violence*. Berkeley: University of California Press, 2000.

Kant, Immanuel. *Kant: Political Writings*. 2nd ed. Ed. Hans Siegbert Reiss, trans. H. B. Nisbet. Cambridge: Cambridge University Press, 1991.

Karam, Azza M. *Women, Islamisms, and the State: Contemporary Feminisms in Egypt*. New York, St. Martin's, 1998.

Kedourie, Elie. *Nationalism*. Oxford: Blackwell, 1993.

Kerr, Malcom H. *Islamic Reform: The Political and Legal Theories of Muhammad Abduh and Rashid Rida*. Berkeley: University of California Press, 1966.

Khadduri, Majid. "Islam and the Modern Law of Nations." *American Journal of International Law* 50 (1956): 358–72.

———, trans. *Islamic Jurisprudence, Shaft'i's Risala*. Baltimore: Johns Hopkins University Press, 1961.

———. *The Islamic Law of Nations: Shaybani's Siyar*. Baltimore: Johns Hopkins University Press, 1966.

———. *War and Peace in the Law of Islam*. Baltimore: Johns Hopkins University Press, 1955.

Khadduri, Majid, and Herbert J. Liebesny, eds. *Law in the Middle East*, vol. 1, *Origin and Development of Islamic Law*. Washington, D.C.: The Middle East Institute, 1955.

King, Noel. *Christians and Muslims in Africa*. New York: Harper & Row, 1971.

Kluckhohn, . . . "Universal Categories of Culture." In *Readings in Cross-Cultural Methodology*, ed. Moore.

Koskenniemi, Martin, ed. *International Law*. Aldershot: Dartmouth Publishing, 1992.

———. "The Normative Force of Habit: International Custom and Social Theory." In *Finnish Yearbook of International Law* I, 1991: 77–153.

Kothari, Rajne. "Human Rights: A Movement in Search of a Theory." In *Rethinking Human Rights: Challenges for Theory and Action*, ed. Smitu Kothari and Harsh Sethi. New York: New Horizon Press, 1989.

Kratochwil, Friedrich, Richard Falk, and Saul H. Mendlovitz. "Conceptual Thinking About the Individual in International Law." In *International Law: A Contemporary Perspective*, ed. Falk, Kratochwil, and Menlovitz.

Kroeber, A. L., and Clyde Kluckhohn, eds. *Culture: A Critical Review of Concepts and Definitions*. New York: Vintage, 1963.

Kruse, Hans. "The Islamic Doctrine of International Treaties." *Islamic Quarterly* 1 (1954): 152–194.

Kuriym, K. "Athar Siyasat al-Islah al-Iqtisady ala al-Usar Mahdudat al-Dakhl wa al-Atfal bi-Masr" (The Impact of Policies of Economic Reform on Limited-Income Families and Children in Egypt). Prepared for Third World Forum, Middle East Office, and UNICEF. Egypt, n.d..

Kymlicka, Will, ed. *The Rights of Minority Cultures*. Oxford: Oxford University Press, 1995.

Kymlicka, Will, and Wayne Norman. "Return of the Citizen: A Survey of Recent Work on Citizenship Theory." *Ethics* 104, 2 (1994): 352–81.

Labib, Tahir. "The Arab Child: Between the Needs and the Institutions." In *Al-Tufula wa al-Tanmiya fi al-Watan al-Araby*, ed. General Secretariat, Administration of Social Affairs, Arab League, Tunis, 13–15 November 1986, Part II.

Ladd, John. "The Poverty of Absolutism." *Acta Philosophica Fennica* 34 (1982): 158–80.

Lapidus, Ira M. *A History of Islamic Societies*. 2nd ed. New York: Cambridge University Press, 2002.

Leary, Virginia A. "The Effect of Western Perspectives on International Human Rights." In *Human Rights in Africa*, ed. An-Na'im and Deng.

Liebesny, Herbert J. *The Law of the Near and Middle East*. Albany: State University of New York Press, 1975.

Leibfried, Stephan. "Towards a European Welfare State? On Integrating Poverty Regimes into the European Community." In *New Perspectives on the Welfare State in Europe*, ed. Catherine Jones. London: Routledge, 1993.

Lillich, Richard, ed. *International Human Rights Instruments*. Buffalo, N.Y.: Hein, 1985.

Lindholm, Tore. "Prospects for Research on the Cultural Legitimacy of Human Rights." In *Cross-Cultural Perspectives*, ed. An-Na'im.

Loenen, M. L. P., and J. E. Goldschmidt, eds. *Religious Pluralism and Human Rights in Europe: Where to Draw the Line?* .Antwerp: Intersentia, 2007.

Lovelace v. Canada. Canada Human Rights Year Book 1 (1983).

Lowe, Richard G. *Agricultural Revolution in Africa? Impediments to Change and Implications for Farming, for Education, and for Society*. London: Macmillan, 1986.

Luard, Evan, ed. *The International Protection of Human Rights*. London: Thames and Hudson, 1967.

MacDonald, Duncan B. *Development of Muslim Theology, Jurisprudence and Constitutional Theory*. Lahore, 1903.

MacDonald, Ian. "Group Rights." *Philosophical Papers* 18(2) (1989): 117–136.

MacLean, Iain S. *Opting for Democracy: Liberation Theology and the Struggle for Democracy in Brazil*. New York: Peter Lang, 1999.

Macmullen, Ramsay. *Christianizing the Roman Empire*. New Haven, Conn.: Yale University Press, 1984.

Madjid, Nurcholish. "The Necessity of Renewing Islamic Thought and Reinvigorating Religious Understanding." In *Liberal Islam: A Source Book*, ed. Charles Kurzman. New York: Oxford University Press, 1998. 284–94.

Mahmassani, Subhi. *Falsafat al-Tashri fi al-Islam* (The Philosophy of Jursiprudence in Islam). Trans. Farhat J. Ziadah. Leiden: Brill, 1961.

Mahmood, Saba. *Politics of Piety: The Islamic Revival and the Feminist Subject*. Princeton, N.J.: Princeton University Press, 2005.

Makdisi, George. "The Juridical Theology of Shafi'i: Origins and Significance of Usul Al-Fiqh." *Studia Islamica* 59 (1984): 5–47.

Malinowski, Bronislaw. "Culture." In *Encyclopaedia of the Social Sciences*, vol. 4. London: Macmillan, 1931.

Mandaville, Peter G. *Transnational Muslim Politics: Reimagining the Umma*. London, Routledge, 2001.

Mann, Michael. "Dealing with Oriental Despotism: British Jurisdiction in Bengal 1772–93." In *Colonialism as Civilizing Mission: Cultural Ideology in British India*, ed. Harald Fischer-Tiné and Michael Mann. London: Anthem, 2004.

Marks, Stephen P. "Emerging Human Rights: A New Generation for the 1980's?" In *International Law*, ed. Falk, Kratochwil, and Mendlovitz.

Marsden, George. *Fundamentalism and American Culture*. New York: 1982.

Marshall, T. H. "Citizenship and Social Class." In Marshall, *Citizenship and Social Class, and Other Essays*. Cambridge: Cambridge University Press, 1950.

Marty, Martin, and Frederick E. Greenspan, eds. *Pushing the Faith: Proselytism and Civility in a Pluralistic World*. New York: Crossroad, 1988.

Massell, Gregory J. "Law as an Instrument of Revolutionary Change in a Traditional Milieu: The Case of Soviet Central Asia." *Law and Society Review* 2, 2 (1968): 179–228.

Masud, Mohammad Khalid, Brinkley Morris Messick, and David Stephan Powers. "Muftis, Fatwas, and Islamic Legal Interpretation." In *Islamic Legal Interpretation: Muftis and Their Fatwas*, ed. Masud, Messick, and Powers. Cambridge, Mass.: Harvard University Press, 1996.

McChesney, Allan. "Aboriginal Communities, Aboriginal Rights and the Human Rights System in Canada." In *Cross-Cultural Perspectives*, ed. An Na'im.

McCracken, John. *Politics and Christianity in Malawi 1875–1940*. Cambridge: Cambridge University Press, 1977.

McDonald, Michael, ed. *Collective Rights*. Special issue, *Canadian Journal of Law and Jurisprudence* 4 (1991).

McMurray, O. K. "Inter-Citizenship: A Basis for World Peace." *Yale Law Journal* 27, 3 (January 1918): 299–316.

Mernissi, Fatima. *The Veil and the Male Elite: A Feminist Interpretation of Women's Rights in Islam*. New York: Perseus, 1991.

———. *Women in Islam: An Historical and Theological Enquiry*. Trans. M. J. Lackland. Oxford: Blackwell, 1991.

Meron, Theodor, "A Report on the N.Y.U. Conference on Teaching International Protection of Human Rights." *New York University Journal of International Law and Politics* 13, 4 (1981): 881–957.

Messick, Brinkley Morris. *The Calligraphic State: Textual Domination and History in a Muslim Society.* Berkeley: University of California Press, 1993.

Meyer, Peter. "The International Bill: A Brief History." In *The International Bill of Human Rights*, ed. Paul Williams. Glen Ellen, Calif.: Entwhistle, 1981.

Mickolus, Edward. *The Literature of Terrorism: A Selectively Annotated Bibliography.* Westport, Conn.: Greenwood Press, 1980.

Miladi, Samir, and Jiega H. Serag El Din, eds. *The State of the Child in the Arab World 1990.* Cairo: Arab Council for Childhood Development, 1990.

Miller, David. "Bounded Citizenship." In *Cosmopolitan Citizenship*, ed. Kimberly Hutchings and Roland Dannreuther. London: Macmillan, 1998.

———. "Citizenship and Pluralism." *Political Studies* 43, 3 (1995): 432–50.

Milne, A. J. M. *Human Rights and Human Diversity: An Essay in the Philosophy of Human Rights.* Albany: State University of New York Press, 1986.

Mlinar, Zdravko. "Individuation and Globalization: The Transformation of Territorial Social Organization." In *Globalization and Territorial Identities*, ed. Mlinar. Brookfield, Vt.: Avebury, 1992.

Mohammad, Noor. "The Doctrine of Jihad: An Introduction." *Journal of Law and Religion* 3 (1985): 381–97.

Moltmann, Jürgen. "Political Theology and Theology of Liberation." In *Liberating the Future: God, Mammon and Theology*, ed. Joerg Reiger. Minneapolis: Augsburg Fortress, 1998. 61–80.

Momen, Moojan. *Introduction to Shiʿi Islam: The History and Doctrines of Twelvers Shiʿism.* New Haven, Conn.: Yale University Press, 1985.

Moore, Frank W., ed. *Readings in Cross-Cultural Methodology.* New Haven, Conn.: Hraf Press, 1961.

Morrison, Karl Frederick *Understanding Conversion.* Charlottesville: University of Virginia Press, 1992.

Morsink, Johannes. "The Philosophy of the Universal Declaration." *Human Rights Quarterly* 6 (1984): 309–34.

Mukhtasar Tafsir ibn Kathir. Summarized and ed. Muhammad Ali al-Saban. Beirut, 1400 Hijri (corresponding to 1979).

Murdock, George Peter. "The Cross-Cultural Survey." In *Readings in Cross-Cultural Methodology*, ed. Moore.

Musa, Mahmud Ahmed. "Arabic: The Role of Education in the Rearing of the Arab Child." In *Al-Tufula wa al-Tanmiya fi al-Watan al-Araby* (Childhood and Development in the Arab Homeland: Proceedings of the Conference on Childhood and Development). General Secretariat, Administration of Social Affairs, Arab League, Tunis, 13–15 November, 1986. Part I.

Nanda, Ved P., James R. Scarritt, and George W. Shepherd, Jr., eds. *Global Human Rights:*

Public Policies, Comparative Measures and NGO Strategies. Boulder, Colo.: West-view, 1981.

Nandy, Ashia. *The Intimate Enemy: Loss and Recovery of Self Under Colonialism*. Delhi: Oxford University Press, 1983.

Neier, Aryeh. "The Military Tribunals on Trial." *New York Review of Books* 49, 2 (2001): 11–15.

Nelson, Jack L., and Vera M. Green, eds. *International Human Rights: Contemporary Issues*, Standfordville, N.Y.: Human Rights Publishing Group, 1980.

Nickel, James W. "Cultural Diversity and Human Rights." In *International Human Rights: Contemporary Issues*, ed. Nelson and Green.

Norton, Augustus, and Martin Greenberg. *International Terrorism: An Annotated Bibliography and Research Guide*. Boulder, Colo.: Westview, 1980.

Nussbaum, Martha C. *Cultivating Humanity: A Classical Defense of Reform in Liberal Education*. Cambridge, Mass.: Harvard University Press, 1997.

O'Connell, Daniel P. *International Law*. 2nd ed. London: Stevens & Sons, 1970.

Okoth-Ogendo, H. W. "Constitutions Without Constitutionalism: Reflections on an African Political Paradox." In *State and Constitutionalism: An African Debate on Democracy*, ed. Shivji.

Opler, Marvin K. "Cultural Evolution and the Psychology of Peoples." In *Essays in the Science of Culture*, ed. Dole and Carneiro.

Othman, Shehu, "Postscript: Legitimacy, Civil Society and the Return of Europe." In *Legitimacy and the State in Twentieth-Century Africa: Essays in Honour of A. H. Kirk-Greene*, ed. Terence Ranger and Olufemi Vaughan. London: Macmillan, 1993.

Ottenberg, Simon. "Ibo Receptivity to Change." In *Continuity and Change in African Cultures*, ed. Bascom and Herskovits.

Parekh, Bhikhu C. *Gandhi*. Oxford: Oxford University Press, 1997.

Paust, Jordan J. "Antiterrorism Military Commissions: The Ad Hoc DOD Rules of Procedure." *Michigan Journal of International Law* 23 (2002): 677.

———. "Post-9/11 Overreaction and Fallacies Regarding War and Defense, Guantanamo, The Status of Persons, Treatment, Judicial Review of Detention, and Due Process in Military Commissions." *Notre Dame Law Review* 79 (2004): 1335.

Pearl, David, and Werner Menski. *Muslim Family Law*. London: Sweet and Maxwell, 1998.

Pentney, William. "*Lovelace v. Canada*: A Case Comment." *Canada Legal Aid Bulletin* 5 (1982).

Pfister, Thomas. "Citizenship and Globalization, Review Essay." In *Citizenship and Migration: Globalization and the Politics of Belonging*, ed. Stephen Castles and Alastair Davidson. London: Palgrave, 2000.

Pinsky, Robert. "Eros Against Esperanto." In *For Love of Country*, ed. Martha C. Nussbaum and Joshua Cohen. Boston: Beacon Press, 2002.

Pipes, Daniel. *In the Path of God: Islam and Political Power*. New York: Basic Books, 1983.

Piscatori, James P. *Islam in a World of Nation-States*. Cambridge: Cambridge University Press, 1986.

———, ed. *Islam in the Political Process*. Cambridge: Cambridge University Press, 1983.

Pocock, J. G. A. "The Ideal of Citizenship Since Classical Times." *Queen's Quarterly* 99, 1 (Spring 1992): 35–55.

Polat, Ülger. "Baden-Wurttemberg's Conscience Test Zeitgeist of Fear and Prejudice." Trans. M. Lawton. *Qantara*, February 16, 2006; http://www.qantara.de/webcom/ show_article.php/ _c-478/_nr-402/i.html.

Pollis, Adamantia, and Peter Schwab, eds. *Human Rights: Cultural and Ideological Perspectives*. New York: Praeger, 1979.

Preiswerk, Roy. "The Place of Intercultural Relations in the Study of International Relations." *Year Book of World Affairs* 32 (1978).

Prentoulis, Nikos. "On the Technology of Collective Identity: Normative Reconstructions of the Concept of EU Citizenship." *European Law Journal* 7, 2 (2001): 196–218.

Provizer, Norman W. "Defining Terrorism." In *Multidimensional Terrorism*, ed. Martin Slann and Bernard Schechterman, Boulder, Colo.: Westview, 1987.

Pruess, Ulrich K., Michelle Everson, Mathias Koenig-Archibugi, and Edwige Lefebvre. "Traditions of Citizenship in the European Union." *Citizenship Studies* 7, 1 (2003): 3–14.

Rahman, Fazlur. *Islam*. 2nd ed. Chicago: University of Chicago Press, 1979.

Rambo, Lewis. *Understanding Religious Conversion*. New Haven, Conn.: Yale University Press, 1993.

Ranger, Terence O., and Isaria N. Kmambo, eds. *The Historical Study of African Religions*. Berkeley: University of California Press, 1972.

Rapoport, David C. "Fear and Trembling: Terrorism in Three Religious Traditions." *American Political Science Review* 78 (1984): 658–77.

Rawls, John. "The Idea of an Overlapping Consensus." *Oxford Journal of Legal Studies* 7 (1987): 1–25.

Redfield, Robert. *The Primitive World and Its Transformations*. Ithaca, N.Y.: Cornell University Press, 1953.

Reformed Ecumenical Council. *Acts of the Reformed Ecumenical Council Athens 1992*. Grand Rapids, Mich.: Reformed Ecumenical Council, 1992.

Reisman, W. Michael et al., eds., *International Law in Contemporary Perspective*. St. Paul, Minn.: Thomson-West, 2004.

Renteln, Alison Dundes. "A Cross-Cultural Approach to Validating International Human Rights: The Case of Retribution Tied to Proportionality." In *Human Rights Theory and Measurements*, ed. D. L. Singranelli. Basingstoke: Macmillan, 1988.

———. *International Human Rights: Universalism Versus Relativism*. Newbury Park, Calif.: Sage, 1990.

———. "Relativism and the Search for Human Rights." *American Anthropologist* 90, 1 (1988): 56–72.

——. "The Unanswered Challenge of Relativism and the Consequences for Human Rights." *Human Rights Quarterly*, 7 (1985): 514–40.

Richard, Pablo. "La Teología de la Liberación en la nueva coyuntura." *Pasos* 34 (March–April, Segunda Época, 1991): 1–8.

Riddell, James C., and Carol W. Dickerman, *Country Profiles of Land Tenure: Africa 1986*. Madison: University of Wisconsin-Madison Land Tenure Center, 1986.

Riesenberg, Peter. *Citizenship in the Western Tradition: Plato to Rousseau*. Chapel Hill: University of North Carolina Press, 1992.

Robinson, B. A. "Religion in the United Kingdom" Ontario Consultants on Religious Tolerance, February 19, 2003, http://www.religioustolerance.org/uk_rel.htm.

Rouse, Ruth. "The Missionary Motive." *International Review of Missions* 25 (1936): 250–258.

Rowland, Christopher, ed. *The Cambridge Companion to Liberation Theology*. Cambridge: Cambridge University Press, 1999.

Sachs, Albie. *Advancing Human Rights in South Africa*. Capetown: Oxford University Press, 1992.

Safwat, Safia M. "Offenses and Penalties in Islamic Law." *Islamic Quarterly* 26 (1982): 149–181.

Sanders, Douglas. "Collective Rights." *Human Rights Quarterly* 13 (1991): 217–419.

Sanneh, Lamin. *The Crown and the Turban: Muslims and West African Pluralism*. Boulder, Colo.: Westview, 1997.

——. *Encountering the West: Christianity and the Global Cultural Process: The African Dimension*. Maryknoll, N.Y.: Orbis, 1993.

Sathirathai, Surakiart. "An Understanding of the Relationship Between International Legal Discourse and Third World Countries." In *International Law*, ed. Koskenniemi et al.

Schabas, William A. *An Introduction to the International Criminal Court*. 2nd ed. Cambridge: Cambridge University Press, 2004.

Schacht, Joseph. *An Introduction to Islamic Law*. Oxford: Clarendon, 1964.

——. *The Origins of Muhammadan Jurisprudence*. Oxford: Clarendon, 1950.

Schmid, Alex. *Political Terrorism*. New Brunswick, N.J.: Rutgers University Press, 1983.

Schneider, Harold K. "Pakot Resistance to Change." In *Continuity and Change in African Cultures*, ed. Bascom and Herskovits.

Schoffeleers, Matthew, and Wim Van Binsbergen, eds. *Theoretical and Methodological Explorations in African Religions*. London: Kegan Paul, 1985.

Schwedler, Jillian. "Introduction: Society and the Study of Middle East Politics Civil." In *Toward Civil Society in the Middle East? A Primer*, ed. Schwedler. Boulder, Colo.: Lynne Reinner, 1995. 1–30.

Sen, Amartya. *Development as Freedom*. New York: Knopf, 1999.

——. "How to Judge Globalism." *American Prospect: Globalism and Poverty* 13, 1 (2002): A2–A6.

Sewall, Sarah B., and Carl Kaysen, eds. *The United States and the International Criminal*

Court: National Security and International Law. Lanham, Md.: Rowman and Little-field, 2000.

Shah, Ghanshyam. "Tenth Lok Sabha Elections: BJP's Victory in Gujarat." *Economic and Political Weekly*, December 21, 1991, 2921–24.

Shaltut, Mahmud. *Al Islam wa al-ʿalaqat al-Dawliya* (Islam and International Relations). Cairo, 1951.

Sharevskaya, Berta I. *The Religious Traditions of Tropical Africa in Contemporary Focus*. Budapest: Center for Afro-Asian Research of the Hungarian Academy of Sciences, 1973.

Shaw, Robert. "The Enlightenment Concept of Citizenship, Rights and Governance in Modern and Postmodern States." http://www.porirua.net/CitizenshipShawpdf.pdf

Shepherd, George W., Jr. "Transnational Development of Human Rights: The Third World Crucible." In *Global Human Rights*, ed. Nanda, Scarritt, and. Shepherd.

Shihata, Ibrahim. "Islamic Law and the World Community." *Harvard International Club* 4(1) (1962): 101–114.

Shils, Edward. *Tradition*. Chicago: University of Chicago Press, 1981.

Shivji, Issa G., ed. *State and Constitutionalism: An African Debate on Democracy*. Harare, Zimbabwe: Southern African Political Economy Series (SAPES) Trust, 1991.

———. "State and Constitutionalism: A New Democratic Perspective." In *State and Constitutionalism*, ed. Shivji.

Shweder, Richard A., and Robert A. LeVine, eds. *Culture Theory: Essays on Mind, Self, and Emotion*. Cambridge: Cambridge University Press, 1984.

Spiro, Melford E. "Culture and Human Nature." In *The Making of Psychological Anthropology*, ed. George Spindler. Berkeley: University of California Press, 1978.

———. "Some Reflections on Cultural Determinism and Relativism with Special Reference to Emotion and Reason." In *Culture Theory*, ed. Shweder and LeVine.

Steiner, Henry, and Philip Alston. *International Human Rights in Context: Law, Politics, Morals*, Oxford: Clarendon, 1996.

Stocking, George W., Jr. *Race, Culture, and Evolution: Essays in the History of Anthropology*. Chicago: University of Chicago Press, 1982.

Strawson, John. "Islamic Law and English Texts." In *Laws of the Postcolonial*, ed. Eve Darian-Smith and Peter Fitzpatrick. Ann Arbor: University of Michigan Press, 1999.

Streeck, Wolfgang. "From Market Making to State Building? Reflections on the Political Economy of European Social Policy." In *European Social Policy: Between Fragmentation and Integration*, ed. Stephan Leibfried and Paul Pierson, Washington, D.C.: Brookings Institution, 1995.

Sullivan, Donna J. "Gender Equality and Religious Freedom: Toward a Framework for Conflict Resolution." *New York University Journal of International and Policy* 24 (1992): 791–856.

Sundara Raj, M. "Awakening of Human Rights." In *Human Rights in India: Historical, Social and Political Perspectives*, ed. C. J. Nimral. New York, Oxford University Press.

Swidler, Leonard, ed. *Religious Liberty and Human Rights in Nations and Religions*. Philadelphia: Temple University Press, 1986.

Taha, Mahmoud Mohamed. *The Second Message of Islam*. Trans. and intro. Abdullahi Ahmed An-Naʿim. Syracuse, N.Y.: Syracuse University Press, 1987.

Terchek, Ronald J. *Gandhi: Struggling for Autonomy*. New York, Rowman and Littlefield, 1998.

Thompson, Kenneth W., ed. *The Moral Imperatives of Human Rights: A World Survey*. Washington, D.C.: University Press of America, 1980.

Thornberry, Patrick. *International Law and the Rights of Minorities*. Oxford: Clarendon, 1991.

Tombs, David. "Latin American Liberation Theology Faces the Future." In *Faith in the New Millennium*, ed. Stanley E. Porter, Michael A. Hayes, and David Tombs. Sheffield: Sheffield Academic Press, 2001. 32–58.

Toprak, Binnaz. "Islam and the Secular State in Turkey." In *Turkey: Political, Social and Economic Challenges in the 1990s*, ed. Çigdem Balim-Harding, Ersin Kalaycioglu, Cevat Karatas, Gareth Winrow, and Feroze Yasamee. London: Brill, 1995. 90–96.

Trimingham, Spencer. *The Influence of Islam upon Africa*. New York: Praeger, 1968.

Tucker, Robert W. *The Inequality of Nations*. New York: Basic Books, 1977.

Turner, J. D. *An Introduction to Liberation Theology*. Lanham, Md.: University Press of America, 1994.

———. "Marxism and Liberation Theology." In *The Cambridge Companion to Liberation Theology*, ed. Rowland. 199–217.

UNESCO. *Human Rights: Comments and Interpretations*. London, Allan Wingate, 1949.

UNICEF. *The State of the World's Children*. London: Oxford University Press for UNICEF, various years.

United Nations Development Programme. *Human Development and Human Rights Report on the Oslo Symposium*. 1998.

———. *Human Development and Human Rights Report on the Oslo Symposium*. 2000.

———. *What Is Human Development*. http://hdr.undp.org/en/humandev/

Van Dyke, Vernon. "Collective Rights and Moral Rights: Problems in Liberal Democratic Thought." *Journal of Politics* 44 (1982): 21–40.

———. *Human Rights, Ethnicity and Discrimination*. Westport, Conn.: Greenwood Press, 1985.

Vasak, Karel. *Birthright of Man: A Selection of Texts Prepared Under the Direction of Jeanne Hersch*. New York: UNESCO, UNIPUB, 1969.

———, ed. *The International Dimensions of Human Rights*. Rev. Philip Alston. 2 vols. Westport, Conn.: Greenwood Press, 1982.

Vesey-Fitzgerald, Seymour G. "Nature and Sources of the Shariʿa." In *Law in the Middle East*, ed. Khadduri and Liebesny.

Vincent, R. J. "The Factor of Culture in the Global International Order." *Year Book of World Affairs* 34 (1980): 252–264.

Voll, John O. *Islam: Continuity and Change in the Modern World.* Essex: Longman, 1982.

Vroom, H. M. "Scripture Read and Interpreted: The Development of the Doctrine of Scripture and Hermeneutics in Gerefomeerde Theology in the Netherlands." *Calvin Theological Journal* 28 (1993): 352–71.

Vuola, Elina. *Limits of Liberation: Feminist Theology and the Ethics of Poverty and Reproduction.* Helsinki: Suomalainen Tiedeakatemia, 1997.

Wadud, Amina. *Qur'an and Woman: Rereading the Sacred Text from a Woman's Perspective.* Oxford: Oxford University Press, 1999.

Wafi, Ali Abdel Wahid. "Human Rights in Islam." *Islamic Quarterly* 2 (1967): 64–75.

Wardlaw, Grant. *Political Terrorism.* Cambridge: Cambridge University Press, 1982.

Watkins, Kevin, and Penny Fowler. *Rigged Rules and Double Standards: Trade, Globalization, and the Fight Against Poverty.* Oxford: Oxfam Publications, 2002.

Watt, Montgomery. *Islamic Philosophy and Theology.* Edinburgh: University Press, 1962.

Weiss, Bernard, and Arnold H. Green. *A Survey of Arab History.* Cairo: American University in Cairo Press, 1987.

Welch, Claude E., Jr., and Virginia A. Leary, eds. *Asian Perspectives on Human Rights.* Boulder, Colo.: Westview, 1990.

Wells, Charlotte Catherine. *Law and Citizenship in Early Modem France.* Baltimore: Johns Hopkins University Press, 1995.

Williams, D. T. *Capitalism, Socialism, Christianity and Poverty.* Capetown: Van Schaik, 1998.

Williams, Raymond. *Keywords: A Vocabulary of Culture and Society.* Oxford: Oxford University Press, 1976.

Wolfe, Michael. "Review of Law and Citizenship in Early Modern France." *Renaissance Quarterly* 50, 1 (1997): 291–92.

Woodrow Wilson International Center for Scholars. Event Summary, Conference: Muslims in the United States: Demography, Beliefs, Institutions, and Political Participation (June 18, 2003); http://www.wilsoncenter.org/topics/pubs/Muslim_Thought_final.pdf, viewed April 9, 2010.

Woolley, Mary E. "Progress, Man's Distinctive Mark Alone," Address, National Education Association Convention, New York, 27 June 1938, In *Vital Speeches of the Day*, 4: 21.

Yates, Timothy. *Christian Mission in the Twentieth Century.* Cambridge: Cambridge University Press, 1994.

Young, Crawford. *The African Colonial State in Comparative Perspective.* New Haven, Conn.: Yale University Press, 1994.

Young, Oran. "Compliance in the International System." In *International Law: A Contemporary Perspective*, ed. Richard Falk, Friedrich V. Kratochwil, and Saul H. Mendlovitz. Studies on a Just World Order 2. Boulder, Colo.: Westview, 1985. 99–111.

Young, Robert J. C. *Postcolonialism: An Historical Introduction.* Malden, Mass.: Blackwell, 2001.

Yuval-Davis, Nira. "The Multi-Layered Citizen: Citizenship in the Age of Globalization." *International Feminist Journal of Politics* 1, 1 (1999): 119–36.

Zaman, Habiba. "The Taslima Nasrin Controversy and Feminism in Bangladesh: A Geo-Political and Transnational Perspective." Special Issue, *Sexual Economics. Atlantis* 23, 2 (1999): 42–54; http://www.forms.msvu.ca/atlantis/frame/volumes.htm, April 8, 2010.

Zayd, Mustafa. *AI-Nasikh wa al-Mansukh* (The Abrogator and the Abrogated in the Qur'an). 2 vols. Cairo: Dar al-Fikr al-Arabi, 1963.

Index

Acknowledgments

I am grateful for the funding provided by the Center for the Study of law and Religion (CSLR) of Emory University School of Law for the editing of this collection of essays under a major project of the Center that is generously sponsored by the Henry Luce Foundation in New York City. However, this book is published independently by the Human Rights Series of the University of Pennsylvania Press in accordance with their own academic standards and decision-making process, and not under the auspices of the CSLR project.

I also wish to express my appreciation to Mr. Simon Kress, Ph.D. Candidate, Department of English, Emory University, assisted by Ms. Andrea Leon Ramirez of Emory University School of Law, for carefully editing these essays and preparing them for publication.

My most affectionate and profound appreciation and gratitude is to my wife Sara, Aisha Osman, and to our children, for their patience and unfailing support that sustained me through the years. It is to them that I dedicate my life and all my work.